PROPAGANDA
AND
PERSUASION

PROPAGANDA AND PERSUASION

Garth S. Jowett ▪ **Victoria O'Donnell**
University of Houston   Montana State University

FOURTH EDITION

SAGE Publications
Thousand Oaks ▪ London ▪ New Delhi

For information:

Sage Publications, Inc.
2455 Teller Road
Thousand Oaks, California 91320
E-mail: order@sagepub.com

Sage Publications Ltd.
1 Oliver's Yard
55 City Road
London EC1Y 1SP
United Kingdom

Sage Publications India Pvt. Ltd.
B-42, Panchsheel Enclave
Post Box 4109
New Delhi 110 017 India

Library of Congress Cataloging-in-Publication Data

Jowett, Garth S.
Propaganda and persuasion / Garth S. Jowett and Victoria O'Donnell.— 4th ed.
    p. cm.
Includes bibliographical references and index.
ISBN 978-1-4129-0897-9 (cloth) — ISBN 978-1-4129-0898-6 (pbk.)
    1. Propaganda. 2. Persuasion (Psychology) I. O'Donnell,
Victoria. II. Title.

HM1231.J68 2006
303.3′75—dc222   2005023032

This book is printed on acid-free paper.

09   10   11   12   13   7   6   5   4   3

Acquisitions Editor:	Margaret H. Seawell
Editorial Assistant:	Sarah K. Quesenberry
Production Editor:	Astrid Uirding
Copy Editor:	Gillian Dickens
Typesetter:	C&M Digitals (P) Ltd.
Indexer:	Juniee Oneida
Cover Designer:	Michelle Lee

*To Ada and May, who lived through two world wars
and who, in another time and place, took me to the movies.*

Garth S. Jowett

*I continue to dedicate this book to the memory of
my mother, Helen A. O'Donnell, a very special woman.*

Victoria O'Donnell

Contents

Preface to the First Edition

This book grew out of the discovery that both authors were interested in the study of propaganda; however, we come to this interest from the perspectives of different academic disciplines: Professor Jowett from that of communication history and Professor O'Donnell from persuasion and rhetoric. To any discerning reader, this will make the primary authorship of the individual chapters obvious, but to keep the record straight, Professor Jowett wrote Chapters 2, 3, and 5; Professor O'Donnell wrote Chapters 1, 4, and 6. Chapters 7 and 8 are the result of the joint exchange of ideas.

We were both intrigued with how poorly propaganda had fared in recent years as part of general communication studies, and further informal investigations revealed that few students were being given the opportunity or encouragement to examine this subject in a systematic manner. When we questioned our colleagues, we were assured that propaganda as a topic within the communication curriculum still held great interest but that because the subject was so vast in scope, it was difficult to cover it in anything but the most cursory way. This problem was compounded by the lack of suitable classroom materials designed to allow a systematic treatment, without forcing the student to consult a wide array of disparate sources. This book was written with a view to solving some of these problems by presenting an overview of the history of propaganda, as well as a review of the social scientific research on its effects and an examination of its applications. We have tried to restrict the narrative so that it will serve as a guide to further reading on specific issues rather than be encyclopedic in scope.

In the past 70 years, many hundreds of books have dealt with various aspects of propaganda; an almost equal number of books and journal articles have dealt with persuasion. Very often, those two subjects have come to be regarded as synonymous. With the growth in the study of persuasion in the last two decades, propaganda has received scant attention as a subject in its own right within the spectrum of communication studies. With the advent of a whole range of new communication technologies and the imminent promise of a myriad of channels for disseminating information, the opportunities for increased propaganda activities are obvious. For this reason, we believe that the time has come to revive the study of propaganda as a separate topic and of great significance at this point in time.

This book is offered as a modest treatment of a very old subject, and we trust that the reader will be sympathetic to the fact that we could include neither a detailed history of propaganda nor a lengthy review of all the research ever done to evaluate its effectiveness in specific campaigns. Our aim was to provide the reader with a challenge to become involved in the fascinating world of propaganda in the hope that it would stimulate further research discussion. We both owe an intellectual debt to T. H. Qualter (1962), whose excellent slim volume *Propaganda and Psychological Warfare* was all that was available for a long time and whose recent detailed monograph, *Opinion Control in Democracies* (1985), is a landmark study but unfortunately was only received after this volume had been sent to the printer. Other than Qualter and the important work by David L. Altheide and John M. Johnson, *Bureaucratic Propaganda* (1980); the three-volume compilation of important articles by Harold D. Lasswell, Daniel Lerner, and Hans Speier, *Propaganda and Communication in World History* (1979); and Richard A. Nelson's (1986) forthcoming detailed bibliography on the subject, there have been very few systematic examinations of propaganda in recent years, and it is the intention that this book fill some of the gaps in the current literature.

What may appear to the reader to be a relatively short book is, in fact, the result of several years of reviewing a vast literature, which unfortunately is reflected only in a minor way in the bibliography. We chose to present in this book both a digest of important and classic ideas on the subject and our original ideas. It has been our goal to produce a work that will enable students of modern-day propaganda to recognize, analyze, and evaluate propaganda in their midst while giving them an appreciation of its history and development. Although respectful of the work of Jacques Ellul, we could not incorporate many of his ideas within the text of the book. We aimed to clarify and distinguish propaganda as a form of communication but found that we could not do so with Ellul's view of the pervasiveness of propaganda. Also, advertising, though presented as the most prevalent form of propaganda in the United States, does not receive extensive treatment. We thought that advertising as propaganda is such a complex and extensive subject that it required an entire series of studies in itself and that such a treatment was beyond the scope of this book.

Writing a book should always be a learning experience, and the book taught us that we all have a great deal to learn about the role and practice of propaganda in our everyday society. We have also learned that in order not to fear propaganda, we must first understand it.

—Garth S. Jowett
Houston, Texas

—Victoria O'Donnell
Denton, Texas

Preface to the Second Edition

In the 6 years since the first edition of this book appeared, we have been gratified by the increased interest in the field of propaganda studies. Although it would be premature to declare that the study of propaganda is now an accepted part of all communication studies or political science programs, nevertheless, indications are that more and more such courses are appearing. As time separates the study of propaganda from the political ideologies that hovered over academe in the Cold War period, there is a clear revival of interest in the important role of propaganda in many aspects of modern life, not necessarily related to international intrigue and military campaigns.

The publication of the first edition of this book proved to be an important development in both our academic careers. We presented joint workshops on teaching propaganda studies as part of the communication curriculum for the Speech Communication Association, which were well attended by enthusiastic participants and from whom we learned as much as we taught. Several things were made very clear in these workshops, as well as from correspondence with others: First, it is very difficult to get anyone to agree on an exact definition of propaganda, although the definition offered in this book is now (thankfully) widely cited; second, it is a formidable task to get instructors and students to view propaganda as a "neutral" technique, which only in its specific application becomes either "positive" or "negative"; and third, this subject is guaranteed to raise emotions in the classroom no matter how it is taught. Also, we have discovered that, in the classroom, only with a determined effort can discussions of propaganda be removed from an association with war (and even more specifically, Nazi propaganda activities). This is a testament to the especially negative connotation the term *propaganda* has acquired in our society and to the persistent and somewhat troublesome strength of Nazi mythology and imagery (this last fact is a topic that requires its own full-length treatment). It is one of our stated intentions that the approach outlined in this book, which provides a wider and more systematic examination of propaganda throughout history and in the modern world, will help enlarge the dimension of the propaganda discourse beyond these limiting subjects.

In the past 6 years, although the number of books dealing with propaganda in a systematic manner has not been as large as we would like to have seen, several publications deserve special mention. Ted Smith III edited a splendid collection of original essays, *Propaganda: A Pluralistic Perspective* (1989), that contributes to opening the discussion of what encompasses the discourse of propagandistic activities. A recent book by Anthony Pratkanis and Elliot Aronson, *Age of Propaganda: The Everyday Use and Abuse of Persuasion* (2001), is admirable in its sociopsychological examination of many aspects of propaganda in contemporary society. Also, the work of Michael Sproule in a series of articles on the history of propaganda analysis in the United States has significantly reshaped our understanding of this topic. Several books that have contributed to the reevaluation of propaganda are Maureen Honey, *Creating Rosie the Riveter: Class, Gender, and Propaganda During World war II* (1984); Richard W. Steele, *Propaganda in an Open Society: The Roosevelt Administration and the Media, 1933–1941* (1985); Benjamin Ginsberg, *The Captive Public: How Mass Opinion Promotes State Power* (1986); Shearon Lowery and Melvin DeFleur, *Milestones in Mass Communication Research* (1988); Philip G. Zimbardo and Michael Leippe, *The Psychology of Attitude Change and Social Influence* (1991); and Holly Cowan Shulman, *The Voice of America: Propaganda and Democracy, 1941–1945* (1990). These and other specialized studies are collectively helping give shape to the role and dimensions of propaganda in American society.

We have welcomed the opportunity to write a second edition of this book, as much for the chance to enlarge on certain topics as to try to keep up with current events. The few years since the first edition have been witness to several important historical events that have contributed to the appreciation of propaganda in modern society. Perhaps the decade will be best remembered for the sudden demise of communism in Eastern Europe. The first edition was written during a period when the USSR was still "the Evil Empire" described by Ronald Reagan. It was a strange experience in this edition to have to rewrite all the descriptions of Soviet propaganda activities in the past tense. Even as this book is going to press, we still do not know what types of propaganda may emerge from the region. (Today's newspapers, January 3, 1992, are full of stories about the dismantling and replacement of the previous Soviet propaganda symbols, such as the giant statues of Lenin and Marx.) The fact is that we just have no clear idea of what type of propaganda will now dominate the international scene. We can only be sure that the battle for the "hearts and minds" of the world's population will continue and that the decade of the '90s might see the emergence of an international polarization more along economic than political lines. The differences between the "have" and "have-not" nations will become more obvious, and this will generate its own type of propaganda battle.

This book has been greatly enlarged in certain areas. Much historical material was added, including a case study of the Crusades, the demagoguery of Huey Long and Father Charles Coughlin, and the specific propaganda activities of the Korean and Vietnam conflicts. The Persian Gulf War, though somewhat anticlimactic in the end, was a textbook example of both the positive and negative uses of propaganda and provided a useful new case study for this edition. The section in Chapter 1 that defines propaganda has been greatly expanded based on our classroom experience with the first edition and has two new models that conceptualize disinformation. The sections on the theoretical aspects of propaganda have been updated to include the latest research that pertains to persuasion and mass media effects and cultural studies. Only one of the original case studies, that involving the tobacco industry, has been retained, but a historical study about the U.S. government and women's work in World War II has been added, and every chapter contains revisions and expansions. (Victoria O'Donnell is making a documentary film about the Vanport City, Oregon, case study. It will be available for education uses.)

In the preface to the first edition, we noted that writing this book had been a learning experience for us. This learning experience has not stopped, for the more we attempt to understand the subject of propaganda, the more we discover what remains yet to be learned. In particular, the past 6 years have witnessed the increasing use of professional "manipulators" of public opinion, especially in the political arena. Unchecked, this trend threatens, at worst, to subvert the very foundations of our democratic society and, at best, to make the public even more suspicious about politics and the mass media. We need to be continuously vigilant about giving over our democratic rights to these highly skilled operators. It has been our experience that students who have studied propaganda are extremely adept at spotting, and even hostile to, such professional manipulation of public opinion. It is our fervent wish that all who use this book will acquire such skills because the future of democracy and free expression of ideas depend upon it.

—Garth S. Jowett
University of Houston

—Victoria O'Donnell
Montana State University

Preface to the Third Edition

When the first edition of *Propaganda and Persuasion* was published in 1986, we hoped that the study of propaganda would become a more mainstream part of communication studies curricula in colleges and universities. In the preface to the second edition, we indicated that evidence suggested this was happening. Now, 12 years later, with this third edition, we are optimistic that interest in the study of propaganda as a more specialized topic in communication studies is increasing. It has been our pleasure to be a part of this modest growth, and we have been grateful for the citations this book has received in the communication literature. The danger in becoming a "standard" text is the temptation to remain petrified in order not to jeopardize the book's status in the field. We have wholeheartedly rejected this stance, and consequently this third edition is considerably revised, updated, and expanded. That the practice of propaganda is constantly shifting in purpose, technology, and ideology is both exciting and challenging; however, it behooves constant study and evaluation. We have tried to cover many of the new developments in this edition, including two new case studies regarding controversies in the tobacco and pharmaceutical industries.

Of course, the study of the history of propaganda and persuasion does not stand still either, and we are pleased to see that, in 6 years since the second edition was published, several new studies have appeared that make significant contributions to the literature on the subject: Mark U. Edwards, *Printing, Propaganda, and Martin Luther* (1994); Hilmer Hoffman, *The Triumph of Propaganda: Film and National Socialism, 1936–1945* (1996); Michael Kammen, *Mystic Chords of Memory: The Transformation of Tradition in American Culture* (1993); T. Jackson Lears, *Fables of Abundance: A Critical History of American Advertising* (1994); and J. Michael Sproule, *Propaganda and Democracy: The American Experience of Media and Mass Persuasion* (1997).

At the conclusion of the Persian Gulf War in 1991, few books dealt with this event. The short duration of this conflict provided an ideal opportunity for scholars from different disciplines to examine the role of propaganda in precipitating and supporting this military action. Douglas Kellner's *The Persian Gulf TV War* (1992) and Philip M. Taylor's *War and the Media: Propaganda and Persuasion in the Gulf War* (1992) are extremely useful examples of lengthy propaganda case studies. The study of wartime propaganda is also enhanced by the publication of Caroline Page's *U.S. Official Propaganda During the Vietnam War 1965–1973: The Limits of Persuasion* (1996) and Philip M. Taylor's *Munitions of the Mind: War Propaganda From the Ancient World to the Nuclear Age* (1990). The appearance of these books within the context of mainstream academic disciplines such as communication, history, music, political science, psychology, and sociology provides clear evidence that the study of propaganda is emerging in its own right.

In anticipation of a fourth edition of this book, we encourage and welcome comments from those who read or use this book regarding how we might enhance it. For this edition, our publisher, Sage, generously allowed us to add many more pages of information, enabling us to update and expand various sections, add new sections and case studies, and examine the increasingly important role of the Internet in the dissemination of propaganda. Although two of the case studies remain under the same topical headings, they, too, have been extensively rewritten and revised. We hope it is apparent to the reader that the components of a propaganda case study can be systematically examined according to the methodology of propaganda analysis presented in Chapter 6.

We continue to enjoy teaching this subject to students, and we acknowledge that their interest and enthusiasm for the subject is most gratifying. The advent of the Internet has made this generation of students much more conscious of the implications of the spread of information. We find that students are more critical of government, large corporations, and advertising, and perhaps this is a good thing. We hope this third edition, which for us was a worthwhile intellectual journey, will assist in providing the tools for sound analysis and evaluation of the myriad aspects of propaganda that surround us in contemporary society.

—Garth S. Jowett
University of Houston

—Victoria O'Donnell
Montana State University

Preface to the Fourth Edition

W e have decided to continue the tradition established through the first three editions of this book, that is, to retain the previous prefaces. We have done this for several reasons: First, it allows us to comment on the state of the field of propaganda studies every few years; second, it enables us to make special note of new contributions to the field, even if we miss a few. New developments, we hope, will be picked up in a following edition. Finally, it allows us to comment on the general state of the world as seen from the point of view of propaganda scholarship.

In the almost 20 years since the first volume appeared in 1986, there has been a definite increase in the interest in the study of propaganda. The study of persuasion continues to be at the forefront of communication studies. There is, however, a discernible trend for independent courses in propaganda studies being offered under the umbrella of communication, journalism, public relations, and political science. The growing divide in American politics has generated a daily stream of political propaganda. The media appear to exacerbate these tendencies by contributing to the biases and heightening the conflict. It is also obvious that if one peruses the agendas of academic conferences dealing with communication and political science, the subject of propaganda is fairly prominent, due no doubt to the pervasive discussion of the role of the media in modern society and the climate of international tension that surrounds us.

As in previous years, several new studies have been published since the last edition that make a substantial contribution to our understanding of the important but often subtle role that propaganda and persuasion play in modern society. In no particular order these would include the following: Jennings Bryant and Dolf Zillmann (2002), *Media Effects: Advances in Theory and Research;* Toby Clark (1997), *Art and Propaganda in the Twentieth Century;* Steve Coll (2004), *Ghost Wars: The Secret History of the CIA, Afghanistan, and bin Laden, From the Soviet Invasion to September 10, 2001;* Nicholas Cull, David Culbert, and David Welch

(2003), *Propaganda and Mass Persuasion: A Historical Encyclopedia, 1500 to the Present;* Nicholas Cull (1996), *Selling War: The British Propaganda Campaign Against American "Neutrality" in World War II;* Stanley Cunningham (2002), *The Idea of Propaganda: A Reconstruction;* Allison B. Gilmore (1998), *You Can't Fight Tanks With Bayonets: Psychological Warfare Against the Japanese Army in the Southwest Pacific;* Clayton D. Laurie (1996), *The Propaganda Warriors: America's Crusade Against Nazi Germany;* Michael Nelson (1997), *War of the Black Heavens: The Battles of Western Broadcasting in the Cold War;* Shawn Parry-Giles (2002), *The Rhetorical Presidency, Propaganda, and the Cold War: 1945–1955;* Sheldon Rampton and John Stauber (2003), *Weapons of Mass Deception: The Uses of Propaganda in Bush's War on Iraq;* Nancy Snow (2003), *Information War: American Propaganda, Free Speech and Opinion Control Since 9/11;* Oliver Thomson (1999), *Easily Led: A History of Propaganda;* and Donald Warren (1996) *Radio Priest: Coughlin, the Father of Hate Radio.* Most significant was the publication of a classic in the literature that had not been available since its original publication in 1928—Edward Bernays's (1928/2005) *Propaganda,* with an informative introduction by Mark Crispin Miller. These as well as many studies published in communication and psychology journals have enriched the field of propaganda and persuasion studies.

Once again, we are extremely grateful for the number of citations this book has received in the growing literature on propaganda, and we are particularly pleased to see graduate research that has made use of our models and the adoption of our suggestions for "how to analyze propaganda" as a template for further study. We would like to stress, however, that while such usage is flattering, we do not recommend that students slavishly adopt these templates but rather use them as starting points for developing their own analytical strategies.

In this new edition, we have included, where relevant, references and sections dealing with the new reality caused by the shocking events of September 11, 2001. The destruction of the Twin Towers of the World Trade Center in New York City fundamentally altered our modern world in ways that are still too early and too complex to fully comprehend. Yet, in the little niche occupied by those of us who study propaganda, it has brought about a renewed sense of urgency that we should work toward understanding how propaganda operates in this new world of "the war on terrorism," "jihads," "weapons of mass destruction," and "regime change." We hope that this book will contribute toward increasing that understanding by alerting the reader to the important role that propaganda plays in our lives.

Acknowledgments

The preparation of this fourth edition would not have been possible without the encouragement and assistance of our companions at Sage Publications. Our editor, Margaret Seawell, was, as usual, a paragon of patience. She provided the encouragement and guiding hand throughout the revision. The coordination of the project was greatly assisted by the outstanding work of our editorial assistant at Sage, Sarah Quesenberry, who performed the heroic task of pulling it all together, searching for illustrations, and generally keeping us focused with her cheerfulness and firm guiding hand. Our copy editor, Gillian Dickens, and project editor, Astrid Virding, also greatly contributed to the project. We also thank Jill Meyers, former editorial assistant at Sage, for her assistance, and Jayme Stoutt, who did the graphics for the models in Chapters 1 and 8.

Garth Jowett wishes to acknowledge the contribution of his undergraduate and graduate students studying propaganda. They have, through their enthusiastic embracing of the subject, provided continuous inspiration, while at the same time applying a subtle pressure to remain current in this growing and increasingly complex field. Their "show-and-tell" examples of propaganda in our daily lives have often provided source material for this and past editions of this book.

Victoria O'Donnell expresses her gratitude to the Montana State University librarians who acquired numerous books and articles for her research. She also wishes to acknowledge Clara Sprague, University Honors Program Administrative Assistant, who assisted her with computer techniques and kept the office going during some of the writing phases of this book. She especially thanks her spouse, Paul Monaco, for his loving support and interest in her work.

That the two authors are separated by more than 1,500 miles is no longer a factor of any consequence because modern technology has removed the barriers of separation. We worked via telephone, overnight mail, and, with increasing frequency, through e-mail. As usual, we take responsibility for our individual chapters—Victoria for Chapters 1, 4, and 6; Garth for Chapters 2, 3, and 5. Chapters 7 and 8 were joint endeavors. Of course, we also take complete responsibility for the book as a whole and willingly share the blame for any errors.

1

What Is Propaganda, and How Does It Differ From Persuasion?

Propaganda is a form of communication that attempts to achieve a response that furthers the desired intent of the propagandist. Persuasion is interactive and attempts to satisfy the needs of both persuader and persuadee. A model of propaganda depicts how elements of informative and persuasive communication may be incorporated into propagandistic communication, thus distinguishing propaganda as a specific class of communication. References are made to past theories of rhetoric that indicate propaganda has had few systematic theoretical treatments prior to the 20th century. Public opinion and behavioral change can be affected by propaganda.

Propaganda has been studied as history, journalism, political science, sociology, and psychology, as well as from an interdisciplinary perspective. To study propaganda as history is to examine the practices of propagandists as events and the subsequent events as possible effects of propaganda. To consider propaganda as journalism is to understand how news management or "spin" shapes information, emphasizing positive features and downplaying negative ones, casting institutions in a favorable light. To examine propaganda in the light of political science is to analyze the

The Roman
Catholic Church

1

ideologies of the practitioners and the dissemination and impact of public opinion. To approach propaganda as sociology is to look at social movements and the counterpropaganda that emerges in opposition. To investigate propaganda as psychology is to determine its effects on individuals. Propaganda is also viewed by some scholars as inherent thought and practice in mass culture. A more recent trend that draws on most of these allied fields is the study of propaganda as a purveyor of ideology and, to this end, is largely a study of how dominant ideological meanings are constructed within the mass media (Burnett, 1989, pp. 127–137). Ethnographic research is one way to determine whether the people on the receiving end accept or resist dominant ideological meanings.

This book approaches the study of propaganda as a type of communication. Persuasion, another category of communication, is also examined. The terms *propaganda* and *persuasion* have been used interchangeably in the literature on propaganda, as well as in everyday speech. Propaganda employs persuasive strategies, but it differs from persuasion in purpose. A communication approach to the study of propaganda enables us to isolate its communicative variables, to determine the relationship of message to context, to examine intentionality, to examine the responses and responsibilities of the audience, and to trace the development of propagandistic communication as a process.

We believe there is a need to evaluate propaganda in a contemporary context free from value-laden definitions. Our objectives are (a) to provide a concise examination of propaganda and persuasion, (b) to examine the role of propaganda as an aspect of communication studies, and (c) to analyze propaganda as part of social, religious, and political systems throughout history and contemporary times.

Propaganda Defined

Propaganda, in the most neutral sense, means to disseminate or promote particular ideas. In Latin, it means "to propagate" or "to sow." In 1622, the Vatican established the *Sacra Congregatio de Propaganda Fide,* meaning the sacred congregation for propagating the faith of the Roman Catholic Church. Because the propaganda of the Roman Catholic Church had as its intent spreading the faith to the New World, as well as opposing Protestantism, the word *propaganda* lost its neutrality, and subsequent usage has rendered the term pejorative. To identify a message as propaganda is to suggest something negative and dishonest. Words frequently used as synonyms for *propaganda* are *lies, distortion, deceit, manipulation, mind control, psychological warfare, brainwashing,* and *palaver.* Resistance to the word *propaganda* is illustrated by the following example. When the legendary film director John Ford assumed active duty as a lieutenant commander in the U.S. Navy and chief of the Field Photographic Branch of the Office of Strategic Services during World War II, he was asked by his editor, Robert Parrish, if his film, *The Battle of Midway,* was going to be a propaganda film. After a long pause, Ford replied, "Don't you ever let me hear you use that word again in my presence as long as you're under my command" (Doherty, 1993, pp. 25–26). Ford had filmed the actual battle of Midway, but he also included flashbacks of an American family at home that implied that an attack on them was an attack on every American. Ford designed the film to appeal to the American people to strengthen their resolve and belief in the war effort, but he resisted the idea of making films for political indoctrination. According to our definition, *The Battle of Midway* was a white propaganda film, for it was neither deceitful nor false, the source was known, but it shaped viewer perceptions and furthered the desired intent of the filmmaker to vilify the enemy and encourage American patriotism.

Terms implying propaganda that have gained popularity today are *spin* and *news management,* referring to a coordinated strategy to minimize negative information and present in a favorable light a story that could be damaging to self-interests. *Spin* is often used with reference to the manipulation of political information; therefore, press secretaries and public relations officers are referred to as "spin doctors" when they attempt to launder the news (Kurtz, 1998). Besides being associated with unethical, harmful, and unfair tactics, propaganda is also commonly defined as "organized persuasion" (DeVito, 1986, p. 239). Persuasion differs from propaganda, as we will see later in this chapter, but the term is often used as a catch-all for suspicious rhetoric. Sproule (1994) references propaganda as organized mass persuasion with covert intent and poor or nonexistent reasoning: "Propaganda represents the work of large organizations or groups to win over the public for special interests through a massive orchestration of attractive conclusions packaged to conceal both their persuasive purpose and lack of sound supporting reasons" (p. 8).

When the use of *propaganda* emphasizes purpose, the term is associated with control and is regarded as a deliberate attempt to alter or maintain a balance of power that is advantageous to the propagandist. Deliberate attempt is linked with a clear institutional ideology and objective. In fact, the purpose of propaganda is to send out an ideology to an audience with a related objective. Whether it is a government agency attempting to instill a massive wave of patriotism in a national audience to support a war effort, a terrorist network enlisting followers in a jihad, a military leader trying to frighten the enemy by exaggerating the strength of its army, a corporation pursuing a credible image to maintain its legitimacy among its clientele, or a company seeking to malign a rival to deter competition for its product, a careful and predetermined plan of prefabricated symbol manipulation is used to communicate an objective to an audience. The objective that is sought endeavors to reinforce or modify the attitudes, or the behavior, or both of an audience.

Many scholars have grappled with a definition of the word *propaganda*. Jacques Ellul (1965, p. xv) focused on propaganda as technique itself (notably, psychological manipulation) that, in technological societies "has certain identical results," whether it is used by communists or Nazis or Western democratic organizations. He regarded propaganda as sociological phenomena, not as something made or produced by people of intentions. Ellul contended that nearly all biased messages in society were propagandistic even when the biases were unconscious. He also emphasized the potency and pervasiveness of propaganda. Because propaganda is instantaneous, he contended, it destroys one's sense of history and disallows critical reflection. Yet, Ellul believed that people need propaganda because we live in mass society. Propaganda, he said, enables us to participate in important events such as elections, celebrations, and memorials. Ellul said that truth does not separate propaganda from "moral forms" because propaganda uses truth, half-truth, and limited truth. Leonard W. Doob, who defined propaganda in 1948 as "the attempt to affect the personalities and to control the behavior of individuals towards ends considered unscientific or of doubtful value in a society at a particular time" (p. 390), said in a 1989 essay that "a clear-cut definition of propaganda is neither possible nor desirable" (p. 375). Doob rejected a contemporary definition of propaganda because of the complexity of the issues related to behavior in society and differences in times and cultures.

Both Ellul and Doob have contributed seminal ideas to the study of propaganda, but we find Ellul's magnitude and Doob's resistance to definitions troublesome because we believe that to analyze propaganda, one needs to be able to identify it. A definition sets forth propaganda's characteristics and aids our recognition of it.

Psychologists Anthony Pratkanis and Elliot Aronson (2001) wrote a book about propaganda for the purpose of informing Americans about propaganda devices and psychological dynamics so that people will know "how to counteract their effectiveness" (p. xv). They regarded propaganda as the abuse of persuasion and recognized that propaganda is more than clever deception. In a series of case studies, they illustrated propaganda tactics such as withholding vital information, invoking heuristic devices, using meaningless association, and other strategies of questionable ethics. They defined propaganda as "mass 'suggestion' or influence through the manipulation of symbols and the psychology of the individual" (p. 11), thus emphasizing verbal and non-verbal communication and audience appeals.

Other scholars have emphasized the communicative qualities of propaganda. Leo Bogart (1995), in his study of the U.S. Information Agency (USIA), focused on the propagandist as a sender of messages:

> Propaganda is an art requiring special talent. It is not mechanical, scientific work. Influencing attitudes requires experience, area knowledge, and instinctive "judgment of what is the best argument for the audience." No manual can guide the propagandist. He must have "a good mind, genius, sensitivity, and knowledge of how that audience thinks and reacts." (pp. 195–196)

(The quotations enclosed are from the original six-volume classified study of the USIA done in 1954 that Bogart's work condenses. The study was released in abridged form in 1976, and the introduction to it was revised in 1995.)

Scholars have studied propaganda in specific institutions. Alex Carey (1997) regarded propaganda in the corporate world as "communications where the form and content is selected with the single-minded purpose of bringing some target audience to adopt attitudes and beliefs chosen in advance by the sponsors of the communications" (p. 2–1). Noam Chomsky, in his introduction to Carey's collection of essays, said that Carey believed that "the twentieth century has been characterized by three developments of great political importance: the growth of democracy, the growth of corporate power, and the growth of corporate propaganda as a means of protecting corporate power against democracy" (p. ix). Carey said that "commercial advertising and public relations are the forms of propaganda activity common to a democracy. . . . It is arguable that the success of business propaganda in persuading us, for so long, that we are free from propaganda is one of the most significant propaganda achievements of the twentieth century" (pp. 1–4, 2–1).

Shawn J. Parry-Giles (2002), who studied the propaganda production of the Truman and Eisenhower Cold War operations, defined propaganda as "conceived of as strategically devised messages that are disseminated to masses of people by an institution for the purpose of generating action benefiting its source" (p. xxvi). She indicated that

> Truman and Eisenhower were the first two presidents to introduce and mobilize propaganda as an official *peacetime* institution. In a 'war of words,' propaganda acted as an integral component of the government's foreign policy

operation. To understand propaganda's influence is to grasp the means by which America's Cold War messages were produced and the overall impact that such strategizing had on the ideological constructions of the Cold War. (p. xvii)

Bertrand Taithe and Tim Thorton (2000) see propaganda as part of a historical tradition of pleading and convincing and therefore

as a form of political language, however, propaganda is always articulated around of system of truths and expresses a logic of exclusive representation. It is the purpose of propaganda to convince, to win over and to convert; it has therefore to be convincing, viable and truthful within its own remit. . . . The shaping of the term propaganda is also an indication of the way the political nation judges the manner in which political messages are communicated. . . . Propaganda promotes the ways of the community as well as defining them. (pp. 2–4)

Terence H. Qualter (1962) emphasized the necessity of audience adaptation: "Propaganda, to be effective, must be seen, remembered, understood, and acted upon . . . adapted to particular needs of the situation and the audience to which it is aimed" (p. xii). Influencing attitudes, anticipating audience reaction, adapting to the situation and audience, and being seen, remembered, understood, and acted on are important elements of the communicative process.

Pratkanis and Turner (1996) defined the function of propaganda as "attempts to move a recipient to a predetermined point of view by using simple images and slogans that truncate thought by playing on prejudices and emotions" (p. 190). They separated propaganda from persuasion according to the type of deliberation used to design messages. Persuasion, they said, is based on "debate, discussion, and careful consideration of options" to discover "better solutions for complex problems," whereas "propaganda results in the manipulation of the mob by the elite" (p. 191). Coombs and Nimmo (1993) regarded propaganda as "an indispensable form of communication" and "a major form of public discourse;" however, they presented propaganda as "the mastery of all modern forms of palaver"—that is, "the use of guile and charm" (p. 45). Their approach is similar to Ellul's, for they state, "The volume and sophistication of the new propaganda is so vast, and growing, that we increasingly take it for granted as natural and, thereby, we find it exceedingly difficult to distinguish what is propaganda from what is not" (p. 16). Although their major interest is political propaganda, they also focus on advertising, marketing, and sales pitches. These definitions vary from the general to the specific, sometimes including value judgments, sometimes folding propaganda into persuasion, but nearly always recognizing propaganda as a form of communication.

Jowett and O'Donnell's Definition of Propaganda

We seek to understand and analyze propaganda by identifying its characteristics and to place it within communication studies to examine the qualities of context, sender, intent, message, channel, audience, and response. Furthermore, we want to clarify, as much as possible, the distinction between propaganda and persuasion by examining propaganda as a subcategory of persuasion, as well as information. Our definition of propaganda focuses on the communication process—most specifically, on the purpose of the process: *Propaganda is the deliberate, systematic attempt to shape perceptions, manipulate cognitions, and direct behavior to achieve a response that furthers the desired intent of the propagandist.*

Let's examine the words of the definition to see what is precisely meant. First, *deliberate* is a strong word meaning "willful, intentional, and premeditated." It implies a sense of careful consideration of all possibilities. We use it because propaganda is carefully thought out ahead of time to select what will be the most effective strategy to promote an ideology and maintain an advantageous position. *Systematic* complements *deliberate* because it means "precise and methodical, carrying out something with organized regularity." Governments and corporations establish departments or agencies specifically to create systematic propaganda. Although the general public is more aware of propaganda agencies during wartime, such agencies exist all the time, for they are essential. For example, as you will see in the case study "Premarin: A Bitter Pill to Swallow," in Chapter 7, a pharmaceutical company, with the help of a public relations company and a massive advertising campaign, waged a campaign to both present its drug as superior and prevent other companies from getting government approval of the generic version. Advertising campaigns, as you will see in Chapter 3, are forms of systematic propaganda. Of particular interest are the advertising strategies of the pharmaceutical industries. Marcia Angell (2004a), author of *The Truth About the Drug Companies: How They Deceive Us and What to Do About It,* reveals that in the 1990 drug industry annual reports to the Securities and Exchange Commission and to stockholders, 36% of sales revenues went into marketing and administration. Angell said this category "includes what the industry calls 'education,' as well as advertising and promotion" (Angell, 2004b, p. 55). Because of the "rapacious pricing and other dubious practices of the pharmaceutical industry," according to Angell, the public has begun to resist and protest. As a result, she says, the "drug companies are now blanketing us with public relations messages. And the magic words, repeated over and over like an incantation, are *research, innovation,* and *American*" (Angell, 2004b, p. 52). The pharmaceutical ads that are prolific on television visually depict healthy people and their families enjoying life in the beautiful outdoors while, according to Angell, the verbal messages say something like this:

> "Yes, prescription drugs are expensive, but that shows how valuable they are. Besides, our research and development costs are enormous, and we need to cover them somehow. As 'research-based companies,' we turn out a steady stream of innovative medicines that lengthen life, enhance its quality, and avert more expensive medical care. You are the beneficiaries of this ongoing achievement of the American free enterprise system, so be grateful, quit whining, and pay up." (Angell, 2004b, p. 53)

However, as Angell explains, "The prices drug companies charge have little relationship to the costs of making the drugs and could be cut dramatically without coming anywhere close to threatening R&D [research and development]" (p. 54). It is not our intent to target drug companies with this example, but Angell's research reveals that these kinds of propaganda campaigns are both deliberate and systematic.

The goal of propaganda is to "attempt," or try, to create a certain state or states in a certain audience; thus, propaganda is an attempt at directive communication with an objective that has been established a priori. The desired state may be perceptual, cognitive, behavioral, or all three. Each one of these is described with examples as follows:

Shaping perceptions is usually attempted through language and images, which is why slogans, posters, symbols, and even architectural structures are developed during wartime. How we perceive is based on "complex psychological, philosophical, and practical habitual thought patterns that we carry over from past experiences" (Hayward, 1997, p. 73). *Perception* is the process of extracting information from the world outside us, as well as from within ourselves. Each individual has a perceptual field that is unique to that person and formed by the influences of values, roles, group norms, and self-image. Each of these factors colors the ways a person perceives (O'Donnell & Kable, 1982, p. 171). Johnson, in his book *In the Palaces of Memory* (1991), offered a colorful description of perception and recognition according to the activity of neural networks in the brain:

> Looking out the window at the ocean, we might notice a bright light in the night sky hovering on the horizon. Deep inside the brain one neural network

responds to this vector, dismissing it as just another star. But its intense brightness causes another network to guess that it is Venus. Then the light starts getting bigger, brighter, creating a different vector, a different set of firing patterns. Another network associates this configuration with approaching headlights on a freeway. Then two more lights appear, green and red. Networks that interpret these colors feed into other networks; the pattern for *stop light* weakly responds. All over the brain, networks are talking to networks, entertaining competing hypotheses. Then comes the roar, and suddenly we know what it is. The noise vector, the growing-white-light vector, the red-and-green vector all converge on the network—or network of networks—that says *airplane.* (p. 165)

Johnson went on to say, "How a perception was ultimately categorized would depend on the architecture of the system, that which a person was born with and that which was developed through experience. Some people's brains would tell them they had seen a UFO or an angel instead of a plane" (p. 165). Because members of a culture share similar values and norms as well as the same laws and general practices, it is quite possible to have group perceptions or, at least, very similar perceptions within a cultural group.

Our language is based on a vast web of associations that enable us to interpret, judge, and conceptualize our perceptions. Propagandists understand that our constructed meanings are related to both our past understanding of language and images and the culture and context in which they appear. Perception is dependent on our attitudes toward issues and our feelings about them. For example, legislation designed to increase timber thinning in national forests has been labeled a "Healthy Forests Initiative." Environmental groups protested the legislation on the grounds that it was unhealthy to cut down healthy trees and harm wildlife. Michael Garrity, executive director of the Alliance for the Wild Rockies, revealed that the U.S. Forest Service will make about $312,000 by cutting 4.5 million board feet of timber in southern Montana's Gallatin National Forest alone ("Gallatin National Forest Thinning Plan Moves Ahead," 2005). What is "healthy" depends on our associations.

"Operation Desert Shield" was changed to "Operation Desert Storm" when U.S. forces invaded Iraq in January 1991. Changing *Shield* to *Storm* enabled people to alter their perception of the U.S. military operation from "protective" armies to "raging" forces. The second invasion of Iraq in March 2003 failed to achieve a successful slogan. "Shock and Awe" was tried, but it only lasted for 1 week. Frank Rich, editorialist for *The New York Times,* said that the television images from the Arab network Al Jazeera that depicted American soldiers who had been killed or taken prisoner by Iraqi forces contradicted the slogan. "For the first time we could smell blood, American blood, and while that was shocking, it was far from awesome" (Rich, 2003).

The war against the Taliban and Al Qaeda had a more successful slogan with "Operation Enduring Freedom." President George W. Bush began to use the phrase "the war on terror" shortly after the attack on the World Trade Center on September 11, 2001, and continuing through his reelection campaign in 2004. Gilles Kepel, in *The War for Muslim Minds* (2004), said, "The phrase was engineered to heighten fear while simultaneously tapping the righteous indignation of citizens in 'civilized nations' against barbaric murderers who would perpetrate despicable atrocities on innocent victims" (p. 112). The president, however, made a serious gaffe when, in impromptu remarks, he described America's goal to annihilate Al Qaeda's Taliban hosts in Afghanistan as a "crusade." In the Muslim world, "crusade" represented medieval European Christianity's Crusades against Islam. There was an uproar over the religious connotations of the word, which suggested that Bush wanted to conquer Islam. Bush retracted the term immediately and promptly visited a mosque in Washington, D.C., in an attempt to nullify the impression that American mobilization against Al Qaeda was aimed at Muslims or at Islam in general (Kepel, 2004, p. 117). Osama bin Laden, however, was quick to pick up the term and use it in his Al Qaeda propaganda messages denouncing American crusaders. Nevertheless, as Kepel stated, "From both a military and a psychological point of view, the Afghan operation appeared to be a triumph for the United States" (p. 120). Operation Enduring Freedom did not, however, eradicate Al Qaeda's effectiveness because it continued its fight via the Internet Web sites, satellite television links, clandestine financial transfers, and a proliferation of activists (Kepel, 2004, p. 121).

Perceptions are also shaped by visual symbols. During the second Iraq war, as in the first, symbolic yellow ribbons have been put on trees, fences, buildings, automobiles, and jewelry to indicate support of the U.S. military. The ritual of tying yellow ribbons can be traced back to the American Civil War, when women wore yellow ribbons for their loved ones who were away at war. The 1949 John Wayne film *She Wore a Yellow Ribbon* reflects the theme of remembering someone who is away. For television messages about progress in the second Iraqi war, a designer who had worked for Hollywood film and television studios built a $250,000 set for General Tommy Frank's briefings in Qatar (Rich, 2003, p. 1). President Bush, wearing combat clothing, visited troops on the aircraft carrier USS *Abraham Lincoln* on Thanksgiving Day 2003 where, beneath a banner that said "Mission Accomplished," he held up an artificial replica of a roasted turkey.

With digital technology, images can go out to television, newspapers, and the Internet instantly. Photographs are easily doctored, making it difficult to tell what is real and what is not. A video of a man and his 12-year-old son, Mohammed al-Dura, cowered behind a concrete structure in the Gaza strip while Israeli soldiers and Palestinian fighters engaged in gun battle, was widely circulated in September 2000. The boy appeared to be killed and the father wounded in the crossfire. A clip of the boy's death was widely circulated on television worldwide, and stills appeared on the front pages of newspapers. This visual became a symbol of continuing atrocities for the Palestinian intifada, causing riots to break out in the West Bank and violent outbreaks against Jews not only in Israel but also elsewhere around the world. According to an article in *Reader's Digest* ("Seeing Isn't Believing," 2004, pp. 144–146), there were many indications that the video was staged.

As the dangerous eating disorder anorexia nervosa reaches epidemic proportions among young girls and women, hundreds of pro-anorexia Web sites keep appearing on the Internet. These Web sites, which appear to be put up by young anorexic females and friends, offer advice on dieting tips for drastic weight loss, strategies to trick parents into believing that their daughters are eating, and praise on behalf of extreme thinness. Visual propaganda on these *Pro-Ana* (anorexia is personified as "My friend Ana") Web sites features photographs of famous models and movie stars that have been altered to make them appear even thinner than they actually are. Photographs of extremely obese women are also shown to trigger extreme fasting.

There is nothing new about propagandists exploiting the media to get their visual messages across, for historical propagandists did so as well in order to shape perceptions. In 1914, Mary Richardson went into the National Gallery in London and slashed a painting, *The Rokeby Venus*, a 1650 masterpiece by Diego Velasquéz. At her trial, she said her motive had been to draw attention to the treatment of the suffragette leader Emily Pankhurst, who was on a hunger strike in prison. Toby Clark (1997) said,

> The attack on the painting would have been partly understood as an extension of the suffragettes' tactic of smashing department store windows, which assaulted feminized spaces of consumerism like a parodic inversion of shopping. By moving the battle to the nation's foremost art museum, Richardson brought the values of the state's guardians of culture into the line of fire, and by choosing a famous picture of a nude woman, she targeted the point of intersection between institutional power and the representation of femininity. . . . Richardson had not destroyed the picture, but altered it, making a new image—the slashed Venus—which was widely reproduced in photographs in the national press, as Richardson had surely anticipated. Though the

newspapers' response was hostile, demonizing "Slasher Mary" as a monstrous hysteric, Richardson had succeeded in using the mass media to disseminate "her" picture of a wounded heroine, in effect a metaphorical portrait of the martyred Pankhurst and of the suffering of women in general. (pp. 28–29)

As perceptions are shaped, *cognitions may be manipulated*. One way that beliefs are formed is through a person's trust in his or her own senses (Bem, 1970). Certainly, an attitude is a cognitive or affective reaction to an idea or object, based on one's perceptions. Of course, once a belief or an attitude is formed, a person's perceptions are influenced by it. This does not happen in a vacuum. The formation of cognitions and attitudes is a complex process related to cultural and personal values and emotions. The Voice of America during World War II had a stated directive to manipulate the cognitions of both the enemy and America's allies. It was to "spread the contagion of fear among our enemies but also to spread the contagion of hope, confidence and determination among our friends" (Shulman, 1997, p. 97). A study done at the University of Massachusetts during the 1991 Gulf War found that the more people watched the news of the war on television, the stronger their attitudes that the United States should be involved in the war (National Public Radio broadcast, June 26, 1991). Although it is tempting to say that the television images and patriotic messages created positive attitudes toward the war, it is possible that viewers who leaned toward support of the war watched more television. Without assigning particular causality to the media coverage or anything else, one can conclude that the first President Bush had his nation's support. Polls taken during the war indicated very strong support of the war and of President Bush. In mid-February 1991, pollsters found 80% approval of Bush's handling of the Gulf crisis (Ajemian, Goodgame, & Kane, 1991) and 86% approval of a ground war in Iraq (Duffey & Walsh, 1991). Contrasted with those during the Vietnam War, the government's efforts to elicit national support for Operation Desert Storm were successful. Even people who participated in antiwar demonstrations said they supported U.S. troops in the Persian Gulf. While there have been many heroes among the troops fighting in the second Iraq war, the story of Private Jessica Lynch received nonstop coverage in the media. One story in the *Washington Post* (April 3, 2003), whose headlines claimed, "She Was Fighting to the Death," led us to believe that the nineteen-year-old supply clerk had fought fiercely against her Iraqi attackers but was riddled with bullet and knife wounds. As a prisoner of war, the papers said she was abused and finally rescued in a daring night raid. A revised story (June 17, 2003), with the headline "A Broken Body, a Broken Story, Pieced Together," disclosed that Lynch had not been shot or stabbed but that a Humvee accident shattered her bones. Her rifle jammed, thus she never fired, and her captors were gone before she was rescued. As Ellen Goodman wrote in her column entitled "Jessica Lynch a Human, Not Symbolic, Hero" (June 22, 2003), "By making Jessica into a cartoon hero, we may have missed the bravery of the young soldier now recovering in Walter Reed Army Medical Center. . . . Jessica Lynch has now become a redefining story of the war, with skeptics asking whether the Pentagon spun the media or the media hyped the story" (p. B4). Whether it was the Pentagon or media hype, the public's cognitions were manipulated. Beliefs and attitudes are discussed in more detail later in this chapter.

Often, the *direction of a specific behavior* is the intent of a propaganda effort. During war, one desired behavior is defection of enemy troops. In the 1991 Gulf War, the U.S. Fourth Psychological Operations Group dropped 29 million leaflets on Iraqi forces to attract defectors. A U.S. radio program, *Voice of the Gulf,* featured testimonials from happy Iraqi prisoners of war, along with prayers from the Koran and the location of the bomb targets for the next day. Seventy-five percent of Iraqi defectors said they were influenced by the leaflets and the radio broadcasts ("A Psy-Ops Bonanza," 1991). The same tactic was used in the 2003 Iraq war when leaflets that said, "Do Not Risk Your Life and the Lives of Your Comrades. Leave Now and Go Home. Watch Your Children Learn, Grow and Prosper" were dropped on Iraqi military forces. At the beginning of the 2001 war on the Taliban, U.S. military radio broadcasts into Afghanistan by Air Force EC-130E Commando Solo aircraft warned the Taliban in two of the local Afghan languages that they would be destroyed not only by U.S. bombs and missiles but also by American helicopters and ground troops:

> Our helicopters will rain fire down upon your camps before you detect them on radar. . . . Our bombs are so accurate we can drop them right through your windows. Our infantry is trained for any climate and terrain on earth. United States soldiers fire with superior marksmanship and are armed with superior weapons.

This tactic to frighten the enemy was successful in directing a specific behavior, for Rear Admiral John Stufflebeem, deputy director of operations for the U.S. Joint Chiefs of Staff, said "I have not seen any reports that they are returning fire on our aircraft" ("Troops Ready for Action," 2001).

Beliefs, attitudes, and behaviors are desirable end states for propagandistic purposes and determine the formation of a propaganda message, campaign, or both. Because so many factors determine the formation of beliefs, attitudes, and behaviors, the propagandist has to gather a great deal of information about the intended audience.

To continue with the definition, propaganda seeks to *achieve a response,* a specific reaction or action from an audience *that furthers the desired intent of the propagandist.* These last words are the key to the definition of propaganda, for the one who benefits from the audience's response, if the response is the desired one, is the propagandist and not necessarily the members of the audience. People in the audience may think the propagandist has their interest at heart, but in fact, the propagandist's motives are selfish ones. Selfish motives are not necessarily negative, and judgment depends on which ideology one supports. For example, people who listened to the Voice of America (VOA) broadcasts behind the Iron Curtain during the Cold War found satisfaction for their hunger for information, and thus it appeared that VOA had altruistic motives. The information they received from VOA, however, was ideologically injected to shape positive perceptions about the United States and its allies and to manipulate attitudes toward democracy, capitalism, and freedom. Most Americans would not regard these practices as negative, but the communist government officials did. Later in the chapter, in the section on subpropaganda, we give examples of seemingly altruistic communication that was deliberately designed to facilitate acceptance of an ideology.

When conflict exists and security is essential, it is not unusual for propagandists to try to contain information and responses to it in a specific area. Recipients of propaganda messages are discouraged from asking about anything outside the contained area. During wartime, members of the press complain about restrictions placed on them in reporting the events of the war. Newspaper reporters covering the Civil War complained in the 1860s, as journalists did during the Gulf War in 1991. Tom Wicker (1991), of the *New York Times,* wrote, "The Bush administration and the military were so successful in controlling information about the war that they were able to tell the public just about what they wanted the public to know. Perhaps worse, press and public largely acquiesced in this disclosure of only selected information" (p. 96). When Iyad Allawi was selected as the interim prime minister of Iraq in August 2004, he closed down Al Jazeera's Baghdad bureau in retaliation for unfavorable coverage (Galbraith, 2004, p. 70). Complaints regarding information control during wartime is not unusual. Consider the saying "The first casualty during war is truth."

Although contemporary technology is capable of instantaneous transmission of messages around the world and because of the tremendous expansion of exposure to all the mass media throughout the world, it is difficult for a country to isolate its citizens from ideas and information that are commonly known in the rest of the world. Despite the availability of the Internet and the World Wide Web, China has attempted to prevent people from receiving information. Chinese-born Tian Suning, educated in the United States, is attempting to use the Internet to inform the Chinese people about their environmental problems. He says that the Chinese government blocks access to sensitive Internet sites. "In China," wrote *Washington Post* columnist Steve Mufson (1998), "information has been treated as political propaganda" (p. 7). Tian Suning, however, persists in his efforts and compares the Internet to the invention of the printing press for purposes of spreading information to the people of the world. Chinese television, considered the "mouthpiece" of government propaganda, recently has been allowed to engage in live news presentation and investigative reporting. One program, *Jiaodian Fangtan (Focal Report)*, on CCTV tracks down and exposes problems. Chinese authorities, however, require the program to carry positive propaganda on occasions such as national holidays. The program has become very popular with the public, and its commercial success has increased government support for its investigative programs, although they are carefully managed and directed (Bin, 1999).

Television transmission crosses political boundaries as well. Certainly, as communist governments toppled in Poland, Czechoslovakia, Hungary, East Germany, and Romania in 1989, the world saw dramatic evidence that propaganda cannot be contained for long where television exists. People living under the austere regime of East Germany received television from West Germany and saw consumer goods that were easily had and a lifestyle that was abundant rather than austere. Also, the technology of the portable video camera enabled amateurs to capture and display footage of the Czech police on the rampage, the massacre of Georgian demonstrators in Tiblisi, and the bloodbath in Tiananmen Square. When a communist government controlled Czechoslovakia, rebellious protestors produced the "Video Journal" on home video cameras and sent it into Czech homes via rented satellite dishes. In Poland, Lech Walesa said that the underground Solidarity movement could not have succeeded without video. In Romania, while the crowds protested against Nicolae Ceausescu, the television showed fear and doubt in his eyes and encouraged people to continue to fight against his regime despite his army's violence. Ironically, the center of the intense fighting between the army and Ceausescu's loyalists was the Bucharest television station. For a time, the new government was in residence there, making the television station the epicenter of the revolution and the seat of the provisional government.

In this age of instantaneous television transmission, containment of information is no longer easy. Yet, propaganda itself, as a form of communication, is influenced by the technological devices for sending messages that are available in a given time. As technology advances, propagandists have more sophisticated tools at their service. ABC's *Nightline* reported in December 1991 the first recorded use of a fax machine for propaganda purposes. Leaflets describing how to prepare for a chemical warfare assault, presumably sent by the Hussein propagandists, came through thousands of Kuwaiti fax machines. The Internet and satellites are major propaganda outlets for Al Qaeda, which reaches its followers in 68 countries. Videotapes of executions of Coalition personnel in Iraq appear immediately after they occur. The elusive insurgent leader in Iraq, Abu Mousab al-Zarqawi, exhorts followers to seek martyrdom in suicidal assaults against American soldiers, Christians, and Iraqi policemen through cell phone calls to his lieutenants, on Web sites, and in motivational videotapes. He has lured hundreds of followers to join him by representing Iraq as the new home of global jihad.

The study of contemporary propaganda in both oppressed and free societies is a complex endeavor. We acknowledge that one's perception of a form of communication determines what is self-evident and what is controversial. One person's propaganda may be another person's education. In our definition, the elements of deliberate intent and manipulation, along with a systematic plan to achieve a purpose that is advantageous to the propagandist, however, distinguish propaganda from a free and open exchange of ideas.

Forms of Propaganda

Although propaganda takes many forms, it is almost always in some form of activated ideology. Sometimes propaganda is *agitative,* attempting to rouse an audience to certain ends and usually resulting in significant change; sometimes it is *integrative,* attempting to render an audience passive, accepting, and nonchallenging (Szanto, 1978, p. 10). Propaganda is also described as white, gray, or black, in relationship to an acknowledgment of its source and its accuracy of information.

White propaganda comes from a source that is identified correctly, and the information in the message tends to be accurate. This is what one hears on Radio Moscow and VOA during peacetime. Although what listeners hear is reasonably close to the truth, it is presented in a manner that attempts to convince the audience that the sender is the "good guy" with the best ideas and political ideology. White propaganda attempts to build credibility with the audience, for this could have usefulness at some point in the future.

National celebrations, with their overt patriotism and regional chauvinism, can usually be classified as white propaganda. International sports competitions also inspire white propaganda from journalists. During the 1984 Summer Olympics, many complaints were voiced about "biased" coverage by the American reporters, particularly from the British Broadcasting Corporation (BBC). The absence of the Soviet Union's athletes in Los Angeles provoked a less than enthusiastic reaction to the multiple victories of Americans from non-American news sources. Although gold medalists of past games lauded American performances, the home countries of other athletes exclaimed "unfair." Daley Thompson, the decathlon winner from Great Britain, appeared on television wearing a T-shirt that read, "But what about the coverage?" Coverage by the American Broadcasting Company (ABC) was accurate reporting of the events and white propaganda. It appeared to stir up American patriotism deliberately while being genuinely excited about the American athletes' achievements. Doubtless, this was also intended to convey a message to the Soviet government: "We do not need you at the Games." The 1998 Winter Olympics in Nagano, Japan, had all the usual nations represented, but in addition to the events themselves, American television primarily focused on biographical profiles of American athletes. It also persistently held the cameras on the American figure skater, Tara Lipinski, off the rink in many settings, whether she was shopping or watching the events. The same thing happened during the 2004 Olympics, only this time the cameras focused on the U.S. swimmer Michael Phelps, who was expected to win seven gold medals. He won six gold medals, dropping out of a race to let his teammate have a chance to win one. One has to ask whether television viewers watch the Olympics out of national pride or interest in international athletics. Greece, the host for the 2004 Olympics, concerned about poor advance ticket sales, produced white propaganda in promoting the nation as a "safe destination," "technically excellent," and a "modern European country." Through opening ceremonies, speeches, and advertisements, what the Olympics 2004 home page called a "new Greek identity" emerged. Surveys given to 2001 respondents in the United States, United Kingdom, Spain, Germany, and France immediately after the games in September 2004 indicated that the majority felt positive about Greece after the games based on what they saw or heard (from the home page for the 2004 Olympics [http://www.athens2004.com]).

Black propaganda is when the source is concealed or credited to a false authority and spreads lies, fabrications, and deceptions. Black propaganda is the "big lie," including all types of creative deceit. Joseph Goebbels, Hitler's propaganda minister, claimed that outrageous charges evoke more belief than milder statements that merely twist the truth slightly (Bogart, 1995, p. xii). During World War II, prior to Hitler's planned invasion of Britain, a radio station known as "The New English Broadcasting Station," supposedly run by discontented British subjects, ran half-hour programs throughout the day, opening with "Loch Lomond" and closing with "God Save the

King." The station's programming consisted of "war news." This was actually a German undercover operation determined to reduce the morale of the British people throughout the Battle of Britain.

The same technique was used on the French soldiers serving on the Maginot Line from the autumn of 1939 until the spring of 1940. Radio broadcasts originating from Stuttgart and hosted by Paul Ferdonnet, a turncoat Frenchman who pretended to be a patriot, warned the French soldiers to save France before the Nazis took it over. The French soldiers heard Ferdonnet sympathize with their discomfort in crowded and damp conditions in barrack tunnels, and they enjoyed the latest gossip about Paris. He then went on to tell them that French officers had dined at a famous restaurant in Paris, where they ate delicious six-course lunches (Roetter, 1974, p. 3). He also described British soldiers in French towns. Because they earned higher pay than their French counterparts, he said they spent a lot of money and made love to French women. He also said the French soldiers were dupes to fight England's war and urged them to support a "new" government for France. The French soldiers were already miserable because of the conditions on the Maginot Line, and they resented the differences in pay between themselves and the British soldiers. Ferdonnet's broadcasts, though designed to weaken the French soldiers' morale, provided entertainment but not thoughts of defection. Perhaps the French soldiers were not deceived because they also received obvious Nazi propaganda in the form of pornographic cartoons showing British soldiers fondling naked French women. Huge billboards were set up within their view that said, "SOLDIERS OF THE NORTHERN PROVINCES, LICENTIOUS BRITISH SOLDIERY ARE SLEEPING WITH YOUR WIVES AND RAPING YOUR DAUGHTERS." The French soldiers put up their own sign that said, "WE DON'T GIVE A BUGGER, WE'RE FROM THE SOUTH" (Costello, 1985, pp. 242–243). The French soldiers listened to Ferdonnet because they knew he would be more entertaining than their own official radio broadcasts (O'Donnell & Jowett, 1989, p. 51).

Radio Free Hungary made its appearance 10 years later with very successful black propaganda broadcasts. This station attracted world attention and sympathy in 1956 when the Soviets sent their tanks into Budapest to squelch the popular revolution that tried to overthrow the communist regime. Radio Free Hungary's fervent pleas for help from the United States aroused sympathy from the Free World. The atrocities of the Soviets were described in hideous detail, and the Soviets were cursed and denounced in every transmission. The station was actually a brilliant fake operated by the KGB with the intention of embarrassing the United States. The chance that the United States would send troops to Hungary was small, even though

Radio Free Europe had suggested that Americans would support a popular uprising in Hungary. The Soviet Union used Radio Free Hungary to demonstrate that the United States could not be relied on to help a country in revolt. Radio Free Hungary was so effective that the U.S. Central Intelligence Agency (CIA) did not know it was a Soviet propaganda device until after it ceased broadcasting (Kneitel, 1982, pp. 15–16).

Even allies target friendly nations with black propaganda. British intelligence operations attempted to manipulate the United States to go to war in the 2 years before Pearl Harbor was attacked by the Japanese. British Security Coordination (BSC) established itself in New York City's Rockefeller Center for covert action techniques. They wrote stories that were fed to the *New York Herald Tribune* about Nazi spies in America and infiltrated WRUL, a radio station in New York. BSC subsidized the radio station and furnished it with material for news bulletins and specially prepared scripts for talks and commentaries. One example was a propaganda campaign by the British to deter Spain from entering the war on Germany's side. Because the radio station had an ethics standard and a rule against broadcasting material that had not appeared in the American press, the BSC inserted its own material into friendly newspapers and then quoted it for radio broadcasts. BSC also conducted a campaign against German-controlled corporations in the United States by placing articles in newspapers and magazines, organizing protest meetings, and bringing picket lines to certain properties belonging to I. G. Farben Corporation. The British activities were discovered after the bombing of Pearl Harbor when the U.S. State Department pronounced that "British intelligence operations in America were out of control and demanded that offensive covert operations end" (Ignatius, 1989, pp. 9–11).

Black propaganda includes all types of creative deceit, and this type of propaganda gets the most attention when it is revealed. The exhibit "Fake? The Art of Deception" was featured in the British Museum in 1990 and included among the art forgeries several examples of propaganda. One type of forgery was the postage stamp (see Figures 1.1, 1.2, and 1.3). Both British and German versions were displayed, and the exhibition catalogue reported that 160 different stamps were produced by both sides during the two world wars (M. Jones, 1990, p. 75).

The success or failure of black propaganda depends on the receiver's willingness to accept the credibility of the source and the content of the message. Care has to be taken to place the sources and messages within a social, cultural, and political framework of the target audience. If the sender misunderstands the audience and therefore designs a message that does not fit, black propaganda may appear suspicious and tends to fail.

Gray propaganda is somewhere between white and black propaganda. The source may or may not be correctly identified, and the accuracy of the information is uncertain. In 1961, when the Bay of Pigs invasion took place in Cuba, the VOA moved over into the gray area when it denied any U.S. involvement in the CIA-backed activities. In 1966–1967, Radio Free Europe was organized, financed, and controlled by the CIA, which publicly denied any connection. A fund appeal on American television, radio, and mail indicated that Radio Free Europe was dependent on voluntary contributions, known as "truth dollars." The actual purpose of the appeal was to fortify the deception and dispel rumors about a CIA relationship (Barnouw, 1978, p. 143). When the Soviet Union invaded Afghanistan, Radio Moscow used gray propaganda when it attempted to justify the action. The documentary *Afghanistan: The Revolution Cannot Be Killed* appeared on Soviet television on December 25, 1985. The program left the impression that the conflict had been instigated by outsiders, and maps with routes leading from Pakistan and Iran into Afghanistan were shown. Film clips suggested that the guerrillas were mercenaries. A captured man identified as a Turkish national said he had been sent to Afghanistan by the CIA. The film ended with music about the Afghan homeland and pro-Soviet troops being cheered by crowds (Ebon, 1987, p. 345). In each of these cases, the source of the message was correctly identified, but the information was inaccurate. Gray propaganda is also used to embarrass an enemy or competitor. Radio Moscow took advantage of the assassinations of Martin Luther King Jr. and John F. Kennedy to derogate the United States. VOA did not miss the opportunity to offer similar commentaries about the invasion of Afghanistan or the arrests of Jewish dissidents.

Parry-Giles (1996), by reviewing internal documents of the Truman and Eisenhower presidencies, revealed how the U.S. government used the domestic news media to propagandize the American public during the Cold War by giving journalists the texts to be published in the newspapers in the 1940s and 1950s. By controlling the content and favoring journalists who cooperated, the government covertly disseminated propaganda to a domestic audience. This example of gray propaganda expands the definition to include, according to Parry-Giles, the attribution of the source to a nonhostile source (p. 53). An example of gray propaganda coming from a nonhostile source is as follows. Letters describing the successes of rebuilding Iraq, presumably written by American soldiers in Iraq in 2003, appeared in newspapers across the United States. A Gannett News Service (GNS) search found identical letters in 11 newspapers, and thus they appeared to be form letters. Six soldiers, whose names appeared on the letters, were questioned by GNS, and they denied having written them. A seventh soldier did not know about the

Figure 1.1   A German "black" parody of a British stamp, c. 1944. Note how the traditional crown has been replaced with a "Star of David" at the very top of the stamp.

letter bearing his name until his father congratulated him for getting it published in his hometown newspaper. All of the interviewed soldiers said they agreed with the information in the letters even though they did not write them. The actual source has not been uncovered. This is clearly gray propaganda with acceptable information attributed to a nonhostile source that was not the actual source.

Gray propaganda is not limited to governments. Companies that distort statistics on annual reports, advertising that suggests a product will achieve results that it cannot, films that are made solely for product placement, and television evangelists who personally keep the money they solicit for religious causes all tend to fall in the gray propaganda category.

Another term used to describe propaganda is *disinformation.* Disinformation is usually considered black propaganda because it is covert and uses

Figure 1.2   In this "black" parody, c. 1944, the Germans used the image of the Russian leader Stalin in place of the traditional image of Queen Elizabeth. Other political symbols visible on this stamp include the Star of David and the Hammer and Sickle. The function of such parody stamps was more to create a symbolic awareness of the political association between the USSR and Britain than to undermine the economy of the postal system.

false information. In fact, the word *disinformation* is a cognate for the Russian *dezinformatsia,* taken from the name of a division of the KGB devoted to black propaganda.

Disinformation means "false, incomplete, or misleading information that is passed, fed, or confirmed to a targeted individual, group, or country" (Shultz & Godson, 1984, p. 41). It is not misinformation that is merely misguided or erroneous information. Disinformation is made up of news stories deliberately designed to weaken adversaries and planted in newspapers by journalists who are actually secret agents of a foreign country. The stories are passed off as real and from credible sources. Long before the Cold War, a *New York Times* journalist successfully circulated stories that portrayed the Soviet Union in a positive light. Walter Duranty, the *Times* Moscow correspondent, was an active agent of Soviet propaganda and disinformation. He reported false stories about Josef Stalin and distorted and suppressed information. He was awarded the Pulitzer Prize for correspondence in 1932. In 1933, when Stalin conducted a savage campaign for collective farming in the Ukraine that resulted in widespread famine and more than 6 million deaths, Duranty denied the existence of the famine in his reports. He is still

Figure 1.3   The "battle of the stamps" continued with this British "black" parody of a German stamp. The meaning of the iconography is obvious. Here again, this stamp was probably more effective as anti-Nazi propaganda in Britain than in Germany itself.

on the list of Pulitzer Prize winners, but a subcommittee of the Pulitzer board is reviewing his award with the possibility of revoking it (Rutten, 2003).

Ladislav Bittmann, former deputy chief of the Disinformation Department of the Czechoslovak Intelligence Service, in testimony before the House Committee on Intelligence of the U.S. Congress in February 1980, said,

> If somebody had at this moment the magic key that would open the Soviet bloc intelligence safes and looked into the files of secret agents operating in Western countries, he would be surprised. A relatively high percentage of secret agents are journalists. . . . There are newspapers around the world penetrated by the Communist Intelligence services. (Brownfield, 1984, p. 6)

Allan C. Brownfield (1984), reporter for the *Washington Inquirer,* wrote,

The documentation of the manner in which Moscow has placed false stories in the non-Communist press is massive. In one instance, Alezander Kasnechev, the senior KGB officer in Rangoon, Burma, who defected to the U.S. in 1959, described the Soviet effort to plant such stories. His department was responsible for receiving drafts of articles from Moscow, translating them into Burmese, and then seeing that they were placed in local publications to appear as if they had been written by Burmese authors. The final step was to send copies back to Moscow. From there they were quoted in Soviet broadcasts of publications as evidence of "Burmese opinion" that favored the Communist line. (p. 6)

Among the more sensational Soviet disinformation campaigns was one that charged the United States with developing the virus responsible for acquired immune deficiency syndrome (AIDS) for biological warfare. The story first appeared in the October 1985 issue of the Soviet weekly *Literaturnaya Gazeta,* and it quoted the *Patriot,* a pro-Soviet newspaper in India. Although it was a Soviet tactic to place a story in a foreign newspaper to give it credibility, this time no such story had appeared in India. Despite denials by the U.S. Department of State, the story appeared in the news media of more than 60 countries, including Zimbabwe, while the nonaligned countries were having a conference there and in the October 26, 1986, issue of London's *Sunday Express* after *Express* reporters interviewed two people from East Berlin who repeated the story. Subtle variations continued to appear in the world press, including an East German broadcast of the story into Turkey that suggested it might be wise to get rid of U.S. bases because of servicemen infected with AIDS. On March 30, 1987, Dan Rather read the following news item on *CBS Evening News:*

A Soviet military publication claims the virus that causes AIDS leaked from a U.S. army laboratory conducting experiments in biological warfare. The article offers no hard evidence but claims to be reporting the conclusions of unnamed scientists in the United States, Britain, and East Germany. Last October, a Soviet newspaper alleged that the AIDS virus may have been the result of Pentagon or CIA experiments. ("CBS Spreads Disinformation," 1987, p. 7)

Increasing evidence indicates that disinformation is widely practiced by most major world powers, and this reflects the reality of international politics. For a long time, the United States denied using disinformation, yet a U.S. disinformation effort charged the Sandinistas in El Salvador with cocaine running. The Iran-Contra hearings in 1987, along with Admiral

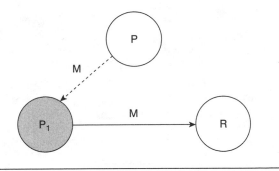

Figure 1.4   Deflective source model

Poindexter's papers, however, revealed that the CIA and the Contras were involved in a massive Central American drug-smuggling connection. The CIA had conducted a complex covert anti-Sandinista guerrilla movement that was financed through the illegal sale of parts to the Iranian air force. Other disinformation stories planted by the United States during the Cold War were about carcinogenic Soviet spy dust, Soviet sponsorship of international terrorism, and attempts by Bulgarians to assassinate the pope (Alexandre, 1988, pp. 114–115). The CIA began covert work in Afghanistan as early as 1979 when the Soviet Union invaded (Coll, 2004). According to Ahmed Rashid (2004), the Pakistan, Afghanistan, and central Asia correspondent for the *Far Eastern Economic Review* and the *Daily Telegraph*, "The CIA has a long record of manipulating the press and television and putting out its own interpretation of events" (p. 19).

As a communication process, disinformation is described according to two models we have developed (see Figures 1.4 and 1.5). In Figure 1.4, the propagandist (P) creates a *deflective source* (P_1), which becomes the apparent source of the message (M). The receiver (R) perceives the information as coming directly from P_1 and does not associate it with the original propagandist (P). In Figure 1.4, the propagandist secretly places the original message (M_1) in a *legitimating source* (P_2). This message (now M_2), as interpreted by P_2, is then picked up by the propagandist (P) and communicated to the receiver (R) in the form M_3, as having come from P_2. This legitimates the message and at the same time dissociates the propagandist (P) from its origination. One can see in both models that the propagandist's intent is to obscure the identity of the message originator, thus creating a high degree of credibility for both message and apparent source.

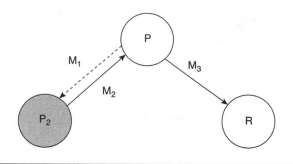

Figure 1.5   Legitimating source model

SOURCE: Reprinted by permission of Greenwood Publishing Group, Inc., Westport, CT, from Victoria O'Donnell and Garth Jowett, "Propaganda as a Form of Communication," in *Propaganda: A Pluralistic Perspective* by T. J. Smith III. Copyright by T. J. Smith III and published in 1989 by Praeger Publishers.

Propaganda thus runs the gamut from truth to deception. It is, at the same time, always value and ideology laden. The means may vary from a mild slanting of information to outright deception, but the ends are always predetermined to favor the propagandist.

Subpropaganda/Facilitative Communication

Another dimension of propaganda is what Doob (1948) called "subpropaganda." Here, the propagandist's task is to spread an unfamiliar doctrine, for which a considerable period of time is needed to build a frame of mind in the audience toward acceptance of the doctrine. To gain the target audience's favor, various stimuli are used to arouse the attention of the audience and the related encoders and agents who mediate communication. L. John Martin (1971), a research administrator in the USIA for 9 years, called subpropaganda "facilitative communication" (p. 62)—that is, an activity designed to keep lines open and maintain contacts against the day when they will be needed for propaganda purposes.

Facilitative communication most frequently takes the form of financial aid, radio newscasts, press releases, books, pamphlets, periodicals, cultural programs, exhibits, films, seminars, language classes, reference services, and personal social contacts. These are all arranged in an effort to create a friendly atmosphere toward those who may be needed later. W. Phillips Davison (1971) gave examples of influencing journalists to give favorable press to the United States by offering rides and other services such as office space provided by the U.S. Committee on Public Information, parties, conducted tours of foreign cities, and news scoops.

Facilitative communication itself may not be propaganda, but it is communication designed to render a positive attitude toward a potential propagandist. In 1969, 450 active registrations of agencies distributing propaganda were on file with the U.S. government on behalf of foreign agencies. Davison pointed out that most were concerned with tourism, investment, or trade. This did not include activities by embassies or consulates, nor did it include mail and shortwave radio from abroad. Bogart (1995) said that within the USIA, both in 1953 and today,

> It is widely believed that a sense of affinity is developed by showing the people of other nations American documentary films and giving them free access to American books and publications. Such exposure fosters friendship that has great, intangible value, quite apart from any immediate political benefits. An even more powerful impression is made by bringing foreign nationals to the United States, where they can meet Americans and get a first-hand look at the society. (p. xxxiii)

In 1998, the USIA maintained more than 200 posts in 143 countries "to explain and support American foreign policy and promote U.S. national interests" (www.usia.gov/abtusia/factsh.htm, 1998). This agency alone published magazines and commercial bulletins in 20 languages, had a wireless file information service in 5 languages, produced films, operated a radio-teletype network, maintained a World Wide Web site, supported a speaker program abroad, supported public-access libraries, sponsored exchange and visitor programs, and broadcasts more than 900 hours a week through VOA in 47 languages, including English. Radio Free Europe/Radio Liberty broadcasts more than 500 hours a week in 23 languages. VOA "WORLD-NET" is a satellite television network established in 1983. News, educational, and cultural programs are broadcast 24 hours a day to millions of viewers through American embassies, U.S. Information Services (USIS) posts, and foreign television and cable networks. The USIA was moved back into the State Department during the Clinton administration and became known as the Bureau of International Information Programs (IIP). President Clinton called the propaganda from the bureau one of "the most effective foreign policy tools we have" (Parry-Giles, 2002, p. 191). Under the George W. Bush administration, the IIP is "the principal international strategic communications entity for the foreign affairs community" (http://www.state.gov/r/iip/). Its mission statement is to "inform, engage, and influence international audiences about U.S. policy and society to advance America's interests." The outreach is for international audiences, including media, government, opinion leaders, and the public in more than 140 countries around world. The bureau produces news articles; electronic and print publications; products on U.S. values, culture, and daily life in America; and lectures, workshops, and seminars to promote understanding of U.S. policies. President Bush's weekly radio addresses as well as all electronic and print articles are available in 7 languages—English, Arabic, Chinese, Spanish, French, Russian, and Persian (see http://usinfo.state.gov).

Another form of facilitative propaganda is helping societies restore their institutions after war or conflict. American soldiers in Afghanistan have been rebuilding schools in Paktia with the objective of winning enough gratitude and loyalty from the local Afghans to undercut any support for the defeated Taliban movement (Constable, 2002, p. 15).

The use of propaganda is prevalent in the world today. It is not only obvious in war-torn countries, divisions between and among ethnic groups, and struggles for power, but dissemination of propaganda is easier than it has ever been. Communication networks have expanded and changed, and information tends to be more accessible. The institutions of modern society, government, business, and religion retain the need to manipulate responses deliberately.

A Model of Propaganda

The literature of propaganda often refers to "mass persuasion," suggesting that propaganda is persuasion on a one-to-many basis. Propaganda tends to be linked with a general societal process, whereas persuasion is regarded as an individual psychological process. Propaganda has not been altogether successfully differentiated from persuasion by other writers. The model in Figure 1.6 is our attempt to differentiate between them and to demonstrate a separation according to purpose and process. The model also reveals the similarity between persuasion and propaganda, with subtle differences of technique used according to purpose.

Communication Defined

Communication is a process in which a sender transmits a message to a receiver through a channel. This process has been represented by both linear and transactional models. One of the earliest models of communication was developed by Aristotle (333 B.C.E.), who described a speaker, a speech, and an audience as the major components of the communication act. A linear model that influenced communication research was developed by Shannon

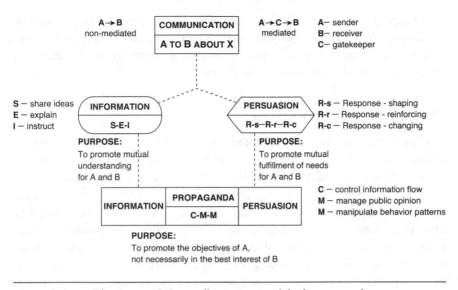

Figure 1.6   The Jowett/O'Donnell purpose model of propaganda

and Weaver in 1949 for the study of electronic engineering. Its components were source, message, transmitter, signal, and receiver. Other linear communication models that followed were similar to Shannon and Weaver's because they emphasized source, message, channel, and response.

Communication involves attempts to share meaning through a process of symbolic interaction between and among human beings. Communication has been defined as "an essential life process of exchange through which humans create, acquire, transmit, and utilize information" (O'Donnell, 1993, p. 8). Communication is built around an exchange of information that has both intended and perceived meaning. Information exchange can reduce uncertainty after several cycles of exchange. The tendency is for the sender and the receiver to move toward one point, for one to move toward the other, or for both to unite in a common interest or focus.

A straightforward definition of the communication process is that which happens when *A* (sender) communicates to *B* (receiver) about *X* (Westley & MacLean, 1977). *A* may be a person, a group, or a social system. *B* may be a person, a group, or a social system as well. Communication is often a human face-to-face transaction, but it is also often a mediated interaction whereby *A* communicates to *B* through *C* about *X*. Here, *C* is a gatekeeper, an encoder of a message, or quite possibly an agent for *B* (Westley & MacLean, 1977).

It is important to examine both the message and the response to it in the study of communication. Responses may be in the realm of feedback, or they may be examined as effects on the audience. The elements of face-to-face or mediated communication or both must be examined in the light of the context in which they occur, both in a specific and an immediate sense and in the social-cultural framework of the times.

Propaganda and Information

Communication has been defined as a process of exchange in which sender and receiver, either through mediated or nonmediated means, create, acquire, transmit, and use information. When the information is used to accomplish a purpose of sharing, explaining, or instructing, this is considered to be informative communication. People seek information when they need to understand their world. Once gained, information tends to reduce uncertainty. Uncertainty reduction is usually acquired through the communication of messages; thus, messages can be analyzed in terms of the amount of uncertainty they remove. Informative messages affect receivers by allowing them to acquire information, understand their world, and learn.

Generally, *informative communication* is thought to be neutral because it is characterized by a very special and limited use of language. Informative discourse is communication about subject matter that has attained the privileged status of being beyond dispute. Whenever information is regarded as disputable by either the sender or the receiver, the communication has difficulty proceeding as information. An informative communicator differs from other kinds of communicators by having the purpose of creating mutual understanding of data that are considered to be accurate, concepts that are considered to be indisputable, and ideas that are based on facts.

Propaganda uses informative communication in a similar fashion. The difference is that the purpose exceeds the notion of mutual understanding. The purpose of propaganda is to promote a partisan or competitive cause in the best interest of the propagandist but not necessarily in the best interest of the recipient. The recipient, however, may believe that the communication is merely informative. As we pointed out in the example of VOA, white propaganda is very similar to informative communication. Information is imparted from an identifiable source, and the information is accurate. The distinction between white propaganda and informative communication is that white propaganda informs solely to promote a specific ideology. Techniques of informative communication are also used in gray and black propaganda, but the information is not likely to be accurate or even based in reality. The propaganda bureau of Nazi Germany was known as the "Ministry of Information," an excellent example of black propaganda parading as information.

Many writers grapple with the distinction between propaganda and informative communication in educational practices that include the communicative purpose of instructing for mutual understanding. Elliot Aronson (1980, p. 60) questioned whether educators are merely imparting knowledge or skill. One subject area that Aronson questioned is arithmetic. He pointed out that most examples in elementary school arithmetic texts deal with buying, selling, renting, working for wages, and computing interest. He also cited Zimbardo, Ebbeson, and Maslach (1977), who thought these examples did more than simply reflect the capitalist system in which education occurs. The point is that arithmetic problems with a capitalist ideological base endorse the system, legitimate it, and suggest that it is the natural and normal way. Aronson said that interpretation of an instructional practice depends largely on the values of the person interpreting it. Four authors were asked by university researchers if their management textbooks are propaganda. Although their responses varied, "all four authors [said that they] write their textbooks to support a managerial ideology." The researchers concluded that the managerial ideology "would seem to serve the interest of other groups who are also currently most powerful in management education" (Cameron, Ireland, Lussier, New, & Robbins, 2003, pp. 726–728). (William E. Griffith, in his essay on communist propaganda, referred to *propaganda* and *education* interchangeably. He said that educating the masses has been the same as propaganda [cited in Lasswell, Lerner, & Speier, 1980, pp. 239–258].)

By evaluating educational practices according to their ends rather than their means, however, one can observe the use of informative communication as a means of achieving a propagandistic end in practices such as the ones described above.

Propaganda and Persuasion

Persuasion Defined

Persuasion as a subset of communication is usually defined as a communicative process to influence others. A persuasive message has a point of view or desired behavior for the recipient to adopt in a voluntary fashion. Victoria O'Donnell and June Kable (1982) defined persuasion as

a complex, continuing, interactive process in which a sender and a receiver are linked by symbols, verbal and nonverbal, through which the persuader attempts to influence the persuadee to adopt a change in a given attitude or behavior because the persuadee has had perceptions enlarged or changed. (p. 9)

Persuasion has the effect, when it is successful, of resulting in a reaction such as "I never saw it that way before." What happens is that the recipient of the persuasive interaction relates to, or contrasts the message with, his or her existing repertoire of information, experiences, or both. The process of persuasion is an interactive one in which the recipient foresees the fulfillment of a personal or societal need or desire if the persuasive purpose is adopted. The persuader also has a need fulfilled *if* the persuadee accepts the persuasive purpose. Because both persuader and persuadee stand to have their needs fulfilled, persuasion is regarded as more mutually satisfying than propaganda.

Persuasion Is Transactional

People respond to persuasion that promises to help them in some way by satisfying their wants or needs. That is why the persuader must think in terms of the persuadee's needs, as well as his or her own. Persuasion is a reciprocal process in which both parties are dependent on one another. It is a situation of interactive or transactive dependency. *Interactive* suggests turn taking, whereas *transactive* suggests a more continuous and dynamic process of co-creating meaning. The persuader who understands that persuasion is interactive or a transaction in which both parties approach a message-event and use it to attempt to fulfill needs will never assume a passive audience. An active audience seeks to have its needs fulfilled by the persuader, and an active persuader knows how to appeal to audience needs in order to ask the audience to fill his or her needs by adopting the message-purpose. A politician seeking votes must address the needs of the voters. If the voters are convinced that the politician will fulfill their needs, then they will fulfill the needs of the politician by casting positive votes at election time.

Responses to Persuasion   3 responses

Persuasion attempts to evoke a specific change in the attitudes or behaviors of an audience. The change sought is a specific response from the audience. Three different forms of response are possible (Roloff & Miller, 1980, p. 16).

First is *response shaping*. This is similar to learning, wherein the persuader is a teacher and the audience is a student. A persuader may attempt to shape the response of an audience by teaching it how to behave and offer positive reinforcement for learning. If audience responses favorable to the persuader's purpose are reinforced by rewards to the audience, positive attitudes are developed toward what is learned. The audience has a need for positive reinforcement filled, and the persuader has a need for a desired response from the audience filled.

Second is *response reinforcing*. If the people in the audience already have positive attitudes toward a subject, the persuader reminds them about the positive attitudes and stimulates them to feel even more strongly by demonstrating their attitudes through specified forms of behavior. Much persuasion in today's society is response reinforcing (e.g., blood drives, fund-raising, pep rallies, helping others), but people have to be motivated to go out and do these things year after year. Very little controversy surrounds these situations, but people's emotional needs have to be aroused to get them to get out and give blood or money or team support and other activities requiring effort, time, and money. ← ·toughest one

Third is *response changing*. This is the most difficult kind of persuasion because it involves asking people to switch from one attitude to another ("Favor the flat tax"), to go from a neutral position to a positive or negative one ("Support the community's recycling program"), to change behavior ("Practice safe sex"), or to adopt a new behavior ("Host an international student for the summer"). People are reluctant to change; thus, to convince them to do so, the persuader has to relate the change to something in which the persuadee already believes. This is called an anchor because it is already accepted by the persuadee and will be used to tie down new attitudes or behaviors. An anchor is a starting point for change because it represents something already widely accepted by potential persuadees. Anchors can be beliefs, values, attitudes, behaviors, and group norms. In 1943, during World War II, the illustrator Norman Rockwell used the anchors of the four freedoms declared by President Franklin D. Roosevelt (freedom from want, freedom from fear, freedom to worship, and freedom of speech) in posters to get people to buy savings bonds. The freedom of speech poster proclaimed "Save freedom of speech, buy war bonds" (see Figure 1.7).

Beliefs

A *belief* is a perceived link between any two aspects of a person's world (Fishbein & Ajzen, 1975, p. 131). A belief expresses a relationship between two things ("I believe that a laptop computer will help me get better grades") or a thing and a characteristic of that thing ("I believe that life once existed on Mars"). We have thousands of beliefs. To change old beliefs or to create new ones, a persuader has to build on beliefs that already exist in the minds of the audience. A persuader has to use anchors of belief to create new belief. The stronger the belief of a receiver, the more likely it is to influence the formation of a new belief.

Figure 1.7   Norman Rockwell poster. The setting is a New England town meeting. The speaker's hands are those of a laborer conveyed by color and texture. The detail conveys the idea that in a democracy, everyone has an equal voice regardless of social and economic status.

Values

A *value* is a special kind of belief that endures and is not likely to change. A value is a belief that is prescriptive and a guideline for a person's behavior. A value can be a standard for behavior (honesty, sensitivity) or a desired end (success, power). Values are concepts of right and wrong, good and bad, or desirable and undesirable. Schwartz and Bilsky (1987, p. 551), after a review of the literature on values, designated five features that are common to most definitions of values: (a) concepts or beliefs (b) about desirable end states or behaviors (c) that transcend specific situations, (d) guide selection or evaluation of behavior or events, and (e) are ordered by relative importance.

Personal values are derived from cultural values that tend to be utopian, mythic, and pragmatic. For example, many people share a national vision that embraces the belief in popular participation of people in government, in the right to say what you think without restriction, and in good conquering evil. A West European research organization, Futuribles, through a grant from the United Nations Educational, Scientific, and Cultural Organization (UNESCO), conducted a study of 1,125 experts throughout the world to predict their countries' core values for the year 2000. The experts from North America, primarily the United States, predicted that the top-ranked values would include possession of material wealth, health, jobs and work, individual liberty, and social equality. In contrast, the experts from Latin American countries predicted survival as the top priority, whereas African experts feared the loss of liberty. Schwartz and Bilsky (1987) surveyed subjects from Israel and Germany and found seven dominant motivational values: enjoyment, achievement, restrictive conformity, security, prosocial (active concern for the welfare of others), maturity, and self-direction.

When situations arise that pose a conflict between national and personal values, people often find it difficult to adapt. A nation's decision to go to war to protect economic assets creates conflict for the people whose children may die in battle. People regard their values as very personal and get quite upset when these are attacked; thus, the values make strong anchors for both persuasion and propaganda.

Attitudes

An *attitude* is a readiness to respond to an idea, an object, or a course of action. It is an internal state of feeling toward, or an evaluative response to, an idea, person, or object. It is expressed in a statement that clarifies a position ("I like milk in my coffee" or "I disagree with political correctness codes"). An attitude is a relatively enduring predisposition to respond; therefore, it already resides in the minds of audience members and can be used as an anchor. As people form beliefs about an object, idea, or person, they automatically and simultaneously acquire attitudes toward it. Whereas each belief is an association of an attribute with an object, an attitude is essentially an attribute evaluation.

Attitude change is often the desired response in persuasion; thus, attitudes may be used as anchors ("If you prefer to be physically fit, then you should exercise regularly") or as persuasive end states ("Patients should be allowed to sue health maintenance organizations"). People have thousands of attitudes—some important, others inconsequential. A persuader and a propagandist can use strongly held attitudes as anchors to promote related attitude change.

Behavior

Behavior can be used as an anchor not only because it is an overt expression of a way of being but also because behavioral patterns are fair predictors of future behaviors. When a behavior is recurrent, a script for behavior develops to the point that a great deal of consciousness is not necessary to continue the same behavior. References to successful behavior can be motivational. By reminding persuadees that their behavior has meant need fulfillment in the past, a persuader can urge them to use the same or similar behavior in the future. Conversely, if a certain behavior has negative consequences, the persuader can urge persuadees to avoid the consequences by discontinuing the behavior.

Another successful motivational strategy is to show persuadees models of behavior. Modeling influences new behavior in persuadees because it offers new information about how to behave (Bandura, 1986). Albert Bandura's model of observational learning includes the necessity of symbolic representation in words and images for retention of a behavior and identification of the subject with the model. Powerful modeling can simultaneously change observers' behaviors, thought patterns, emotional reactions, and evaluations. Observational learning includes knowledge of the rules of thought, as well as behavior itself.

Group Norms

Group norms are beliefs, values, attitudes, and behaviors derived from membership in groups. Group norms can be used as anchors because people have a tendency to conform to the norms of the groups to which they belong. Psychologist Daryl Bem (1970, p. 75) said that the major influence on people is people. Peer pressure influences how people dress, talk, and behave. When they are uncertain about what position to take or what to do, people often adopt the attitudes and behaviors of their peers. They also succumb to peer pressure because it is easier to conform than to depart from the norms of their groups.

Another form of group norm is derived from the norms of a reference group. *Reference groups* are groups admired or disliked by nonmembers who may be influenced in a positive or negative direction by those groups. People may admire the norms of a group such as Amnesty International or be repulsed by the norms of the Skinheads.

Resonance

A persuader who is well prepared knows the audience. Anchors can be discovered from knowledge of the audience members' affiliation with groups as well as from insight into their beliefs, values, attitudes, and behaviors. Because these categories constitute important attributes of the audience, they can be used to motivate the audience to accept the purpose of the persuader. Both persuasion and propaganda tend to produce messages of *resonance;* that is, the recipients do not perceive the themes of messages to be imposed on them from an outside authority to which they are required or committed to defer. Rather, the recipients perceive the anchors on which the message is based as coming from within themselves. Paul Kecskemeti (1973) defined the propagandist's ideal role in relation to the recipient of the message as that of an alter ego: "Someone giving expression to the recipient's own concerns, tensions, aspirations, and hopes. . . . Thus, propaganda . . . denies all distance between the source and the audience: the propaganda voices the propagandee's own feelings" (p. 864). Nazi propaganda relied on resonance by representing legends of the past, familiar music, and street theater in its propaganda. There was a bizarre play performed for German railroad workers in 1933. Hitler was compared to Jesus Christ in a Christmas nativity play. The performers, dressed as crusaders, acted out the struggle of light and darkness while Stormtroopers marched to the nativity scene carrying swastika flags. An announcer spoke over a loudspeaker: "God sent us a savior at the moment of our deepest despair; our Fuhrer and our wonderful Stormtroopers" (T. Clark, 1997, p. 52).

Identification must take place between the persuader and the persuadee in persuasive communication. Common sensations, concepts, images, and ideas that make them feel as one are shared. A persuader analyzes an audience to be able to express its members' needs, desires, personal and social beliefs, attitudes, and values, as well as their attitudes and concerns about the social outcome of the persuasive situation. The persuader is a voice from without, speaking the language of the audience members' voices within. Yet, persuasive communication may be dialectic in nature and preclude homogeneity. Conversely, the propaganda message is more often homogeneous because it is more likely to be sent to a mass audience than to one person in an interpersonal setting. Exceptions to this exist, of course, when the propagandist works one-on-one with various subjects.

Persuasion Seeks Voluntary Change

In general, practitioners of persuasion assume that the audience has access to information about the other side of a controversial issue as well as exposure to counterpersuasion. In other words, there is a recognition that any change that occurs within audience perceptions, cognitions, or behaviors will be voluntary change. Both parties, persuader and persuadee, will perceive the change due to persuasion as mutually beneficial.

Misleading and Manipulating an Audience

Of course, a persuader can mislead an audience regarding the true intention. Sometimes an audience is aware of this, which gives an aura of voluntary compliance; that is, the audience can decide to consent to change while knowing quite well that the persuader has a hidden agenda. Sometimes an audience will believe a persuader's spoken intent, and consequently, it will be manipulated and used without knowing what is happening. This we regard as propaganda. More commonly, however, the propagandist exploits an audience's beliefs or values or group norms in such a way as to fan the fires of prejudice or self-interest. When the audience goes along with such practices, a certain kind of mutual reciprocity occurs because both parties have needs fulfilled. The audience's needs—the reinforcement of prejudicial or self-serving attitudes—get fulfilled and spoken, but the persuader's needs—the attainment of a selfish end through the audience's compliance—get fulfilled but not spoken. A 1993 Roper poll revealed that 22% of U.S. adults and 20% of U.S. high school students believed it was possible that the Holocaust did not happen. Deborah Lipstadt (1993) attributed this to partial ignorance on the part of those surveyed but also recognized that Holocaust denial stems from "a mélange of extremist, racist, and nativist sentiments" (p. 4).

In contrast, no audience members, no matter how perverse their own needs, will put up with hearing that they are being manipulated and used to fulfill another's selfish needs. Thus, the propagandist cannot reveal the true intent of the message.

Rhetorical Background and the Ethics of Persuasion

Since the beginnings of the study of rhetoric, which was synonymous with persuasion until the early 20th century, theorists and practitioners have been concerned with ethics. The form of government in ancient Greece encouraged public speaking. Citizens voiced their opinions openly and were encouraged to share in making political and judicial decisions. Because civic responsibility was presumed, encouragement to be honorable citizens and to acquire skill in public statement was strong. The Athenian system disqualified any speaker who was "suspected of certain dishonorable acts . . . he could be prosecuted, not for the offense, but for continuing to speak in the assembly after committing the offense" (Bonner, 1933, p. 80). People studied the art of rhetoric almost as an entire system of higher education, if not a way of life (Hunt, 1925, p. 3).

Plato opposed the place of rhetoric in Athenian life as well as whatever part rhetoric had in influencing public opinion. As Hunt (1925) said, "He despised mere opinion almost as much as he did the public" (p. 3). He believed in a government ruled by philosopher-kings and not a government in which rhetoric was employed by those who did not possess true wisdom or knowledge. As a result, two of his writings, the *Gorgias* and the *Phaedrus,* attacked rhetoric as a system capable of making the worse appear the better reason. In the *Gorgias,* Plato criticized the study of rhetoric for misleading people into believing that, by attempting through words to achieve what is good, they could do good. Without insight and wisdom, a person who studied rhetoric was likely to become what we would call a propagandist. Plato, through his spokesman Socrates, posed the following questions:

Do the rhetoricians appear to you always to speak with a view to what is best, aiming at this, that the citizens may be made as good as possible by their discourses? or do they, too, endeavor to gratify the citizens, and neglecting the public interest for the sake of their own private advantage, do they treat the people as children, trying only to gratify them, without being in the least concerned whether they shall become better or worse by these means? (cited in Cary, 1854, pp. 125–126)

In the *Phaedrus,* Plato admonishes the rhetorician to have high moral purpose and knowledge of truth or else not attempt rhetoric at all. Through the exhibition of three speeches about love, which represent three different kinds of speakers, Plato contrasted the neutral, the evil, and the noble lovers/speakers. The second lover/speaker is evil and insincere and attempts to exploit, deceive, and manipulate his audience, whereas the third lover/speaker is noble and has a genuine desire to help the audience and to actualize its ideals. Plato summed up the best of the speakers by having Socrates say,

A man must know the truth about each particular of which he speaks or writes. . . . Not till then can discourses be artistic as far as it lies in the nature

of their genus to be made so, to be controlled by art for the purpose of instruction or persuasion. (cited in Bailey, 1965, p. 51)

Aristotle, the great philosopher and social interpreter of fourth-century
Greece, produced many classical works about the nature of ideas and
people. The work that is seminal in the field of persuasion is *Rhetoric*
(L. Cooper, 1932). Although Aristotle studied with Plato at the academy and
embraced many ideas that Plato expressed in the *Phaedrus*, *Rhetoric* tends
to be detached from issues of morality. Rather, it is an amoral and scientific
analysis of *rhetoric,* defined as "the faculty of discovering in the particular
case what are the available means of persuasion" (L. Cooper, 1932, p. 7).
Yet, in *Rhetoric,* Aristotle establishes the concept of *credibility* (*ethos*) as a
form of proof and mode of persuasion. *Ethos,* an artistic proof established
within the discourse itself, provides the audience with insight into the persuader's character, integrity, and goodwill. Other forms of proof are emotional appeal (*pathos*) and the speech itself, its reasoning and arguments
(*logos*), defined by Aristotle as "when we have proved a truth or an apparent truth from such means of persuasion as are appropriate to a particular
subject" (cited in L. Cooper, 1932, p. 9).

Central to the study of rhetoric is the audience, which Aristotle classified
and analyzed. Logic is established through audience participation in an interactive reasoning process. Known as the *enthymeme,* this practical device is
regarded by many as a syllogism with some part or parts missing. In fact, the
enthymeme enabled the persuader and persuadees to co-create reasoning by
dialectically coming to a conclusion. It requires the audience mentally to fill
in parts of the reasoning process, thus stimulating involvement. Aristotle
regarded the enthymeme as a way of guarding truth and justice against false-
hood and wrong. He believed that audiences could not follow close and
careful logical reasoning related to universal truths but could participate
in reasoning related to probability in the sphere of human affairs. In his
Nicomachean Ethics, Aristotle dealt with his expectations for high moral
principles and analyzed virtue and vice to provide strategies for *ethos,* or
character of the speaker. With regard to persuasion, he indicated that a
crafty person could artfully manipulate the instruments of rhetoric for either
honest or dishonest ends. Depending on which end is desired, the use of
rhetorical devices is judged accordingly: "If . . . the aim be good, the cleverness is praiseworthy; but if it be bad, it becomes craft" (cited in Browne,
1850, VI, pp. xii, 8). MacCunn (1906) interpreted this to mean that the
Aristotelian thesis postulates that "cleverness and character must strike alliance" (p. 298). MacCunn also saw Aristotle's general point of view as judg-
ing the means according to the ends sought: "He who would win the harper's

skill must win by harping; he who would write, by writing; he who would heal the sick by healing them. In these, as indeed in all the arts, faculty is begotten of function, and definite proclivity comes of determinate acts" (p. 301). Aristotle believed that the ethics of rhetoric could be judged by the speaker's intent, the means used in the speech to further the argument, and accompanying circumstances. He also thought the integration of reason and emotional appeals was acceptable as long as the speaker advocated for the general public good.

Quintilian, the premier teacher of imperial rhetoric in Rome during the first century C.E., wrote the *Institutes of Oratory,* in which he advocated the necessity of credibility, arguing on behalf of Cato's definition: "An orator is a good man, skilled in speaking" (cited in Benson & Prosser, 1969, p. 118). This concept was reiterated by St. Augustine in his fifth-century work on Christian preaching and rhetoric, *On Christian Doctrine.* Insistence on truth as the overall objective of public speaking is the cardinal tenet of this treatise. St. Augustine was concerned about using rhetorical techniques for false persuasion, but he thought the way it was used did not reflect on rhetoric itself:

> There are also rules for a more copious kind of argument, which is called eloquence, and these rules are not the less true that they can be used for persuading men of what is false, but as they can be used to enforce the truth as well, it is not the faculty itself that is to be blamed, but the perversity of those who put it to a bad use. (cited in J. F. Shaw, 1873, IX, p. 5)

Classical concepts of rhetoric, especially that of the good man speaking well, were revitalized throughout the Middle Ages, the Renaissance, and the Reformation. Neoclassicism held forth in theoretical works on persuasion despite the appearance of despotic princes and authoritarian rulers in the same countries in which the rhetorical works were published. In 1513, Machiavelli wrote *The Prince,* advocating that deception to gain and maintain control be used, that the ends justified the means, and that the public was easily corrupted. He said, however, that force was needed to coerce the public as well:

> The populace is by nature fickle; it is easy to persuade them of something, but difficult to confirm them in that persuasion. Therefore one must urgently arrange matters so that when they no longer believe they can be made to believe by force. (Machiavelli, 1513/1961, p. 19)

Machiavelli accurately described the demagogue/propagandist—"everyone sees who you appear to be, few sense who you really are"—and elaborated thusly:

A prince, therefore, need not necessarily have all the good qualities I mentioned above, but he should certainly appear to have them. . . . He should appear to be compassionate, faithful to his word, kind, guileless, and devout. . . . But his disposition should be such that, if he needs to be the opposite, he knows how. (pp. 55–56)

In the same century, rhetorical theorists such as Philipp Melanchthon, the humanist educator, contemporary of Martin Luther, and major religious reformer of Germany; Leonard Cox, the first to write a treatise on rhetoric in the English language; and Thomas Wilson, Elizabeth I's secretary of state, whose *Arte of Rhetorique* was published eight times in 30 years from 1553 to 1583, were turning out works that echoed the ethical principles of Plato, Cicero, and Quintilian.

Even after the *Sacra Congregatio de Propaganda Fide* became an official organ of the Roman Catholic Church in 1622, no rhetorical theorist addressed its implications with regard to persuasion. The major rhetorical works of the 17th century were Francis Bacon's four treatises—adapting classical rhetoric to the needs of the scientist and affirming the value of ornamentation and imaginative coloring in rhetoric—and the early elocutionists Robert Robinson and John Bulwer, whose works on delivery foreshadowed the rhetorical movement that placed major emphasis on delivery and pronunciation.

Rhetoric and Propaganda

The study of persuasion in the theories of rhetoric laid down throughout the centuries emphasized adherence to the truth and sound reason in revealing the real intent of the persuader, demonstration of a conclusion based on evidence and reasoning, and a sincere concern for the welfare of the audience. These are the humanistic concerns of the classicists. It can be argued that the humanists were concerned with eloquence and consequently preferred rhetoric to logic. No major rhetorical theories have come from nations whose governments have been totalitarian; thus, the history of rhetoric hardly includes the study of propaganda except for allusions to misuse of rhetorical techniques for dishonest ends. The Bolsheviks had Eisenstein to describe and demonstrate the use of propaganda in film, and the Nazis had Hitler's *Mein Kampf* and Goebbels's diaries as guidelines for propaganda, but these have not been part of the history of rhetorical theory. The reason for this comes from the rhetorician's insistence on a consideration of ethics in rhetoric. Not until Kenneth Burke, the American literary critic, wrote

"*The Rhetoric of Hitler's 'Battle'*" in 1939 (in Burke, 1973) did a serious rhetorical critic tackle and analyze propaganda while simultaneously contributing new ideas to rhetorical theory.

Drawing on what he called the Dramatistic Pentad—five interrelated motivational or causal points of view—Burke (1941/1973) analyzed the *act* (what took place in thought or deed), the *scene* (the background of the act, the situation in which it occurred), the *agent* (the actor or person or institution that performed the act), the *agency or agencies* (the means or instruments used by the agent), and the *purpose* (the motive or cause behind the act). Burke determined that, in *Mein Kampf*, (a) the *act* was the bastardization of religious thought; (b) the *scene* was discordant elements in a culture progressively weakened by capitalist materialism; (c) the *agent* was Hitler; (d) the *agencies* were unity identification such as "one voice" (the Reich, Munich, the army, German democracy, race, nation, Aryan, heroism, etc.) versus disunity identification such as images, ideas, and so on of the parliamentary wrangle of the Hapsburgs, Babel of opinion, and Jewish cunning, together with spiritualization and materialization techniques; and (e) the *purpose* was the unification of the German people. Burke's description of Hitler's strategies to control the German people is a masterful criticism of propaganda, yet it also is heavily flavored with moralistic judgment. It warns the reader about "what to guard against if we are to forestall the concocting of similar medicine in America" (p. 191).

Donald C. Bryant's (1953) seminal essay, "*Rhetoric: Its Function and Scope*," devotes a few pages to propaganda, which includes advertising and certain political discourse, as "partial, incomplete, and perhaps misused, rhetorics" (p. 413). He characterized propaganda by technique—excluding competing ideas, short-circuiting informed judgment, ignoring alternative ideas or courses of action, and in general subverting rational processes. Although Bryant did not engage in propaganda analysis or add new insight into understanding propaganda, he acknowledged that the understanding of propaganda is grounded in the understanding of rhetoric. His stance is a classical one, for he said, "The major techniques of this propaganda are long known rhetorical techniques gone wrong" (p. 415).

Although few rhetorical theorists discussed propaganda, the study of persuasion blossomed in the 20th century as an inquiry into behaviorism. This happened almost concurrently with the serious study of propaganda by social scientists. This development and synopsis of the resulting research is presented in Chapter 4. Now let's return to the model that depicts propaganda as a special form of communication.

Propaganda as a Form of Communication

Propaganda may appear to be informative communication when ideas are shared, something is explained, or instruction takes place. Information communicated by the propagandist may appear to be indisputable and totally factual. The propagandist knows, however, that the purpose is not to promote mutual understanding but rather to promote his or her own objectives. Thus, the propagandist will attempt to control information flow and manage a certain public's opinion by shaping perceptions through strategies of informative communication.

A persuader, likewise, shares ideas, explains, or instructs within the purpose of promoting the mutual satisfaction of needs. In fact, a persuader skillfully uses evidence to teach potential persuadees with the intent of response shaping. Evidence itself does not persuade, but it can enhance a persuader's credibility (McCroskey, 1969). Persuaders, however, do not try to appear as informers. An effective persuader makes the purpose as clear as possible in order to bring about attitude or behavior change. The explicitly stated conclusion is twice as likely to get the desired audience response compared with the suggested one (Biddle, 1966; Hovland & Mandell, 1952). The propagandist may appear to have a clear purpose and certainly an explicitly stated conclusion, but the true purpose is likely to be concealed.

Concealed Purpose

The propagandist is very likely to appear as a persuader with a stated purpose that seems to satisfy mutual needs. In reality, however, the propagandist wants to promote his or her own interests or those of an organization— sometimes at the expense of the recipients, sometimes not. The point is that the propagandist does not regard the well-being of the audience as a primary concern. The propagandist is likely to be detached from the recipients. Not only does the propagandist not care about the audience, but also may not believe in the message that is being sent. In fact, concealment of purpose may not be the only deviousness. Often, propagandists do not want their identity known.

Concealed Identity

Identity concealment is often necessary for the propagandist to achieve desired objectives and goals. The propagandist seeks to control the flow of information, manage public opinion, and manipulate behavioral patterns. These are the kinds of objectives that might not be achieved if the true intent were known or if the real source were revealed.

Control of Information Flow

Control of information flow takes the form of withholding information, releasing information at predetermined times, releasing information in juxtaposition with other information that may influence public perception, manufacturing information, communicating information to selective audiences, and distorting information. The propagandist tries to control information flow in two major ways: (a) controlling the media as a source of information distribution and (b) presenting distorted information from what appears to be a credible source. Using journalists to infiltrate the media and spread disinformation is one way to present distorted information. A public relations expert, Victoria Clarke, developed the Pentagon's media operation, including the program to embed American journalists with American troops in Iraq in 2003–2005. This may have been intended as a form of controlling information flow because the journalists get emotionally attached to their units, thus causing their reporting to be emotional.

Slobodon Milosevic of Serbia and Franjo Tudjman of Croatia seized control of most of the media and used newspaper, radio, and television reports of atrocities to fan the fires of hatred on both sides during the Serbian-Croatian war in the former Yugoslavia. The reporting on Belgrade television was so biased that thousands of people staged a huge demonstration to protest. In Croatia, Tudjman removed personnel at Croatian television and the newspaper *Vjesnik* and replaced them with his own people.

Altheide and Johnson (1980) made a case for what they called "bureaucratic propaganda," in which organizations as diverse as the military, television networks, and evangelical crusades release official reports containing what appears to be scientifically gathered and objective information to influential groups with the purpose of maintaining the legitimacy of the organizations and their activities. The information in the official reports is often contrived, distorted, or falsely interpreted. This information, according to Altheide and Johnson, may never be seen by the public but rather by a congressional committee or some citizens group and may be used for some action or program.

Other reasons for corporate information control are secrecy in new product development or suppression of data about products that are hazardous to human health and the environment.

Minority opinion may be suppressed to maintain an appearance of a strong base of support. Colluding sources of information that support the propagandist's intent will be disseminated, whereas opposing sources are likely to be suppressed. When Chinese students demonstrated in Tiananmen Square in Beijing in 1989, the government blacked out news reports of the protest to smaller cities and the countryside. Chinese citizens in these areas never knew about the Beijing unrest and the demands for reforms. The world saw the demonstrations because the media were in Beijing to cover Mikhail Gorbachev's visit there. When the government brutally massacred student protestors fleeing from tanks and grenades, it distorted the truth by claiming that thugs and counterrevolutionaries had murdered soldiers of the People's Republic of China, who fired back in self-defense. Here, the Chinese government successfully controlled information flow to its own people, but other people of the world knew about it.

Expansion of access to information around the world through new mass communication technologies has made control of information flow difficult. CNN and the BBC World Service bring television news to almost everyone except where they have been banned in Singapore, India, and China (Bogart, 1995, p. xxxiii). In the Mexican state of Chiapas, where land reforms promised following the 1919 revolution have still not been carried out, the Zapatista National Liberation Army, a revolutionary group, declared war on the Mexican army and the administration of President Carlos Salinas de Gortari. The Mexican government has attempted to control the information flow to prevent sympathy for the Zapatistas; however, the revolutionaries have promulgated their cause through the World Wide Web. A Zapatista "Solidarity" page can be found at www.ezln.org, with multiple links explaining not only their cause but also the causes of other groups as well. Likewise, Htun Aung Gyaw, who was sentenced to death in absentia in Burma for leading the student resistance to the Burmese military regime and who escaped to the United States, runs the Civil Society for Burma over the Internet from Ithaca, New York (www.csburma.org). He gets information to supporters in Burma, who then smuggle it to the resistance workers. He also sends faxes to foreign companies that do business in Burma to detail the atrocities of the military regime (Ryan, 1998, p. 12).

The Management of Public Opinion

Propaganda is most often associated with the management of public opinion. Public opinion has been defined by Land and Sears (1964) as "an implicit verbal response or 'answer' that an individual gives in response to a particular stimulus situation in which some general 'question' is raised" (quoted in Mitchell, 1970, p. 62). Walter Lippmann (1922) regarded public opinion as that which emanated from persons interested in public affairs, rather than as a fixed body of individuals. He believed that public opinion was effective only if those interested persons supported or opposed the "actors" in public affairs. Speier (1950) thought public opinion exists when a unique "right" is granted to a significant portion of extragovernmental persons:

In its most attenuated form this right asserts itself as the expectation that the government will reveal and explain its decisions in order to enable people outside the government to think and talk about these decisions, or to put it in terms of democratic amenities, in order to assure "the success" of the government's policy. (quoted in Altheide & Johnson, 1980, p. 7)

Mitchell (1970) gave four forms that public opinion usually takes: (a) popular opinion as generalized support for an institution, regime, or political system (as opposed to apathy, withdrawal, or alienation); (b) patterns of group loyalties and identifications; (c) public preferences for select leaders; and (d) intensely held opinions prevalent among a large public regarding public issues and current affairs (pp. 60–61). Mitchell likened the propagandist's management of public opinion to "a burning glass which collects and focuses the diffused warmth of popular emotions, concentrating them upon a specific issue on which the warmth becomes heat and may reach the firing-point of revivals, risings, revolts, revolutions" (p. 111).

The Manipulation of Behavior

Ultimately, the goal of propaganda is to manipulate behavior and behavioral patterns; external rather than internal public opinion is sought. Voting, buying products, selecting entertainment, joining organizations, displaying symbols, fighting for a cause, donating to an organization, and other forms of action responses are sought from the audiences who are addressed by the persuader and the propagandist. These are *overt* behaviors that can be observed as both verbal and nonverbal responses.

According to Triandis (1977), other categories of behavior are *attributive* behavior, derived from the conclusions drawn about the internal states of others from observations of their behavior, and *affective* behavior, emotional reactions to people and events. An example of an attributive behavior is a manufacturer concluding, "Consumers buy our product regularly; therefore, they must like it." Examples of affective behaviors are cheering and yelling for a political candidate and experiencing a burst of pride when the national anthem is sung. Triandis pointed out that behaviors become habits or behavioral patterns when they are performed repeatedly over a long period of time. Patterns in past behaviors or habits are fair predictors of future behaviors. In other words, they become "scripts" for behavior in similar situations. When a similar situation is encountered, carrying out the same behavior does not require a great deal of consciousness (Roloff & Miller, 1980, p. 50). Robert Coles's book *The Political Life of Children* (1986), which is about how children learn about political loyalties from language, religion, and family, tells, for example, about the children of war-torn Northern Ireland. The Protestant children believe that God is on their side, and Coles relates how their parents sang "God Save the Queen" to them while rocking them to sleep in the nursery.

A propagandist or persuader will have difficulty changing behavior if the audience already has habits to the contrary. This is especially true when a habitual behavior is triggered by emotion (Triandis, 1977, p. 25). The point is that behavioral change is not easy to bring about. Both persuaders and propagandists are well aware of this and actively seek information regarding variables related to behavioral change and predictors of behavior.

Thus, we have seen how propaganda is a form of communication and how it uses both informative and persuasive communication concepts to promote its own objectives by controlling the flow of information, managing public opinion, and manipulating behavioral patterns. Propaganda is a subset of both information and persuasion. Sharing techniques with information and persuasion but going beyond their aims, propaganda does not seek mutual understanding or mutual fulfillment of needs. Propaganda deliberately and systematically seeks to achieve a response that furthers the desired intent of the propagandist.

Overview of the Book

The modern study of propaganda came about after World War I and, interestingly, led the way to the social scientific study of persuasion. At the same time, as Doob (1966) pointed out, the word *propaganda* became less used and was replaced by words such as *communication, information,* and *persuasion* because they imply no value judgment and tend to embrace the development of new communication technologies as well as the "intricate perplexities inherent in developing societies and international diplomacy" (p. vi).

The historical development of propaganda and the developing media and audiences are the subjects of Chapters 2 and 3. Chapter 4 reviews the theories and research regarding persuasion and propaganda. Chapter 5 examines the use of propaganda in psychological warfare and the emerging fear of propaganda in mass society. The remainder of the book concentrates on modern propaganda methods of analysis (Chapter 6), four case studies (Chapter 7), and a process model that depicts how propaganda works in modern society (Chapter 8).

2

Propaganda Through the Ages

The use of propaganda has been an integral part of human history and can be traced back to ancient Greece for its philosophical and theoretical origins. Used effectively by Alexander the Great, the Roman Empire, and the early Christians, propaganda became an integral part of the religious conflicts of the Reformation. The invention of the printing press was quickly adopted by Martin Luther in his fight against the Catholic Church and provided the ideal medium for the widespread use of propagandistic materials. Each new medium of communication was quickly adopted for use by propagandists, especially during the American and French revolutions and later by Napoleon. By the end of the 19th century, improvements in the size and speed of the mass media had greatly increased the sophistication and effectiveness of propaganda.

In the 20th and 21st centuries, we have witnessed an unprecedented growth in the scope and speed of communication technologies, which has far outstripped the ability to control the continuous flow of information that emanates from a myriad of sources. This development has greatly enhanced the ability of a would-be propagandist to spread a message quickly, efficiently, and often without challenge from countervailing sources. The result has been a worldwide proliferation of propagandistic information on a wide range of subjects. In particular, since the dramatic events surrounding the attack on the World Trade Center in New York on September 11, 2001, there has been a significant growth in satellite-based television news broadcasting vying for the attention of an international audience. The influence of these new global networks will undoubtedly play a major role in how propaganda is used on the international stage in the immediate future.

The use of propaganda as a means of controlling information flow, managing public opinion, or manipulating behavior is as old as recorded history. The concept of persuasion is an integral part of human nature, and the use of specific techniques to bring about large-scale shifts in ideas can be traced back to the ancient world. Many artifacts from prehistory and from earliest civilizations provide us with evidence that attempts were being made to use the equivalent of modern-day propaganda techniques to communicate the purported majesty and supernatural powers of rulers and priests. In a largely preliterate age, dazzling costumes, insignia, and monuments were deliberately created symbols designed to evoke a specific image of superiority and power that these early propagandists wished to convey to their audience.

As was noted in Chapter 1, the first systematic attempt to use and analyze propaganda was in ancient Greece. The use of deliberate forms of speech carefully calculated to deliver a persuasive message can also be found in the writings of Confucius in his *Analects,* where he suggests that the use of "good" rhetoric, together with the proper forms of speech and writing, could be used to persuade men to live meaningful lives. Bruce L. Smith pointed out in 1958 that this Platonic admonition was echoed in our modern world by the leaders of communist China, only it was called "brainwashing" (pp. 579–580). Although many changes have taken place in China during the past 30 years, the Chinese government still creates and promotes these systematic and deliberate propaganda messages aimed at creating a cohesive communist society among the diverse population.

The history of propaganda is based on three interweaving elements: first, the increasing need, with the growth of civilization and the rise of nation-states, to win what has been called "the battle for people's minds"; second, the increasing sophistication of the means of communication available to deliver propagandistic messages; and third, the increasing understanding of the psychology of propaganda and the commensurate application of such behavioral findings. Throughout history, these three elements have been combined in various ways to enhance and encourage the use of propaganda as a means of altering attitudes and for the creation of new ideas or perspectives. Only in comparatively modern times, however, have scholars and scientists begun to understand and assess the role of such mass propaganda techniques as an aspect of the social process. The history of propaganda does not develop as a clear linear progression, but certain significant historical benchmarks are worth examining as illustrations of how propaganda has been used at different times. In each case, those wishing to control or manage others (the propagandists) have made maximum and intelligent use of the forms of communication (the media) available to them while also accurately gauging the psychological susceptibility of their audiences so that their messages could be tailored to ensure the best possible reception. The successful propagandist is able to discern the basic beliefs, needs, or fears of the audience and to play upon those.

Ancient Greece and Alexander the Great

The ancient world, prior to 500 B.C.E., provides many examples of effective propaganda techniques being used by rulers, mostly in support of war or religious persuasion. As Philip M. Taylor (1990, p. 23) observed, a gradual shift occurred from war being fought in the name of a god to war being fought in the name of the king, often as the embodiment of "the living god." Egyptian pharaohs best exemplified this trend, and they devised their own unique, personalized style of propaganda in the form of spectacular public monuments, such as the Sphinx and the pyramids. "The Pharaohs were among the first to recognize the power of public architecture on a grand scale to demonstrate prestige and dynastic legitimacy" (P. M. Taylor, 1990, p. 23).

Although the ancient kingdoms of Sumer, Babylonia, Assyria, Egypt, and others all used techniques of propaganda, such applications were sporadic and lacked a philosophical (one could say "psychological") base (see P. M. Taylor, 1990, pp. 13–23). Not until the emergence of Greek civilization after approximately 800 B.C.E. do we find the first systematic application of propaganda in both warfare and civil life. After 750 B.C.E., the Greek city-states became the basis of an increasingly structured society, albeit one in which each state had its own gods, culture, and social hierarchy. Given these differences, warfare between these city-states competing for cultural domination as much as for trade was inevitable. In such an atmosphere, the "iconography" of propaganda flourished, and great temples, monumental sculptures, and other edifices became significant symbols of the power of the state.

The long struggle between the two most powerful of these city-states—Athens and Sparta—yielded a host of legends that have become part of modern history and mythology. In their joint struggle against the Persians under King Darius and his son Xerxes (490–449 B.C.E.), we find one of the first deliberate uses of disinformation as a propaganda ploy. When Xerxes began his expedition to conquer all of Greece in 480 B.C.E., he quickly achieved a notable series of victories, including the conquering of Athens. When the situation looked hopeless for the Greeks, the Athenian naval commander, Themistocles, instituted a classic disinformation campaign of deflection. Themistocles arranged to have a series of messages delivered to Xerxes, apparently from Xerxes's own sources, suggesting that the many Greek troops from the smaller city-states of Thessaly, Thebes, and Argos who had joined his army in the wake of his military successes were unreliable and on the verge of revolt. Xerxes chose not to deploy these troops. Themistocles continued his plan of disinformation when Xerxes was led to believe that his Greek troops at Salamis (in Cyprus) were planning to leave, and Xerxes subsequently deployed half of his fleet to try to trap them. Themistocles was able to use yet a third successful disinformation ploy to induce Xerxes to attack the Greek fleet under these unfavorable conditions. Thus, the Battle of Salamis (September 28, 480 B.C.E.) proved to be a turning point in human history, and the Greeks' victory decided the war in their favor. After the Persian army was defeated at Plataea in 479 B.C.E., the Persians, despite having captured Athens, were eventually forced to leave Greece. Why was Themistocles's disinformation propaganda ploy so successful? As P. M. Taylor (1990) pointed out, "The simple fact of the matter was that this type of defection was so common in ancient Greece that Xerxes had little reason not to believe [the disinformation of] Themistocles!" (p. 26). This is a very salient point because propaganda firmly grounded in the realm of "possibility" or "truth" is much more likely to be successful, and Themistocles certainly understood this.

Alexander the Great

Alexander III, known as "The Great" (356–323 B.C.E.), as King of Macedonia (336–323 B.C.E.) created a Greek empire that stretched from India in the east, to Scythia in the north, and to Egypt and the Persian Gulf in the south, thereby introducing a new period of history known as the Hellenistic Age. He was only 20 when he succeeded to the throne after the assassination of King Philip II, his father. This precocious young man fulfilled his father's destiny by uniting Greece against its external enemies and created the League of Corinth, which included all the Greek states except Sparta. From his earliest years, he had impressed distinguished men with his intelligence and astute political sense. By all accounts, he was virtuous and abstained from large quantities of food and drink, which was normal among his officers. For his time, he was extremely magnanimous to those whom he defeated, understanding that more could be gained by incorporating these subjugated peoples into his empire than by destroying them.

Alexander never lost a battle, and when possible, he explored the territory alone or with a local guide. He was one of the first to study openly the "psychology" of his enemies, including their weapons and methods of warfare. His troops were well trained, and he was fair with them, never making a promise he did not intend to keep. He led by the example of his own courage and never lavished great riches on himself, giving gifts to others instead. His strategic military instincts were legendary, and no one was able to move armies as swiftly as Alexander. But he was also a master propagandist who knew the importance of significant events. As an example, in his attempt to unite the Macedonians and the Persians in his last years, he married Barsine, the eldest daughter of the late Persian King Darius. As well, he also arranged the marriages of 80 of his officers to Persian noblewomen and 10,000 of his troops to the Persian concubines who had followed his army through Asia. In this way, Alexander indicated his sincere desire to create a unified empire under his leadership and to underscore his belief that all his "subject" peoples were equal in his eyes. This symbolic act of propaganda reconciled the two cultures in a way that no political treaty ever could.

In 324 B.C.E., Alexander requested that he be deified so that he could carry out a scheme of repatriating 20,000 Greek exiles, which was contrary to the established laws of the League of Corinth. He became the son of Zeus, and his face soon appeared on coins, replacing that of Heracles, the real mythological son of Zeus. He commissioned, or allowed to be built, many statues and monuments in his honor, and representations of his portrait were to be found everywhere in his empire, adorning pottery, coins, buildings, and formal art (P. M. Taylor, 1990, p. 31). Alexander was the first to recognize that to maintain cohesion and control over his vast empire, such propaganda symbols could serve as a constant reminder of the various subjugated populations just where the center of power resided. These strategies are still widely used today.

Alexander died from fever at the age of 33, but he had been so successful in creating his own cult of personality and legends that they are as powerful today as they were 2,000 years ago. Even though we have very few contemporary accounts of his life and actions, the work of later historians ensured that his name has become synonymous with power and military might. He is, without doubt, one of the greatest figures in human history, and other notable individuals who followed him, such as Hannibal, Julius Caesar, Napoleon Bonaparte, and even 20th-century military generals, have all expressed admiration for Alexander and his achievements.

Imperial Rome

The Imperial Roman Empire, between 50 B.C.E. and C.E. 50, applied systematic propaganda techniques that used all available forms of communication and symbology to create an extremely effective and extensive network of control. The resulting "image" of Imperial Rome remains strong and has become an integral part of our popular culture, as we can all identify with the trappings associated with this great empire. Roman emperors developed their propaganda strategies to meet a very real need. Following in the footsteps of Alexander the Great, the Romans quickly found that the geographic extent of their far-flung conquests had created a difficult problem of control over their empire and necessitated the development of a strong, highly visible, centralized government. The wealth and power that had come with the conquests were used to maximum advantage as vast sums of money were spent on symbolizing the might of Rome through architecture, art, literature, and even the coinage. Coordinated from Rome, the policy of the Caesars was to combine all these symbols into a form of "corporate symbolism" reminiscent of modern-day advertising plans, which projected the image of an all-powerful, omnipresent entity.

Whereas the Greek city-states had already discovered that judicious use of sculpture, poetry, building, music, and theater could project the desired image of sophistication, the skill of the Caesars, as one historian noted, was in expanding and mass-producing this means of communication so that it was projected successfully over a long period to a very large area (Thomson, 1977, p. 56). Other factors contributed to the success of the Romans, for they were able to exploit a political and spiritual vacuum that made their imperial subjects much more susceptible to the sophisticated offerings of their conquerors. The Roman Empire was able to offer more than military protection: It provided both a moral philosophy and a cultural aesthetic that was adopted by the local peoples. In this way, the art and architecture of Rome was as much a symbol of imperial power as were the garrisons of armored legions, and the cultural legacy remained much longer.

Julius Caesar (100–44 B.C.E.) was particularly adept at using sophisticated propaganda techniques throughout his rise to power and during his move to assert totalitarian power. Initially, he used stories of his military exploits abroad, combined with actual terror tactics at home, to put fear into the populace. One prime communication channel for conveying these messages was coins; they were widely used to boast of victories or to show the emperors in various guises such as warlord, god, or protector of the empire. Coins were the one social document that the Romans were certain would be seen by the widest possible range of subjects under their control. Caesar also

Figure 2.1   One of Julius Caesar's coins. Coins were the first genuine form of mass propaganda, in that they were widely circulated and clearly were intended to represent the power of the state with the symbology stamped on them.

made maximum use of the spectacle, spending lavishly on massive triumphal processions—more than four in 1 month at one point—each representing a victory in the civil war and each different from the other. The cumulative effect of all this pomp and show of power helped create an atmosphere that enhanced Julius Caesar's reputation and seemed to justify his careful hints that he was descended from the goddess Venus. It was no accident that he chose the phrase "I came, I saw, I conquered," which in Latin is reduced to the alliterating and rhyming words *veni, vidi, vici*.

Julius Caesar was a master propagandist, equaled only by Napoleon and Hitler in his understanding of meaningful symbols and in his ability to understand instinctively the psychological needs of his audience. He understood the need to use such symbols of power and sophistication as a means of converting subject populations to the Roman way of life. This was far less expensive than maintaining elaborate garrisons of legionnaires and induced obedience to the new regime through cooperation and identification, rather than subjugation. Significantly, subject peoples were often granted the right to become Roman citizens under certain circumstances, thus increasing personal identification with the conqueror.

Caesar created his own legends out of ordinary events, and by making himself seem supernatural, he was able to set in motion the psychological changes in the minds of the Roman people that would lead away from republicanism and toward the acceptance of monarchical rule and the imperial goals. It is not surprising that, throughout history, evocations of the Caesarist image have been repeated by those who aspire to leave their mark on the world. Thus, not only Charlemagne, Napoleon, Mussolini, and Hitler have invested themselves in Caesarist trappings, but so has almost every parvenu monarchy in Europe. Whether the image of the eagle, the armored breastplate, the man-god on the white horse, or the powerful orator, the propagandistic legacy of the Roman Empire is still much in evidence in our own world.

Propaganda and Religion

When considering the effect of long-range propagandistic activities, no campaigns have been more successful than those waged by the great proselytizing religions of Buddhism, Christianity, and Islam. Although each of these great religions has used different strategies to achieve its purpose, they have all relied on the use of charismatic figures, heavy symbolism, a simple and incessant moral philosophy, and an understanding of their audience's needs. In each case, the new religion had to find a way to replace the existing religious beliefs and to win over the minds and hearts of the populace.

It should also be made clear that the propagandistic aspects of religions change over time and are subject to variations, depending on a variety of social and political factors at any point in time. The somewhat humane practices of proselytizing of the early Christians were not followed in the coercive techniques of the Spanish Inquisition in the 16th century, and even today quite wide differences are found in the use of propaganda in different Christian denominations, such as fundamentalist Southern Baptists or Methodists. In the case of Islam, in which religion permeates all aspects of life, including politics (Islam does not recognize the concept of "secular" authority), many shifts have occurred in the strict application of religious laws in various Islamic countries over the centuries. Today, we are witnessing a renewed propaganda effort by fundamentalist Muslims to use Islam as a means of achieving both the cultural and political goal of creating unity among the Arabic nations. The fundamentalists see strict adherence to the religious (and therefore political) laws of Islam as being the only way to counteract the inroads made by more materialistic Western influences (Patai, 1983).

This issue of Islamic fundamentalism has taken on a much greater significance in the wake of the events of 9/11 and is the source of a great deal of conflict and consternation in current international politics. In the effort to destroy the source of the terrible attack on the World Trade Center, the American military essentially removed an extreme form of Islamic fundamentalism in Afghanistan, where the Taliban regime not only had severely restricted the education of females but also had gone so far as to forbid television viewing, radio listening, dancing, and the playing and singing of nonreligious music. A new government, supposedly more tolerant of religious and cultural practices, was eventually voted in by the citizens. As a result, it was hoped that the "new" Afghanistan would now become less of a threat to the region, and to world peace itself, than had the fundamentalist and terrorist-supportive Taliban government. However, history has constantly demonstrated that the long-term results of such imposed "regime shifts" are very difficult to predict, and the country continues to struggle with entrenched cultural practices, such as the unequal treatment of women and the continuation by large parts of the population to offer loyalty to local warlords, which threatens the power of the central government to control the country.

Religions can be used very effectively as propaganda vehicles for broader social or political purposes. Beginning with the Chinese-Japanese War (1894–1895), the Japanese military used the Shinto religion as one important element in providing public support for their expansionist policies. This was done by turning the previously benign practice of Shinto into a supra-religious national cult. This act allowed the cult of Shinto to be imposed on the entire nation while still giving lip service to the modernistic notion of freedom of religious belief that the Japanese were eager to convey to the outside world. In the name of this Shinto cult of supra-nationalism, the emperor cult (worshipping of the emperor as a living god) was artificially devised, and a course in *shushin* (moral teaching) was made the basis of compulsory education for all. In this way, Shinto was manipulated by the militarists and jingoistic nationalists as the spiritual weapon for mobilizing the entire nation to guard the safety and prosperity of the emperor's throne. Japanese soldiers were sent into battle, propagandized in the belief that they were fighting "for the emperor!" After the defeat of Japan in 1945, the Allied powers prohibited the practice of State Shinto, although the pure religion was allowed to return, and today it continues to be an important part of Japanese life.

The use of religion continues to be a very important ingredient in modern propaganda practices. The Irish Republican Army—especially its military wing, the Provisional Irish Republican Army (PIRA)—in its efforts to force the British out of Northern Ireland, continues to emphasize the differences between the living conditions (e.g., housing, jobs, schooling) for the British-favored Protestants and its own followers in the Roman Catholic community (Wright, 1990). Even when a provisional settlement was reached between the warring factions in Northern Ireland in mid-1998, the uneasy peace was being threatened by the deep-seated cultural differences fostered by three

Figure 2.2   *The Leaflet Seller,* an etching by Amman from 1588. Illustrated leaflets have been a staple form of propaganda since the 16th century, and the leaflet seller was a common sight in town and cities. The combination of pictures and text was used for entertainment in the form of stories but also for propaganda purposes in religious and political conflicts.

centuries of religious confrontation. The Protestant Orange Order, an important cultural organization, insisted on its right to continue its marches through Catholic neighborhoods, symbolizing the victory of Protestant forces over Catholics at the Battle of the Boyne on July 12, 1690. These propagandistic marches, anachronistic as they may seem, have become an integral part of Protestant life and serve as a means of socialization for many young men into Protestant culture.

In South Africa, until the late 1980s, the Dutch Reformed Church (DRC) provided a religious justification for the establishment of the government's policies of apartheid. The DRC used its interpretation of certain biblical texts to propagandize actively in favor of racial separation. As Allister Sparks (1990) noted,

While the state has implemented the political philosophy, the church has supplied the theological justification for it. Thus has Afrikanerdom been largely relieved of what Leon Festinger [a psychologist] would call the "cognitive dissonance" of a devoutly religious people imposing a discriminatory, oppressive and manifestly unjust system on others of God's children. More than that, the church's endorsement gave a great impetus to the apartheid idea. It replaced the sense of guilt with a sense of mission, teaching not only that apartheid is not sinful but that it is in accordance with the laws of God. To implement it is therefore a sacred task which the Afrikaner people have been specially "called" to perform. (p. 153)

In one of the most dramatic shifts in South African history, the DRC eventually renounced its theological position in the late 1980s and apologized to those it had harmed by propagating these false interpretations of the Bible. This decision demolished the theological justification for political separation of the races and removed one major stumbling block in the dismantling of apartheid. In the period since 1991, after the release of the African leader and hero Nelson Mandela, the DRC has attempted to play a mediating role in bringing about racial and social harmony in the new "rainbow nation," as postapartheid South Africa calls itself. Although this new role for the church has not succeeded in eliminating all remnants of racist ideology among its former adherents, those whites who have chosen to remain in the DRC have demonstrated a genuine desire to see the fledgling multiracial society succeed.

Religious ideology can also propagandize for the good of society. As an example, in the United States, we have witnessed a similar shift in attitude (essentially religious "beliefs") in the Church of Jesus Christ of Latter Day Saints (the Mormon Church). Until recently, Mormon credo was similar to that of the DRC in South Africa, interpreting the Hebrew Scriptures to link black skin color to curses from God. In 1978, the church decided to admit all worthy of priesthood, regardless of race or color. However, the church was also eager to retract certain statements without undermining the credibility of church figures who are revered as prophets and whose pronouncements Mormons believe were inspired by God. As the membership in the church grew in Africa and other foreign countries, it became a necessity to disavow these earlier "racist legacies." The Los Angeles Times (May 18, 1998) reported that church leaders were secretly meeting to consider how to achieve this. Clearly, if the Mormons are to succeed in their overseas missions, they will have to find a way to erase this unacceptable part of their history.

In the United States, churches have traditionally played a significant role in furthering (or sometimes hindering) civil rights causes. Thus, in the battle for "gay rights," both sides have used religious interpretation to bolster their propagandistic campaigns. Those against claim that the Bible clearly condemns homosexuality; those in favor call attention to the most fundamental tenet of Christianity: "love thy neighbor." In recent years, we have seen an increasing campaign by sectors of the "religious right" to try to convince homosexuals and lesbians that, through the use of specific Christian-based "counseling," they could become "straight." Backed by full-page advertisements in major newspapers, this campaign has become a controversial battleground for the question of whether homosexuality is genetic or behavioral in origin.

In the presidential election of 2004, the issue of "gay marriage" (the legal right for homosexuals to marry) was a galvanizing one for many people, especially those who identified themselves as "born-again" or evangelical Christians. The issue became a focus of major propaganda campaigns on both sides of the argument and was ultimately credited with being a salient factor in the reelection of George W. Bush. To many political observers, this particular propaganda campaign was the forerunner of a much more systematic attempt on the part of conservative religious and political elements to make homosexuality a major issue in all local and national elections.

The Rise of Christianity

To examine the propagandistic strategies and techniques of a religion in no way demeans it; on the contrary, it provides a clear example that not all propagandistic messages are negative but are often aimed at some positive social or political purpose. The example of the rise of Christianity demonstrates how, by skill and understanding of the audience, a specific appeal was made that eventually altered the shape of the world. Christianity was aimed to a large extent at the defeated, the slaves, and the less successful part of the Roman Empire. It had to compete with literally hundreds of other similar religions for this audience at the time of the dissolution of the Roman Empire, and considering that Christ and his followers did not have control over the existing communications media at the time, the ultimate level of adoption of Christianity must be considered one of the great propaganda campaigns of all time.

When the strategy of Christian techniques is broken down, we find a masterful use of images and emotion. The legacy of the Jewish synagogue preacher was well established, but Christ and his followers took what were basically traditional messages and put them into a new form. The use of parables, dramatic gestures on the floor of the temple, graphic metaphors (e.g., the seeds on stony ground, the eye of the camel, the shepherd and his flock), and the personal factor of singling out individuals as human metaphors (e.g., Peter "the Rock," Simon "the Fisherman") combined to provide a powerful, emotional, and easily understood message. The keynote was simplicity and a promise of humanity and dignity for those who had often been denied such treatment. Early organizers of the Christian religion also developed the concept of cellular proselytizing, later to be adopted and developed by Lenin in the Russian Revolution and other revolutionaries since then. This was exemplified by the choice of 12 disciples as the dedicated core who would carry the message to other groups, who in turn would spread the word through personal contact in a system resembling today's pyramidal marketing schemes. Each cell would have its own leaders, and the loyalty and faith of cell members were solidified by the rituals of baptism and communion (Thomson, 1977). Nearly three centuries after the death of Christ, the cross became the symbol of Christianity, but during that time, the use of the two curved intersecting lines symbolizing a fish was widely used.

Not only was this symbol easy to draw, but it also had mystical overtones in that it derived from an acronym for the Greek words for "Jesus Christ, Son of God, savior," *ichthus*, which means "fish." The theme of the fish was particularly suited to a religion that relied on recruitment, and the metaphor of the apostles as "fishers of men," which many of them were in real life, was most appropriate. Initially used as a secret sign during the time when Christians were persecuted by the Roman authorities, the fish symbolized the mission of the group it represented and did so simply and effectively; as a result, it was found scrawled on walls, trees, in the dust, and any place where Christians wished to leave their mark to communicate their increasing numbers and strength to others. Even graffiti have a powerful propaganda value (Dondis, 1981).

The early Christians persevered against great odds, not only in the form of persecution and competition from other religions but also from dangerous internal schisms and heresies from dissident groups. One factor that eventually allowed Christianity to flower was the rejection of attempts made to absorb it into a universal world-religion (Gnosticism) or to restrict it to the select few (Montanism). From the outset, Christianity had asserted that it was catholic, or universal, in its message and appeal long before it became Roman Catholic in fact. What helped Christianity was its syncretic nature; it absorbed and used aspects from both Greco-Roman classicism and the new Germanic culture, as well as elements from ancient Oriental religions. When combined with the dramatic gospel of a savior who had died to save the entire world, and told in the common Greek or "Koine" that was the universal literary language of the Roman Empire, the religion thus possessed identity as well as universality for its increasingly wider audience.

After Constantine I adopted Christianity for a mixture of personal and political motives about the year 313, Christianity became for all intents and purposes the official religion of the emperors and was eventually adopted by the Germanic tribes that inherited the remnants of the empire. It took several hundred years for the full panoply of Christian symbolism to develop, but aided by the resilience of the infrastructure and communication system developed during the Roman Empire, the religion spread remarkably quickly. Its theme of universal love and a promise that the humble and the meek would inherit the earth was a dramatic reversal of the established order, but it found a sympathetic ear and gained audience empathy. The success of Christianity must also be considered within the sociohistorical period of late antiquity. The period 100 to 300 was an extremely religious age, evidenced by an increasing interest in the "other world." The material world, beset by barbaric invasions, plagues, disintegrating governments, and incessant warfare, was increasingly considered to be a place of evil, and humans were regarded as strangers in this world. Christianity, more than other religions, emphasized the mortification of the flesh and the spiritual separation from the material world and also promised a glorious afterlife to the faithful (Forman, 1979).

In succeeding centuries, the full symbolism of Christianity would be adopted—the cross, the lion and the lamb, the virgin and child, and even the horned and tailed figure (surely taken from pagan symbols) of the devil. These symbols have endured for nearly 1,500 years, and today Christianity is practiced by several billion people. The continued success of Christianity is a testament to the creative use of propaganda techniques applied to universal humanistic principles.

The Crusades

As was noted earlier, religious faith has been one of the most potent sources of propaganda in human history. Of all the wars that have been fought in the name of religious faith, none have been so bloody or more protracted than the Christian Crusades of the Middle Ages. For nearly 200 years, between 1095 and 1291, the forces of Christendom tried to wrest control of the Holy Land at the eastern end of the Mediterranean from the Islamic forces that controlled it. The origin of the Crusades can be traced directly to the exploitation of the almost mystical religious fervor of this period by a series of popes and monarchs seeking to consolidate their own power in the ongoing controversy between church and state. In fact, the basic concern that the holy places of Christendom were in the control of Moslem "infidels" was not really a problem, for although Christian pilgrims were often taxed, the Moslems had seldom denied religious visitors access to these sacred sites.

More practical political and economic considerations fueled the crusading impulse. The Roman Catholic Church saw an opportunity to spread its influence eastward into the sphere of its archrival, the Eastern Orthodox Church, from which it had been separated since 1054 as a result of a dramatic quarrel over doctrine. Feudal monarchs and lords of Western Europe dreamed of the riches that could be obtained from new lands and subjects. Also involved were the promise of penance for all sins and the forgiveness of debts for those going on Crusades. All these factors were exploited in the church's exhortations for people to take up arms to recover the soil where Jesus had trod.

The most significant propaganda events of the Crusades were the circumstances surrounding the original plea for the Crusades made by Pope Urban II in 1095. The Byzantine emperor Alexius Comnenus, responding to increasing inroads made by the Seljuk Turks on his territory, appealed to Pope Urban II for military assistance to protect "Christianity." The pope carefully staged his response at the Council of Clermont, held in November 1095 in southeastern France. He had previously announced that he would make a great public speech, thus assuring a significant audience. The splendor of the convocation was impressive, with cardinals, bishops, and nobles resplendent in their robes while the common folk gathered outside the church. After the ecclesiastical business had concluded, Urban moved outside to mount a large platform specially built for this occasion. According to one version (Freemantle, 1965, p. 54), he began by saying,

> It is the imminent peril threatening you and all the faithful which has brought us hither. From the confines of Jerusalem and from the city of Constantinople a horrible tale has gone forth . . . an accursed race, a race utterly alienated from God . . . has invaded the lands of those Christians and has depopulated them by the sword, pillage and fire.

Urban then enumerated the atrocities the Moslems had supposedly committed, including the ravaging of churches and their use in Islamic rites, the rape of Christian women, and the defiling of Christian altars.

He was graphic in his details, reporting that one technique used by the Turkish with their victims was to "perforate their navels, and dragging forth the extremity of the intestines, bind it to a stake; then with flogging they lead the victim around until the viscera having gushed forth the victim falls prostrate upon the ground." As the crowd stirred with emotion, Pope Urban II asked, "On whom, therefore, is the labor of avenging these wrongs and for recovering this territory incumbent, if not upon you? . . . Enter upon the road to the Holy Sepulcher; wrest that land from the wicked race, and subject it to yourselves" (Freemantle, 1965, p. 55). Urban skillfully balanced his appeal to the emotions with these atrocity stories, with a practical vision of what he was offering to those who would undertake this holy Crusade. He reminded his audience that the land to which he was urging them to go "floweth with milk and honey . . . like another paradise of delights," whereas the land they would be leaving was "too narrow for your population" and notably poor in food production.

Once Urban had announced the Crusade, and even before he had completed his speech, individuals in the crowd were calling out, "Deus Volt! Deus Volt!" (God wills it!). Whether this response was spontaneous or the result of deliberate planning we will never know, but Urban lost no opportunity and declared then and there that "Deus Volt!" would become the battle cry against the heathen foe and, furthermore, that each man embarking on the Crusade would wear the sign of the cross on his clothing. Next, the bishop of Puy, possibly briefed beforehand, stepped forward and shouted, "I confess!" Volunteers came forward, and before an emotionally charged crowd, the Christian crusade to liberate the holy city of Jerusalem was launched (Thomson, 1977, pp. 71–72).

Even before the crowds had dispersed, many had already ripped their clothing to make two strips forming a cross. This gesture was soon repeated by scores of thousands all across Europe. The cry for revenge on the infidels and in favor of a holy crusade was propagated by priests and preachers, and a significant number of written tracts were distributed describing the nature of Moslem atrocities on Christian people. Woodcuts of a monstrous Turk trampling the cross were circulated from village to village (Freemantle, 1965). All these propaganda strategies would not have been so effective if an underlying mood of piety had not been established a century earlier. Significant numbers of people had already experienced lengthy religious pilgrimages to such places as Rome, Venice, or even the Holy Land. The idea of undertaking such an arduous trip in the name of God for a clearly devout purpose officially sanctioned by the Church was not as far-fetched as might be imagined.

While Pope Urban II and the feudal monarchs were organizing official expeditions, the common people, roused to a fever pitch, surged forth on their own with little preparation. At this point, one of the most significant figures of the Crusades mythology appeared—Peter the Hermit. A priest of Amiens, a town in France, Peter was one preacher whose propagandistic eloquence attracted thousands of ordinary people to take part in what has been called the People's Crusade of 1096. Peter was very much like one of the Old Testament prophets with his wild hair, rolling eyes, and torrential speech. He claimed to be carrying a personal letter from God and was frequently subject to visions. He was so revered that the hairs of his donkey's tail were plucked to be kept as holy relics by worshippers. He arrived in Constantinople in July 1096 with only a remnant of the original ragtag band of almost 50,000 pilgrim-crusaders who had left France and Germany. There, he joined the other band of commoners, led by Walter the Penniless, which had managed to make its way eastward. Despite the warnings of the Christians living in Byzantium, these unprepared pilgrims began hostilities against the Turks, and they were systematically cut to pieces. Peter eventually joined forces with the princes of the first official Crusade, but his moment of glory had vanished, and in the end he returned to France, where he died in 1151.

The People's Crusade may have failed, but the First Crusade of the Princes was a great success, and by 1097, four expeditionary forces converged on Constantinople by land and sea. The climax of a series of Crusader victories came on July 15, 1099, when, after a 5-week siege, the forces entered Jerusalem to kneel in prayer at the site of the Holy Sepulcher. The Crusader kingdoms maintained a strong presence in the Holy Land for nearly 200 years afterward.

The entire crusading ethos fostered a new element of propaganda—the rise of chivalry. In the 12th century, a series of epic poems, the *Chansons de Geste,* were widely spread along the pilgrim routes by wandering troubadours. These stories about the feats of valor of Roland and his friend Olivier, who sacrificed themselves in the service of their king, served to provide role models for the chivalric ideal of knighthood. These epic poems were a form of propaganda for the idea of combat in the noble cause and helped establish the romance of all the attendant pomp and ceremony associated with chivalry. In many ways, the romantic notion of chivalry was as dangerous as later beliefs in nationalism and race, in that it created a romantic ideal of knighthood in which young men were asked to prove themselves in war or combat.

The Crusades started with great religious fervor and ended in disillusionment and political disarray, but in the end the propaganda that created the Crusades served a positive end. Despite the eventual loss of both Jerusalem and Constantinople, the contact with the civilizations of Byzantium and Islam brought many new ideas into Europe, such as glass making, silk weaving, and the use of sugar and spices in cooking. But an even greater consequence of the Crusades was the changes in the structure of feudalism brought about by the decline in wealth of the great feudal families. Towns now became wealthier and freemen more assertive in demanding their rights. Tradesmen and artisans prospered in this new climate of freedom, and the use of money began to replace the previous system of barter. Finally, the Roman Church, the moral and propagandistic force behind the Crusades, was able to solidify its power in the face of declining feudalism.

The Crusades continue to have a very special resonance in modern society as the battle between extremist elements of Moslem fundamentalism and the American government-sponsored "war against terrorism" has created deep divisions in the Arab world. It should be remembered that from the historical perspective, Arab culture has traditionally interpreted the Crusades in a very different light, essentially seeing the crusaders as rapacious foreign interlopers, whose main ambitions were not so much religiously motivated as they were seeking land, wealth, and power. These views, like those in the West that see only the religious and chivalrous aspects of the crusaders, have not changed for nearly a thousand years. Therefore, it was a very propagandistic faux pas when, a few days after the assault on the World Trade Center, president George W. Bush speaking spontaneously, without the aid of advisers or speechwriters, put a word on the new American effort to combat terrorism that both shaped it and gave it meaning. "This crusade," he said, "this war on terrorism." For George W. Bush, *crusade* was an offhand reference, no doubt colored by his strong Christian beliefs, but many, in both the Arab and Western worlds, saw it as an accidental probing of unintended but nevertheless real meaning. It was felt that while the president had used the word inadvertently, it nonetheless suggested his perspective on the nature of the conflict and was an unmasking of his most deeply held feelings. People, especially in the Arab nations, were outraged at the use of this term. Later, his embarrassed aides suggested that he had meant to use the word only as a synonym for struggle, but Bush's own syntax suggested that he defined crusade as war. This seemingly small, albeit innocent, mistake has continued to provide a rationale for many in the Arab world to view the "war on terrorism" with anger and suspicion and as a 21st-century version of the Crusades of the Middle Ages.

The Reformation and Counter-Reformation

In the history of propaganda, Christianity figures prominently, as both proponents and adversaries of the various denominations have used every conceivable technique to maintain their power and spread their ideas. Development of the movable-type printing press in the mid-15th century created a totally new form of communication that was almost immediately put to use as a major channel of propaganda in the titanic struggle for power between the Roman Catholic Church and Martin Luther.

An explanation of the causes of the struggle between the Roman Catholic Church and the "reformists" is beyond the scope of this book, but it essentially involved disagreements with increasingly corrupt practices in the established church (e.g., the sale of indulgences for vast sums of money) and a desire to establish direct contact with God without having to go through priests. This latter desire ultimately manifested itself in a call for the establishment of a simplified liturgy and Bible in the vernacular German language, rather than in Latin, which prevented full participation by the congregation. Martin Luther provided the first vernacular liturgies in 1526 (the "Deutsche Messe"), and his major literary achievement, the German-language Bible, was first printed in complete form in 1534. (A translation of the New Testament had appeared earlier in 1522.) The printed Bible, which went through many editions in Luther's lifetime, was the highest achievement of the Reformation and the direct result of the application of a new technology to the furthering of a specific cause. As noted Reformation historian A. G. Dickens (1968) pointed out,

> Between 1517 and 1520, Luther's thirty publications probably sold well over 300,000 copies. . . . Altogether in relation to the spread of religious ideas it seems difficult to exaggerate the significance of the Press, without which a revolution of this magnitude could scarcely have been consummated. . . . For the first time in human history a great reading public judged the validity of revolutionary ideas through a mass-medium which used the vernacular languages together with the arts of the journalist and the cartoonist. (p. 51)

The development of the printing press was a quantum leap in the speed of communication, and in the 16th century, printing speeds increased from about 20 sheets per hour to more than 200; although this was slow in comparison with modern printing presses, it was nevertheless an important step toward the evolution of true mass media. Luther's works were widely circulated by printers using aggressive sales tactics, but then their appeal for the increasingly literate population was enhanced by his vigorous, entertaining style, as well as the use of woodcut illustrations by leading artists of the time, such as Lucas Cranach. These early cartoons were able to convey in a simplified manner Luther's attack on the papacy and Catholicism and greatly increased the effectiveness of his message.

As a study in propaganda, the Reformation, particularly the role played by Martin Luther and his followers, is a perfect example of how the channeling of the message, couched in an empathic emotional context and provided with an effective means of delivery, can bring about mass changes in attitudes. Luther used plain German language laced with common idiomatic expressions of Northern Germany and Austria and based his sermons on metaphor and folk wisdom; these factors allowed effective communication over a wide area and with a heterogeneous audience of Germans of all social classes. Basing his operations in the small town of Wittenberg, he distributed his stirring pamphlets all over Northern Europe, taking advantage of the lack of effective censorship in the divided German states.

Using a novel and entertaining "dialogue" style in his printed sermons, Martin Luther was able to attack precisely those aspects of the established church practices, such as the sale of indulgences, the buying and selling of church offices, the open hypocrisy of clerical celibacy, and papal corruption, all of which had already received wide attention among the general public. Luther used the basic strategy of widely disseminating and emphasizing information that had previously been a part of what can be called the "general public paranoia," thus confirming the public's fears and increasing the potential for attitude change on a mass scale. But he was also able to offer a positive message of hope as a counter to this aggressive negativity; now the people could control their own religious destinies and, using a language they understood, could participate more meaningfully in the religious ceremony. What Luther encouraged, in essence, was the idea that individuals could communicate directly with God without the intervention of the church. Comparing the hold of the Catholic Church over the German population to that of the Hebrews held in captivity in Babylon, he struck a very sympathetic chord with his audience.

Luther made sure his religious activities were supported on the political front, once again demonstrating a masterful grasp of the elements of a successful propaganda campaign. Immediately after he had been condemned by the papacy in 1520, he penned a manifesto titled *The Address to the Christian Nobility of the German Nation* (the first edition of 4,000 was sold out within a week), which was pointedly aimed at the rulers of Germany—the princes, the knights, and cities—that, under the young Emperor Charles V, had a series of grievances against Rome. Although the emperor was himself a devout Catholic, for political reasons (the Turkish menace was a constant problem) he seemed powerless to act against Luther, and Luther suddenly found himself swept along with the tide of national resentment against Rome. Luther was thus able to exploit the political disorganization in Germany at this time to serve his own purposes, pitting the German nobility, Protestant and Catholic, against each other.

Luther did not limit his propaganda strategies to the sermon or the pamphlet but rather used a range of other techniques. The dramatic public act of

Die offinbarung

Figure 2.3   The Dragon of Revelation Wearing the Papal Tiara. This
illustration from the first edition of Gutenberg's *German New
Testament* was printed in 1522. The depiction of the papacy in this
manner was very controversial, and later editions often excised the
two top crowns, which represented the role of the kings and
nobility, because of pressure from German royalty. It is estimated
that one quarter of all the editions of Luther's bible contained this
clear visual identification of the pope with the antichrist.

nailing his *Ninety-Five Theses* to the church door in Wittenberg on the eve
of All Saint's Day in 1517 was a major propagandistic gesture. Luther knew
that simply sending a copy of his document to the leaders of the church
would not have served his purpose. This very public act moved his action
from one of persuasion to a deliberately planned propaganda strategy. Had

Figure 2.4   *The Devil With Bagpipes,* by Erhard Schön, 1535. This colored
woodcut is an explicit criticism of the clergy, showing a monstrous
devil sitting on the shoulders of a friar and playing his head as if it
were a bagpipe. The meaning here is obvious: The clergy speaks
the language of the devil. This is a particularly effective and direct
form of visual propaganda, even for those who could not read the
accompanying text.

it not been for the printing press, only a few copies of this protest may have
circulated among the people of Wittenberg, but with the new technology,
this gesture was turned overnight into a manifesto that swiftly circulated
throughout Germany, attracting an ever-widening audience and eventually

becoming the precipitating factor in the greatest crisis in the history of the Western church.

In the 16th century, despite the inroads of the printing press, most information was still obtained and circulated orally. Luther, recognizing the continued importance of the oral tradition, used not only the sermon (which he then had printed) but also the emotional power of music in the form of the vernacular hymn. Of special importance was the poetic version of Lutheran doctrine put to verse by Hans Sachs, the most prolific German poet and dramatist of his age. Propagandistic activities in the form of theatrical presentation were also very influential in an age when most people could not read.

The work of artist and engraver Lucas Cranach (1472–1553) was of most assistance to Luther's propagandistic efforts. His portraits of the reformers and the Protestant princes were widely circulated, thus giving them greater personal identification with the audience and turning them into visual embodiments of heroic proportion; however, Cranach's engraved caricatures satirizing the pope or depicting the Catholic Church as the Babylonian woman of the Revelation had the greatest propaganda value. These were easily identifiable and provided a measure of entertainment, as well as underscoring political and religious tensions. From all accounts, these caricatures and portraits sold extremely well in the Protestant sections of Germany.

One aspect of Luther's propaganda strategies was particularly effective: He succeeded in convincing his defenders that the papacy was, in fact, the Antichrist. This allowed Luther to assume a special position within the sacred history and legends of the Christian church. As Edwards (1994) pointed out in his detailed study of Luther's propaganda techniques,

> He was spoken of in biblical terms, taking the attributes of the prophesied opponents of the Antichrist. He was not just any monk, doctor, or man of the Bible, however learned. Fitted to the role of revealer of the papal Antichrist, he possessed an authority and inspired a deference that no other man of his age could claim, at least in the religious realm. (p. 92)

The Protestant movement was not limited to the activities of Martin Luther in Germany. Other Protestant reformers, such as John Calvin in Switzerland and John Knox in Scotland, also used sophisticated propaganda techniques, extending the mere persuasive aspects of the pulpit by the judicious use of the printing press to refine their particular theological philosophies. In fact, one significant feature of the Protestant Reformation was the many different Protestant sects that came into existence. Although there were differences in the theological interpretations of these groups, their propaganda strategies were almost identical. First, their propaganda efforts had two main objectives: a negative one to emphasize and exploit the wide discontent with the practices of the old church and a positive one to associate themselves with the aspirations and expectations of a new religious order. Second, their propaganda was as much secular (especially political) as it was spiritual (Roelker, 1979). This latter strategy was especially effective in areas in which new political allegiances based on territorial or cultural identifications were being formed. The end result of the Protestant Reformation was a fundamental restructuring of both secular and religious power in Western society.

The Counter-Reformation

The established Roman Catholic Church did not quietly acquiesce to the demands and actions of the Protestant reformers. The Catholic Church soon began its own propaganda campaigns to prevent further inroads on its powers. One of the most important figures of the Counter-Reformation was Ignatius Loyola, founder of the Jesuits, who developed his own highly effective and instinctual propaganda techniques. The Society of Jesus, which was the official name of the Jesuits, was organized into a cellular structure, and Loyola created in his followers a highly emotional, almost mystical fanaticism. He understood the significant power of education as a means of altering and then fixing attitudes in the young, and he insisted on total obedience from those in his order.

The Jesuits became the major force in the church's attempt to counter the Protestant Reformation, and under Loyola, they achieved some remarkable successes. Austria was restored completely to the Catholic position, and the Polish peasantry were converted to Catholicism in the face of strong opposition from the reformers (Thomson, 1977). Later, through the use of Jesuits, the Catholic Church began to expand its missionary efforts in other continents, most notably South America and Asia (China in particular). For his efforts, Ignatius Loyola was made a saint by Pope Gregory XV in 1622. The Society of Jesus continues as a major teaching arm of the Roman Catholic Church today, a fitting tribute to the power of propaganda.

Also in 1622, Pope Gregory XV, after examining the state of the church in Europe, decided to establish on June 22 of that year the Sacra Congregatio Christiano Nomini Propaganda or, as it was more commonly known, the Sacra Congregatio de Propaganda Fide (Congregation for the Propagation of the Faith), which was charged with carrying "the faith" to the New World and with reviving and strengthening it in Europe as a means of countering the Protestant revolution. This unified and centralized Roman Catholic Church missionary activities, and within a few years, in 1627, Pope Urban VII founded the Collegium Urbanum, the seminary that served as the training ground for the Propaganda.

It is interesting that the methods and strategies to be used by the missionaries of the Propaganda were left to the discretion of those in the field. The object was to bring women and men to a voluntary, not coerced, acceptance of the church's doctrines. Pope Gregory's plan laid the foundation for modern propaganda techniques in that it stressed the control of opinions and, through them, the actions of people in the mass. It also provided a convenient term for the description of the practice of public opinion control. At first, the word *propaganda* was applied to any organization that set out to propagate a doctrine; then it was used to describe the doctrine itself; and finally it came to mean the techniques employed to change opinions and spread the doctrine. Thus was born the modern-day usage of *propaganda* (Qualter, 1962).

In his study of propaganda, Qualter (1962) pointed out that the Catholic origins of the word gave it a sinister connotation in the northern Protestant countries that it does not have in the southern Catholic countries. He cited an English encyclopedist of the mid-19th century, W. T. Brande, as saying of Gregory's organization: "Derived from this celebrated society the name propaganda is applied in modern political language as a term of reproach to secret associations for the spread of opinions and principles which are viewed by most governments with horror and aversion" (pp. 4–5). This largely negative connotation, as we saw in Chapter 1, continues to cloud the discussion of propaganda.

After the development of the printing press and its judicious use in the Reformation, the adoption of propaganda techniques became a normal part of the strategies devised by those seeking to control or manipulate others. Now, all major conflicts in society, whether religious or territorial, provided an opportunity for the contesting forces to use whatever techniques they could find for disseminating propagandistic information. As an example, both sides in the Thirty Years' War (1618–1648), that titanic struggle waged all over Germany and Northern Europe by competing religious forces, turned out massive quantities of leaflets, pamphlets, and line drawings, including vicious caricatures of the religious and secular leaders. A new development of some importance in this conflict was the printing of posters from copper plates, which made possible a much wider distribution than was possible from woodcuts. Both sides engaged in writing about the atrocities the other had committed (a technique widely used even today), and roving bands of uncontrolled soldiers produced printed materials warning towns of starvation if they resisted and promising booty to those who joined with them. Historians have noted about the Thirty Years' War that, despite the low level of literacy, all classes of the population were reached by one or more of the various propaganda techniques (Davison, 1971; Taylor, 1990; Thomson, 1977, 1999).

The Emergence of Propaganda

The 18th century was one of revolution, and much of the increasing political agitation as subject populations sought to march toward a greater degree of political freedom was fueled by developments in printing and improvements in transportation. As the century progressed, so did the technology of printing and paper making, and with improved efficiency and speed in transportation, it was possible to disseminate messages to increasingly wider audiences. The availability of printed materials provided an impetus for the increase in the rates of literacy among the general population of most countries, and written propaganda messages became quite sophisticated in their appeal to the reader.

The path to literacy has not always been a smooth progression, for at various times there have been political, economic, or social reasons for discouraging literacy in a society. Those in power may wish to prevent literacy as a means of controlling the flow of information, or people may have no real economic incentive to devote the time to acquiring literacy skills. Also, the internal values of the society itself may not encourage the need to read and write in the majority of the population. As an example of the danger of generalizing about literacy, in certain countries, women were not encouraged to become literate, whereas in others, far more women than men were literate (Graff, 1981).

The use of political cartoons and other visual material that established direct communication with the audience became quite common, and satirical prints were a staple of most 18th-century propaganda campaigns, creating a new visual "language." In his detailed historical study of the use of print in propaganda, Robert Philippe (1980) noted,

> Caricature is the most usual and familiar mode of this language. It was by means of such distortion that prints appealed to a wider public and gained universal popularity. The metamorphosis of the political print was linked, as indeed was its first appearance, to the developments in printing techniques. The spirit and general tendency of this form of visual expression have remained steadfastly the same for five hundred years. The print is a mass medium—universal, direct, immediate, and pithy. (p. 9)

But how do such cartoons and satirical drawings work, and why do they have such strong propagandistic potential? Philippe (1980) suggested a possible answer when he noted,

> Prints are partisan. They espouse causes. Exaggeration is second nature to them. Their methodology is accumulation and synthesis—and hence events, places, moments and people acquire an extraordinary intensity and power. A print is neither historic evocation nor narrative, but rather a conjunction of

symbols and allusions. It enlarges, shrinks, or disguises people, to reveal their many facets at a glance. The synthesizing power of the print expresses both what is visible and what is concealed. To what is, it adds what has been and what will be. The image is thus liberated from the grammar of space and time and the print remains dynamic, aggressive, fertile and creative. (p. 9)

This was the age of the great English graphic satirists and propagandists William Hogarth (1697–1764), James Gillray (1757–1815), and Thomas Rowlandson (1756–1827), whose drawings were sold to bolster rival political activities or to make telling moral points for their eager audiences. Gillray became the most obvious propagandist, devoting his entire output to creations of social or political satire, many of which were circulated widely throughout Europe and even in North America. King George III—"Farmer George"—and his family suffered widely at Gillray's hands, and after Gillray's conversion to conservatism as a result of his dismay at the French Revolution, he launched a long series of political attacks ridiculing Napoleon and the French while glorifying John Bull and the common Englishman.

Gillray's work was very influential on 19th-century political satirists such as the American Thomas Nast (1840–1902). Nast was most famous for his crusade against the political machine of William Marcy Tweed in New York City. Tweed was reported to have said, "Stop them damn pictures. I don't care so much about what the papers write about me. My constituents can't read. But, damn it, they can see pictures" (Hess & Kaplan, 1975, p. 13). The members of the Tweed Ring were eventually driven from office, and many of them were tried and sentenced to prison. Tweed himself escaped to Spain, where he was recognized 5 years later, thanks to a Nast cartoon showing him in prison garb with two young urchins in tow. Nast had drawn the cartoon as an indication that Tweed was apprehending minor criminals while major criminals went unmolested. The Spanish police, however, interpreted it to mean that Tweed was wanted for kidnapping, and the word *Reward* also caught their eye. Tweed was promptly extradited to the United States, where he died in the New York City jail in 1878 (St. Hill, 1974). This propaganda campaign has now become a historical legend and constitutes the most dramatic instance of deliberate propagandistic cartooning in American politics. Nast, however, was only one of several American cartoonists whose work was influential in shaping political opinions in an age when journalism was not required to be objective and politically biased reporting was normal.

The American Revolution

Historians agree that the philosophical underpinnings of the revolution of the American colonists against their British rulers can be found in a variety of sources. The most notable is the series of political writings beginning during the 17th century, including the work of John Locke (1632–1704), especially his *Treatises on Government* (1690), in which he refuted the divine right of kings and the absolutist theory of government. Written in defense of the coming to the British throne of King William III in 1689, as an aftermath of the beheading of King Charles I earlier in 1649, these documents had a significant effect on subsequent political action in the American colonies. Essentially, Locke suggested that the people are the ultimate sovereign and that they always have the right to withdraw their support and overthrow the government if it fails to fulfill its trust. (During the Vietnam War period of the 1960s and 1970s, many opposed to the war espoused a similar philosophy.) Such ideas had a profound influence on the writers and pamphleteers whose propagandistic work was so instrumental in helping foment and sustain the energy of the American Revolution. Bernard Bailyn (1967), in his important book *The Ideological Origins of the American Revolution,* noted,

> The American Revolution was above all else an ideological, constitutional, political struggle and not primarily a controversy between social groups undertaken to force changes in the organization of the society or the economy. . . . [I]ntellectual developments in the decade before Independence led to a radical idealization and conceptualization of the previous century and a half of American experience, and it was this intimate relationship between Revolutionary thought and the circumstances of life in 18th-century America that endowed the Revolution with its peculiar force and made it so profoundly a transforming event. (pp. vi–vii)

The American colonists were remarkably literate and well informed on political matters; therefore, the spread of ideas through the printed word was a major factor in the development of a revolutionary ideology. In particular, the ideas contained in Richard Price's *On Civil Liberty* (1776), which sold 60,000 copies in hardback and 120,000 unbound, and Thomas Paine's *Common Sense* (1776), which sold nearly as well, were widely distributed throughout the colonies (Wish, 1950). Thomas Paine (1737–1809) can be considered the first great propagandist of the American Revolution, and George Washington claimed that *Common Sense,* an emotional pamphlet that contained persuasive arguments for independence from England, had been a powerful influence on the minds of many men prior to the war. The son of a Quaker corset maker from Norfolk, England, Paine came to America in 1774 and worked for Benjamin Franklin, editing the *Pennsylvania Journal.* Paine used a simple, forthright writing style, not unlike Luther's, and shocked his readers by his boldness while also using wit and satire to bring opposing ideas into sharp ridicule. His appeals were equally balanced between the head and the heart, and he noted that his aim was to "fit the powers of thinking and the turn of the language to the subject, so as to bring out a clear conclusion that shall hit the point in question and nothing else."

The newspaper provided the major vehicle for the dissemination of propagandistic information, and the development of these had been steady after 1740 despite various attempts by the British to tax such periodicals. When the war began on April 19, 1775, with the battles of Lexington and Concord, 37 newspapers were being published in the colonies. At the highest point, however, 70 newspapers were being published during the Revolutionary War. When the war concluded 6½ years later, 35 newspapers were in business. The war had taken its toll on some newspapers, but others had been established in their place. No sooner did a newspaper close down than it would reappear under another name, and precisely because of this, newspaper editors were willing to print inflammatory material, knowing that they could restart anytime they wished. Also, printing attacks on the colonial powers was sure to increase circulation among an audience primed to accept such information.

The demand for news during the war increased newspaper readership to 40,000 households, but this did not include multiple readers for each copy and the extent to which such information was then further disseminated by word of mouth. One problem editors faced was that they had no way to organize systematic news gathering. The principal means of obtaining news was through exchanges with other newspapers or chance letters and official messages. Even when reports of major events were picked up, they often constituted little more than short paragraphs. Worst of all was the slowness of message dissemination during this crucial period. It took more than 6 weeks for the news of Lexington and Concord to reach Savannah in Georgia (Emery & Emery, 1984). In the absence of fast, hard news, it was no wonder that false information and rumors spread quickly and widely. Printing materials were also in short supply, and fearing that the patriotic newspapers would not be able to continue their important role, printers made special pleas to contribute rags for paper making.

A classic example of newspaper propaganda was the so-called Boston Massacre, which took place in 1770. British troops had been quartered in Boston for a year and a half, against the wishes of the citizens, and they were forced to face continuous harassment, a situation not helped by the historical aloofness of British troops toward the colonists. On March 5, 1770, a crowd looking for trouble started pelting snowballs, sticks, and oyster shells at 10 soldiers outside the Boston customshouse, daring the soldiers to fire.

Figure 2.5   A facsimile of the front page of *The Pennsylvania Journal* of
October 31, 1765, showing the black mourning border and other
emblems of death symbolizing the death of freedom of the press as
a result of the imposition of the Stamp Act.

Eventually they did fire, and 11 of the unarmed rioters were injured, 4 of them fatally (a fifth died later). This event provided the impetus for numerous propaganda attacks on the British in which the facts of the event were blown out of proportion or exaggerated to emphasize British tyranny. The most famous of these attacks was Paul Revere's engraving, which, masquerading as a realistic portrayal of the event, was in fact a political cartoon deliberately created as propaganda for the anti-British forces. Revere's engraving included a sign "Butcher's Hall" above the British customshouse, and interestingly, he also changed the race of one of the victims, Crispus Attucks, who was, in reality, a towering black man. The cartoon was considered to be so inflammatory that when the soldiers were brought to trial, their lawyer warned the jury not to be swayed by drawings that add "wings to fancy" (Hess & Kaplan, 1975). This cartoon was widely reprinted in the colonial press and was followed by other Revere efforts, including an engraving of four coffins above which were the initials of the American dead.

The political cartoon proved to be a potent propaganda weapon throughout the Revolutionary period. As early as 1754, Benjamin Franklin had drawn his famous snake, severed into eight pieces to symbolize the separate colonies, with the legend "Join, or Die." This was the first cartoon to appear in an American newspaper. Published first on May 9, within a month it had been reprinted by virtually every newspaper on the continent. Although the snake was ridiculed by those loyal to the British side, the serpent won out in the end, and in his equally famous cartoon, James Gillray, the British satirist sympathetic to the American side, drew the defeated British camp completely surrounded by a large rattlesnake.

People had a macabre fascination with the symbology of death in American political cartoons, as we noted with Paul Revere's work. The most obvious example took place on October 31, 1765, when eight newspapers, being shut down as a result of the imposition of the notorious Stamp Act, used black mourning border and symbols from tombstones on their front pages to symbolize their death. William Bradford's *Pennsylvania Journal* included the masthead motto "EXPIRING: In hopes of a Resurrection to Life again." The association of death with the lack of freedom was a simple one for the colonials to grasp, and as individual freedoms were restricted by the British powers, these were symbolized as "deaths." The restriction of the freedom of the press was a particularly galling one for the Americans, as this was the chief means of disseminating both political and commercial information and binding the colonists together into a cohesive opposition to British tyranny.

Samuel Adams was considered to be the chief architect of the anti-British propaganda activities, and he based all his plans on the achievement of five

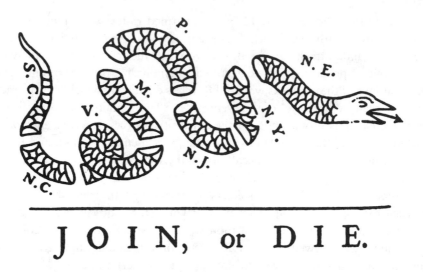

J O I N, or D I E.

Figure 2.6   Benjamin Franklin's famous cartoon in support of a "Plan of Union" for the colonies. It first appeared in *The Pennsylvania Journal* on May 9, 1754, and was based on the superstition that a snake that had been severed would come back to life if the pieces were put together before sunset. Each segment represents one colony. This cartoon was revived at the time of the Stamp Act Crisis in 1765 and again at the start of the American Revolution in 1774.

main objectives: (a) The aims of the revolution needed to be justified, (b) the advantages of the victory needed to be advertised, (c) the masses needed to be roused to action by creating hatred for the enemy, (d) logical arguments from the opposition needed to be neutralized, and (e) all issues needed to be stated in clear black-and-white terms to ensure that even the common laborer could understand (Emery & Emery, 1984). Adams devoted his life to the Revolutionary cause and became known as "Master of the Puppets" because of his ability to orchestrate and manipulate others. Nor was he the most scrupulous individual, and many of his numerous attacks on the British, printed under a variety of names, painted the actions of governors, customs men, and judges in the darkest possible colors.

Adams was also a master of organization, helping elect men sympathetic to his cause and procuring the passage of resolutions he favored. Operating from his base as a journalist with the *Boston Gazette*, Adams put together his Committee of Correspondence in 1772, and this group became the propaganda organization for the Revolution. He had his agents covering every

Figure 2.7   Benjamin Franklin's "snake" cartoon had been widely ridiculed
and parodied in the British press. However, in October 1776,
when General Cornwallis surrendered at Yorktown, the famous
English caricaturist, James Gillray, who opposed British policies in
the American colonies, drew this cartoon that showed the defeated
British camp completely encircled by a rattlesnake. Franklin's
snake had the last laugh.

important meeting and gathering to collect "news" that was immediately
relayed back to Adams's central committee, where the information was pro-
cessed and disseminated to the appropriate areas.

Perhaps Adams's greatest individual propaganda coup was the organization of the Boston Tea Party, which symbolized the opposition to the Tea
Act of 1773, although he took no personal part in the dumping of tea into
Boston Harbor. The incident is a classic example of provocation that was
turned into a major item of propaganda when the British predictably retaliated, as Adams knew they would, by the passing of the Boston Port Bill,
which closed the harbor and ruined trade. This action just served to increase
the hostility of the colonists, particularly after more troops were dispatched
to the city; the stage for open revolt was being carefully set. Eventually,
it would come at Concord in 1775, when British troops sent to confiscate
weapons and ammunition stored by the skeleton colonial army engaged in a
skirmish that eventually led to a full-scale war. This incident also served as
the background to another important, albeit inaccurate, American legend—
Paul Revere's famous ride to warn the inhabitants of Concord, "The British

are coming! The British are coming!" In fact, Paul Revere's famous ride only took on its legendary status after the publication of Henry Wadsworth Longfellow's poem "Paul Revere's Ride" in 1861. Even then, Longfellow, basing his poem on Revere's account, got some facts wrong: Revere never waited for signals from lanterns, and he carried the news to Lexington, not Concord (Hart, 1965, p. 639).

During the Revolutionary War itself, relatively minor incidents, such as the skirmishes at Lexington and Concord, were turned into major victories; Washington's crossing of the Delaware River in the dead of winter and the misery endured by the tattered troops at Valley Forge took on an almost mythical status. Many events and personalities associated with the Revolution were embellished over the years and have now been enshrined as an integral part of the nation's mythology. The propaganda value of such "foundation myths" is an essential part of nation building and is found in every country. These myths form the "core of culture" and are revived when needed to remind the population "what this society and its values are all about."

Samuel Adams, Benjamin Franklin, Thomas Jefferson, and even George Washington wanted to instill into the colonists a belief that not only was their cause just but that their "native" skills were also more than a match for the trained soldiers and mercenaries of the British army. To this end, they became skillful propagandists by manipulating (and even creating) information to their advantage or making appeals to the emotions. George Washington had Tom Paine's *American Crisis* read to his troops, words written on a drumhead that have survived through the centuries as inspiration in the darkest times in a nation's history:

> These are the times that try men's souls. The summer soldier and the sunshine patriot will, in this crisis, shrink from the service of his country. . . . Tyranny, like hell, is not easily conquered; yet we have this consolation with us, that the harder the conflict the more glorious the triumph. What we obtain too cheap, we esteem too lightly. (Emery & Emery, 1984, p. 82)

Written on December 19, 1776, these words were broadcast widely during the difficult period in the early days of World War II. It is also to Washington's and Paine's credit that, a week after hearing those inspirational words, the frozen and tattered colonial forces won a solid victory in Trenton.

Thomas Jefferson was a master propaganda strategist, with his draft of the Declaration of Independence one of the great propaganda statements in all of history. Based on a combination of the ancient Greek and Roman philosophy of the rationalist "laws of nature" earlier expounded by Locke and the modern philosophy of a secular natural law derived from Isaac Newton's scientific work, Jefferson was able to write a document in which he emphatically declared, "We hold these truths to be self-evident, that all men are created equal." Dropping all pretense at the fiction that a good king had been misled by evil advisers, Jefferson listed a long series of charges against King George III and suggested that because all appeals for redress had been rebuffed, there was now no alternative but to "alter or abolish" a government destructive of the principles of freedom. The Declaration thus became the legal and philosophical justification for the Revolution sought by Adams as one of his objectives.

Benjamin Franklin also proved to be an instinctual master of propaganda, using his talents as journalist, scientist, and diplomat to great advantage. In his role as diplomat, he was assigned to the French court to plead the colonists' case. Dressing in a fur hat and openly wearing spectacles, he became a living symbol of the unsophisticated nobility of the New World seeking to free itself from its feudal masters. His portrait began to appear on a wide range of popular culture objects, from snuff boxes to chamber pots, and his company was eagerly sought by scientists, politicians, and fashionable ladies, in whose company he reveled. Going out of his way to promote his new status as a cult figure, he used these contacts to enormous advantage, pleading for both financial and military assistance in the fight against the British; he was so successful that his personal popularity endured in France for many generations.

In his role as a journalist, Franklin had, of course, many years of experience both as an editor and as what we would today call a publicist, having promoted a wide variety of schemes and ideas during his lifetime. He was particularly famous for his series of *Poor Richard's Almanacs,* which contained a collection of maxims and proverbs culled from the world's literature and given a pragmatic American flavor—"Early to bed, early to rise, makes a man healthy, wealthy, and wise." He became a master of both white and black propaganda during the Revolutionary War. He published *The Sale of the Hessians,* which dealt with the British press gangs in Germany forcibly recruiting mercenaries, and later was responsible for a fake issue of the *Boston Independent,* in which the British appeared to be boasting of scalp hunting, a practice that was particularly repugnant to the American colonists (Thomson, 1977). In many respects, Franklin was a man ahead of his time, including his clear grasp of the rudiments of the psychology of modern propaganda techniques.

With the end of the Revolutionary War, the press had proved itself an indispensable factor in the creation of the public opinion leading up to the war and an important rallying point during the fighting. (As an example, the Declaration of Independence appeared in print in colonial newspapers before it was issued as an official manifesto. It was included in its entirety in the *Pennsylvania Evening Post* on July 6, 1776, just 2 days before it was adopted by the Continental Congress. As soon as it was ratified, it appeared in most other newspapers in the colonies.) Now that the colonists had won their freedom from Britain, it would be necessary to implement the new democratic political philosophy. Although the press had won its own freedom from the restraints of the British Crown, how this freedom would be institutionalized by the new government that had not yet taken shape was uncertain.

Once the Revolutionary War was over, the young nation was faced with developing its own propaganda campaigns to ensure its commercial and political survival in the face of a skeptical world. All the trappings of rampant patriotic nationalism were required to give the new nation a clear identity of its own, separate from the mother country, and thus were created the military uniforms, the flags, the patriotic songs and slogans, and the diplomatic stances such as the Monroe Doctrine, which proclaimed the sphere of interest of the United States in the New World. The development and international publicity attendant on the framing of the "democratic" Constitution was perhaps the greatest propaganda vehicle of all for gaining the attention of the rest of the world. Eventually, the image of the United States would be most successfully propagandized through its industrial and commercial achievements, together with the enormous output of material from its developing mass communication industries.

The French Revolution and Napoleon

The French Revolution was a complex political event that has had wide political and philosophical implications for the course of modern Western history. Taking their inspiration from the American patriots' revolution against their colonial masters, the French overthrew their despotic monarchy in an attempt to establish an entirely new form of government. Such action meant denying the concept of the divine right of kings and overturning the "natural order" and required a major shift in the philosophical underpinnings of French society. To accomplish this change, leaders of the Revolution resorted to a massive propaganda campaign, the purpose of which was to "sell" these new ideas and the resulting alterations in the structure of French society and culture.

By 1788, newspaper readership in France was well developed, and pamphlets were appearing at the rate of 25 a week; this reached a climax of information in 1789, when more than 60 new newspapers were started. Although much of the information offered was contradictory, the tone was becoming steadily more radical and critical of the monarchy and government. Many of the critics were the skilled propagandists known as the Encyclopedists, who had worked on Diderot's famous compendium of human knowledge. Key events of the eventual revolution were themselves all carefully orchestrated pageants of propaganda. The storming of the Bastille—the dreaded symbol of oppression full of tortured prisoners—has remained with us as an archetypal image when, in fact, the prison was almost empty, containing only seven individuals. Furthermore, the destruction of the building (which took place 2 days after the "storming") has assumed mythical proportions. Total demolition was still incomplete in 1792. Destruction of the physical edifice, however, was symbolic of the overthrow of the old regime.

The adoption of specific forms of dress was a major propaganda device during the ebb and flow of the French Revolution, as were other symbolic devices. The national colors of red, white, and blue were seen everywhere, as was the Phrygian stocking cap and the tricolor sash. Crowds were manipulated by fireworks displays, the burning of effigies of hated politicians and aristocrats, and especially patriotic music, in which the great theme of La Marseillaise remains even today a stirring tribute to the power of musical propaganda. The Revolution even had its own official propagandistic artist, the great Jacques Louis David (1748–1825), whose works had been an incitement to revolution before 1789 and who served in this capacity through the reign of Napoleon. David was far more than a painter, directing the artistic affairs of the new Republic until he, too, fell out of favor at the time of the downfall of Robespierre in 1794. He was later restored to his former glory by Napoleon, for whom he created a very specific imperial image. David's style used a sense of realism that sought to create art for the middle classes and was entirely appropriate to the revolutionary context of the times. His work continues to serve as an inspiration to later political regimes seeking to glorify their exploits through works of art.

The French revolutionaries used a wide variety of media to export their doctrines throughout the world at the end of the 18th century. W. Phillips Davison (1971) pointed out that even their style of dress was worn by revolutionary sympathizers throughout Europe. This form of symbolic propaganda was countered when a conservative German prince, the Langraf of Kassel, seeking to combat these subversive styles, ordered that all prisoners be dressed in them and sent out to sweep the streets. This provides an excellent example of counterpropaganda. Despite small victories of this sort, the French Revolution was so devastating to the existing social and political structure of Europe that entirely new forms emerged, and these required that new myths and heroes be created to provide the necessary social and cultural cohesion.

Out of the chaos of the destruction of the old French society, the "man on the white horse" emerged—Napoleon Bonaparte—who must be considered one of the greatest masters of the use of propaganda in history. He recognized the power of manipulation of symbols early in his career as an army officer, and throughout his life, he learned to glory in his victories while placing the blame for his failures at the feet of others. Like Caesar before him, he wrote self-congratulatory accounts of his military exploits and created for himself a swashbuckling image of the dashing commander. Napoleon was among the first of the modern propagandists to understand the need to convince the population that the rights of the individual were less important than the willingness to sacrifice one's life for emperor and nation. In this way, he was able to gather large, populist armies even in the worst of times.

The visual image of the romantic hero was created with the assistance of the artist Jacques Louis David, who helped design the clothes, hairstyle, and other accoutrements that have come down to us today as an unmistakable symbol of the diminutive French leader. Napoleon's portrait appeared everywhere, accompanied by his ubiquitous eagles, and he took the lead in designing a specific form of imperial architecture that was a mixture of Roman, Etruscan, and Egyptian styles, all great empires of the past. Triumphal arches and massive victory columns were erected, again evoking images of the Roman Caesars.

At his coronation at Notre Dame Cathedral on December 2, 1804, Napoleon achieved one of his great propaganda triumphs when he took the imperial crown from the hands of Pope Pius VII and placed it on his own head, symbolizing that he owed allegiance to no one and that he was a self-made emperor. The imperial regime that followed his coronation had its own symbols, with the Roman eagle figuring prominently above the tricolor flag, and the use of princely titles was brought back for members of Napoleon's family.

Napoleon quickly learned to exploit the power of the press to his advantage as a political weapon, devising new propaganda techniques that caught his opponents by surprise. Like most other European governments of the time, he maintained domestic censorship, but he went out of his way to plant pro-French items in foreign-language newspapers on the continent. Several newspapers were even founded by the French in occupied German territories, and in Paris a newspaper called the *Argus of London* appeared, allegedly edited by an Englishman but, in actuality, produced by the French Foreign Office. Supposedly written from an English viewpoint, the newspaper attacked the "war-mongering journals" back in London and was widely distributed throughout the West Indies and to British prisoners of war in places such as Verdun (Thomson, 1977). Napoleon also made wide use of leaflets distributed before his invading armies; he projected a promise of French "liberty" to countries such as Italy, where oppression had been the normal political way of life and a hint of freedom was bound to create widespread excitement. Even the *Napoleonic Code,* an easily translated volume of law, was an impressive demonstration of revolutionary imperial power that could be readily transported to other European countries. One of his major internal propaganda weapons was the use of the plebiscite, in which the population was asked to vote on an issue, the outcome of which was already clearly decided, and then the results published as an unequivocal indication of his popularity. As an example, in May 1802, the French people were asked to vote on the following question: "Shall Napoleon Bonaparte be consul for life?" The result was an overwhelming majority of 3,500,000 votes in favor over fewer than 10,000 opposed. Two years later, he became emperor when another plebiscite approved the change.

The use of such predetermined plebiscites has been a favorite technique of modern dictators and political regimes such as Hitler and the former Soviet Union, who were eager to give international recognition to the apparent popularity of their internal programs. This type of staged plebiscite was also used by the Baltic nations of Lithuania, Latvia, and Estonia to demonstrate clearly the level of internal cohesion and support in their attempts to win their independence back from the Soviet Union.

So successful were Napoleon's propaganda techniques in creating his imperial image that his legend became even stronger after his death in 1821. Hundreds of books appeared, some attacking him but most praising him, and finally in December 1840, his body, accompanied by the king's son François, Prince de Joinville, was returned from the remote island of St. Helena to a magnificent funeral in Paris. Nearly a million people watched as his remains were conveyed through the Arc de Triomphe in the Place de l'Etoile to his specially built tomb in the Hotel Des Invalides. Napoleon left behind an enormous legacy of important institutions, such as his legal code, the French internal administrative system, the national banking system, the military academies and universities, and, most important, a dramatic symbol of French might and glory so deeply ingrained into Western popular culture that it continues to have useful propaganda value even today.

Figure 2.8   At an early stage in his career, Napoleon is shown as the heroic leader. Note the stormy setting in the background with the implication that Napoleon, pointing forward, would lead the country through this troubled period. The romantic imagery was consistent with the general public mood in France at this time.

Propaganda in the 19th Century: The American Civil War

The main development in propaganda techniques during the 19th century was the increase in the speed with which messages could be conveyed to increasingly urban-based audiences. The importance of printing, especially

Figure 2.9   Napoleon shown as the "Emperor of Europe." Once Napoleon
had consolidated his power in France and begun his conquests, his
propagandistic image changed to that of a near-Greek God. This
fanciful engraving shows him astride the world, with the light of
the Gods shining down on him, as he leads the way forward to
further conquest.

after the introduction of steam-driven and later electricity-driven printing
presses, created new opportunities for refining propaganda as a political and
economic weapon. Although few major international conflicts occurred during the 19th century, the American Civil War (1860–1865) proved to be a

Figure 2.10   Voyage to the island of Elba; anonymous print from the period of
Napoleon's imprisonment. This print uses the same symbols of
grandeur but in a satirical vein; the imperial eagle was now merely
a vehicle for transporting the emperor to his exile, and his now
useless crowns dangling from its claws. Surrounded by the bees
from his coat of arms, Napoleon is carrying his pronouncements
on military conscription and mass enlistment.

devastating conflict, when the technology and effectiveness of armaments
had far outstripped the medical assistance for wounded soldiers, and the
resulting death toll was extremely high. The Civil War also provided an
opportunity to test the efficacy of the new communications infrastructure,
based on the telegraph in combination with increases in printing speed. At
the start of the conflict, more than 500 war correspondents were attached
to the Northern armies. The full promise of these new technologies was not
to be realized, however, because war correspondents were not always
allowed near the battlefields; military censorship was also considerable, with
the result that many erroneous reports were dispatched to newspapers. To

maintain home front morale, readers were often deliberately given false reports about the outcome of battles. (The Battle of Bull Run was initially reported as a victory for the North, when its was, in fact, a devastating defeat.) This was particularly true in the South, where telegraph lines were destroyed and communication had to rely on letters and dispatches from the battlefronts. The Southern press was far more partisan than the more contentious Northern newspapers and magazines, and this left a legacy that hampered the North-South relationship for many years afterward. In terms of propaganda, both sides used atrocity stories, and fictitious engravings (photographs were still not printable in newspapers at this time) of brutalizations by soldiers were published. Despite the problems associated with getting prompt and accurate reports from the war, Americans, particularly those in the North, became a nation of newspaper readers eager to gain the latest information.

At the conclusion of the American Civil War, the two sides were left to try to reunite themselves into one nation. These efforts at reconciliation took a long time but were aided enormously by the extensive communication infrastructure left in the war's aftermath. The telegraph had been extended all across the country, and many of the magazines and newspapers that had been established to supply war news now became staple reading matter for the growing population. By 1870, about 4,500 newspapers were active in the United States, with the major growth coming from daily newspapers. The possibilities for propagandistic activities increased enormously. As one English writer, looking at the phenomenon of this growth of newspapers, observed,

> America is a classic soil of newspapers; everybody is reading; literature is permeating everywhere; publicity is sought for every interest and every order; no political party, no religious sect, no theological school, no literary or benevolent association, is without its particular organ; there is a universality of print. (Emery & Emery, 1984, p. 405)

In 1866, the transatlantic cable was successfully completed, and now the United States was directly connected to the news flow from Europe, thus greatly extending the possibilities of propaganda activities, this time on a more international scale. The ability to print engravings and, after 1880, photographs added further impact to the printed word. As each new form of mass communication found an audience, it was immediately seized on as a vehicle for conveying propaganda. Thus, newspapers, then magazines, and later motion pictures were each used by propagandists in their attempts to capture the public's attention.

The development of democratic political institutions was the most important impetus to the growth of the use of propaganda in the 19th and 20th centuries. As Qualter (1962) so eloquently stated,

> Even those whose attitude toward the role of public opinion in politics did not change found that of necessity they had to learn the mechanics of peaceful persuasion by propaganda. With an extended franchise and an increasing population it was becoming too expensive to do anything else. Where at one time voters could be bought, they now had to be persuaded. Politicians had, therefore, to become interested in propaganda. (p. 33)

The combination of the demands created by democratic political institutions and the increasing sophistication of propaganda techniques used in warfare marked the emergence of an awareness of propaganda as an ubiquitous force in the late 19th and early 20th centuries. We must also not overlook the increasing importance of advertising as an integral part of economic development and the emergence of consumerism, for many techniques developed to persuade customers to purchase products were later adopted by other propagandists. One significant aspect of 20th-century propaganda is the symbiotic relationship between advertising and other forms of propaganda, particularly as techniques for reaching audiences become more sophisticated and reliable. Propaganda began to emerge as a modern force in the 19th century; it became an integral part of the social, political, and economic life of the 20th century. As was noted earlier, the development of a wide range of new communication technologies—from cell phones to iPods, from communication satellites to wi-fi networks for computers, and from digital cameras (often in cell phones) to PDAs (personal digital assistants)—offers the potential for ingenious new methods of spreading propaganda messages in the 21st century.

3

Propaganda Institutionalized

The late 19th and early 20th centuries were periods of great expansion of propagandistic activities. The growth of the mass media and improvements in transportation led to the development of mass audiences for propaganda, increasing its use and effectiveness. Each of the mass media—print, the movies, radio, and then television—contributed its unique qualities to new techniques of propaganda. Radio in particular brought into existence the possibility of continuous international propaganda, whereas television has increased the problem of "cultural imperialism," in which one nation's culture is imposed on another nation's. This led to a call for a New World Information Order by many Third World countries in the latter part of the 20th century. Since the 19th century, advertising has become the most pervasive form of propaganda in modern society and is now disseminated on a global scale.

The 19th and 20th centuries saw an unprecedented explosion in the field of communication and transportation, a trend that shows no indications of slowing down at the beginning of the 21st century. Initially, the limitation on both the speed of communication and the difficulties experienced in transportation in an age of rough roads and horse-drawn traffic severely restricted the flow of information between geographically separated points.

Even the growing urban centers, which were now a common manifestation of the push toward industrialization, had problems in circulating and controlling information to a large number of people within a short period of time. Newspapers and commercial news sheets of the early 19th century did not have wide circulation, and despite the increase in the literacy rate among the middle class, books were not yet as widely available for the general population as they would be later in the century. Public oratory, though important, also had the inherent handicaps of a limited audience and irreproducibility. The result was that rumor and gossip continued to be an important means of maintaining communication links between groups and individuals wishing to circulate specific messages.

The major problem with rumor as a means of communication is it lacks the necessary control to ensure that the message content is not distorted. As Shibutani (1966) explained,

> Content is not viewed as an object to be transmitted but as something that is shaped, reshaped, and reinforced in a succession of communicative acts. . . . In this sense a rumor may be regarded as something that is constantly being constructed; when the communicative activity ceases, the rumor no longer exists. (p. 9)

Clearly, although rumors have been a highly effective way to circulate information with amazing speed, they are not a reliable means of disseminating propaganda. This strategy may work splendidly if a rumor continues to take the direction intended, but rumors have a life of their own, and they could just as easily turn on the original propagandists. Witness the difficulties that one of the world's largest manufacturers of household products, the Procter and Gamble Company, has had fighting a rumor that its trademark of the moon and stars was, in reality, a satanic symbol. Despite the enormous sum of money the company had spent on advertising trying to create a specific public image, this rumor was widely circulated, largely by fundamentalist Christian groups and independent operators under the umbrella of another company, The Amway Corporation. Ultimately, because of its failure to halt the economic damage caused by the continuance of this rumor, the company considered going as far as changing its trademark (Kapferer, 1990). Subsequently, after several court battles, the trademark was retained, but the belief that this image, which depicts the man in the moon and stars, is satanic continues to be the source of widespread Internet rumors.

Before the practice of propaganda on a mass scale could proceed, new forms of communication that provided a greater degree of message control and targeting of audiences had to emerge. This is exactly what did happen in the 19th and 20th centuries, and propaganda became increasingly more sophisticated, widely practiced, and accepted as part of modern society.

The New Audience

The introduction of new forms of communication created a new historical phenomenon—the mass audience. For the first time in history, the means now existed to disseminate information to large, heterogeneous groups of people within a relatively short period of time. With the introduction of the *New York Sun* on September 3, 1833, the era of the "penny press" was begun, and the entire shape of news was altered. The penny press was not so much a revolutionary development but rather the inevitable result of the gradual shift away from selling newspapers only through monthly or annual subscriptions. Founders of the penny press, such as Benjamin Day of the *Sun* and James Gordon Bennett of the *New York Herald,* recognized that a growing audience of middle- and working-class readers was willing to pay for a newspaper on a daily basis (Crouthamel, 1989). Whereas the earlier commercial press had disdained much interest in everyday events, the penny press deliberately sought to cultivate the audience's interest in local events and everyday occurrences. Also, as Schudson (1978) noted,

> The new journalism of the penny press . . . ushered in a new order, a shared social universe in which "public" and "private" would be redefined. . . . With the growth of cities and of commerce, everyday life acquired a density and a fascination quite new. (p. 30)

The formation of these new mass publics came about at the same time democracy as a political process was gradually being introduced into many countries. And although the United States had been founded on entirely democratic principles, the young nation was still struggling to internalize exactly how this rather novel experiment of "government by the people" would work in practice. Historians have often labeled the 1830s the era of "Jacksonian democracy" because of the emergence of a clear populist sentiment at this time. We must view the introduction of the mass press against this historical-political background. Schudson (1978), after examining this important historical event, suggested that the penny press was a response to what he called the emergence of "democratic market society," created by the growth of mass democracy, a marketplace ideology, and an urban society. He noted,

The penny press expressed and built the culture of a democratic market society, a culture which had no place for social or intellectual deference. This was the groundwork on which a belief in facts and a distrust of the reality, or objectivity, of "values" could thrive. (p. 60)

As the newspaper assumed a larger and more consistent role in the dissemination of information, the public came to depend on such daily information to a much greater degree than ever before and for several reasons. First, as yet, there were few competing voices besides the remaining commercial newsletters and the occasional book. Second, even those competing news sources could not match the newspaper for timeliness and consistency. Third, newspapers made no pretense at being politically neutral in this early period, and therefore they appealed directly to the biases of their readers. Fourth, the demands of a democratic political system required that the electorate have a continuous knowledge of the workings of the political system, and only newspapers were able to provide this continuity. Fifth, the average working-class or middle-class citizen did not have the time or the organization at his or her disposal to keep up with political or economic developments and therefore was forced to rely on the news-gathering abilities of the newspaper. Last, the newspaper provided more than just political and economic information; it also offered entertainment and local news that created a sense of social cohesion in an increasingly fragmented world. The reader was made aware that he or she was part of a wider world sharing and reacting to the news.

The existence of this shared experience made it possible for propaganda to work, for propaganda can be successful only when it is targeted toward specific groups without having to diffuse the message through a variety of channels. Not only did the gradual increase in importance of the mass media throughout the 19th century and into the 20th century bring into existence viable and reachable publics, but the media themselves also began to assume the mantle of "expertise." This proved to be a potent combination, for now the media were both collectors and disseminators of information, and this placed them in a powerful position to act as the channel for all types of persuasive messages, from merely informative advertising to the most blatant forms of propaganda for specific causes.

The Emergence of Mass Society

More important than the real power of these new media was their perceived power, for politicians and others reacted to what they assumed this power

Figure 3.1   The cartoon by Thomas Nast caused William Marcy "Boss"
Tweed to be arrested in Spain. The Spanish police misinterpreted
the illustration to mean that Tweed was wanted for kidnapping.
The word *reward* on the bottom left also caught the eye of the
police. First published in *Harper's Weekly*, July 1, 1876.

to be. This was an age when the study of the psychology of human
communication was still in its infancy, and it was naturally assumed that
people would react in a homogeneous manner to whatever stimulus was
exposed to them. Much of the concern for the power of the media stemmed
from the growing body of sociological literature in the 19th century that
suggested that the shift from a rural society to an urbanized, industrial
society was creating something known as "society." Bramson (1961) noted
that European sociological pessimism on the subject of mass society

stemmed from the 19th-century notion of the breakdown of the traditional community. Thus, European sociology of this period had a preoccupation with "social disorganization" and "social disintegration" caused by the emergence of an industrialized and urbanized, large-scale society. The end result was that

> this perspective of nineteenth century sociology is recapitulated in the twentieth century theory of mass society, particularly in its view of the past. By contrast with the anarchic individualism of life in the cities, the impersonality of social relationships, the peculiar mental qualities fostered by urban life with its emphasis on money and abstraction, theorists of mass society idealized the social aspects of the traditional society of the later middle ages. (p. 32)

The role of the emerging mass media in this shift from the traditional type to the modern type of society was seen as crucial, for through the popular media the public was acquiring new ideas. It was also suggested that the media encouraged a cultural blandness that satisfied public tastes at the lowest possible level and thereby severely hampered attempts to elevate humankind to its full potential. Furthermore, from the perspective of the socialist and communist thinkers whose ideas were beginning to gain some credence at the turn of the century, the mass media were seen as the handmaidens of the capitalist system, lulling the populace into a political lethargy that prevented them from realizing their true plight as victims of the capitalist system.

The dominance of the negative concept of mass society in intellectual circles in the first part of the 20th century was a salient factor in shaping the attitudes and subsequent attempts to control the perceived power of the mass media. Subsequent developments in propaganda must be examined within this intellectual context, for early propagandistic efforts using the new mass media seemed to justify all the fears and doubts surrounding these new channels of information and their potentially dangerous ability to manipulate their audiences.

The Emergence of the Propaganda Critique

One major concern that emerged at the end of the 19th century was the future of the democratic process in the face of the new possibilities of manipulation of public opinion through increasingly skillful propaganda techniques. The potential for such manipulation led many theorists to reject even democracy

Figure 3.2   "A Group of Vultures Waiting for the Storm to 'Blow Over'"—
"Let Us Prey." It was Thomas Nast's cartoons such as this one that
caused Boss Tweed so much anguish and eventually resulted in his
downfall. First published in *Harper's Weekly*, September 23, 1871.

as a viable political system. Qualter (1962) cited the case of the English
philosopher Graham Wallas, who in his book *Human Nature in Politics*
(1908) suggested that men were not entirely governed by reason but often
acted on "affection and instinct" and that these could be deliberately aroused

and directed in a way that would eventually lead to some course of action desired by the manipulator. Qualter noted of Wallas,

> Given a greatly expanded franchise, with its corollary of the need to base authority on the support of public opinion, political society invited the attention of the professional controller of public opinion. When to the demand for new methods of publicity there were added revolutionary advances in the techniques of communication, and the latest discoveries in social psychology, mankind had to fear more than ever "the cold-blooded manipulation of popular impulse and thought by professional politicians." (p. 51)

Although he never used the word *propaganda,* preferring the phrase "the manipulation of popular impulse" (the word *propaganda* did not become part of common usage until after 1918), Graham Wallas was but one of many concerned with the future of democracy in a world in which propagandistic manipulation seemed to be increasing (Qualter, 1985).

In the United States in the early part of the 20th century, concern for the increasing potential of mass media to manipulate human emotions and behavior took a different form from that of the European philosophers who had developed the "mass society" theories. The important revisionist work of Michael Sproule (1987, 1989, 1991, 1997) provides us with a useful overview of the emergence of what he called "Propaganda and American Ideological Critique" (1991). Sproule pointed out that the American intellectual tradition was to treat public opinion as "enlightened discussion," rather than as the European intellectuals' concern about the "rise of the masses." This tradition came about because, in the United States, the alienation between the government and its citizens was far less than that found in European countries. Also, inherent in democracy was the faith that public opinion would ultimately be rational because it would be judged by an educated citizenry. Whereas European Marxist-based theories tended to treat social class and the political state as the prime shapers of ideology, the major concern of the propaganda critique that emerged in the United States in the Progressive Era was for "the implication for democratic social organization of the new marriage between private institutions and the emerging professions of mass communication" (Sproule, 1991, p. 212).

The widespread and potent use of propaganda in World War I was clearly a watershed moment in the history of propaganda studies, in Europe as much as in the United States. Sproule (1991) suggested that

> while progressive propaganda criticism did not begin with the state as the archetypal source of ideological manipulation, the Great War did show that

the American government was capable of pursuing an ideological hegemony. However, unlike Marxists, progressive critics treated state propaganda in the Great War as less a central problem and more a harbinger of how various private institutions and interest groups would compete after the war. Working from this perspective, American progressives developed a body of criticism focused on the array of social forces that competed for control of what Marxists would call the ideological apparatuses of civil society: education, news, religion, and entertainment. (p. 214)

In the period immediately after 1918, the concerns of the progressive propaganda critics were articulated in Walter Lippmann's *Public Opinion* (1922) and *The Phantom Public* (1925). Lippmann gradually shifted his concerns away from the potential for institutional manipulation to a more general concern about the ability of the public to be able to make decisions in the complex modern era. The philosopher John Dewey, in his books *The Public and Its Problems* (1927) and *Liberalism and Social Action* (1935), also examined the new complexities of social interaction brought about by the increasing importance of the mass media in modern society. Many others were part of this movement. As Sproule (1991) noted,

> During the 1920s and 1930s, the progressive propaganda critics developed a wide-ranging program to combat the problem of partisan ideological diffusion through news, religion, entertainment, education, and government. In contrast to Marxist scholars, however, progressives were optimistic about the public's ability to withstand propaganda, especially since progressives believed they would turn the ideological apparatuses, particularly education, into weapons against the powerful propagandas.
>
> With its wide popular audience, progressive critique became the dominant school of thought on propaganda during the years between the two world wars. . . . Progressives had faith in the essential cognitive competence of the public, believing that all that was necessary to combat propaganda was to inform the public about how modern institutions diffused their ideologies through news, religion, entertainment, education, and government. (pp. 219–220)

Propaganda analysis was both an important journalistic and scholarly activity in the interwar period. (The role of propaganda analysis in the interwar period is examined in greater detail in Chapter 5.) Much of this scholarly activity was devoted less to pure theorizing than to analyzing the methods by which propagandists worked, often making this knowledge public in the hopes of affecting some type of reform. In one famous study, using Federal Trade Commission data, Ernest Gruening (1931) exposed the propaganda activities of the National Electric Light Association (NELA). The NELA had co-opted educators, subsidized the writing of textbooks, bribed news reporters and editors, and supplied classroom material for schools all in the hope of developing a favorable impression of the monopolistic activities of their member companies.

In Sproule's (1997) history of the "propaganda critique" movement in the United States, he pointed out that almost all forms of communication and entertainment came under critical examination as potential vehicles for propaganda. Thus, the new media such as movies and later radio, as well as the more traditional forms of journalism—newspapers and magazines—were all subjected to intense analysis in the period between the two world wars. The progressive propaganda critics also directed their attention to religious preaching and teaching, now more widely disseminated through the new media. In particular, they indicated a deep concern for the increasing role of federal government propagandistic activities in the aftermath of the Creel revelations about the extent of propaganda in World War I. As Sproule (1997) noted, this group was concerned that "despite the demise of the Committee on Public Information (CPI), agencies of the federal government continued to spend the people's money to tell the people what to believe" (p. 45).

One exception to this activist position was the political scientist Harold D. Lasswell (1927; Lasswell & Blumsenstock, 1939), an important pioneer in the scholarly analysis of propagandistic activities. Although he did eventually take political positions, particularly during World War II, in this early period, Lasswell was much more concerned with developing a theoretical perspective of propaganda and less interested in public policy. As an example, his case study *World Revolutionary Propaganda: A Chicago Study* (in Lasswell & Blumsenstock, 1939) is a meticulously assembled collection of data on the precise methods of propaganda used by Communist Party groups in Chicago in the Depression years to instill in that city's workers a concept of *world revolution*. He stated his aims quite clearly: "We are interested in the facts. We have taken care to find them. But we are chiefly concerned with the meaning of the facts for an understanding of the future" (p. v.). For Lasswell, understanding and discerning patterns in the propaganda process would reveal its strategies and ultimate effectiveness. He also took the position that manipulation of the mass public was possible because individuals tend to react to emotional impulses rather than to sober analytic statements. As the various forms of mass communication developed into their powerful institutional structures, employing skillful manipulators of information, such views as Lasswell's would increase, particularly after the apparent spectacular success of propaganda in World War I.

The New Media

Each major form of mass communication that emerged in the 19th and 20th centuries had its own peculiar set of strengths and weaknesses. What they all had in common was their ability to establish direct contact with the public in such a manner as to bypass the traditional socializing institutions, such as the church, the school, the family, and the political system. Because of this historically unique and very significant ability, the media were feared by those concerned with the moral welfare of society but welcomed by those who sought to use this "direct contact" to present their own cases to the mass audience, whether it be an advertiser trying to convince the public to purchase a new product or a politician "selling" policies.

Print Media

We noted earlier in this chapter how significant the penny press was in the early part of the 19th century in the creation of the first modern media publics. Throughout the rest of that century and into the 20th, the mass press continued to grow both in size and in significance as a purveyor of information and as a shaper of ideas. During the fight for the abolition of slavery and the American Civil War, newspapers on both sides played significant roles as propaganda agents, and in the postwar years, the newspaper business grew spectacularly. Emery and Emery (1984) noted,

> Between 1870 and 1900, the United States doubled its population and tripled the number of its urban residents. During the same 30 years the number of daily newspapers quadrupled and the number of copies sold each day increased almost sixfold. . . . The number of English-language, general circulation dailies increased from 489 in 1870 to 1967 in 1900. Circulation totals for all daily publications rose from 2.6 million copies in 1870 to 15 million in 1900. (p. 231)

Another feature of the last half of the 19th century was the spectacular rise of magazines as important sources of information. Spurred on by inexpensive postal rates established by Congress in 1879, magazines such as *Ladies' Home Journal* and *Saturday Evening Post* soon had circulations that exceeded half a million. These popular periodicals, though not blatantly propagandistic, nevertheless presented a particular perspective that proved to be a major influence in shaping domestic life in the United States. Particularly after 1899, under the editorship of George Horace Lorimer, the *Saturday Evening Post* became a major vehicle of mass culture in the United States (Cohn, 1989). As an example, in World War I, the *Saturday Evening Post,* which was read by nearly 10 million people a week, took a decided anti-German editorial perspective, and

> the constant repetition of these themes in editorials, articles, fiction, and car-
> toons worked to create a broad-based acceptance for the terms of Lorimer's
> Americanism. As Will Irwin, a major *Post* writer during the war years, cyni-
> cally expressed it, "In pouring the plastic American mind into certain grooves,
> [Lorimer] had a great social influence." (Cohn, 1989, p. 103)

Smaller "literary" publications, such as *Harper's Weekly* (1857), *Atlantic Monthly* (1857), and *Nation,* though limited in circulation, nevertheless had a profound influence on public opinion. Many other magazines of political and social opinion also contributed to the shaping of the public agenda on issues such as poverty, immigration, business corruption, and public health (Tebbel, 1969). Magazines were and continue to be a very personalized medium, creating strong reader identification and association with the editorial tone and content. It was in magazines that most of the political and social muck-raking took place.

By the beginning of the 20th century, the major daily newspapers in the United States had clearly established themselves as leaders and shapers of public opinion on a wide range of issues. This was the era of yellow journalism, in which the major New York dailies—Joseph Pulitzer's *World* and William Randolph Hearst's *Journal*—competed with each other for the coveted circulation by seeing who could cover or create the most spectacular news. One famous example of the increasing potential of the press to create propaganda in this period was the battleship *Maine* incident. As a result of their direct intervention in a series of incidents fomenting the Cuban insurrection (1895–1898), the major daily newspapers in America were accused of having created an extreme war psychosis in the minds of the American people, leading up to the mysterious sinking of the *Maine* in the Havana harbor in 1898 and to the subsequent Spanish-American War of the same year. A satisfactory answer has never been offered to why the *Maine* sank, but this did not stop Hearst's *New York Journal* from offering a $50,000 reward for information leading to the arrest of the alleged criminals while the paper's headlines screamed for war (Wilkerson, 1932; Wisan, 1934). Once war was declared, the newspapers spent enormous sums of money covering it, with the *Journal* proclaiming, "How do you like the *Journal*'s war?" (Emery & Emery, 1984, p. 295).

Although newspapers declined in readership in the 20th century, they still provide a continuous source of propaganda in our society. During both world wars, newspapers were the major source of information for the general public and, as such, were used for propaganda purposes rather extensively. Despite the significant inroads made by broadcast journalism, newspapers are still read for in-depth information and perspectives on news and events; as such, under the guise of both straight news reporting and editorializing, they do carry propaganda messages. Nothing in the U.S. Constitution forces a newspaper publisher to be totally neutral and objective in reporting the news, and thus whether it be in clearly labeled editorial opinions or in the particular slant of an "innocent" news report or in paid advertising, newspapers are a prime source of propaganda in our society. This is equally true for the large newsmagazines such as *Time* and *Newsweek*, in which both the selection of the specific stories to be featured and the way those stories are treated can be considered to be propaganda. Even an apparently harmless publication such as *Reader's Digest* can, in fact, be carefully constructed to be a propaganda vehicle for the values and politics of the owner (Schreiner, 1977).

In 2003, nearly 2.3 billion books were sold in the United States, a figure that was down from the 3 billion sold in 1997 ("Book Sales," 2005). This decline matches similar statistics for other forms of reading material such as magazines and newspapers. Whether this indicates the rise in importance of newer media forms such the Internet, video, DVD, and cable television is still too early to state with any certainty, but the signs for reading are ominous. Although books are still an important source of propaganda, they are somewhat limited in their circulation and seldom have a mass audience. Nevertheless, they can and do have an impact far beyond their primary readership circle, as the opportunity to develop specific ideas in-depth makes the book a particularly potent source of propagandistic information. Throughout history, books have played a pivotal role in the shaping of ideas and attitudes on a large scale certainly beyond their actual primary readership. The Bible, even for those who do not read it, continues to be the source of social and cultural values that shape a great portion of our lives. Depending on the specific theological interpretation, the Bible also serves as the source of a great deal of religious and political propaganda on such issues as abortion and homosexuality. In the past, such books as Charles Darwin's

Origin of the Species (1859/1982) or Harriet Beecher Stowe's *Uncle Tom's Cabin* (1852/1991) were the sources of major conflicts in our society. In our own age, books continue to have a major impact, but now this medium is forced to compete with the more instantaneous and accessible visual media. Now "propagandistic" ideas developed in books are often picked up and magnified by television, thus creating an audience much larger than a book could.

Although not deliberately propaganda, the work of Sigmund Freud cannot be ignored as an important factor in shaping 20th-century thought about the nature of human beings. Unfortunately, one of the most significant propagandistic books in the past century was largely ignored when first published. In fact, had the world taken Adolf Hitler's *Mein Kampf* (*My Struggle*) seriously in 1926, when it appeared in Germany, rather than waiting until the first English edition in 1939, the international diplomatic approach to Hitler's conquests throughout the 1930s might have been quite different.

In recent years, a spate of books has achieved great popularity by propagandizing the theme that American moral standards have declined significantly and that American society is in the state of a "cultural war" (see Davison Hunter, 1991, for a detailed history of this movement). The book *See, I Told You So,* by conservative talk show host Rush Limbaugh (1993); *The Book of Virtues* (1994) and a whole industry of similar titles by William Bennett, former U.S. Secretary of Education and former head of the National Endowment for the Humanities; and philosopher Alan Bloom's best-selling *The Closing of the American Mind* (1987) are examples of such books that have achieved best-seller status by attacking such wide-ranging subjects as television, rap music, abortion, "humanistic" education, political liberalism, and even the "worldview" of the United Nations as being the sources for American cultural decline.

In the 2 years preceding the 2004 presidential election, a surprising number of books espousing varied political positions appeared in American bookstores. It seemed as if every week, there was yet another best seller, written usually by a television or radio talk show host, which told the American public what was wrong with the country and how, by electing their candidate (or not electing the other one), they would make everything whole again. Many of these books were highly propagandistic, some bordering on outright lies or, at the least, containing unsupportable accusations aimed at discrediting the opposition. Thus, President George W. Bush was the subject of many books aimed at his apparent lack of intellect, his suspect service record in the National Guard, and his motivations for leading us into the Iraq War. John Kerry was subjected to intense scrutiny for his exploits in Vietnam, his voting record in the Senate, and even the manner in which

he spent his considerable wealth. Much to everyone's surprise, books had suddenly become a major battleground in the political wars of the 21st century.

These books, usually argued in a highly one-sided manner, have a significant impact on those readers who already subscribe to the notion that
"something is wrong with our society" and are widely cited by their admir-
ers as reliable sources. Attempts to "counterpropagandize" these arguments
with a wider range of perspectives almost never make any inroads with those
already converted to this position. Clearly, the commitment of time an individual makes to actually "read" a polemical book is a strong psychological
base for increasing the potential success of the propaganda message.

Movies

It is rather surprising that, despite the enormous inherent appeal of
the motion picture, this medium has never become the powerful vehicle of
"direct" propaganda that its critics feared it would. In fact, perhaps precisely
because of its popularity as one of the world's great entertainment forms,
rather than as a medium of conscious information dissemination, it has
failed to fulfill its initial promise as both an educator and a channel for the
propagandist. Of all the mass media, the motion picture has the greatest
potential for emotional appeal to its audience, offering a deeper level of identification with the characters and action on the screen than found elsewhere
in popular culture. The motion picture can also make audiences laugh, cry,
sing, shout, become sexually aroused, or fall asleep; in short, it has the ability to evoke an immediate emotional response seldom found in the other
mass media. Yet, systematic attempts by governments or other groups to use
the motion picture as a channel for the delivery of deliberate propagandistic
messages have not, on the whole, been very successful.

In contrast, the motion picture has been extremely successful in influencing its audiences in such areas as courting behavior, clothing styles, furniture
and architectural design, speech mannerisms, and eating and drinking habits
(Jowett, 1982). In these and other areas, the motion picture is an excellent
shaper of subtle psychological attitudes and, under the right circumstances,
can be a potent source of social and cultural information. In his famous
study *Movies and Conduct*, social psychologist Herbert Blumer (1933), after
examining hundreds of diaries kept by young moviegoers, noted,

> For many the pictures are authentic portrayals of life, from which they draw
> patterns of behavior, stimulation to overt conduct, content for a vigorous life
> of imagination, and ideas of reality. They are not merely a device for surcease;
> they are a form of stimulation. . . . [M]otion pictures are a genuine educational

institution . . . in the truer sense of actually introducing him [the student] to and acquainting him with a type of life which has immediate, practical and momentous significance. (pp. 196–197)

is all movies care about now

One could argue that movies do, in fact, succeed as propaganda vehicles in a much subtler way by presenting one set of values as the only viable set. Over a period of years, these values can both reflect and shape society's norms.

Immediately after projected motion pictures were introduced in 1896, they were used for propaganda purposes in a variety of ways. Raymond Fielding (1972), in his history of the newsreel, recounted fake news films of the Dreyfus affair in France in 1896, whereas actual political events were also the subjects of early films, including fake footage of the charge up San Juan Hill and the sinking of the Spanish fleet in Santiago Bay in the Spanish-American War. The pure visual power of the motion picture can be seen in one of the first films to be made after the declaration of war against the Spanish. Made by Vitagraph studios, it was titled *Tearing Down the Spanish Flag* and simply showed a flagpole from which a Spanish flag was flying. The flag was abruptly torn down, and in its place an American flag was raised. In the words of Albert E. Smith, one founder of the Vitagraph Company,

> Projected on a thirty-foot screen, the effect on audiences was sensational and sent us searching for similar subjects. . . . The people were on fire and eager for every line of news. . . . With nationalistic feeling at a fever pitch we set out to photograph what people wanted to see. (Fielding, 1972, pp. 29–30)

The fear of the motion picture's power both to communicate and to educate resulted in early and consistent attacks on it from all those institutions and individuals who had the most to lose from its inherent appeal. Thus, throughout the world, clergy, social workers, educators, and politicians were all involved in trying to make the motion picture more responsive to their call for social control of this obtrusive new form of information (Jowett, 1976). In the United States, the Supreme Court refused to allow the motion picture the right of free speech granted by the First Amendment to the Constitution. In the landmark case *Mutual vs. Ohio* (1915), Justice McKenna, speaking for the unanimous Court, noted,

> [Motion pictures are] not to be regarded, nor intended to be regarded as part of the press of the country or as organs of public opinion. They are mere representations of events, of ideas and sentiments published or known; vivid, useful and entertaining, no doubt, but . . . capable of evil, having power for it, the greater because of their attractiveness and manner of exhibition. (Jowett, 1976, p. 120)

Thus, of all the various forms of mass communication that have been introduced into the United States, only the motion picture has been subjected to systematic legalized prior censorship. This situation continued until the mid-1950s, at which time the Supreme Court began to strike down the various censorship restrictions against the medium (Randall, 1968).

During World War I, crude attempts were made to use the motion picture as a propaganda device, including such films as *The Kaiser, The Beast of Berlin,* and *My Four Years in Germany,* but the most important of these propaganda efforts, aimed at molding public opinion in favor of the United States entering the war, was *Battle Cry of Peace* (1915), produced by J. Stuart Blackton (whose hand had earlier ripped down the Spanish flag in 1898). This film showed the Germans attacking New York by sea and reducing the city to ruins, but it also had a reverse effect, in that the pacifist movement used the film to expose the war profiteers and armament manufacturers who would benefit from U.S. entry into the war (Campbell, 1985). Before 1916, most American films were decidedly pacifist in tone, reflecting the mood of the American people; as an example, in *War Brides* (1916), the peace-loving heroine commits suicide rather than give birth to a future soldier (Furhammer & Isaksson, 1971). Once the United States declared war in 1917, encouraged by public sentiment, a flurry of anti-German films were made.

All the Allied countries made propaganda films, with the British government going so far as to import the great American director D. W. Griffith to direct *Hearts of the World* (1918), featuring the Gish sisters in a plot set against authentic war-shattered backgrounds from the western front (Reeves, 1986). In the United States, the CPI, formed by the government to become the propaganda agency for the war effort, worked with the film industry in making films with patriotic content, including offering suggestions for stories and military expertise and props as required by the studios. The significant role of the movies in World War I did much to establish and legitimate the movie industry as an important part of American society. By the end of the war, President Woodrow Wilson and other high government officials were not averse to being seen in the company of movie stars at war bond drives and other social occasions—something that would have been unthinkable before 1916. This testified to the increased awareness of politicians about the potential power of the motion picture (Ward, 1985).

In Germany in 1917, Chief of Staff General Ludendorff sent a letter to the Imperial Ministry of War, in which he noted,

The war has demonstrated the superiority of the photograph and the film as means of information and persuasion. Unfortunately our enemies have used their advantage over us in this field so thoroughly that they have inflicted a great deal of damage. . . . For this reason it is of the utmost importance for a successful conclusion to the war that films should be made to work with the greatest possible effect wherever any German persuasion might still have any effect. (Furhammer & Isaksson, 1971, p. 11)

By the time the German government got around to setting up its filmic propaganda arm, the war was nearly over, but this same organization, Universium Film Aktiengesellschaft (UFA), survived to become a major propaganda agency for the Nazis during the 1930s and through World War II.

The period between the two world wars was known as the "golden age" of the commercial cinema, as the medium achieved heights of popularity not thought possible for an entertainment that had started out in cheap storefront nickelodeons. The Hollywood product dominated world screens as the European film studios were still recovering from their devastation from the war. Audiences were so used to seeing commercial escapist material that getting them to view anything that appeared to be educational was extremely difficult. The only propaganda films ever seen in commercial theaters were the often innocuous newsreels and the occasional documentary such as *Nanook of the North* (1926), which was a surprising commercial success even though it had originally been made as a propaganda film for a fur company. If audiences were being propagandized, then it was under the guise of entertainment, and they numbered in the hundreds of millions every week.

In 1928, the Motion Picture Research Council was given more than $200,000 by the philanthropic Payne Fund to conduct the most extensive research ever undertaken into the influence of the movies on American life. This research was conducted by a distinguished group of social scientists on a nationwide basis and aimed at determining the degrees of influence and effect of films on children and adolescents. The research was carried out over a 4-year period (1929–1933) and was eventually published in 10 volumes. The origins of the Payne Fund studies point out the shift that was then taking place in assessing the significance of media in shaping the lives of their audiences. Reverend William Short, the man most responsible for setting up the studies, wanted scientific evidence he could use to foster his campaign to place the motion picture industry under a more stringent form of social control. By the late 1920s, it was no longer acceptable to present evidence that could not be empirically verified. The research itself became the center of a propaganda campaign when a popularized version of some of the research findings was published in the book *Our Movie-Made Children,* by journalist Henry James Forman in 1933. Forman had been employed to simplify and, in some cases, distort the research to arouse public concern in favor of the establishment of a national film censorship commission. Although this ploy did not work in the end, the Payne Fund studies (usually as interpreted by Forman) were widely quoted in all types of media and formed the platform for launching many critical essays on the state of the motion picture industry (Jowett, Jarvie, & Fuller, 1996, pp. 92–121).

In the Soviet Union, films were controlled more firmly by the political authorities than anywhere else in the world (R. Taylor, 1979). The theme of revolution was fundamental to almost all Soviet films, with Lenin as the central figure. To achieve the maximum emotional impact, Soviet filmmakers developed a visual technique called *montage,* in which various film images were juxtaposed to create a specific response from the viewer. The idea was that the skill of the director could create a reality from the different pieces of film that would almost assault the visual sensibilities of the audience and achieve the desired psychological effect. The great Russian propaganda films such as Sergei Eisenstein's *Battleship Potemkin* (1925), Vsevolod Pudovkin's *Storm Over Asia* (1928), and Alexander Dovzhenko's *Earth* (1930) all used montage as a central technique for eliciting the proper audience response.

But even in the Soviet Union, despite the achievements of the filmmakers of the early revolutionary period, authorities were not satisfied with the medium's role, and with the coming to power of Joseph Stalin in the late 1920s, the Soviet cinema began to concentrate on socialist realism. This meant that all films were to be comprehensible to, and appreciated by, the millions, and their one aim was to be the glorification of the emerging Soviet state (Furhammer & Isaksson, 1971, p. 20). As a result of this edict, Soviet films were drained of their vitality, and they only regained their original powers of propaganda in the mid-1930s, after Hitler came to power and several successful antifascist films were produced. These included Eisenstein's *Alexander Nevsky* (1938), which used the theme of a 13th-century battle as an obvious prophesy of what was to come.

After the war, the Soviet film industry turned its attention to making blatant anti-American propaganda films until the death of Stalin (1953), at which time a change in tone occurred. Until the recent period of *glasnost,* the Soviet cinema continued to be a mixture of politics and art, and there was little pretense about trying to achieve propagandistic goals. In its last few years, with the relaxation of government control, the Soviet cinema industry began to explore themes (poverty, sexual dysfunction, domestic violence, political corruption) it would not have been allowed to examine during the previous hard-line communist regime.

With the collapse of the communist regimes in Eastern Europe after 1991, their national film industries faced an enormous dilemma. Ironically, the communist governments in countries such as Czechoslovakia, Hungary, Poland, and East Germany, as well as the Soviet Union, had heavily subsidized their film industries not only to use them as propaganda vehicles but also to demonstrate a subtle "artistic superiority" to the crassly commercial cinema of the noncommunist world. Of course, it was well known that many of these films were, in fact, attacks on the communist system itself, although the governments seemed to ignore this reality. Such films were very often praised in the West for their artistry and "courage" and given international awards. They also quite often proved to be successful at the box office, bringing in much-needed hard currency from outside the communist bloc. With the demise of these paternalistic communist governments, filmmakers in these countries found themselves without funds and were forced, like their non-communist counterparts, to seek funds from the private commercial sector.

At this point, some of these filmmakers have been more successful than others in altering their production style away from its original propagandistic perspective to the more audience-pleasing style favored by commercial film studios. For example, the Russian film *Burnt by the Sun* (1994), written and directed by Nikita Mikhalkov, examined the human side of betrayal during the Russian Revolution and won the Academy Award for Best Foreign Film in 1995. Just a few years later, the Czech film *Kolya,* by director Jan Sverak, featured a much more sentimental story of the relationship between an old man and a young child, and in 1997 it, too, won the Academy Award for Best Foreign Film. Many other directors have not made this transition and find themselves without commercial sponsorship to make the more artistic, introspective films possible with state support of the arts for propaganda purposes.

The enormous Hollywood film industry has never lent itself to overt propaganda on any grand scale, but at times, even commercial filmmakers have used their entertainment medium for promoting a specific idea. As an example, after several years of conspicuous silence, motivated no doubt by international marketing considerations and not wishing to alienate the important German market, Hollywood finally produced its first anti-Nazi film in 1939, more than 6 years after Hitler had come to power. (In fact, the Nazi menace was already surfacing in Germany by 1928.) This film, *Confessions of a Nazi Spy,* was based on the exploits of a former FBI agent who had cracked a spy ring inside the German-American Bund. Once war broke out in Europe in 1939, Hollywood countered with such films as *Devil Dogs of the Air, Here Comes the Navy,* and *Miss Pacific Fleet,* which were deliberately designed as recruiting films for the still neutral U.S. armed services by presenting this as an attractive lifestyle. These became known as the "preparedness films," and they immediately aroused the suspicion and anger of those who did not wish to see the United States become involved in a European war.

Figure 3.3   A scene from *Confessions of a Nazi Spy*, showing George Sanders as the Gestapo agent rallying members of the German-American Bund. Released in April 1939, this film was the first out-and-out anti-Nazi film from a major American studio and immediately aroused enormous controversy, including precipitating a senatorial hearing into propaganda activities in the American motion picture industry. The film was based on a true series of events and suggested that spies, fifth columnists, and Bundists were a serious threat to American security. The last 10 minutes, involving a trial scene, was a direct blast at the menace of fascist ideology. It was the first film to name Hitler directly and was quickly followed by other anti-Hitler films.

In 1941, the isolationist senator from North Dakota, Gerald P. Nye, recognized the potential power of the movies in a famous radio speech when he criticized the Hollywood studios for their role in bringing America "to the verge of war." He was perceptive in his assessment of the movies' potential for successful propagandizing when he noted,

> But when you go to the movies, you go there to be entertained. You are not figuring on listening to a debate about the war. You settle yourself in your seat with your mind wide open. And then the picture starts—goes to work on you, all done by trained actors, full of drama, cunningly devised, and soft passionate music underscoring it. Before you know where you are you have actually listened to a speech designed to make you believe that Hitler is going to get you if you don't watch out. . . . The truth is that in 20,000 theaters in the United States tonight they are holding war mass meetings, and the people lay down the money at the box office before they get in. (Nye, 1941, p. 722)

Figure 3.4   A still from the American movie, *I Wanted Wings,* directed by Mitchell Leisen and released in March 1941. This was one of the most popular of the "preparedness films" in the prewar period. Filmed on location at Randolph and Kelly fields near San Antonio, Texas, with the cooperation of the Army Air Corps, this film followed the lives and training of three young men—a wealthy playboy (Ray Milland), a college athlete (Wayne Morris), and an automobile mechanic (William Holden)—seen here with Brian Donlevy (second from the left) as their training sergeant. The film was well received both critically and at the box office and undoubtedly was responsible for increasing enlistments.

Movies promote "Man's world" values. These are some good examples.

Once the United States entered World War II in December 1941, the movie industry did contribute toward the total war effort, but not only by making war films, for less than one third of all the films released in the United States from 1942 to 1944 actually dealt with the war (Jowett, 1976). What the Hollywood industry did so well was to provide morale-building films for consumption on the home front and overseas, for during the war, entertainment was not only a luxury but also an emotional necessity. American films managed to develop a most potent combination of being able to entertain and propagandize at the same time, thus "getting the message across" while also attracting the large audiences that obvious propaganda and documentary films were seldom able to do.

In November 1941, a prominent and articulate Hollywood producer, Walter Wanger, noted that motion pictures should be used in the upcoming conflict "to clarify, to inspire and to entertain." He continued,

The determination of what ought to be said is a problem for our national leaders and our social scientists. The movies will make significant contributions to national morale only when the people have reached some degree of agreement about the central and irrefutable ideas of a nation caught in the riptide of war. (p. 381)

Wanger was stressing the fact that although movies were merely a medium of entertainment, they were very popular and therefore had a powerful potential to gain the public's attention. For this reason, it was essential that the content of the propaganda "messages" carried in movies during this time of crisis should be based on national interests and not left up to the patriotic whims of the heads of the studios. Once the war did begin for the Americans in 1941, that is precisely the dictum that was followed.

Film was an important medium for propaganda during World War II, but seldom in the way the official propagandists intended. In many cases, audiences were far more sophisticated than expected, and the result was a rejection of blatant efforts to bring about changes in existing opinions. When filmic propaganda was most successful, it was usually based on a skillful exploitation of preexisting public emotions, eliciting an audience response that closely matched public sentiment. A good example is the Nazi film *Baptism of Fire* (1940), which was a skillful compilation of documentary footage dramatically illustrating the supposed invincibility of the German armed forces as they battered the Polish army out of existence in under 3 weeks. When this film was screened in those countries threatened with German invasion, it had a definite intimidation effect. American films, in contrast, were most successful when they stressed positive themes, particularly as they depicted normal life on the home front. Hollywood studios, because of their prior experience at developing strong characterizations, were particularly adept in their war films at depicting the inner strength of ordinary fighting men, usually in groups carefully balanced to underscore the various ethnic origins of Americans such as Irish, Italians, Jews, and so on. In fact, many of the most successful American films during the war did not concern themselves with the fighting at all.

In a study of the contribution made by movies to the war effort, Dorothy Jones (1945), of the Office of War Information (OWI), found that between 1942 and 1945, only about 30% of Hollywood films actually dealt with the war itself. Although she was critical of the movie industry for "lacking a real understanding of the war," she ignored the established fact that, by 1943, having grown tired of war films, not only the home front audience but also the combat forces preferred to see the spate of musicals, comedies, and escapist romances the movie industry was only too happy to turn out. This

Figure 3.5   A still from *Wake Island*, showing Macdonald Carey, Robert
Preston, and Brian Donlevy. This was the first major film about
Americans at war and was released in September 1941. Few
American war films aroused emotions as much as this one did
when it was released. The story was based on the fictionalized
account of a real event—the Japanese capture of the American
base on that Pacific island, after the heroic to-the-last-man
defense immediately after Pearl Harbor. The film succeeded as
both wartime propaganda and as rousing entertainment and
was an enormous hit with the public. This type of propaganda
"entertainment" film was far more successful in reaching
the public than most documentaries deliberately created for
that purpose.

blend of war films and escapist material, most of which tended to emphasize positive aspects of the "American way of life," combined to create a
potent propaganda source for morale building during this difficult period in
American history. Of equal significance was the appeal these domestic films
had among both America's allies and conquered enemies, where their popularity was exceeded only by the demand for American food. Recognizing this
fact, at the end of the war, the U.S. government made serious efforts to make
available to the occupied countries only those films that showed the United
States and its democratic institutions in a favorable light.

Since the end of World War II, little systematic use of film for propaganda purposes on a large scale has been made. Occasional commercial
films propagandize in the sense that they espouse a particular point of view

about a controversial subject. Examples of such films are *The China Syndrome (1979)*, which dealt with the dangers of nuclear power; *Missing (1982)*, which dealt with American complicity in the overthrow of the Chilean government; *Salvador (1986)*, which detailed U.S. complicity in the political upheaval in El Salvador; and *JFK (1991)*, which put forward director Oliver Stone's personal vision of the assassination of President John Kennedy. Of all the current filmmakers, Oliver Stone has been criticized the most for openly "propagandizing" various political perspectives or causes. His film *Nixon (1995)* and his examination of "violence and the media" in *Natural Born Killers (1996)* have been the subject of much criticism and discussion. Stone publicly admits that his films are meant to present a biased examination of the subject matter, leaving the final judgments on the issue of "truth" to the audience. The ideology espoused in individual movies (particularly if they are successful and feature a glamorous star) can still capture the public's imagination, often resulting in specific behavior. As an example, director Tony Scott's very popular *Top Gun* (1986), which romanticized the rigorous training navy pilots undergo, significantly increased the number of applicants at naval recruitment centers. This film, made with the cooperation of the U.S. Navy, also had a strong propaganda theme that emphasized U.S. military "superiority" over vaguely "Middle Eastern" forces.

It is important to point out that the films mentioned above are not part of an organized campaign on behalf of a recognized propaganda agency. This was not always so, for in the most intense part of the Cold War period (roughly 1947–1965), the American film industry was actively solicited by the U.S. government to make commercial films that pointed out the dangers of communism. This contrasted wildly with the pro-Russian films that Hollywood had turned out once Hitler had marched into Russia in 1942, and the American public had to be convinced that we were all now allies. Previously exposed to films such as *The North Star* (1942), *Mission to Moscow* (1943), and *Song of Russia* (1944), the American film audience was now treated to *The Iron Curtain* (1948), which confusingly starred Dana Andrews, who only a few years before had been featured in a sympathetic role in *The North Star* as a Russian partisan; *The Red Menace*, which cataloged the methods of communist subversion in the United States; *Whip Hand* (1951), which dealt with communists running a prison camp in a small town in the United States to test biological weapons; *I Was a Communist for the FBI* (1951), which later became the basis of a television series; *My Son John* (1952), which examined the reaction of patriotic parents when they discover that their son has become a communist; and *Big Jim McLain* (1952), which featured John Wayne hunting communists in Hawaii.

Figure 3.6   A scene from *The North Star,* showing Walter Huston exhorting
his fellow Russian villagers to defend themselves from the invading
German army. Released in November 1943, this film was written
by Lillian Hellman and was reported to have cost producer Samuel
Goldwyn more than $3 million in 18 months of production. The
film was deliberately designed to increase American sympathy and
understanding toward our Russian allies in their fight against
fascism, but it eventually proved to be an embarrassment to
the makers who attempted to "explain it away" at the House
Un-American Activities Committee Hearings in 1947. However,
when it was released, it received both critical and public acclaim.

(It was no coincidence that the name McLain was used to identify the hero
closely with noted anticommunist Senator Joseph McCarthy.)

The fate of the film *The North Star* in the postwar period is particularly
interesting. The film was produced by Sam Goldwyn from a script by the
political activist author Lillian Hellman and distributed by RKO studios
with a big-name cast and major studio production values, ostensibly to solidify Soviet-American relationships at the height of the war. The story dealt
with a Russian village defending itself against the invading German forces,
and although the inner strength of the Russian peasants was stressed, nowhere in the film were the words *communist* or *communism* mentioned. But
even this was too much in the hysteria of the Cold War red scare. When the
film was shown on television in 1957, the title was changed to *Armored
Attack,* and comments were inserted into the film to repudiate the original
sentiments, innocent though they may have been. A new ending was added

showing Russian tanks invading Hungary in 1956, with the voice-over reminding viewers that the heroism of the Russian peasants in World War II should not obscure the brutality of the communist leaders in the postwar period. At the very end, another voice-over apologizes for any pro-Soviet impressions the film may have given (Whitfield, 1991).

It was no coincidence that much of the focus of the House Un-American Activities Committee on communist subversion in the United States in the period after 1947 was on ferreting out potential communists in the Hollywood community. Not only did the committee gain national media attention by questioning entertainment personalities who were widely recognized public figures (who cared about anonymous government employees?), but there was a genuine fear that because the film industry was very powerful, it would be dangerous to allow communist sympathizers to use it as a propaganda tool. Much the same could be said for the attention given to both radio and television, for the commercial media were considered to be potent sources of propaganda disguised as entertainment, as Senator Nye had pointed out in 1941.

Since the breakup of the large Hollywood studios and the emergence of largely independent producers, little attempt has been made to use the motion picture industry for organized propagandizing. Show business personalities, in contrast, are increasingly using their media-obtained popularity to espouse political causes. The majority of the public seems clearly able to distinguish the on-screen persona of the actor from the off-screen political causes with which he or she might be identified. As an example, there was and continues to be considerable hostility toward Jane Fonda for her antiwar activities during the Vietnam War and subsequent support of liberal causes, but she still had an enormous number of fans willing to ignore her political stances and pay money at the box office to see her in such films as *Nine to Five* (1980) or to buy her fitness videos. (It is interesting to note that *Nine to Five* was a political film dealing with significant issues of feminism; however, audiences did not really perceive it as such.) When Jane Fonda made a comeback film in 2005, *Monster-in-Law,* there were independent movie theater owners who, 30 years after the events, were still not willing to exhibit this film, despite the fact the movie was the top box office draw the week it was released.

In recent years, such first-rank stars as John Travolta and Kirstie Alley have actively propagandized, as private citizens and not in their films, for the Church of Scientology in the face of sometimes very hostile reactions. The propaganda value of such personalities lies mainly in their ability to gain media attention for their favorite causes; however, the public seldom sees them as credible sources. On the one hand, Fonda could create public interest in the issues of Vietnam, but she was not considered to be an expert in foreign policy. On the other hand, both Travolta and Alley credit the Church of Scientology with giving them the spiritual comfort to revitalize their flagging careers and, in the case of Alley, to break her drug and later food addiction. In these cases, the public is likely to be much more receptive to such endorsements. In similar fashion, a popular actor such as Richard Gere can focus the public's attention on a sensitive international issue—the Chinese "occupation" of Tibet and destruction of Tibetan culture; the Dalai Lama has obviously learned that his cause will receive far more attention if he associates with glamorous movie stars and public personalities.

The difference between a star deliberately pushing a personal cause and merely being associated with a politician or political campaign is subtle but important. Richard Brownstein, in his detailed examination of the relationship between Hollywood and politics, *The Power and the Glitter* (1990), noted that the specific image a star projects can lend an aura to the politician who associates with him or her and that this association sends a cultural message to the audience. Brownstein continued,

> For their fans, these entertainers embody memories, lifestyles, places and times, shared experiences. They suggest a way of looking at the world, symbolizing not only experiences but also values; you can often tell a lot about someone by how they feel about John Wayne or Sylvester Stallone, or whether they prefer Bob Dylan to Elvis Presley. They are all part of the code people use to recognize others like themselves. . . .
>
> These cultural messages can help politicians make themselves more three-dimensional, particularly to the many voters who pay little attention to elections. . . .
>
> To play these cultural roles, stars need not be personally credible messengers on public policy, the way they must to push individual causes; what matters instead is how their image affects the way voters see a politician who associates with them. (pp. 369–370)

When Hollywood attempted to make so-called message films in the period after World War II, it quickly became obvious that most people do not go to the movies to have their consciences disturbed. Subsequent research has clearly demonstrated that movies, like other mass media, rarely bring about a major change of opinion; however, we also know that consistent exposure to a specific point of view when the audience has none of its own stands a good chance of making some impact. Thus, the cumulative effect of filmic propaganda is greater than any individual film. On one hand, foreign audiences, often knowing little about the United States, will, after years of exposure to American films, develop very specific beliefs and attitudes about the American way of life. On the other hand, no single film can change an individual's racial attitudes ingrained after years of socialization.

The U.S. government is still very concerned about the potential for filmic propaganda from both inside and outside the country. In 1983, the U.S. Department of Justice labeled three documentary films produced by the National Film Board of Canada "propaganda." One of these films, *If You Love This Planet,* about the nuclear arms race, subsequently won an Academy Award (Rosenberg, 1983). This labeling issue was challenged in court, and on April 27, 1987, the U.S. Supreme Court upheld the federal law under which this decision was made, stating that the labeling was "neutral and evenhanded" and did not constitute an infringement of freedom of the press. (For an excellent, full account of this important case, see Gustainis, 1989.) American films being exported are also subject to censorship for propagandizing. Through a little-known program, under the Beirut Agreement adopted by the United Nations in 1948 to "facilitate the international circulation of visual and auditory material of educational, scientific and cultural character," the U.S. Information Agency (USIA) provides "Certificates of International Educational Character" to all films wishing to be exempt from export duties. Over the years, the many films that have been denied such certificates fall into one of three categories: (a) blatant promotion of a specific product or service, (b) offensive religious proselytizing, or (c) political propaganda. In 1983, *The Killing Ground,* an Emmy-winning ABC News documentary on toxic wastes, was denied a certificate on the basis that it was "emotional rather than technical" and because "the primary purpose or effect of the film appears to be less to instruct or inform in an educational sense than to present a special point of view" (Rosenberg, 1983, p. 40). John Mendenhall, who ran the program at the USIA at the time, said, "If we feel that the purpose of the film is to advocate a cause or is persuasive of one point of view, that's one type of propaganda, and we deny it a certificate" (Rosenberg, 1983, p. 41). The fact that no similar incidents of film censorship have occurred in the past 10 years indicates that a more enlightened perspective is the current policy at the USIA and its successor agencies, but a change in administration ideology could alter that.

Michael Moore and Fahrenheit 9/11

In the midst of the heated 2004 presidential race between incumbent George W. Bush and Senator John Kerry, the possibilities of movie propaganda somewhat unexpectedly appeared in full force. The documentary filmmaker Michael Moore, who had previously made well-received but contentious films on such subjects as General Motors's treatment of its workers

(*Roger and Me,* 1996) and gun ownership in the United States (*Bowling for Columbine,* 2001), turned his attention to examining President George Bush's role in fomenting the Iraq War. Using a variety of old and new film clips, Moore constructed an incendiary version of the president's deliberate actions in bringing about this conflict while also raising questions about the president's service record. Overall, the movie appeared to be a devastating attack on the Bush administration and the president personally, and it was highly acclaimed by those opposed to the war and the president's reelection. However, there were others who were equally hostile in their opposition to the film, and it was quickly labeled as nothing but "left-wing propaganda" and a scurrilous character assassination.

The publicity surrounding the film and the passions associated with the upcoming election made the film into a significant box office success. It subsequently become the largest grossing documentary film in movie history, making more than $222 million worldwide and winning several prestigious international awards such as the Palme D'Or at the Cannes International Film Festival. When released as a home video, just weeks before the election, it shattered all records for sales by a documentary (previously held by Moore's own *Bowling for Columbine*). In early 2005, there was additional controversy when the film was excluded from the Academy Awards documentary category, and questions were raised as to whether this really was a documentary at all.

There is little doubt that *Fahrenheit 9/11* is a skillful propagandistic construction. The psychologist Dr. Kelton Rhoads (2004), in his perceptive and detailed analysis of the film, noted at the end the following: "Call it what you will. For my part, I see a consistent, effective, and clever use of a range of established propaganda tactics. If only a few of these tactics were used, or if the attempt to deceive weren't as apparent, I might equivocate. But Moore has located many of the fundamental 'bugs' in the human hardware, and capitalizes on them with skill" (p. 27).

Just how effective was *Fahrenheit 9/11* as a propaganda weapon for the opposition to the president? There is substantial evidence, both anecdotal and by poll measurement, that this film very largely "preached to the choir," in that it garnered substantial support from those who already believed that the United States had been duped into the Iraq War and changed very few minds from the group who felt that the invasion was justified. A poll of those exiting the movie conducted by Opinion Works in July 2004 showed the following results:

Before you saw the movie today, how were you planning to vote this November?

Bush   2%

Kerry   86%

Nader   0%

Another candidate   2%

Undecided   8%

Not planning to vote   2%

After seeing the movie, are you more likely to vote for one of these candidates, or hasn't the movie made a difference?

More likely to vote for:

Bush   2%

Kerry   66%

Nader   0%

Makes no difference in how I will vote   33%

These data indicate that the main constituency for *Fahrenheit 9/11* were those already firmly in the John Kerry camp; only a relatively small number of the audience would have actually changed their minds after viewing the film.

Earlier in the year, another movie, *The Passion of the Christ*, directed by Mel Gibson, had also created considerable public comment. There were two central issues of concern: The first was the film's potential for spreading anti-Semitic feelings over the historical issue of who was responsible for the death of Jesus. The second focused on the possibility that the strong religious content of the film was a not so subtle comment on the normal "immoral" content of Hollywood films and could serve to galvanize evangelical forces for the Republicans in the upcoming election. *The Passion of the Christ* was the largest moneymaker of the year, grossing more than $370 million in the domestic market alone. It was inevitable that this movie would be compared to *Fahrenheit 9/11* in terms of their deliberate "propagandizing" of specific messages, each to apparently opposing ideologies. During the presidential election, the two films became symbols of the increasing cultural differences obvious in the United States. The final word was offered by the Academy of Motion Picture Arts and Sciences, which did not nominate either film for major Oscars in March 2005.

The motion picture is still a highly effective form of information dissemination, but its use as a propaganda vehicle is severely restricted by several factors. First, audiences worldwide have become used to large-budget films with high-quality production values, and this works against the use of low-budget productions. Second, the concept of the fictional story, complete with acknowledged stars as the basic attraction in commercial films, is so well established that generating a mass audience for anything else is very difficult. Third, the distribution system for commercial films is tightly organized and extremely difficult to break into for those outside the mainstream filmmaking community. Last, filmmaking technology has been superseded by video technologies that offer greater opportunities for dissemination of propaganda messages without the need for a large audience base to justify cost. Thus, the motion picture's effectiveness as a propaganda medium is largely limited to the values and ideologies that are an integral part of the plot structure. Such content, though subtle, is in its own right an extremely potent source of modern propaganda and is certainly more powerful in the long run than the deliberate and often clumsy attempts of the past.

Radio

The invention of radio in the late 19th century altered for all time the practice of propaganda, making it possible for messages to be sent across borders and over long distances without the need for a physical presence. Ultimately, radio has become the major medium of full-scale international *white propaganda,* in which the source of the message is clear and the audience knows and often eagerly expects to hear different political viewpoints. Despite the inroads made by television viewing on leisure-time activities in most industrialized countries, there is no indication of any decline in the use of radio for propaganda purposes, and large sums of money are currently spent on the worldwide dissemination of information from a variety of political ideologies.

The first known use of radio for international broadcasting was in 1915, when Germany provided a daily news report of war activities, which was widely used by both the domestic and foreign press that were starved for up-to-date news. Although these broadcasts were in Morse code and therefore not available to all, they served their purpose. Radio was used dramatically by the Soviets in 1917, when under the call sign "To all . . . to all . . . to all . . . ," the Council of the People's Commissars' Radio put out the historic message of Lenin announcing the start of a new age on October 30 (Hale, 1975). The message stated, "The All-Russian Congress of Soviets has formed a new Soviet Government. The Government of Kerensky has been overthrown and arrested. . . . All official institutions are in the hands of the Soviet Government" (p. 16). This was an international call to all revolutionary groups throughout Europe, as well as to those inside Russia, and later broadcasts would be aimed specifically at foreign workers to "be on the watch and not to relax the pressure on your rulers." Soviet radio was quickly placed under the control of the government, for Lenin noted that radio was a "newspaper without paper . . . and without boundaries" and a potentially important medium for communicating his communist ideas to the dispersed workers and peasants in both Russia and the rest of Europe and, ultimately, the world (Hale, 1975, pp. 16–17). By 1922, Moscow had the most powerful radio station in existence, followed in 1925 by a powerful shortwave transmitter, which soon began broadcasting in English.

Interest in radio grew rapidly during the 1920s, and turning the radio dial in the hope of picking up foreign stations became the pastime of millions of listeners in many countries. In the United States, much of the pioneering credit can be given to station KDKA in Pittsburgh, which started the first regularly scheduled radio service in 1920. By the end of 1923, the station had successfully transmitted a special holiday program to Great Britain, which was picked up and rebroadcast from a Manchester station, and later in 1924 and 1925, it broadcast programs to South Africa and Australia, respectively. These early broadcasts set the scene for a regular exchange of radio programs between countries during the late 1920s and early 1930s, and shortwave radio listening became a fascinating hobby for enthusiastic radio fans. The Dutch inaugurated the first regular shortwave broadcasts in 1927, sponsored by the giant electrical engineering company Phillips; by 1930, this station was broadcasting to most parts of the world in more than 20 languages.

Radio Moscow started broadcasting in French in 1929. This action caused an outcry from the French press, which questioned the right of the Soviets to broadcast in a language other than their own, and the League of Nations was asked to consider the matter. Within a year, the French had seen the light and began their own international broadcasts. In 1930, the English-language broadcasts from Moscow had caused sufficient concern to warrant the British Post Office to monitor these on a regular basis. The success of these foreign broadcasts was not lost on the British Broadcasting Corporation (BBC), which in 1929 proposed to the Imperial Conference (where all parts of the British Empire were represented) that a worldwide service be established to maintain the links of the empire. In proposing this service, the BBC submission noted that, in presenting national cultures to other parts of the world, the "boundary between cultural and tendentious propaganda is in practice very indefinite" (Bumpus & Skelt, 1985, p. 13). The Empire Service was begun in 1932 in English only. One week after it opened, King George V delivered a Christmas message to his subjects throughout the world, and the *New York Times* ran the banner headline "Distant Lands Thrill to His God Bless You!" The BBC gained enormous publicity and prestige from this broadcast.

In 1929, Germany also started broadcasting to its nationals abroad from a shortwave transmitter outside Berlin, and Italy set up its service in 1930, broadcasting at first only Italian domestic programs. By 1932, even the League of Nations had its own station broadcasting news bulletins in three languages: English, French, and Spanish. Only in the United States did the government steer well clear of any involvement with international broadcasting, preferring to leave this to the large commercial networks then being established. These stations, of course, broadcast in English only and therefore did not have the same direct propaganda value in foreign countries.

With the coming to power of the National Socialist government in Germany in 1933, the role of international broadcasting was dramatically elevated to major prominence. (The use of radio by the Nazi regime is discussed in more detail in Chapter 5.) Both Hitler and his Propaganda Minister Joseph Goebbels had been impressed with the Soviet Union's German-language service and the development inside Germany of widespread and powerful listener groups for these propaganda broadcasts. By August 1934, the Nazi administration had reorganized German broadcasting, and programs were being beamed to Asia, Africa, South America, and North America. The Germans pioneered in the use of music as a means of attracting listeners, and by all accounts, the quality of the music was superb, with news bulletins and special programs interspersed. One German radio expert was quoted as saying, "Music must first bring the listener to the loudspeaker and relax him" (Grandin, 1939, p. 46). The 1936 Olympic Games in Berlin provided the impetus to construct the world's largest shortwave radio transmitter facilities, and by the end of 1938, the Germans were broadcasting more than 5,000 hours a week in more than 25 languages. The Nazis also introduced medium-wave broadcasts for the neighboring European countries, especially those with pockets of German-speaking minorities.

Italy followed Germany's lead, increasing foreign and Italian broadcasts to both Europe and the Americas, including the provision of Italian-language lessons that cleverly used many passages from Mussolini's speeches as texts. Listeners were asked to send their translations to Rome for correction, and by 1939, more than 35,000 people had done so (Grandin, 1939, p. 30). Japan began its own foreign-language radio service in June 1935 as a means of informing the large number of Japanese living on the Pacific Rim about activities in the home country. This soon changed, for after Japan found itself internationally isolated following its invasion of Manchuria in 1936, Radio Tokyo was used as a propaganda medium for putting across the Japanese government's position on Japan's role in creating a new Asian alliance. Broadcasts were aimed at the United States and Europe, but the quality of these broadcasts was hampered by a lack of personnel trained in foreign languages. Interestingly, the Japanese government did all it could to discourage the ownership of shortwave radio sets to diminish the impact of broadcasts from outside.

By the beginning of World War II in the summer of 1939, approximately 25 countries were broadcasting internationally in foreign languages. The outbreak of war once again brought about an enormous expansion of international radio services. In particular, the BBC was charged with becoming a major arm of the Allied propaganda effort, so by the end of 1940, 23 languages had been added and more than 78 separate news bulletins were being offered everyday, with special attention given to Germany and Italy. Governments in exile in London were also given the opportunity to broadcast to their home countries. By the end of the war, the BBC was the largest international broadcaster by far, programming in more than 43 languages, and because of its earned reputation for total accuracy, even the German troops were tuning in to find out what was happening.

In the United States at the time of the attack on Pearl Harbor, only 12 shortwave transmitters were in action, all owned by private broadcasters. Under the guidance of the Office of War Information (OWI), these stations became collectively known as the Voice of America (VOA). Eventually, the U.S. government rented the stations, and all programs were prepared by the foreign operations unit of the OWI, under the control of playwright Robert Sherwood. By 1943, the number of transmitters had risen to 36, and VOA was broadcasting in 46 languages for some 50 hours a day. (A useful history of the early years of VOA is Shulman, 1990; a detailed examination of the later period is found in Alexandre, 1988.) There was some uncertainty about the future role of the VOA once the war was over, for the U.S. Congress has always been nervous about propaganda activities, whether domestic or foreign. (This fear stems largely from the concern that the administration in power will eventually use such activities to serve its own domestic ends.) Immediately after the war ended, the VOA was severely cut back, but with the start of the Cold War, Congress, believing that the U.S. response to increasing Soviet propaganda actions was inadequate, voted in 1948 to create a permanent role for the VOA as part of the information activities of the U.S. Department of State.

In the decades following World War II, the unprecedented expansion of international broadcasting activities took place. Immediately after the war, the main thrust of such broadcasts was toward Europe, but gradually during the 1950s, 1960s, and 1970s, more attention was given to India, Arabic countries, Africa, Latin America, and Asia. As the dynamics of world politics were being played out, international radio broadcasts became a prominent weapon in the arsenal of propaganda. With the communist takeover in China in 1949, a new major world and radio power appeared while the Soviet Union, threatened with defections in the Soviet bloc, steadily expanded its broadcasts in an increasing number of languages. The noncommunist countries retaliated, with West Germany expanding its facilities, as did all three of the U.S. operations. (Radio Free Europe [RFE] began in 1951; Radio Liberation [RL] started broadcasting in 1953.) By the end of the 1970s, the use of radio as a major medium for international propaganda was greater than it had ever been.

Current International Radio Propaganda

No field of international propaganda has been so affected by the dramatic changes in world politics since the collapse of communism in Eastern Europe than international shortwave broadcasting. Several distinct kinds of international broadcasting systems, however, can still be said to be clearly propagandistic. The most important by far are the national broadcasting organizations that are usually state funded or supported by a group of politically or religiously active citizens eager to reach a specific audience, usually in other countries. More than 80 nations are involved in this type of activity, some operating more than one such service (Bumpus & Skelt, 1985). The United States has the VOA, which is the main international service; RFE, which transmits to five countries in Central and Eastern Europe; Radio Liberty (RL; formerly Radio Liberation), broadcasting to the Soviet states; the newly created Radio Free Asia; and the politically sensitive Radio and TV Marti as a special service aimed at Cuba and other Caribbean countries. Russia has one main station, Radio Moscow, the national service, as well as many regional outlets. Germany has two, Deutsche Welle and Deutschlandfunk. Although the United Kingdom has only one official station, the BBC's World Service, it has an extensive rebroadcasting network throughout the world.

The number of stations is not really important, for these national organizations have access to extremely high-powered transmitters that ensure a wide reception, and technological improvement occurs constantly. Of greater significance is the number of languages in which these international services are offered. Russia broadcasts nearly 2,100 hours a week in more than 80 languages (the number of hours differs for each language). Radio Beijing, of the Chinese People's Republic, broadcasts more than 1,400 hours in 45 languages; the combined American services broadcast more than 2,000 hours in 45 languages; the German stations broadcast more than 780 hours in 39 languages; and the BBC broadcasts more than 720 hours in 37 languages.

Even such minor world powers as North Korea (593 hours), Albania (581 hours), Nigeria (322 hours), and South Africa (205 hours) all transmit their messages over the world's airwaves.

Other kinds of international broadcasters have far less impact as direct propaganda media. In recent years, the number of commercial shortwave radio stations has increased; these stations garner large audiences by targeting their broadcasts to specific listening groups attracted to popular commercial programming. The use of pop music (in a variety of languages) forms the staple content for such stations as Radio Luxembourg, Radio Monte Carlo, and Sri Lanka's All Asia Service. These stations perform a subtle but valuable propaganda role in the international transmission of popular culture. The United States has found that its popular music broadcasts on VOA, particularly jazz, have wide appeal throughout the world, especially in the former Soviet bloc countries.

In the past 30 years, another group of international shortwave broadcasters, devoted mainly to the promulgation of various Christian doctrines, has become a significant addition to the airwaves. Broadcasting more than 1,000 hours a week in a variety of languages, these stations seek to promulgate their own brand of religion to as wide an audience as their transmitters will allow. Usually financed by subscriptions, much of it raised in the United States, they have brought a new type of propaganda to the international scene. Listening to these broadcasts, a person may often find it difficult to separate out the political content from the religious. Vatican Radio began its worldwide service in 1931, the first of the international religious services, and this number grew to more than 40 by 1975 (Hale, 1975, p. 124). In the United States, the 7 worldwide religious operations include Adventist World Radio, World Radio Gospel Hour, and Voice of the Andes. One of Radio Cairo's channels was given over entirely to Islamic teaching—the Voice of the Holy Koran—which used to break off for 1 hour a day to broadcast the Palestine Liberation Organization's propaganda program. (This service has since been discontinued, a further example of the changes in propaganda priorities brought about by shifting political alliances.) Even the BBC uses the powerful lure of Islamic devotion to attract listeners in Arabic countries by broadcasting readings from the Koran in its Arabic service.

In the Iraq War, the Pentagon broadcast a radio propaganda assault using anti–Saddam Hussein messages. The purpose of the broadcasts was to weaken the resolve of Hussein's public supporters and also those in his military. In part, messages said things such as, "People of Iraq . . . the amount of money Saddam spends on himself in one day would be more than enough to feed a family for a year." Other messages were directed at soldiers, which reminded them that how, during the Iran/Iraq war, Hussein had sacrificed thousands of soldiers, and when those who were taken prisoner were returned, he cut off their ears "as punishment for being captured."

Who is listening to all this international flow of propaganda information, and what effect is it having? Here, we must be careful to examine the effects of international broadcasting within the specific historical, social, and cultural context in which it takes place. Of the more than 600 million radios in the world outside the United States, two thirds can receive shortwave broadcasts. In the United States, of the more than 300 million sets, only 3 million can tune in to the shortwave band. The transistor and the subsequent development of printed circuits have made it possible for radios to be made available in the smallest and poorest villages in the remotest parts of the world. From the rural areas of Latin America to the outback of Siberia and Australia, radio is still a major source of outside communication and information, although the advent of the television satellite has made this medium increasingly popular for those who can afford a satellite dish. We must also keep in mind that much of the radio received in these areas originates from within the country itself; however, a great deal of international broadcasting that can clearly be labeled "propaganda" is still attracting audiences.

The main attraction for audiences listening to foreign-language broadcasts in the past was to get something they could not get from their domestic radio services. The most important of these alternatives seemed to be the desire for timely, accurate, objective information that the domestic media of many of these countries failed to provide. Often, internal control of communication for political reasons forced the population to seek outside sources of information, such as occurred in Brazil after censorship was imposed in 1968. At that time, the VOA and BBC became the most reliable sources of news on events in Brazil itself (Ronalds, 1971). The BBC in particular has earned a reputation for being fair and unbiased in its reporting of events, so much so that, during the British-Argentine conflict, British Prime Minister Margaret Thatcher became angry because the service reported the truth about casualties and other information that she considered to be harmful to British domestic morale.

In August 1985, members of the news service of the BBC went on strike to protest government interference in the showing of a television documentary on terrorism that included an interview with a reputed leader of the Irish Republican Army. The government called the interview "dangerous propaganda"; the television news team called it "pertinent information." This strike gained worldwide attention because of the BBC's vaunted reputation for being unbiased. This reputation, earned during World War II, has continued to make the BBC a major international information source for hundreds of millions of listeners who have come to rely on its daily news reports. The VOA also has a reputation for objectivity, and this accounts for the strong reaction whenever presidents attempt to interject their personal political philosophies into the operation of the VOA. Only by maintaining an unblemished history of fairness do these stations carry any weight with their listeners.

In the United States, with its enormous variety of available news sources, all of which are unrestricted by government censorship, there is no clearly perceived need to listen to outside news broadcasts. For this reason, the U.S. population has never had a history of massive shortwave listening, and shortwave radio receivers are not normally found on domestic radio sets. It is estimated that about half a million people in the United States regularly listen to shortwave broadcasts, mainly the BBC and Radio Canada International. Those who do listen on a regular basis do so more out of curiosity and as a hobby than to seek out alternative news sources. Thus, international radio propaganda is essentially ineffective when aimed at the U.S. population, but such propaganda broadcasts are nevertheless routinely monitored by the government because, with careful analysis, they can reveal the strategies and political maneuvering of the originating countries.

International radio propaganda covers a wide spectrum: On one end is the osmotic effect of the BBC, which has, with patience and professionalism, carved a very special niche for itself as a reliable source of information and all the other nonaggressive national news and cultural services; at the other end are the aggressive, sometimes vitriolic broadcasts found on Arab-language stations in the Middle East, certain African countries, Radio Beijing at times, and wherever there is a need to proclaim "a struggle for freedom"; and somewhere in between are the more propagandistic broadcasts of the VOA, RFE, Radio Moscow, Radio Beijing, and other nationalistic services deliberately aimed at promoting a specific political perspective to audiences in other countries.

It is difficult to measure the exact impact of all this international propaganda broadcasting. Clearly, some of it is very effective, particularly when the domestic population is denied access to a variety of alternative news sources and they turn to outside channels of information. By all accounts, most listeners of international broadcasts are sophisticated enough to be wary of blatant propagandizing, although here again the emotional circumstances providing the content of such broadcasts must be taken into consideration. If the message is too much at odds with what the audience believes or suspects to be true, then the end result is less effective than it would have been had it concentrated on a modicum of reality. As Brown (1963) pointed out,

The main lesson to be drawn . . . is how very resistant people are to messages that fail to fit into their own picture of the world and their own objective circumstances, how they deliberately (if unconsciously) seek out only those views which agree with them. (p. 309)

Despite the caution in claiming success for international propaganda broadcasts, however, the fact is that many governments in the recent past have been concerned enough about the provision of alternative news sources to resort to highly costly jamming of signals. (The People's Republic of China still occasionally jams VOA broadcasts aimed at its population.) The jamming of signals has been around since the beginning of radio itself, and many sophisticated and expensive techniques were developed. But in the end, these proved to be largely wasteful exercises and were not always successful, especially in trying to cover large geographic areas. Thus, the USSR, despite its most strenuous efforts, could not prevent some of the signals of VOA, RFE, and RL from reaching target audiences during the Cold War. The United States has never had to resort to jamming signals because, as indicated above, the domestic audience for such broadcasts is not very large or likely to be negatively influenced.

International radio broadcasts have at times been a potent force in shaping the world of propaganda in the 20th century, and they are likely to remain so in the foreseeable future, but with a different emphasis. Clearly, the battle for the "hearts and minds" of listeners will not be the epic battles of the past between communism and capitalism, but probably on a larger world scale between the conflicting cultures of the industrially advanced countries and the less advantaged Third World countries. Since the beginning of the "War on Terrorism" and the ensuing Afghanistan and Iraq conflicts, a new cause for international broadcasting has arisen in the Middle East, and now there are a significant number of clandestine radio stations vying for the attention of Muslim populations, broadcasting largely anti-Western messages. These stations may only exist for a few days or weeks at a time, but the availability of inexpensive, mobile equipment allows them to state their message and then disappear before they can be tracked down. (The interested reader is advised to log on to www.Clandestineradio.com to track the mercurial nature of these radio stations.)

Between the start of the Cold War in the late 1940s and the collapse of communism in the late 1980s, the total number of listeners to foreign radio stations rose, partly as a result of the increase in radio sets but also because of larger populations and the increasing frustration with the inadequacy of the local media in many Third World countries (Hale, 1975). In recent years, the use of television satellites and VCRs has cut into shortwave listening, and local stations in the former Russian satellite countries such as Czechoslovakia, Hungary, and Poland are now free to broadcast whatever they wish. It is not surprising that, in many of these countries, what has emerged with the removal of governmental constraints (and funding) is a form of music-based radio firmly based on the American commercial model.

U.S. Government Propaganda Agencies

With the collapse of communism in Europe, the future need for international shortwave propaganda broadcasting became very uncertain and, some politicians in the United States thought, unnecessary. All jamming of VOA and RFE in Eastern Europe was stopped, and VOA even opened an office in Moscow to monitor more accurately the dramatic changes then taking place inside the former Soviet Union. The sudden change of the world's political configuration in the late 1980s caught the propaganda broadcasters by surprise. Even though VOA, RFE, and RL each stepped forward to take credit for having contributed significantly to the collapse of communism by providing an alternative "truth" to its listeners, they were unprepared for a peacetime role. This was particularly true of RFE and RL, both of which had been specifically created to undermine Soviet influence in Eastern Europe. (For a detailed history of Radio Liberty, see Critchlow, 1995, and Puddington, 2000.) VOA, which falls under the umbrella of the USIA, with its worldwide mandate, was less affected and had already begun to change the basis of its operations away from direct broadcasting to include a major effort at distribution of radio and television material through its "placement" program.

In 1994, the International Broadcasting Act consolidated all nonmilitary, U.S. government international broadcast services under a Broadcasting Board of Governors (BBG) and created the International Broadcasting Bureau (IBB). On October 1, 1999, the BBG became the independent, autonomous entity responsible for all U.S. government and government sponsored, nonmilitary, international broadcasting. This was the result of the 1998 Foreign Affairs Reform and Restructuring Act (Public Law 105–277), the single most important legislation affecting U.S. international broadcasting since the early 1950s.

Every week, more than 100 million listeners, viewers, and Internet users around the world turn on, tune in, and log on to U.S. international broadcasting programs. While the "Broadcasting Board of Governors" is the legal name given to the federal entity encompassing all U.S. international broadcasting services, the day-to-day broadcasting activities are carried out by the individual BBG international broadcasters: the VOA, Alhurra, Radio Sawa, Radio Farda, Radio Free Europe/Radio Liberty (RFE/RL), Radio Free Asia

134

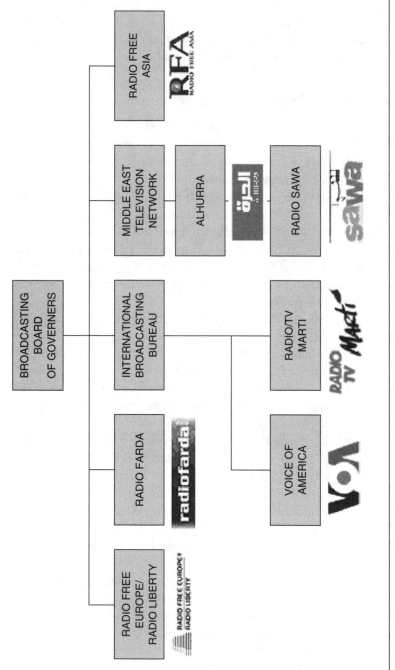

Figure 3.7 International Broadcasting Bureau organizational chart

(RFA), and Radio and TV Marti, with the assistance of the International Broadcasting Bureau (IBB).

The United States prides itself on being a "democracy" and holds itself up to the rest of the world as a model to be admired and emulated. As was discussed in previous chapters, democratic governments have an uneasy relationship with "official" propaganda activities, fearing that such institutions could be used domestically to enhance the fortunes of the party in power. Thus, the establishment of the VOA and other propaganda radio stations was accompanied by very strict rules of how and where these stations could be used. The first VOA broadcast took place on February 24, 1942, aimed at a war-torn world; it now broadcasts almost 900 hours of programming on shortwave and medium-wave radio to an estimated audience of 96 million each week. With more than 1,100 employees, VOA broadcasts in 44 languages, including English, as well as provides programming in 46 languages to more than 1,100 AM, FM, and cable-"affiliated" stations around the world. These additional outlets greatly expand VOA's audience beyond the 96 million who receive the broadcasts directly by tuning in on shortwave and medium-wave radio.

It is worth examining the VOA charter, which became law in 1976, to see how this agency positions itself as part of the mission of the U.S. government:

> The long-range interests of the United States are served by communicating with the people of the world by radio. To be effective, the Voice of America . . . must win the attention and respect of listeners. These principles will therefore govern Voice of America broadcasts:
>
> 1. VOA will serve as a consistently reliable and authoritative source of news. VOA news will be accurate, objective, and comprehensive.
>
> 2. VOA will represent America, not any single segment of American society, and will therefore present a balanced and comprehensive projection of significant American thought and institutions.
>
> 3. VOA will present the policies of the United States clearly and effectively, and will also present responsible discussions and opinion on these policies. (*VOA in 1989 and Beyond,* 1989, p. 2)

VOA's programming is heavily weighted toward news, but research has shown that listeners are equally drawn to the other features, such as call-in shows, English-teaching segments, and, most popularly, music. Perhaps the most blatantly propagandistic aspect of VOA's broadcasts is the "daily editorial" that states the U.S. government's position on various issues, which also fulfills VOA's obligation to "present the policies of the United States."

In all its activities, VOA adopts a strategy of reflecting the culture of target areas to best explain the culture of the United States. Much research is conducted to discover what audiences in these countries need, and this has led to programs with an increased emphasis on how democracies work, the fundamentals of business enterprises, the workings of capitalism, and even export promotion.

Future technological developments, such as direct broadcasting satellites (DBSs), which will enable both listeners and viewers to receive signals directly into their homes from satellite dishes parked in space, pose additional problems that have already been the subject of international rancor. (For a detailed discussion of this issue, see Nordenstreng & Schiller, 1979.)

The recent events in the Middle East following the events of September 11, 2001, have required that the United States increase its propaganda presence in that part of the world. As a result, three new radio services have been started to provide Arab- and Persian-speaking populations with news and information designed to present the American perspective on developments in that region.

The first of these is Alhurra (Arabic for "The Free One"), which is a commercial-free Arabic-language satellite television channel for the Middle East devoted primarily to news and information. In addition to reporting on regional and international events, the channel broadcasts discussion programs, current affairs magazines, and features on a variety of subjects, including health and personal fitness, entertainment, sports, fashion, and science and technology. Alhurra is dedicated to presenting accurate, balanced, and comprehensive news.

The second is Radio Sawa, a 24-hour, 7-days-a-week Arabic-language network that is unique in the Middle East. It broadcasts an upbeat mix of Western and Arabic pop music along with up-to-the-minute news, news analysis, interviews, opinion pieces, sports, and features on a wide variety of political and social issues. Radio Sawa (www.radiosawa.com) originates its programming from Washington and is broadcast across the region, using a combination of medium-wave (AM) and FM transmitters, digital audio satellite, shortwave, and Internet. Radio Sawa will ultimately have six streams tailored to specific parts of the region. Both Alhurra and Radio Sawa have been heavily criticized for not having established themselves as credible news sources. Both use "pop culture" as a means of trying to steer young Arabs away from "hate media," but in doing this, they have shied away from directly confronting many of the issues that are of real concern in the region.

Finally, the last of these new propaganda efforts is Radio Farda, which means "Radio Tomorrow" in Persian, which is a joint effort of two BBG entities: RFE/RL and VOA. Operated from Washington, D.C., and Prague, Czech Republic, Radio Farda produces fresh news and information at least twice an hour, with longer news programming in the morning and the evening. Radio Farda also broadcasts a combination of popular Persian and Western music. The station operates 24 hours a day on medium wave (AM 1593 and AM 1539), digital audio satellite, and on the Internet as well as 21 hours a day on shortwave. Radio Farda complements the VOA's Persian-language radio and television broadcasts into Iran (http://www.bbg.gov/ bbg_aboutus.cfm).

It remains to be seen how successful these new broadcast entities are in getting across a point of view that is often antithetical to that of Muslim tradition and culture and does not take into account long historical animosities and tensions. If we agree that one of the first steps to achieving success with propaganda messages is to "know your audience," then the United States has not done a very credible job. The emotional issues that overwhelmed most Americans in the days and months following the tragic events of 9/11 have prevented us from fully engaging in a thorough, objective analysis of "why" these events took place. Even now there is resistance to acknowledging that, good or evil, we need to understand the reasons—historical, cultural, and political—that motivated the attack on innocent U.S. citizens going about their everyday affairs. Until we do fully understand these reasons and adapt our propaganda strategy accordingly, throwing messages at millions of unsympathetic listeners is unlikely to be successful.

Radio and TV Marti

The idea for Radio Marti originated in the Presidential Commission on Broadcasting to Cuba, which was established by President Ronald Reagan in 1981 to make recommendations on how the Reagan administration could "break the Cuban government's information monopoly" and "satisfy the Cuban people's thirst for reliable information about their own country" (Presidential Commission on Broadcasting to Cuba, quoted in Galimore, 1991, p. 2). The U.S. government was determined to undermine Fidel Castro's censorship barrier by making available to the Cuban people news about world affairs, as well as news about what was going on in Cuba itself. President Reagan signed the Broadcasting to Cuba Act on October 4, 1983, and Radio Marti went on the air on May 20, 1985, broadcasting to Cuba from studios in Washington, D.C., and relayed from a transmitter in Marathon Key in Florida. Named after a famous hero of the Cuban Revolution against Spain, Jose Marti, thus further angering the Cuban government, this station broadcasts continuously on both medium wave (AM) and shortwave. The Cubans jam the AM, but 90% of the Cuban population has access to shortwave. In 1989, Radio Marti's Office of Audience Research confirmed that 85% of the Cuban population older than age 13 were regular listeners to the station.

Radio Marti has proved to be a particularly difficult internal propaganda problem for the U.S. government, in that factions within the large Cuban expatriate community in Florida have continuously pressured for Radio Marti to become more aggressive in encouraging a Cuban revolution against Castro. This tactic would violate the specific guidelines established by the advisory board, which stated that Radio Marti "must not encourage defections nor offer assistance to do so and that its broadcasts must avoid unattributed polemic, argumentation and sweeping generalizations and evaluations, and there must not be incitement to revolution or violence." The aim of the station was to present "the truth, hard facts and dispassionate analysis" (Advisory Board for Cuba Broadcasting, 1989, p. 7). The power struggle for the ideological control of Radio Marti continues as the political situation within Cuba itself becomes more unstable with the collapse of international communism. In 2005, Radio Marti had a staff of 108 and an annual "official" budget of $15 million. (TV Marti is discussed later.)

Opinions about the success of the radio propaganda aimed at Cuba differ, of course. John Spicer Nichols, who has studied the history of clandestine radio propaganda for many years, suggests that the original anti-Castro radio stations run by "shadowy exile groups" broadcasting gray and black propaganda in the 1970s and 1980s were quite successful in establishing connections with the Cuban people. These stations were largely replaced by "professionally produced programs" (essentially, white propaganda) on commercial shortwave stations broadcasting from New Orleans, Nashville, and Miami (Nichols, 1997, pp. 111–112). As Nichols (1997) noted, two factors caused this to happen: First, the Cuban exile community itself gradually moved from being on the political fringe to the political mainstream, and second, the Federal Communications Commission (FCC) was eager to silence all clandestine transmitters on U.S. soil. In the end, virtually all clandestine radio broadcasts to Cuba disappeared, to be replaced by the institutionalized broadcasts of Radio and TV Marti and the other "official" programs. Nichols's assessment of the current political validity of these broadcasts gives us much to think about:

> Separated by 90 miles of water and 35 years from their homeland, the Cuban-American leadership is becoming decreasingly relevant in Havana despite its increasing relevance in Washington. The broadcasts that Cuban exile groups

produce and air on licensed commercial stations or are aired on Radio and TV Marti at the exile's behest are similarly rooted more in the U.S. political reality than in the Cuban political reality. (p. 113)

Television

Because television is essentially a domestic medium, it has not been extensively used as a means of direct international propaganda (with the exception of TV Marti, discussed later). This may change with the introduction of the DBS technology indicated previously, but it is unlikely that many countries would allow the cultural disruptions caused by such daily doses of foreign propaganda. Of far greater current danger is the immense amount of indirect propaganda presented under the guise of entertainment that forms the basis of the worldwide trade in television programming. Much as the motion picture industry has done, the giant television industries of the United States, Great Britain, and Germany have dominated the international market for television programs. Most Third World countries are unable to produce sufficient programming to meet their own needs, and the voracious appetite for television entertainment is met by importing programs from elsewhere. The United States alone sells more than 150,000 hours of television programs annually. (This problem is analyzed in some detail in Lee, 1980, and Negrine & Papathanassopoulos, 1990.)

The content of these programs clearly carries ideological messages, and often they create what is called "the frustration of rising expectations" in viewers from less developed countries by presenting an attractive lifestyle that is beyond their economic means. Ultimately, it is theorized, constant exposure to such a divergence in living conditions will bring about hostility toward the originating country. Schiller (1970) noted,

> To foster consumerism in the poor world sets the stage for frustration on a massive scale, to say nothing of the fact that there is a powerful body of opinion there which questions sharply the desirability of pursuing the Western pattern of development. (p. 114)

One major contributing factor in the collapse of the wall between West and East Germany was the daily dose of television images of "conspicuous consumption" that the East Germans could view in the context of their own relatively drab lifestyles (Hanke, 1990; see also Chapter 1).

In more sanguine times, it was often thought that the worldwide exchange of television programs would lead to greater international understanding and tolerance, but this has not proved to be the case. Today, we have the anomalous situation in which American television programs (particularly those that tend to glamorize the "California lifestyle," such as *Baywatch* and even reruns of older shows like *Dallas*) are followed with almost religious devotion in many countries, while at the same time those same audiences express intense political hostility toward the United States as a symbol of capitalist oppression.

Television does have a major propaganda function in the area of news reporting. Complaints have always been voiced about misrepresentation in the reporting of international (as well as domestic) news, but this issue has recently received an unprecedented amount of attention as a result of complaints from Third World countries that their images are being distorted in the Western press. The issue of the imbalance in the "free flow" of information between industrialized and developing countries became a major topic at international meetings and a significant issue on the agenda of the fundamental political and economic issues in contemporary society. In particular, the United Nations Educational, Scientific, and Cultural Organization (UNESCO) has been the arena of many ardent discussions on the necessity to develop what has been called the New World Information Order (NWIO). At the General Conference of UNESCO in Nairobi in 1976, it was decided that a major study needed to be undertaken of the problem of international communication flows. The subsequent report of what became known as the McBride Commission (Irish statesman Sean McBride was president of the commission), *Many Voices, One World* (McBride, 1980), detailed the extent of the difficulties in reconciling widely differing philosophies on the issue of what constitutes a free flow of information. As the commission report noted,

> It has been frequently stated . . . that due to the fact that the content of information is largely produced by the main developing countries, the image of the developing countries is frequently false and distorted. More serious still, according to some vigorous critics, it is this false image, harmful to their inner balance, which is presented to the developing countries themselves. (McBride, 1980, p. 36)

Predictably, the response in the United States to a call for government involvement to ensure a more balanced flow of communication was negative and based on the historical notion of freedom of the press from all government interference. The issues are complex and easily open to misinterpretation, depending on one's political philosophy (see Nordenstreng, 1982, for a discussion of this issue). By the early 1990s, UNESCO had begun to downplay the great push for a NWIO in the face of more serious problems, such as worldwide famine and AIDS; this was also a deliberate political decision aimed at allaying any fears the United States had about the organization. Ultimately, the concept of developing a NWIO that would provide more balanced coverage to news from developing countries has not had wide acceptance in the West, and images of famine, corruption, and conflicts still predominate on our nightly news broadcasts. In this way, the powerful visual images are presented to television viewers—in broadcasts that seldom have enough time to develop the stories to provide adequate explanations. The "shorthand" nature of television news lends itself to such distortion, thus creating a form of indirect propaganda affecting our perceptions and shaping our attitudes toward a wide variety of issues. We learn to rely on the news media for information, and repeated frequently enough, these images become fixed beliefs, shaping our understanding of the world around us.

No solution to this problem of distortion is clear-cut; it is an inherent part of a free media system in which market forces dictate the content of the media. The difficulties in reconciling this free market media system—in which the commercial mass media allow audience preferences to shape content—with the understandable desire by countries and individuals to present their "best" images are almost insurmountable. Clearly, all parties would like to use the media to propagandize favorably on their behalf, but if news agencies and television networks in the West think their audiences are more interested in learning about political coups, wars, and corruption in Third World countries than about increases in food production, educational advances, and stable political regimes, then that is what will be featured on the news. This type of indirect and unconscious propaganda is a major product of modern media systems. *Where I stopped*

Television, by its visual nature, is vulnerable to misuse as a propaganda medium because it places a premium on using only material with great visual interest to broadcast. The use of "talking heads" to provide expert analysis is only relied on as a last resort when visual support is inadequate. Thus, in the infamous TWA Flight 847 hostage crisis in Beirut in 1985, the American television networks were forced to rely on visual material largely generated by the Lebanese hijackers, almost all of which was aimed at presenting the case for the Shiite Muslims in a favorable light. The networks therefore served as unwitting propagandizers, caught by their desperate need to present whatever visual material they could find and in their desire to compete with each other for the viewing audience. The American public, as we have noted before, is not always receptive to such blatant propaganda messages, and the networks were constantly apologizing for presenting them. Here again, we witness the differences in conditions favoring successful propaganda in two cultures; the Muslim terrorists, in a heightened emotional state of conflict and influenced by years of propaganda for their cause, were naive to think that American television viewers would uncritically accept the images emanating from Beirut. It is also important to note that despite the public nature of the propaganda generated by the terrorists, this did not result in any shift away from the "no concessions to terrorists" policy of the Reagan administration. How much this has to do with the decline in the number of such deliberately staged propagandistic television events in the period since 1988 is unclear.

The most blatant example of television propaganda is the introduction of TV Marti, which began beaming programs into Cuba in August 1990. In 1997, TV Marti had a staff of 86 and was budgeted at $11.1 million. A specially designed antenna was constructed that guaranteed the signals could not be picked up within the United States or interfere with existing domestic or Cuban television reception. The antenna is housed in an aerostat balloon hovering 10,000 feet above the Cudjoe Key, Florida, and aimed at delivering a "Grade A" signal into the heart of Havana. The Cuban government immediately retaliated by jamming the signal into Havana, but according to reports, the station is received on the outskirts of the city and in outlying areas. It has been reported that 28% of households in the potential viewing area receive the signals from TV Marti "at least occasionally." If the station is not seen by the majority of the population, then why is so much money being spent on it? The 1991 *Special Report on TV Marti* suggested several reasons for the need for both Radio and TV Marti.

> For example, wise contingency planning leads us to believe that unforeseen events causing instability in the Cuban government may precipitate a disruption of state broadcasts and/or jamming efforts, causing a disoriented Cuban society to be even more reliant on TV and Radio Marti as credible sources of news and information. . . . And still further in the future, both Radio and TV Marti will be indispensable elements in the U.S. government's efforts to educate Cuban citizens on the ways of democracy and its institutions following a democratic transition in Cuba. (Advisory Council for Cuba Broadcasting, 1991, pp. 7–8)

Both of these stations are bombarding the Cuban people with propaganda in the guise of entertainment, as well as deliberate political messages. The use of these two broadcasting units by the U.S. government is as much a form of psychological warfare as it is a threat to Cuba's economy. The Cuban government is forced to spend a great deal of its already depleted cash reserves on the very expensive jamming operation and has declared that the watching of TV Marti or listening to Radio Marti is "an act of civil disobedience" (Advisory Council for Cuba Broadcasting, 1991, p. 10).

Because of its inherent attractiveness, television offers an opportunity to propagandize in the guise of entertainment. Some countries, such as India and Mexico, have actively used soap operas on television to deliver prosocial messages on issues such as breast-feeding, birth control, and consumer fraud. These programs, designed to be as "involving" to viewers as any "regular" soap opera, have been carefully crafted by script writers working with social scientists to ensure that these "positive" propagandistic messages are smoothly integrated into the plot.

During the Gulf War (1990–1991), the emergence of Cable News Network (CNN) and the invaluable role it played as the major disseminator of news throughout the world took many people by surprise. The Gulf War was the first major conflict of a global nature since the introduction of worldwide television satellite services, and the potential of these systems was dramatically illustrated by the instantaneous broadcasts of events from the embattled area. When CNN reporters remained in Baghdad after the war had actually begun, the world was witness to an unprecedented series of live broadcasts from within the enemy's capital city while it was actually under bombardment. CNN was criticized by some politicians and members of the public for playing into the hands of enemy propaganda, but on the whole, these broadcasts were well received and widely viewed. The question of CNN's unwitting role in "giving aid and comfort to the enemy" by showing the damage to civilian life within Iraq was widely debated at the time, with no clear public consensus emerging except that viewers found the service almost indispensable.

The reporting of the Gulf War also raised new questions about the relationship between the media and the military; it was obvious that the instantaneous technologies available for disseminating news from the battlefields had clashed with the military's need and desire to control what images would actually be seen. The result was that the military denied access to all but a few reporters whom it could control through the use of official "pool" coverage, with military escorts. Although this system was introduced in the name of safety (for troops and reporters), the end result was a great deal of dissatisfaction on the part of the media and a large segment of the public, with the appearance of deliberately manipulated coverage. It was later revealed that many reporters were, in fact, forced to create their own stories from CNN reports but without attributing this source. These are essentially political questions that will take many years to sort out satisfactorily. It was clear by the end of the Gulf War that new communication technologies had fundamentally altered the way all future wars would be reported.

By the time of the second Middle East conflict in 2001 (to be discussed in detail later), this time involving the invasion of Afghanistan and Iraq, CNN had a very lively rival with the emergence of the cable FOX News Network (FNN), heavily funded by owner Rupert Murdock as an alternative to the "mainstream" media and sporting the rather audacious slogan of "Fair and Balanced." FNN was blatantly in support of the administration's actions and provided a largely uncritical evaluation of the events as they unfolded. Once again, reporters for all of the television networks were embedded with the troops, and this brought about similar complaints about the lack of objective reporting. However, the constraints of the battlefield do present real problems, and realistically, reporters cannot safely be allowed to run around in the middle of a firefight trying to get dramatic footage for the audience watching their television sets that evening. Once again, the use of new, more mobile technologies made coverage much more dramatic and personal, far outstripping the ability of the military to control what kinds of images were being sent out to what was now a worldwide audience.

The world of international satellite television, so long dominated by CNN, was also dramatically changed by the emergence of another entity, this time from the Arab world. Launched in 1996 and based in Qatar, Al Jazeera today has more than 30 bureaus and dozens of correspondents covering the entire globe, bringing an entirely new perspective to international news coverage. Their objective, as stated on their Web site, is as follows:

> Free from the shackles of censorship and government control Aljazeera has offered its audiences in the Arab world much needed freedom of thought, independence, and room for debate. In the rest of the world, often dominated by the stereotypical thinking of news "heavyweights," Aljazeera offers a different and a new perspective. (www.Aljezeera.net)

The station has not hesitated to broadcast programming, especially images, which are quite opposite to those distributed in the Western media, and this has given Al Jazeera the reputation of being deliberately inflammatory and propagandistic. With programming focusing primarily on news coverage and analysis, the station has earned the loyalty of an enormous, mostly Arab-speaking audience and the enmity of various critics who argue that Al Jazeera is deliberately sensational by showing bloody footage from various war zones as well as giving disproportionate coverage to various fundamentalist and extremist groups. Criticism from various Western (and sometimes Arab) governments has only served to increase its credibility with an audience that is used to censorship and biased coverage from official government outlets. Al Jazeera is not likely to criticize its own benefactor, the emir of Qatar and the government of Qatar. There is little doubt that

Al Jazeera has opened up the world of cable television news to a much wider audience and has served to heat up the propaganda wars now being fought through satellite television.

It is difficult to predict exactly how much of a role television will play in direct international propaganda in the future. It is doubtful that the use of DBS will be allowed in the same fashion as international radio broadcasting, and the methods of technological control (going so far as to destroy offending satellites) are much easier. It is very likely that we will see a continuation of the argument surrounding the misrepresentation of countries and groups in those countries in which the media are not too tightly controlled by the government. Where governments do have control of the media systems, however, television will continue to play a major role in propagandizing activities, as much through the ideological perspectives of so-called entertainment as through the management of images presented in the news. The potential use of the VCR and the Minicam for the circulation of taped material in a "closed network" is another medium that has just begun to be explored for propaganda purposes. It was widely acknowledged that the circulation of illicit underground tapes in Eastern Europe, even though the number of privately owned VCRs was small, was a significant factor in coalescing opposition groups during the Cold War. In more recent times, the succession of tapes purportedly coming from Osama bin Laden, in which he made personal addresses to Western political leaders or to his own followers and other terrorist leaders being sought in the "war on terrorism," has served to act as quite potent propaganda vehicles. These periodic messages have received wide coverage in the Western media and have often evoked direct responses from heads of state such as President George W. Bush and British Prime Minister Tony Blair. However, as with all such messages, they only have a positive effect with those already in the fold. In the West, they only serve to act as further incentive for his capture. We are only now beginning to realize the enormous potential for television as a major propaganda medium in modern society.

Advertising: The Ubiquitous Propaganda

There is little doubt that under any definition of propaganda, the practice of advertising would have to be included. *Advertising* is a series of appeals, symbols, and statements deliberately designed to influence the receiver of the message toward the point of view desired by the communicator and to act in some specific way as a result of receiving the message, whether it be to purchase, vote, hold positive or negative views, or merely maintain a memory. Also, advertising is not always in the best interest of the receiver of the message (refer to Figure 1.6 in Chapter 1).

The deliberateness of the intention and the carefully constructed nature of the specific appeal distinguish advertising from other forms of persuasive communication; also, in our society, advertising is generally communicated at a cost to the communicator. Whether paid advertising in the traditional sense or the production of leaflets or handbills on a small copier, advertising usually involves the cost of production and distribution. The advertiser (communicator), in turn, hopes this cost will be returned eventually in the form of some benefit, such as the purchase of a product, the casting of a vote, or positive or negative feelings. In fact, advertising is the most ubiquitous form of propaganda in our society. It is found everywhere we look and almost everywhere we listen, and its pressure is felt in every commercial transaction we make. The use of advertising as a means of informing the public about the choices and availability of goods and services is an integral part of the free enterprise capitalist system. Although there have been some exceptions (Hershey's chocolate bar became a big seller, although the company did not do consumer advertising until the early 1970s), advertising is the primary means of stimulating the sales of the products of our consumer-oriented society and, as such, has a direct influence on the economy. Many critics of advertising, however, point out that vast sums of money are spent on promoting an increasingly wider range of choices for an already over-burdened market. After all, does our society really need to choose from more than 30 brands of toothpaste? The debate about the actual economic utility of advertising is also echoed by economists, who disagree about whether advertising increases the costs of goods by creating a larger potential market and thereby lowering unit costs or merely adds to the cost of producing and selling these goods. These arguments have existed ever since advertising became an essential part of modern capitalist economies in the 19th century (Pope, 1983).

Advertising also serves as the financial base for our vast mass communication network, for the structure of our commercialized media system is totally dependent on the revenues from advertising. Even our public broadcasting systems depend to some extent on being underwritten by funds from the business sector. Although advertising may be considered an intrusion into our television viewing, magazine or newspaper reading, or enjoyment of the radio, we accept its existence because we understand its role in making possible our enjoyment of these media. If we really consider the actual structure of the commercial media system, it is the audience that is being delivered to the advertiser and not the other way around.

Institutional Propaganda

In our society, advertising is institutional propaganda at its most obvious level. It serves as a constant reminder that we are being bombarded with messages intended to bring us to a certain point of view or behavior. Yet, we can only absorb so much of what we are expected to, and so we have learned to cope with this enormous information overload. We may look but not really see the television commercial, we may listen but not really hear the radio jingle, and we leaf by print advertisements without paying attention. But every so often, we do see or hear or read, and this is what is intended by the creators of advertising. From the more than 2,000 "messages" we are exposed to every day, we remember at most only about 80 (Heilbroner, 1985).

In 1997, nearly $200 billion was spent on advertising expenditures in the United States. In 2003, more than $249 billion was spent on advertising expenditures in the United States; this was for all types of advertising, from $950,000 commercials on the Super Bowl telecast to the classified advertisements in the local neighborhood newspaper. More than 33,000 nationally advertised brands are for sale in the United States. It is the job of the advertisers (and their appointed advertising agencies) to make their brands stand out from the rest, and so we are inundated with advertising campaigns extolling the specific virtues of individual products, services, institutions, or individuals.

The Science of Advertising

In the late 1950s, the "science" of advertising became the subject of major public debate when Vance Packard published his best-selling book *The Hidden Persuaders* (1957). Cultural historian Jackson Lears (1994) described this book as "a blend of plainspoken outrage at fraud and republican concern about mysterious conspiracies, updated to dramatize postwar preoccupations about mass manipulation" (p. 255). In fact, Packard's book was the culmination of a concern about public "manipulation" by "outside forces" that had begun in the aftermath of the "brainwashing" scare of the Korean War (see Chapter 5 for details of this conflict). At no other time in American history had there been such a close connection between the negative concept of *propaganda* with advertising. The opening paragraph of Packard's book outlines these concerns:

> This book is an attempt to explore a strange and rather exotic new area of American life. It is about the large-scale efforts being made, often with impressive success, to channel our unthinking habits, our purchasing decisions, and our thought processes by the use of insights gleaned from psychiatry and the social sciences. Typically these efforts take place beneath our level of

awareness; so that the appeals which move us are often, in a sense, "hidden." The result is that many of us are being influenced and manipulated, far more than we realize, in the patterns of our everyday lives. (p. 3)

The American public had been alerted to the possibilities of such "hidden persuasion" in the spate of articles and books that appeared in the early 1950s in response to the growing fear that postwar America was becoming a "mass society" (see Chapter 2 for a discussion of the emergence of mass society). Every aspect of the postwar economic boom that had brought about an unprecedented wave of consumerism was critiqued for contributing to a "sameness" in American life that seemed to threaten individuality. Encouraged by the introduction of that most potent of advertising media—television— the American public went on a giant spending spree that gave an enormous boost to the advertising industry but also precipitated concerns about its potential power to manipulate.

Thanks to the popularity of Packard's book (which went into more than 12 printings), as well as the journalistic fallout it precipitated, the American public's attention was alerted to the phenomena of "motivational research" and "subliminal advertising" as two potent and mysterious tools in the advertising agencies' arsenal of consumer research. *Motivational research* was the brainchild of psychoanalyst Ernest Dichter, president of the Institute for Motivational Research, Inc., who coined the term (as well as the term *depth interviews*) in the late 1930s and popularized it as an advertising research technique in the postwar period. Essentially, motivational research used in-depth interviews to try to understand the psychological basis for consumer behavior. In 1958, Packard used the term *subthreshold effects* to describe attempts "to insinuate messages to people past their conscious guard" (p. 42). Later, this practice became more commonly known as "subliminal advertising, which involved embedding verbal or visual messages below the level of the buyers' conscious awareness, keeping them ignorant of being influenced" (Lears, 1994, p. 255). Although no real evidence indicated that subliminal advertising was being practiced on any large scale, the public outcry was strong, and the advertising industry responded that critics were just feeding public paranoia about such manipulation. But these concerns were reflective of the social and cultural situation during the 1950s and the tension of the Cold War. As Lears (1994) noted,

Concerns about advertisers' abuse of motivation research converged with images of "brainwashed" GIs chanting Communist slogans in North Korean prisons. The overall effect of these perceptions was to reaffirm the assumption that the human mind was a pathetic lump of clay. Far more charming than the

Communists, the admaker was nevertheless the American version of a devious master manipulator, orchestrator of a corporate system that to some nervous critics were beginning to work too well. (p. 253)

It is interesting to note that this concern about subliminal advertising has never really disappeared and continues today in such provocative publications as Wilson Bryan Key's series of books, most notably his first, *Subliminal Seduction* (1973). Key provided a series of photographs and other "evidence" of advertisements that he claimed contain subliminal messages or deliberately subliminal images designed to manipulate the unconscious mind of the viewer. A check of the Internet for the subject "subliminal advertising" reveals the continuous and extensive preoccupation with this subject.

These concerns about the manipulative nature of advertising, suggesting that the public was just a "pathetic lump of clay" readily molded to suit the advertiser's needs, were, in fact, just another variation of the outdated "magic bullet" or "hypodermic syringe" model of communications from the turn of the century. It took more sophisticated research in the next three decades to establish that advertising did not work in such a simple manner and that the public's perception of such messages was not monolithic but rather subject to a wide range of possible interpretations (see Chapter 4 for more details on the history of communications research).

In the process of product differentiation, advertising propaganda is selective and often distorting in what it tells the consumer. The desire to appear to be different, to be considered a superior product, or to provide faster, more reliable service encourages the use of hyperbole and exaggeration, and this, in turn, has created a nation of skeptical consumers. To overcome this growing skepticism and to increase the chance of success in an already overcrowded marketplace, advertisers have resorted to a wide range of techniques from the most obvious to the very subtle to attract attention to their specific propaganda strategy. In the act of gaining consumers' attention, we are all too familiar with the blatancy of the bikini-clad woman on the car hood, but most of us are unaware of the effectiveness of the psychologically tested and then readjusted copy for a headache remedy seen on the nightly network news. Increasingly, advertisers are resorting to a variety of scientific testing methods to maximize the expenditure of their advertising budgets by increasing the potential of their message getting through the morass, and this includes close demographic analysis of their target audience, an understanding of the psychological framework of receptivity for their message and whatever adjustments might be necessary to improve this, and a study of the effectiveness of one specific message versus another specific message and even the application of the psychology of color to shape the mood of the audience.

Despite all this expensive scientific analysis, much of advertising remains ineffective, and the list of failed products continues to grow. As we have noted many times in this book, not all propaganda is successful, for a variety of reasons: The message may not be convincing enough to persuade the consumer to change existing behavior (or purchase) patterns, the product may not be seen as utilitarian or cost-effective, or there might just be plain old skepticism, for after all, advertising has a long history of being deceptive or distorting. Of course, advertising can also be extremely effective when the right combination of circumstances comes together, and we have seen many examples of advertising success stories. Despite its proven effectiveness as a "mover of goods," or perhaps because of it, however, public attitudes toward advertising are often very negative. In many ways, a consumer's experience with advertising has made him or her suspicious of all propaganda, and this might prove to be a healthy trend in our society. It will force advertisers and other propagandists to improve the quality of their messages and diminish the possibility of negative propaganda influence. If consumers are aware that they are being propagandized, the choice to accept or reject the message is theirs alone.

The Role of Advertising

In his book *Advertising: The Uneasy Persuasion,* sociologist Michael Schudson (1984) suggested that advertising in the capitalist system serves the same function as the poster art of authoritarian socialism, the state-sanctioned art that was pervasive in the former Soviet Union. We are all familiar with those realistic posters of sturdy men and healthy women working in wheat fields or factories and affirming the joys of socialism; in Schudson's interesting metaphor, advertising serves the same function, depicting equally healthy capitalists driving cars, smoking cigarettes, drinking beer, or wearing designer jeans and essentially enjoying the materialist fruits of the free enterprise system. As Schudson noted,

> American advertising, like socialist realist art, simplifies and typifies. It does not claim to picture reality as it should be—life and lives worth emulating. . . . It always assumes that there is progress. It is thoroughly optimistic, providing for any troubles that it identifies a solution in a particular product or style of life. It focuses, of course, on the new, and if it shows signs of respect for tradition, this is only to help in assimilation of some new commercial creation. (p. 215)

Advertising in our society, therefore, has a symbolic and cultural utility that transcends the mere selling of merchandise, but "the aesthetic of capitalist realism" without a master plan of purposes "glorifies the pleasures and freedoms of consumer choice in defense of the virtues of private life and material ambitions" (p. 218).

Schudson's (1984) unique perspective on advertising provides us with insightful confirmation of precisely why advertising is the most plentiful form of propaganda found in today's society. Like the socialist-realist art it emulates, advertising serves as a constant reminder of the cultural and economic basis of our society. We do not always respond to all the messages we receive, but their pervasiveness provides a sort of psychic comfort that our socioeconomic system is still working.

In recent years, advertisers have been much more careful to "construct" audiences. As costs have increased, advertisers are obviously eager to maximize their potential for reaching the "right" audiences. Turow (1991) noted that companies spend a great deal of time and effort researching exactly how to attract their target audience. Thus, the general abstract concept of *the audience* is turned into a more concrete "construction of reality" in which "certain categories of the audience are chosen over other categories to describe a group of people" (p. 98).

In his very insightful book *Advertising and Popular Culture,* Jib Fowles (1997) provides us with clues to how integrated advertising has become as a part of modern culture. As he noted, "An advertisement or commercial does not stand alone but enters into a number of intertextual relationships, which supply further dynamics to the message" (p. 90). Fowles pointed out that a great deal of current advertising makes assumptions that the audience already has the background to place the content of the advertisements into context. Thus, in the series of commercials for Taster's Choice coffee, which were mini soap operas, the audience had to have seen the entire series of commercials to be "in" on the twists in the story of two star-crossed, middle-aged lovers. Similarly, many commercials, such as those for Nike and Reebok running shoes, actively recognize and acknowledge the audience's familiarity with the competitor's products.

The integration of advertising with other forms of popular culture into a "seamless whole" has the potential of increasing the subtle effectiveness of propaganda messages contained in advertising. Advertising is not seen so much as a separate source of propaganda messages specifically created by sophisticated institutions (the advertiser-advertising agency) to affect behavior (making a purchase) but is accepted as merely another source of (entertaining) information. Nowhere is this integrative process in modern culture more obvious than in the peculiar phenomenon of the proliferation of advertising slogans, labels, and icons that consumers actually wear or display as they go about their daily lives. Such conspicuous display, especially the wearing of designer labels on clothing, can be used as a signifier of success or defiance or whatever specific message the wearer wishes to communicate. The fact that individuals so readily agree to become walking billboards for the designer and often pay handsomely for the privilege in the process is an indication of the success of the integration of advertising and popular culture. Under these conditions, it is little wonder that the majority of the public do not recognize that advertising is, in fact, the most ubiquitous form of propaganda in modern society.

In the final analysis, advertising as propaganda has been largely responsible for the creation of the massive consumer culture in the 20th century, as well as for the fundamental alteration of the nature of political practices in democratic societies. (This theme is developed at length in Qualter, 1991.) Together with the growth of the mass media and improvements in transportation and communication, it is one force that has contributed to the emergence of the mass culture discussed earlier in this chapter. Good or evil, honest or dishonest, economically vital or wasteful, advertising is with us as long as we choose to live in a capitalist economic system, the ultimate success of which is dependent on a high level of consumption of the products and services of this system. The real danger lies in the increasing use of the tactics of this consumer advertising to market dangerous substances (tobacco) and political figures and ideologies. This has resulted in a public that is increasingly ill-informed to make important social and political decisions on a rational basis but that is, instead, becoming more reliant on the sophisticated manipulation of images and symbols.

Propaganda and the Internet

Since the early 1990s, the unexpected growth of the Internet has created a whole new series of difficulties regarding the spreading of rumors as a form of both deliberate and unwitting propaganda. The very "democracy" and accessibility of the World Wide Web has made it the most potent force for the spreading of disinformation yet devised. Tom Dowe (1997), in an article in *Wired* magazine, one of the many publications that have sprung up to meet the public's increasing interest in and use of the Internet, pointed out,

The Net is opening up new terrain in our collective consciousness, between old-fashioned "news" and what used to be called the grapevine—rumor, gossip, word of mouth. Call it *paranews*—information that looks and sounds like news, that might even be news. Or a carelessly crafted half-truth. Or the product of a fevered . . . mind working overtime. It's up to you to figure out which. Like a finely tuned seismograph, an ever more sophisticated chain of Web links, email chains, and newsgroups is now in place to register the slightest tremor in the zeitgeist, no matter how small, distant, or far-fetched. And then deliver it straight to the desktop of anyone, anywhere. (p. 54)

The Internet is now becoming an increasingly important source of information in our society and has begun to take over the role played by traditional journalism sources. This has been particularly true in the world of politics, where the power of the Internet has begun to play a major role in not only the electoral process, but by providing an ongoing forum for the display of public opinion, it is increasingly becoming a factor in shaping how administrations create and implement policy. In many ways, the Internet has become the future nightmare that all politicians dreaded—the source of a daily referendum on their actions. Now, on a daily and sometimes even an hourly basis, the actions of politicians are scrutinized, evaluated, commented on, and either praised or ridiculed. There are continuous updates on news Web sites, or "blogs" (personal columns written by anyone who wishes to act as a journalist on the democratic Internet), which are avidly read by a younger generation attuned to getting their news by reading screens rather than pieces of paper. The potential for propaganda in such a climate is infinite. Anyone can spread a message, true or false, or manipulate information or even alter a picture to suit his or her own ends. The possibilities for serious mischief are enormous and have already been implemented, especially on the political scene. But corporations and individuals are also vulnerable, and there have been some serious cases of damage done to reputations as a result of false information deliberately spread on the Internet.

It is in the realm of national politics that the most obvious use of the Internet for propaganda purposes has been achieved. For example, the administration of President Bill Clinton was under continuous pressure because of information that appeared on the Internet from the time of his inauguration in 1993. The many stories, as diverse as sexual intrigue in the White House and the alleged "murder" of one of his advisers, together with unsubstantiated stories about the Clintons' financial dealings while he was governor of Arkansas, continued unabated, forcing the administration to have to deny or clarify these accusations constantly. These "facts" were presented for everyone to see, but they were usually unsubstantiated and played on the successful propaganda technique of claiming to "confirm" what people are already predisposed to believe to be the truth. The mere appearance of information on the Internet, however, no matter how inaccurate, has the potential for giving the information a degree of veracity and legitimacy, which then has to be ignored, countered, or challenged.

In more recent times, the presidential election of 2004 was in many ways dominated by charge and countercharge largely fought out on competing Internet sites and cable news shows. These two new media forms complemented each other, often with the same personnel doing the speaking and writing. But it was the Internet sites that provided the detailed background analysis, and at times, the documentation fueled the intense hostilities and personal animus that characterized this election. Senator John Kerry's war records, his personal finances, and other details of his life were placed in Web sites for all to see; the same was true of the president's National Guard service records and other documentation that questioned his fitness to serve. There were many questionable (or "black propaganda") sites created that served no purpose other than to propagandize by the spreading of false information. The election of 2004 served to demonstrate clearly that the Internet is now a medium that must be taken seriously in the political arena.

The Internet is also the repository of many urban legends, which continue to circulate years after the event and after the stories have been debunked (see www.Snopes.com for a useful source of urban legends). One prime example of a "story that will not die" is that of TWA Flight 800, a passenger plane that exploded shortly after takeoff in July 1996, killing all 230 people on board. The mysterious circumstances surrounding this tragic flight have proved to be the fodder for an enormous and ongoing series of rumors, conjectures, and ill will circulating among the media, government agencies, and Internet posters about the cause of the mishap. The official government report from the Federal Aviation Administration (FAA), after an exhaustive and painstaking reconstruction of the wreckage, is that an electronic spark in a faulty fuel tank was the cause of the plane exploding. Despite this report (or perhaps precisely because it was issued by an official government agency), the propaganda on the Internet continues to offer a range of alternative scenarios for what may have happened. Most prevalent among these is the claim that the plane was accidentally shot down by an errant military missile fired from a U.S. naval vessel. Numerous Web sites offer up pages and pages of "proof" that this is what really happened. Any attempt to refute these claims is met with skeptical responses on these Web sites that "the government does not want you [the general public] to know the truth."

Many other "conspiracy theories" are available to those who wish to access them by "surfing the Web." A particularly strong antagonism exists between the traditional media organizations and these new sources of information. This is understandable, as the older media, such as newspapers and network television, achieved their success when there was less competition for the public's attention. The advent of newer information sources (e.g., cable television, the Internet) has forced the traditional media to view their news operations more as "products" that are massaged, molded, dressed up, packaged, promoted, and delivered to the consumer as finished commodities. The Internet is perceived as a threat by the mainstream media even though it has, ironically, become a major source for information for these same mass media outlets. Because the Internet operates without any clearly defined rules of journalistic ethics or the need to satisfy the drive for a large audience base as an enticement to advertisers, it functions without constraint in the relatively uncontrolled world of cyberspace. The Internet needs almost nothing in the way of capital investment in expensive electronic equipment, paper, or highly paid on-air "talent." It provides, correctly or incorrectly, instantaneous news and interpretations of the news; it is generally open to immediate public feedback, and it does not rely on "the voices of authority" so prevalent in the mainstream media (the so-called pervasive talking heads with whom we are all familiar). In cyberspace, all voices are accorded equal weight, and, in fact, the very "subversive" nature of the Internet may even diminish the "source credibility" of these usually authoritative voices.

Of course, the Internet also offers an enormous opportunity for "positive" propaganda activities. Already, we have seen the creation of an enormous number of sites that offer much-needed health information to segments of the population either unable to afford a visit to a physician or living in remote areas. Organizations such as the American Cancer Society and American Heart Association have extensive Web sites providing much useful information. Other sites provide information on every conceivable service, from movie starting times to contacts with local, state, and federal politicians. In 1998, the birth of a baby was shown live on the Internet. Although not everyone approved of this incident, many families used this opportunity to provide a sex education experience for their children. Potential uses of the Internet are limited only by people's imaginations.

More specifically, the Internet, as noted previously, offers a unique opportunity to all propagandists. Although access to the World Wide Web is still severely restricted globally (less than 10% of the world's population currently can gain access), the ability to disseminate information, seemingly without a concern for accuracy or the potential for damage, provides the ideal means in the "deliberate, systematic attempt to shape perceptions, manipulate cognitions, and direct behavior to achieve a response that furthers the desired intent of the propagandist" (see the section "Jowett and

O'Donnell's Definition of Propaganda" in Chapter 1). (Web sites very often offer links to other sites or opportunities to send messages to the parties or institutions being scrutinized, a form of direct feedback.) The propagandizing potential of the Internet has become so significant that new companies have been created specifically to monitor what is being said on the network for other companies, institutions, or even individuals (e.g., entertainment figures, politicians, sports figures). Another recent development are sites aimed specifically at monitoring the news for signs of either conservative or liberal bias. Thus, www.Mediamatters.org examines in minute detail comments made by commentators and politicians that are erroneous or exhibit a conservative bias; the Media Research Center at www.Mediaresearch .org does the same thing on the conservative side. In the middle is a rather more objective academic site set up by the Annenberg Public Policy Center at the University of Pennsylvania, www.Factcheck.org. To get close to the truth in a highly subjective arena, one usually has to read all three of these sources.

In the end, we are left to ask whether the Internet poses a serious threat to the orderly dissemination of information on which a democratic form of government depends. At the moment, slightly more than 50% of the American population uses the Internet on a regular basis, but this number increases daily. The following table indicates how the Web is used by the average viewer.

United States: Average Weekly Web Usage

Week ending May 09, 2005

Sessions/visits per person	10
Domains visited per person	24
PC time per person	08:09:02
Duration of a Web page viewed	00:00:49
Active digital media universe	109,384,484
Current digital media universe estimate	202,447,567

Source: http://www.netratings.com/news.jsp?section=dat_to&country=us

All attempts to establish workable "controls" over the Internet have met with public and legal resistance, and the highest courts in the land have declared the Internet to be well protected under the constitutional definition of free speech. This is a medium now in its adolescence, but it has shown itself to have enormous potential power as a propagandizing medium. The

Internet has shown that it can play an important if relatively uncontrollable role in the electoral process, but as politicians and other professional "image manipulators" become more proficient in its use, we can expect it to become an integral and essential part of any modern propaganda campaign. Clearly, the Internet, as it grows in sophistication and accessibility, will bear close scrutiny because of its potential as a propaganda vehicle in which sources can be disguised and deliberate disinformation spread with impunity.

In this chapter, we examined the way propaganda has gradually become institutionalized as a major factor of modern life. The emergence of the mass media in the 19th century afforded an opportunity for the spreading of messages over large distances, to large audiences, and in less time than ever before. These new innovations in information dissemination were extremely useful to a wide range of institutions wishing to propagandize their messages, and each major media form was quickly adapted to this function. Thus, newspapers, movies, radio, and television have all been, and continue to be, used for the dissemination of propaganda, and advertising is now the most prevalent form of propaganda in our society. Finally, we examined how the Internet has become an integral aspect of modern society and a potentially potent propaganda tool.

4

Propaganda and Persuasion Examined

An 85-year history of social science research has yielded much valuable insight into propaganda and persuasion. Researchers began to investigate propaganda after World War I, and by World War II, major studies were being conducted in attitude research. Recent research has included new insights into attitude formation, attitude accessibility, and the study of behavior. It is believed that effects are highly conditional, depending on individual differences, the context in which propaganda and persuasion take place, and a variety of contingent third variables.

The Modern Study of Propaganda and Persuasion

Studies of propaganda in the early part of the 20th century were antecedents to the social scientific study of persuasion. After World War II, researchers stopped referring to their subject of study as "propaganda" and started investigating various constructs of "persuasion," which has become a highly developed subject in communication and social psychology. Today, the research tradition that started in the 1920s continues with various analyses of mass-mediated information about politics, international issues, and trends in news coverage, as well as studies of media content that were related to public concerns. Although many books date the modern study of propaganda

159

and persuasion in the 1930s and 1940s with the beginnings of the scientific study of persuasion, interest in the use of propaganda in World War I prompted earlier investigation.

Propaganda in World War I

The period during World War I was the first time that populations of entire nations were actively involved in a global struggle. The citizens of Europe and America were asked to forgo their own pleasures for the sake of the war effort. Money had to be collected; material comforts had to be sacrificed; families lost their loved ones. All-out public cooperation was essential. To accomplish these ends, attempts were made to arouse hatred and fear of the enemy and to bolster the morale of the people. Mass media were used in ways they had never been used before to propagandize entire populations to new heights of patriotism, commitment to the war effort, and hatred of the enemy. Carefully designed propaganda messages were communicated through news stories, films, photographic records, speeches, books, sermons, posters, rumors, billboard advertisements, and handbills to the general public. "Wireless" radio transmission was considered to be the new medium for shaping public attitudes. It was believed that radio propaganda could weld the masses into an amalgamation of "hate and will and hope" (Lasswell, 1927, p. 221).

Nationwide industrial efforts were mounted with great haste, and the support of civilians who worked in industry was enlisted. The Committee on Public Information (CPI), a civilian committee under the direction of George Creel, was commissioned to "sell the war to America." Creel established a Division of Labor Publications, with former labor organizer Robert Maisel as its head. Maisel's task was to produce and distribute literature to American workers. Another organization, the American Alliance for Labor and Democracy, was formed under the leadership of Samuel Gompers of the American Federation of Labor (AFL) to maintain peace and harmony in the unions in connection with the war effort.

Propaganda was developed and used to bring about cooperation between the industrialized society and the fighting armed forces. Posters, designed to look like movie posters, depicting workers and soldiers arm in arm, were plastered over walls in factories throughout America. The 1914 recruitment poster, "Your Country Needs You," which adorns the cover of this book, turned the British Secretary for War, Lord Kitchener, into an instantly recognizable icon. The image was changed to Uncle Sam by James Montgomery Flagg in 1917 for the "I Want You for the U.S. Army" poster.

The CPI sponsored a National Speakers Bureau on behalf of Liberty Bond sales drives and distributed more than 100 million posters and pamphlets. Wartime propaganda in America and abroad turned out to be very skillful and highly coordinated and was considered by its audiences to be quite powerful.

Although much of the propaganda was factual and accurate, some of it was deceptive and exaggerated. Both the Allies and the Germans circulated false atrocity stories. The Allies told the story of Germans boiling down corpses of their soldiers to be used for fats. The story's inventors deliberately mistranslated *kadaver* as *corpse* instead of *animal* and circulated the story of a "corpse factory" worldwide in an effort to destroy pro-German sentiments. They knew that the German word *kadaver,* which literally means "a corpse," is used in German to refer only to the body of an animal and never to that of a human, but the non-German-speaking audience did not know this. The story, invented in 1917, was not exposed as false until 1925 during a debate in the British House of Commons (Qualter, 1962, p. 66). Atrocity stories, along with other, more tasteful, propaganda efforts, were considered to be quite effective (see also Chapter 5).

The Aftermath of World War I and the Growing Concern About Propaganda

After the armistice, in the early 1920s, the experts involved in the development of wartime propaganda began to have second thoughts about their manipulation of the public. Some of them experienced guilt over the lies and deceptions they had helped spread.

George Creel recounted his experiences with the CPI in *How We Advertised America: The First Telling of the Amazing Story of the Committee on Public Information, 1917–1919,* published in 1920. In his book, Creel tells of the congressional attempt to suppress his report of the CPI's propaganda activities. Creel, who was proud of his activities, discussed in detail the history of the CPI's domestic and foreign activities.

Concern about the power of the developing forms of mass media was widespread, for some people believed that the mass media had extensive, direct, and powerful effects on attitude and behavior change. The belief that the media could sway public opinion and the masses toward almost any point of view was stated by Harold Lasswell (1927) in grandiose language:

But when all allowances have been made, and all extravagant estimates pared to the bone, the fact remains that propaganda is one of the most powerful instrumentalities in the modern world. It has arisen to its present eminence in response to a complex of changed circumstances which have altered the nature of society. . . .

A newer and subtler instrument must weld thousands and even millions of human beings into one amalgamated mass of hate and will and hope. A new flame must burn out the canker of dissent and temper the steel of bellicose enthusiasm. The name of this new hammer and anvil of social solidarity is propaganda. (pp. 220–221)

Lasswell's awe of propaganda was expressed in his pioneer work *Propaganda Technique in the World War* (1927). He noted that the people had been duped and degraded by propaganda during the war. Works such as Lasswell's and Creel's expressed a fear of propaganda, whereas others saw the need to analyze propaganda and its effects. Lasswell based his work on a stimulus-response model rooted in learning theory. Focusing on mass effects, this approach viewed human responses to the media as uniform and immediate. E. D. Martin expressed this approach thusly: "Propaganda offers ready-made opinions for the unthinking herd" (cited in Choukas, 1965, p. 15). Known as the "magic bullet" or "hypodermic needle theory" of direct influence effects, it was not as widely accepted by scholars as many books on mass communication indicate (Hardt, 1989, p. 571; K. Lang, 1989, p. 374; Sproule, 1991, pp. 227–230). The magic bullet theory was not based on empirical generalizations from research but rather on assumptions of the time about human nature. People were assumed to be "uniformly controlled by their biologically based 'instincts' and that they react more or less uniformly to whatever 'stimuli' came along" (Lowery & DeFleur, 1995, p. 400).

As research methodology became more highly developed, it became apparent that the media had selective influences on people. Research concerning important intervening audience variables—for example, demographic background of the audience, selective perception, pre-existing attitudes, patterns of social relationships, and other social and mental states of receivers—disputed the idea of direct influence. Such research led to "limited effects" models that explained the impact of media as a function of the social environment in which they operate. Effects came to be understood as activating and reinforcing preexisting conditions in the audience. Not until the end of the 1920s, however, did human individual modifiability and variability begin to be demonstrable through research.

The Social Sciences and the Study of Propaganda

After World War I, social psychology began to flourish as a research field and an academic discipline. In 1918, Thomas and Znaniecki defined *social psychology* as the study of attitudes. Other social sciences, such as sociology and psychology, were also stimulated by the need to pursue questions about human survival in an age in which social strain grew heavy with concerns about warfare, genocide, economic depression, and human relationships. These questions were about influence, leadership, decision making, and changes in people, institutions, and nations. Such questions were also related to the phenomena of propaganda, public opinion, attitude change, and communication.

Marketing research also began to be developed in the 1920s. Surveys of consumers to analyze their buying habits and the effectiveness of advertising were refined by sampling techniques in the 1930s and were used to poll political as well as consumer preferences. Public opinion research also began to develop. Walter Lippmann's (1922) *Public Opinion* voiced a concern that people were influenced by modern media, especially by the newspapers. In 1937, *Public Opinion Quarterly* began to be published. The Editorial Foreword in the first issue proclaimed,

> For the first time in history, we are confronted nearly everywhere by mass opinion as the final determinant of political and economic action. . . . Scholarship is developing new possibilities of scientific approach as a means of verifying hypotheses and of introducing greater precision of thought and treatment. ("Editorial Foreword," 1937, p. 3)

The Payne Fund studies, discussed in Chapter 3, assessed the effects of films on children and adolescents in the 1930s with respect to individual differences such as economic background, education, home life, neighborhood, gender, and age.

In 1933, the President's Research Committee on Recent Social Trends called the fields of research in propaganda analysis, public opinion analysis, social psychology, and marketing research "agencies of mass impression" (Czitrom, 1982, p. 126). The mass media, then, were considered to be a common denominator from which questions of behavior and attitude change were to be studied. The media industries provided funding for research, along with easily quantifiable data to be analyzed. Applied research also became the by-product of industrial and government institutions and centers, institutes, and universities. Rogers (1994) pointed out that "private foundations and the federal government were more eager to support research that was useful to policymakers but did not raise troubling questions about the interests and motives of the persuaders" (pp. 211–212). Simpson (1994) had a somewhat harsher conclusion: "Sponsorship can, however, underwrite the articulation, elaboration, and development of a favored set of preconceptions, and in that way improve its competitive position in ongoing rivalries with alternative constructions of academic reality" (p. 5). Whatever the sponsors' motives, they enabled a substantial body of behavioral and social scientists to turn their attention to communication studies.

Research in Persuasion

The Study of Attitudes

Although the flurry of research following the end of World War I was related to evaluating propaganda messages, much of the subsequent research had to do with persuasion—specifically, the study of attitudes. During the 1920s and 1930s, research in persuasion was attitude research. Emphasis was placed on conceptually defining attitudes and operationally measuring them. Gordon Allport's (1935) definition of attitude was one of the most important: "An attitude is a mental and neural state of readiness organized through experience, and exerting a directive influence upon the individual's response to all objects and situations with which it is related" (p. 798). The concept of *attitudes* was so central to research that Allport said, "Attitude is probably the most distinctive and indispensable concept in contemporary American social psychology" (p. 798).

Bogardus (1925), Thurstone (1929), and Likert (1932) developed three measures of attitudes. The Likert scale has been one of the most widely used attitude-measurement techniques and is still used for voting and other market research and opinion polls. It consists of categories indicating attitude strength with a *strongly approve* answer graduating down to a *strongly disapprove* response on a 5-point linear scale. The Bogardus and Thurstone scales, which weight a series of attitudinal statements of equal intervals, were used in some of the Payne Fund studies. A representative study that used attitude-measuring scales to determine propaganda effects was done by Rosenthal (1934), who found that Russian silent propaganda films changed socioeconomic attitudes of American students. He also found that stereotypes were easier to create than to eradicate.

Another widely used attitude-measurement instrument was developed by Osgood (Osgood, Suci, & Tannenbaum, 1957). The *semantic differential* focuses on the meaning that people give to a word or concept. This procedure allows people to reveal an attitude by rating a concept on a scale of verbal opposites, such as good and bad, with several blank spaces between the poles. The midpoint in the blank spaces can be an indicator of neutrality. The semantic differential reveals the particular dimensions that people use to qualify their experience, the types of concepts that are regarded as similar or different in meaning, and the intensity of meaning given to a particular concept.

The study of attitude and attitude change received more attention than any other topic in social psychology or communication, yet scholars are still far from achieving conclusive links between attitudes and behavior. One early study of behavior and attitudes was done by Richard Lapiere (1934), who toured the United States with a Chinese couple. They stayed at hotels and ate at restaurants, keeping records of how they were treated. After the trip, Lapiere wrote to all the places they had visited and asked whether they accepted or served Chinese persons as guests. A great majority wrote back and said they did not. From this, Lapiere concluded that the social attitudes of the hotel and restaurant managements had little correspondence with their behavior.

World War II and Research in Communication

After World War II broke out in Europe, researchers turned their attention to studies of propaganda, counterpropaganda, attitudes, and persuasion. Studies conducted during and after the war were primarily undertaken by social psychologists and psychologists who carefully used controls to measure effects. The war caused intense concern about the persuasive powers of the mass media and their potential for directly altering attitudes and behavior. Wartime research was conducted by the U.S. government, which was greatly concerned with the nature of German propaganda, the British communication system in wartime, the means by which the United States Office of War Information bolstered civilian morale, and how to make commercial media fare more relevant to the military struggle (Lazarsfeld & Stanton, 1944).

Paul Lazarsfeld, professor of sociology at Columbia University and head of the Bureau of Applied Social Research, along with other behavioral scientists, produced "Research in Communication" in 1940. This memorandum was a review of the "state of the art" of research at that time. A methodologist, Lazarsfeld was concerned with effects research. Lazarsfeld's approach represented European positivism, the scientific approach of the Vienna Circle influenced by Albert Einstein and Ernst Mach. The Frankfurt school of critical theory was represented by Theodor Adorno and Max Horkheimer, who were also in exile in America. These scholars were concerned with the values and ideological images reflected in media content. Less concerned with immediate effects, they addressed the more subtle and long-term implications of the underlying structure and the implicit themes in the media. Adorno was based in the Princeton Office of Radio Research. Lazarsfeld recalled in his memoirs (Fleming & Bailyn, 1969) the hope to "develop a convergence of European theory and American empiricism" (p. 324). Lazarsfeld perceived critical research in opposition to his practice of administrative research; however, as Hardt (1989, pp. 571–572) pointed out, he failed to consider the role of culture and media in society. Lazarsfeld's focus was on mass media effects that were possibly predictive; thus, his methodology was empirical.

Some wartime research, however, could not measure effects. A study by Speier and Otis, reported in Lazarsfeld and Stanton's (1944, pp. 208–247) *Radio Research, 1942–43*, is representative of the content analyses of newscasts to determine the functions of such newscasts. Speier and Otis (1944) content-analyzed German radio propaganda to France during the Battle of France. They found that the function of propaganda to the enemy in total war is "to realize the aim of war—which is victory—without acts of physical violence, or with less expenditure of physical violence than would otherwise be necessary" (Lazarsfeld & Stanton, 1944, p. 210). They also found that when actual fighting had not yet begun, the propagandist used propaganda as a substitute for physical violence, whereas when actual fighting was going on, propaganda changed into a supplement to physical violence. For example, before fighting began in France, the Germans attempted to terrorize with words, threatening physical violence to get France to negotiate rather than fight. Once fighting actually began, the Germans changed their tactics and chronicled their acts and victories over the radio.

Merton and Lazarsfeld summarized the nature of effect studies in "Studies in Radio and Film Propaganda" (in Merton, 1968, pp. 563–582). These studies used content analysis and response analysis of pamphlets, films, and radio programs. Response analysis was derived through the "focused interview" and a program analyzer, a device that enabled the listener of a radio program to press a button to indicate what she or he liked or disliked. Responses recorded on tape synchronized with the radio program registered approval, disapproval, or neutrality and were plotted into a statistical curve of response. Through response analysis, the researchers were able to determine (a) the effect aspects of the propaganda to which the audience had responded, (b) the many-sided nature of responses, (c) whether the expected responses had occurred, and (d) unanticipated responses. For example, a radio program designed to bolster American morale shortly after the Japanese bombing of Pearl Harbor contained two dominant themes: The first stressed the power and potentiality of the United States to combat defeatism, and the second emphasized the strength of the enemy to combat complacency and overconfidence. Response analysis revealed that the emphasis on the strength of the United States reinforced the complacency of those who were already complacent, and correlatively, references to enemy strength supported defeatism of those who were already defeatist (Merton, 1968, pp. 573–574).

The benchmark for the initiation of sociobehavioral experiments in the area of attitude change, communication, and the acquisition of factual knowledge from instructional media came from studies conducted by a group of distinguished social and behavioral scientists who had been enlisted into service by the U.S. Army. Working within the Information and Educational Division (I&E) of the War Department, the Research Branch assisted the army with a variety of problems involving psychological measurement and evaluation of programs. Some of their experiments were among the first to determine how specific content affected particular audiences. The best known of these experiments was the research that tested the effects of the U.S. Army orientation films, a series called *Why We Fight*.

Frank Capra, the well-known Hollywood director, had been commissioned by the army to make a series of training films for recruits. He produced seven films that traced the history of World War II from 1931 to Pearl Harbor and America's mobilization for war. As they trained to fight in the war, hundreds of thousands of Americans saw these films. The army wanted to find out whether the films did an effective job of teaching the recruits factual knowledge about the war and whether the factual knowledge shaped interpretations and opinions in ways necessary to developing an acceptance of military roles and related sacrifices.

The main team that conducted the studies consisted of Frances J. Anderson, John L. Finan, Carl I. Hovland, Irving L. Janis, Arthur A. Lumsdaine, Nathan Macoby, Fred D. Sheffield, and M. Brewster Smith. The results were published by Hovland, Lumsdaine, and Sheffield in 1949 in a work titled *Experiments on Mass Communication*, which also included other experiments on communication issues. This work touched off considerable interest in the experimental study of persuasion during the postwar years.

Four of the seven *Why We Fight* films were included in the study. Several research procedures were used, including sampling, control groups, matching, pretesting, and measurement. The results showed that the films were not effective in motivating the recruits to serve and fight in the war. The films were also not effective in influencing attitudes related to the army's orientation objectives—for example, deepening resentment toward the enemy, giving greater support to the British, and demanding unconditional surrender. They were somewhat effective, however, in shaping a few attitudes related to the interpretation of the content of the films—for example, that the failure of Germany to invade England during the Battle of Britain was a Nazi defeat. The films were markedly effective, however, in teaching the recruits factual knowledge about the war. In fact, the majority of recruits tested retained the same correct answers when retested 1 week later. Although the films failed to influence the attitudes and motivation of the recruits, they were most successful in presenting information to enhance learning.

Other research on the *Why We Fight* films tested the attitudes of the recruits toward the films themselves. Results showed that the recruits liked the films, accepted the information in them as accurate, and did not perceive them as untruthful propaganda (Lowery & DeFleur, 1995, pp. 148–149). Several characteristics of the audience were tested, including intellectual ability and how it related to learning from the films.

Other studies were conducted to determine whether a one-sided argument was more effective than a two-sided argument. After the German surrender, soldiers in training camps listened to radio speeches that attempted to persuade them to continue the war against Japan. Results indicated that the two-sided message produced greater attitude change than the one-sided message, especially among those who initially opposed prolonging the war. In contrast, the one-sided message brought about greater attitude change among those who initially supported prolonging the war. In addition, the better educated respondents were more favorably affected by the two-sided message, whereas the less well-educated recruits were more responsive to the one-sided message.

The results from the research conducted by the Information and Education Division during the war were very important to the development of communication research. No longer were the media considered to be an all-powerful shaper of attitudes because the effects of films and radio broadcasts were clearly limited. Now, the effects of mass communication were understood to be strongly influenced by individual differences in the audience.

Lasswell developed a five-question model in 1940 to study effects. It grew out of a 10-month-long Rockefeller Foundation–sponsored seminar that included Lazarsfeld and other social scientists. The model—*Who says what to whom in what channel with what effects?* —became the dominant paradigm of American communication research (Rogers, 1994). The model did not include the question *why* and thus focused on effects. Because the model did not concern itself with why those in control of communication made the choices they did to use it for certain functions, it may have steered researchers away from other important topics. Nonetheless, the Rockefeller Communication Seminar was seminal in the development of communication research, for it established networks among communication scholars, and the proceedings volume that came out of it was one of the first books to argue for communication as a field of study (Rogers, 1994). Participants in the seminar moved to Washington, D.C., in 1941 to engage in war-related research. Lasswell's War-Time Communications Project, which used quantitative methods of content analysis of Allied and Axis propaganda, required a neutral observer, thus changing the nature of propaganda research from prewar reformist to objective scientific. "Eventually the value-laden term *propaganda* analysis gave way to *communication research*" (Rogers, 1994, p. 228).

Another research breakthrough occurred during the same era, along with the development of new survey techniques for studying the interrelationship between the media and persuasion in natural settings over time. Lazarsfeld, Berelson, and Gaudet (1948) conducted a panel study during the presidential election of 1940 to determine whether mass media influenced political attitudes. They found that the media tended to reinforce people's existing attitudes rather than introduce new ones. Much more important, as the interviews progressed from month to month, they discovered that the media had been effective in influencing various people who were perceived as leaders. Average citizens were subsequently receiving information and influence from them rather than the media. Face-to-face discussions were found to be a more important source of political influence than the media. The finding was a serendipitous one that had not been anticipated.

After they discovered what was happening, the researchers revised their plans and gathered as much data as they could about interpersonal communication during the campaign. They discovered that people were being influenced by *opinion leaders* who had received their information from the media. From this, they developed the "two-step flow" model of communication effects through discussion with their peers (Lazarsfeld et al., 1948). This model was later revised to become a "multistep flow" model that has people obtaining ideas and information from the media but seeking out opinion leaders for confirmation of their ideas and forming their attitudes. Later research indicated that a highly variable number of relays can exist among the media, the message receivers, and attitude formation (Rogers & Shoemaker, 1971).

Thus, Lazarsfeld and his associates had found that when the political campaign persuaded at all, it served more to activate and reinforce voter predispositions than to change attitudes. Lazarsfeld et al. (1948) concluded, "Exposure is always selective; in other words, a positive relationship exists between people's opinions and what they choose to listen to or read"

(p. 166). This important research introduced the concepts of selective exposure, opinion leader, and two-step and multistep flow into communication research. The research done during World War II reinforced the "limited effects" model of media influence and discovered the importance of gatekeepers.

Kurt Lewin, psychologist and German expatriate, was instrumental in wartime research on how to persuade Americans to change their food-buying and eating habits to accept eating nutritious organ meats such as liver and kidney in times of meat shortages. His studies showed that discussion among shoppers when followed by a group decision was a more effective strategy to produce change than lectures by experts. This led to Lewin's conceptualization of a *gatekeeper,* someone who controls the flow of information. The concept of *gatekeeping* could be applied to other communication situations, according to Lewin: "This situation holds not only for food channels but also for the traveling of a news item through certain communication channels in a group" (cited in Rogers, 1994, pp. 335–336). The gatekeeping function of the media has since become a significant factor that determines what gets into print or on the air (Lang, 1989, p. 371).

The Yale Studies

After the war, Carl Hovland returned to Yale University, gathered a group of 30 colleagues, and developed what has since become known as the "Yale approach" to persuasion. The Yale group examined attitude change in a variety of experimental contexts. Working from a learning theory perspective based on stimulus-response, they investigated the effects of many variables in persuasion. They were among the first researchers to examine the effects of source credibility on information processing. They found that source credibility had no effect on immediate comprehension but that it had a substantial, albeit short-lived, effect on attitude change. Kelman and Hovland (1953) found that because people tend to dissociate source and content over time, the effects of source credibility were not as pervasive as they thought. Kelman and Hovland called this a "sleeper effect." After people have forgotten the name and qualifications of a persuader, the influence of source credibility in changing their attitude disappears, leaving the people with the message content that provided the basis for their attitudes. Contemporary researchers call this a "dissociation hypothesis," rather than a true sleeper effect, which would be the case when a persuasive message results in little initial change followed by a delayed increase in impact on attitude or behavior change (Pratkanis & Greenwald, 1985, pp. 158–160).

Other variables that the Yale group investigated were personality traits and susceptibility to persuasion, the ordering of arguments (primacy-recency), explicit versus implicit conclusions, and fear appeals. The results on fear appeals were surprising to the researchers and of great interest to anyone studying propaganda because weak fear appeals turned out to have more influence on respondents than moderate and strong fear appeals did (Hovland, Janis, & Kelly, 1953, p. 80). Over the next 30 years, researchers continued to study the impact of fear appeals on audiences, with paradoxical results. In some instances, strong fear appeals were found to be persuasive; in others, they were not. Boster and Mongeau (1984) conducted a review of fear-arousing messages since 1952, including a meta-analysis of 25 studies on fear appeals and attitude change. They concluded that a positive correlation between fear-arousing messages and attitude change might exist when certain potentially intervening variables are taken into account: age, certain personality traits, and whether the individual voluntarily exposed herself or himself to the message.

More recent research has indicated that when efficacy, the capacity to produce a desired effect, is high, threatening information contained in a fear appeal is more likely to produce message acceptance (Witte, 1992). In other words, effective fear appeals must include information that threatens the audience but also provides useful action for reducing or eliminating the threat. For example, a health-related message that indicates people as young as 30 are likely to get colon cancer will be more effective if it gives the means of reducing that likelihood (colon cancer screening). Witte (1992) introduced a new model, the *extended parallel process model*, which differentiates between the control of fear and danger to determine a person's reaction to a fear appeal. Her model indicates that when a message creates a strong threat and perceived efficacy, danger control becomes dominant, whereas when perceived efficacy remains low, fear control prevails. When danger control dominates, people will respond to the danger and not to the fear and are likely to accept the recommendation of the message. When fear control is stronger, people are more likely to respond to their fear and to reject the message recommendation. Roskos-Ewoldsen, Yu, and Rhodes (2004) had similar findings in their study of reasoned action and breast self-examination as a means of early detection of breast cancer. Messages to half of the women stressed the danger of breast cancer, while the messages to the other half downplayed the risks of breast cancer. Furthermore, half the messages stressed the effectiveness of self-exam, whereas the other half focused on the limitations of self-exams. They found that regardless of the level of fear appeals, the women who heard the effectiveness of the self-exam message had stronger intentions to perform breast self-examinations (Brock & Green,

2005, p. 58). Sheeran and Orbell (2000) found substantial increases in the number of women who actually took part in cancer screening if an action plan was proposed. Action plans included time and location for the action, so the women could plan and manage their own behavior (Brock & Green, 2005, p. 203).

The 1950s Yale group had wanted to discover the governing laws of persuasion in laboratory settings. Many of the "laws" did not hold up over time, but their work led to a greater understanding of persuasion and stimulated subsequent research in persuasion for years to come.

Consistency Theories

One major grouping of research results that came out of the Yale group's research is known as *consistency theory*. Consistency theorists view the desire or drive for consistency as a central motivator in attitude formation and behavior. *Cognitive consistency* is the mental agreement between a person's notion about some object or event. The underlying assumption is that when new information is contradictory or inconsistent with a person's attitude, it will lead to some confusion and tension. This tension motivates a person to alter or adjust her or his behaviors. For example, most people, including those who smoke, have a positive attitude toward good health and longevity. Information about smoking and secondhand smoke as a cause of disease and death can create tension in smokers. When the tension as a result of inconsistency between attitude and behavior is no longer tolerable, smokers may adjust their behaviors by giving up cigarettes. The same inconsistency has produced new laws and ordinances about smoking in public places, at work, and on public transportation to protect nonsmokers.

All consistency theories are based on the belief that people need to be consistent, or at least to perceive themselves as consistent. The human tendency is toward balance, often called *homeostasis*. When there is imbalance in the human cognitive system, attitude and behavior change tend to result. Most consistency theories (Heider's [1946] balance theory; Osgood & Tannenbaum's [1955] congruity principle) attempt to predict the nature and degree of change that occurs under conditions of inconsistency. The best known of the consistency theories is Festinger's theory of cognitive dissonance.

In 1957, Leon Festinger published his *Theory of Cognitive Dissonance,* which generated a great deal of research, speculation, and argument over the long term. Festinger said that once a person has made an important decision, she or he is in a committed state. If alternatives are presented, the person is susceptible to cognitive dissonance or psychological discomfort. This is based on the need to have consistency among one's cognitive elements. For example, if a person was committed to working for a large corporation and was forced to make a negative speech about it, that person would be put into a state of cognitive dissonance because of the inconsistency. Dissonance can be alleviated in several ways, including rationalization, avoidance, and seeking new support. The person could say that "it's only a job," or not think about the speech after it is given, or look for stronger reasons to support the commitment to the company. If the discrepancy between the commitment and the inconsistent act is high, change is likely to occur. Festinger would say, in the case of wide discrepancy, that the person would change the commitment to the corporation after making a negative speech about it to bring attitude in line with behavior. This theory accounts for the practice of forced behavior producing attitude change.

Recent cognitive dissonance research reveals that people are also driven by interpersonal concerns, such as being perceived as consistent and making a good impression; others are driven by choice and self-perceived responsibility (Tesser, 1995, p. 74). Cognitive dissonance theory influenced Daryl Bem's (1970) theory of self-perception, which states that an individual relies on external cues to infer internal states. Bem used the example of the question "Why do you like brown bread?" with its response "Because I eat it." This is an example of a self-attribution theory, discussed later in this chapter.

Recent research has investigated individual differences in experiencing cognitive dissonance. For example, if people believe they are responsible for inconsistent beliefs, as opposed to being instructed (by a researcher) to act inconsistently with their beliefs, they are more likely to experience dissonance (Brock & Green, 2005, p. 75). People who tend to repress the existence of aversive events are less likely to experience dissonance compared to people who are sensitive to such matters. Cialdini, Trost, and Newsom (1995) developed a new measure to examine individual differences and cognitive dissonance, the Preference for Consistency (PFC) scale. This scale measures people's desire for consistency in three areas: internal consistency, the outward appearance of consistency, and the desire that other people be consistent. They found that people who were high on the PFC were more likely to experience dissonance and subsequent attitude change than those who were low on the scale.

People may also experience dissonance when they vicariously observe someone else behaving inconsistently. Norton, Monin, Cooper, and Hogg (2003) based their study on the presumption that people share a common group membership, strongly identifying with the group. They found that the people who identified with their group changed attitudes to be more consistent with their fellow group members. Those who did not belong to or relate to a group did not change their attitudes.

Theory of Exposure Learning

Social psychologists have amassed considerable evidence that affirms a truism about propaganda—that is, the more people are exposed to an idea, the more they are apt to accept it. Robert Zajonc (1968) conducted a series of studies in which stimuli were exposed to viewers. Regardless of whether the stimuli were meaningful (Chinese characters, nonsense words), respondents who saw them more often liked them better. Zajonc (1980) suggested there is comfort in familiarity. Zimbardo and Leippe (1991) extended this idea with their review of studies of subject exposure to stimuli that were previously liked or disliked. Frequent exposure intensified previous positive and negative attitudes. This "buildup" of attitude intensity is a factor in the polarization of attitudes with repeated exposure.

Social Judgment Theory

Intensity is a key feature of *social judgment theory,* for it not only develops the concept of the direction of an attitude (like-dislike) but also examines the level of ego involvement. *Ego involvement* is the degree of involvement of a person in, and how the person's life is affected by, an issue. A linear scale is used to determine a respondent's latitude of acceptance, rejection, or noncommitment. If a respondent's perception of a message falls within the latitude of acceptance, she or he tends to perceive the message closer to her or his position than it actually is, which results in an assimilation effect. If the message lies in the latitude of rejection, it will be perceived much farther from the person's position than it actually is, which produces contrast effects. The intensity of ego involvement produces a wide latitude of rejection. Social judgment theory is widely used to predict political election outcomes.

Resistance to Persuasion

Most research of the 1950s and 1960s was based on attempts of a persuader to change attitudes in an audience, but William J. McGuire (1964) investigated factors that induced resistance to persuasion, producing work that changed the focus of persuasion research. Using some novel techniques to involve people in creating their own defenses against persuasion, McGuire developed *inoculation theory,* which focuses on a strategy analogous to physical immunization against disease. He used what he called "cultural truisms"—that is, beliefs one holds that are so ingrained within the cultural milieu that they have never been attacked. First, a cultural truism would be mildly attacked. Because the research subject had never dealt with such an attack, she or he needed help in developing a defense against it. Pretreatment in the form of supportive statements and refutational arguments was given by an instructor. If the pretreatment was assimilated, the research subject could then provide counterarguments and defenses against subsequent attacks.

McGuire's Model of Persuasion

McGuire (1968) also developed a *model of persuasion* that emphasized its processes: attention, comprehension, yielding, retention, and action. The model was based on Hovland's work, which took a learning theory approach to persuasion; that is, a message is more likely to change an attitude if, by adopting the position advocated in the message, the person receives positive reinforcement. Attention and comprehension were considered to be receptivity and learning factors, and yielding equaled acceptance of the message purpose or attitude change. Most laboratory studies up to this point stopped there. McGuire extended the idea that persuasion stopped with attitude change by recognizing that, to achieve persuadee action at a later time, retention of the message was necessary. Also, in testing receptivity, McGuire found that receivers with high self-esteem were receptive to persuasive messages because they had confidence in their initial positions. Yet, they were resistant to yielding because they were satisfied with their existing attitudes. He also found that receivers with high intelligence were receptive to a message because they had longer attention spans and were better able to comprehend arguments. Yet, they, too, resisted change because of confidence in existing attitudes. This demonstrated opposite effects on receptivity and yielding in a curvilinear relationship between the variables. This also led him to conclude that receivers with moderate levels of self-esteem and intelligence are more affected by persuasive messages.

Philip Zimbardo and Michael Leippe (1991, p. 136) added steps to the model: exposure at the beginning and, replacing action, translation of attitude to behavior at the end. Exposure precedes attention because people cannot attend a message until they are exposed to it. This is particularly appropriate with advertising on multichannels on television. Although advertisers put their messages on television, there is no guarantee that the right consumers will be exposed to them. Television ratings are important because the more people who watch a program, the more people are exposed to the commercials. Zimbardo and Leippe changed McGuire's "action" to "translation of attitude to behavior" because it recognizes the strength of attitude-consistent behavior. In other words, if a message influences behavior, the new attitude formed by the message must guide behavior in a relevant situation (p. 137).

Diffusion of Innovations

Another development in the late 1960s was the *diffusion of innovations,* developed by James Coleman, who investigated how doctors decided to adopt new antibiotic drugs (Rogers, 1982). Peer networks influenced doctors more than scientific evaluations by university medical schools and pharmaceutical firms. The diffusion process occurred through a combination of mass and interpersonal communication and often took years until an idea had spread. It is a complex process that begins with the people involved who exist within a system. First, their variables, including personality, social characteristics, and needs, are examined. Next, the social system itself has to be looked at in terms of its variables. Third, the characteristics of the innovation are analyzed. The adoption of the innovation itself may vary from optional decision, collective decision, or authority decision. All of this occurs in networks where change takes place. Mass communication and Internet channels may stimulate change, but interpersonal networks are crucial to the process. Innovation occurs as the result of interaction along the links of a network. Recent research, however, has demonstrated that television, the Internet, and mass mailing forge links among viewers even though they may have no direct contact with one another. For example,

> Television evangelists attract loyal followers who adopt the transmitted precepts as guides for how to behave in situations involving moral, social, and political issues. Although they share a common bond to the media source, most members of an electronic community may never see each other. Political power structures are similarly being transformed by the creation of new constituencies tied to a single media source, but with little interconnectedness. Mass marketing techniques, using computer identification and mass mailings, create special-interest constituencies that bypass traditional political organizations in the exercise of political influence. (Bandura, in Bryant & Zillmann, 2002, p. 148)

Individuals can modify innovations as part of the adoption of them. This theory is of particular importance to those interested in attitude and behavior change in a natural setting, such as in a developing nation or an organization.

Recent Research on Attitudes

Research on attitudes at the end of the 20th century focused on the content and formation of attitudinal responses apart from their correlation to behavior change. McGuire (1985, p. 304) predicted that the 1990s would bring renewed interest in attitudes and attitude systems in general and in the structure of attitudes in particular. This research recognized that people have different and even contradictory needs that determine their attitudinal responses. Petty (1995), in a contemporary look at the nature of attitude change, said that beliefs, emotions, and behaviors can separately contribute to people's attitudes but that not all components influence attitude change. Not all three have to be consistent. Petty said,

> Recent research has begun to emphasize the implications of inconsistency and ambivalence among these bases of attitudes. We can feel wonderful when we eat ice cream, but we realize that the fat content in ice cream can produce heart disease. Whether this person's attitude toward ice cream can be predicted is dependent upon whether the affective or cognitive basis is more important. (p. 198)

The *elaboration likelihood model* (ELM) of persuasion (Petty & Cacioppo, 1986) examines centralized processing of information for attitude formation on the basis of a person's motivation to do so, as well as the person's abilities to engage in message- and issue-related thinking. Motivation to engage in persuasive transactions is related to attentional factors, message quality, a person's involvement in the issue, and a person's ability to process persuasive argument. This means that if a person does not care about a topic, she or he is not likely to expend much energy to process the information in the message. Such a person can be expected to rely on extra-message peripheral cues, such as the attractiveness of the persuader or the persuader's credibility. Conversely, if the persuadee cares about the topic at hand in a personal way, she or he is likely to devote great energy to process the message content. In the latter case, evidence becomes important because, if it is sound, the person will be influenced by it (Reinard, 1988, p. 8). In other words, "confront individuals with their concrete social situations, demonstrate the relevancy of an issue for those concerned, and reflection, critical thinking, and subsequent action will occur" (Pratkanis & Turner, 1996, p. 199).

The ELM has generated much attention as a central focus in persuasion research, a great deal of empirical research, and considerable theoretical controversy (see the journal *Communication Theory*, 1993, volumes 1 and 2, for several articles criticizing and defending the ELM). Current research suggests that the amount and nature of one's thinking matters greatly.

Certain variables, such as the persuadee's mood and expertise of the message source, affect attitude change. Attitude change that happens as a result of topic relevance tends to last longer over time, resist attempts to change, and predict relevant behavior (Petty, Cacioppo, Strathman, & Priester in Brock & Green, 2005, pp. 81–111).

Research on Persuasion and Behavior

In the 1970s, experimental research on attitudes waned, and more emphasis was placed on behavior and media influence. Most studies that attempted to link attitude to behavior changes were not able to demonstrate a direct correlation between attitude change and some desired behavior change. Then a new research development measured attitudes toward behavior and intentions to carry out a behavior. Researchers continue to determine what can enable them to predict behavior. Ajzen and Fishbein's (1980) *model of reasoned action* measures the strength of intentions to perform behaviors with strong predictive results. Two important determinants of intentions, however, are related to attitudes. First, the attitude toward the relevant behavior is based on beliefs regarding the behavior and its likely outcomes. Second, the approval or disapproval of significant people, which are attitudes or subjective norms, toward the desired behavior will be taken into consideration.

An attitude may predict behavior when the attitude is strong and clear, when the attitude is relevant to the behavior called for by the situation at hand, when the attitude and the behavior have strong links to the same components of the attitude system, and when the attitude is important to the individual (Zimbardo & Leippe, 1991, p. 192). Kim and Hunter (1993) conducted a meta-analysis of 138 studies about attitude-behavior relationships. With a total sample of 90,908, their findings prompted these researchers to state, "Relevant attitudes strongly predict volitional behavior" (p. 132). The topics of relevance included exercise, family planning, gambling, environmental issues, and race relations. This meta-analysis underscores the need to know one's audience's relevant concerns. When demagogue Huey Long learned that speaking to farmers about their daily chores got a favorable response, he won their votes. His famous pitch, "I know what it is like to slop the hogs" gained him a following that got him elected governor of Louisiana in 1928.

Advertising research reveals that people can have a strong positive attitude toward an advertised product and yet will not buy it. Zimbardo and Leippe (1991) explained that this occurs because the attitude and the buying behavior are connected to different components of the attitude system relative to the product. People may think an advertisement has a cute or lovable image, but they may not take the product seriously enough to purchase it. It may not be relevant enough.

When people are truly committed to an attitude, it is more likely that behavior consistency will occur. Citing the remarkable attitude-behavior consistency of the Chinese student demonstrators in Tiananmen Square in Beijing in 1989, Zimbardo and Leippe (1991) concluded, "People act in accord with their attitudes on matters that matter, sometimes no matter what" (p. 196). Another predictor of behavior is the goal of the person who enacts the behavior. Bandura (1977, p. 161) found that explicitly defined goals create incentive to carry them out.

Bandura's (1986) *theory of observational learning* links behavior and behavior change to modeling that people observe in their homes, among their peers, and in the mass media. According to this theory, modeling influences produce new behaviors because they give people new information about how to behave. Through observation, people acquire symbolic representation of modeled activities that serve as guidelines for their own behavior. Observational learning results when models exhibit novel patterns of thought or behavior that observers did not already possess but that, following observation, they can produce in similar form. Modeling also strengthens or weakens inhibitions over behaviors that have been previously learned. Modeling can also encourage people to engage in behavior they had once perceived as threatening. Modeling influences thus can serve as instructors, inhibitors, disinhibitors, facilitators, stimulus enhancers, and emotion arousers. When people see models express emotional reactions, they are likely to experience emotional arousal. Of course, heightened arousal depends on how the modeled emotional reactions are perceived by the observer. It is obvious that modeling can be an important propaganda strategy, especially where members of an organization wear uniforms, participate in rituals, and reap positive rewards.

Four processes in Bandura's (1986) model are necessary to acquire new behavior: (a) attentional processes, (b) retention processes, (c) motor production processes, and (d) motivational processes. First, a modeled behavior has to be attended to and then subsequently related to. How people relate to others' behavior is determined by perception, motivation, needs, and goals. People are inclined to pay attention to behaviors that have functional value to them. Successful modes of behavior tend to gain more attention than unsuccessful ones. Also, if the person doing the modeling is considered to be attractive or a friend, more attention will be given to observing that person. This is one reason why children in communities with aggressive models for friends may join gangs and engage in aggressive behaviors; they have fewer opportunities to befriend other types or to observe prosocial behaviors than children who live in more pacifistic communities.

Second, what has been observed has to be retained in the memory. Bandura (1986) said that the modeled behavior has to be stored in some symbolic form. His studies found that respondents who expressed modeled behaviors in concise terms or vivid imagery remembered them better.

Third, production processes have to be activated, for they convert symbolic forms into appropriate action. This requires initiation of responses, monitoring, and refinement on the basis of feedback. When a behavior is performed, feedback, coaching, and reinforcement assist its adoption.

Fourth and most important, the actual performance of the modeled behavior requires motivation to do so. The primary motivation is the observation of positive consequences associated with the new behavior. Repeated observation of desirable consequences associated with a behavior provides a strong motivation to perform a behavior. Reinforcement is important to modeling behavior when it is used as an antecedent to the behavior. According to Bandura (1986), the anticipation of positive reinforcement can effectively influence what is observed and the degree of attention paid to the observation of a given behavior. In other words, learning new behaviors through observation can be more successful if those observing the behavior are told ahead of time that they will benefit from performing the behavior.

The whole notion of consequences of behavior as a factor in persuasion is still under consideration. Ward Edwards (1954) developed the *subjective expected utility model* (SEU), based on an economic theory known as *utility maximization theory* or "riskless choice." This model suggests that when faced with behavior choices, people tend to choose the alternative that has the highest expected utility, thus acting in their own interests. Gerald Miller, in the afterword to Cushman and McPhee's (1980, p. 326) work on message-attitude behavior relationships, suggested that people have expectations related to their behaviors and that they may influence reception of related messages. Furthermore, Miller indicated that people may behave according to perceived rewards and punishments for carrying out the behavior. People may not have supportive attitudes but will behave according to perceived consequences.

Marwell and Schmitt (1967) developed a list of strategies for persuasion that focus on persuadee outcome, rather than on the content of the messages used in their study. They developed 16 "compliance-gaining" strategies with both positive and negative consequences, including reward, punishment, debts, altruism, and conformity. Wheeless, Barraclough, and Stewart (1983) concluded in their review of compliance-gaining literature that inherent in a successful compliance-gaining attempt is the persuader's power. Their definition of *power* is "the perceived bases of control that a person has over another person's behavior that would not have otherwise occurred" (p. 120). Perceptions of power vary with an individual's sense of whether external forces are more controlling than internal strength.

A well-known compliance-gaining tactic is *lowballing*. This refers to getting someone to agree to a very attractive transaction—a business deal or sale—and then, on the basis of some excuse, changing the deal so that it costs more. For example, a new car may be advertised at $400 below blue book price. First, the salesperson lets the customer drive the car for a day before sealing the transaction. Next, the salesperson tells the customer that the price has to be higher because of the accessories on the car. By then, the customer has become committed to the purchase and rationalizes, "Well, what's $600 more when this is the car I like."

Another aspect of research into behavior has been *self-attribution research*. When people believe that the cause of a given behavior is derived from an attitude, they will consequently adopt that attitude. Valins (1966) conducted an experiment in which he showed men slides of scantily clothed women. He told them that their physical reactions to the pictures were being measured. The men would hear a heartbeat each time they saw a slide, and each man was told it was his own heartbeat. The supposed heartbeat was manipulated by increasing or decreasing the rapidity of the beats. The men were asked to rate the slides. Predictably, they chose as the best pictures those that were accompanied by rapid heartbeats. People often use their perceived behavior to discover their attitudes.

Recruitment into the religious cult of the Unification Church of Korean Reverend Sun Myung Moon, otherwise known as "Moonies," includes an invitation to a free or inexpensive dinner or weekend retreat. Once there, the recruits find themselves in the company of 20 to 30 pleasant people, eating a delicious meal and enjoying festive dancing and singing. People are very affectionate and attentive. Zimbardo and Leippe (1991, p. 100) pointed out that once recruits find themselves acting like Moonies and enjoying it, they may infer from their behavior that they also like and endorse Moonie ideas. This self-attribution is reinforced by commitment behaviors, such as giving a small donation or contributing some labor. Recruits may then think that because they are making a commitment, they have a positive attitude toward the cult and its beliefs.

Russell Fazio (1986) developed a *model of attitudes as object-evaluation associations in memory* and showed that the strength of this association determines the likelihood that an attitude will be automatically activated on exposure to the attitude object, as well as the extent to which the attitude influences behavior toward the object. In other words, a person has a storehouse of knowledge concerning behaviors that are expected and appropriate in a given situation. An attitude can guide how and what we perceive; thus, it provides a "sizing up" of objects and events in a situation. If an attitude is sufficiently accessible from memory and then is activated as a result of situational cues, it can influence a person's perceptions, definition of the event, and ultimately behavior. Studies have found that attitudes that are highly accessible from memory are more likely to predict behavior than are attitudes that are not accessible from memory.

Research continues on the relationship between attitude and behavior. As a result, a resurgence has occurred in the study of attitudes and their function. Attitude accessibility is an important area of research for developing a better understanding of cognition, memory, and incentives to behave (Roskos-Ewoldsen, 1996).

The Influence of the Media

The rather small number of scholars who devoted their careers to the study of the influence of the media in the 1940s and 1950s spawned several generations of followers. Today, several journals and annuals are devoted exclusively to research on the mass media, plus the thousands of articles in other journals and shelves and shelves of books. Mass communication research has developed as a subdiscipline in its own right. Several works have summarized much of this research (Bryant & Zillmann, 2002; Cantor, 1998; Downing, McQuail, Schlesinger, & Wartella, 2004; Lowery & DeFleur, 1995; MacBeth, 1996; McQuail, 1994; Weimann, 2000; Zillmann & Bryant, 1985). What follows are some highlights of this massive body of research.

Violence and the Media

After the turbulent 1960s, researchers turned their attention to investigations of media influence, especially in relation to violent behavior and other public concerns. In 1968, President Lyndon B. Johnson created the National Commission on the Causes and Prevention of Violence. Seven task forces and five investigative teams produced 15 volumes of reports. One of these reports, *Violence and the Media,* has become a landmark study in the question of media influence. After content analysis of television entertainment programming and survey research on actual violence in America, the researchers concluded that violence not only was a predominant characteristic on television but also was way out of proportion in comparison to actual violence in the real world. Although they acknowledged that the majority of adults who watch television and film are not likely to behave violently as a result, the editors of *Violence and the Media* recognized that long-term and indirect effects of exposure to violence were possible (Lowery & DeFleur, 1995).

Television and Social Behavior, 1969

The *Violence and the Media* report was followed in 1969 by the Surgeon General's Advisory Committee on Television and Social Behavior, which produced several volumes of studies conducted prior to and during the committee's duration. The general conclusion of the researchers was that the viewing of violent entertainment increases the likelihood of subsequent aggressive behavior, but it should be noted that the evidence was derived from laboratory settings and surveys; thus, generalizability is uncertain.

Some of the studies cited were conducted by Albert Bandura and others by Leonard Berkowitz, both of whom had been testing children, adolescents, and young adults in laboratory settings for more than a decade. Their conclusions were more tempered. Both Berkowitz and Bandura and their colleagues were very careful to state that they made no claim to any situation outside the laboratory. They did find, however, that television violence could incite violent behavior in viewers. Berkowitz said it was possible for the research subjects to behave aggressively in later situations if the fantasy situation on film or television seemed justified (Berkowitz, Corwin, & Heironimus, 1963; Berkowitz & Rawlings, 1963). He also indicated that repeated exposure to violence increased the probability of subsequent aggressive acts for some members of an audience but that other factors also determine what may happen—how aggressive the person is, how hostile the media make her or him, how much the person associates the story in film or television with situations in which she or he learned hostile behavior, and the intensity of the guilt or aggression anxiety or both aroused by exposure to the film. Bandura also found that children under certain conditions were apt to reproduce aggressive action after observing adults exhibit novel and aggressive action on the screen (Bandura, 2002; Bandura, Grusec, & Menlove, 1966). Authors of a review (O'Donnell & Kable, 1982, pp. 210–211) of their extensive research concluded that sometimes media violence may be persuasively effective, with the attitude changes consisting more often of modifications than of conversions. With respect to behavior changes, it can be generalized that some types of depicted violence will have some types of effects on the aggression levels of some types of children, adolescents, and young adults under some types of conditions.

One of the most interesting aspects of the experimental evidence concerning the relationship between the media and behavior change is that people tend to be influenced by film and television characters whom they perceive to be similar to themselves. Berkowitz, McGuire, and others found that *viewer identification* is the central concept in the interpretation of film and television effects. The extent to which viewers rated themselves as similar to particular characters influenced their reactions to aggressors in the media.

Television and Behavior, 1982

In 1982, a second Surgeon General's Advisory Committee recommended that other areas of television be investigated. The research that followed was extensive. Already begun in 1972 after the first surgeon general's report, the research consisted of more than 3,000 studies, three fourths of which appeared after 1975 (Lowery & DeFleur, 1995). Because so much information was available, Surgeon General Julius B. Richard recommended that a synthesis and evaluation of the research be undertaken by the National Institute of Mental Health (NIMH). The resulting report, titled *Television and Behavior: Ten Years of Scientific Progress and Implications for the Eighties* (Pearl, Bouthilet, & Lazar, 1982), covered many themes, but the most publicized finding concerned the link between televised violence and later aggressive behavior in children. This link was found in both field and laboratory studies, but much work remains to be done in this area. One study in a related area suggested that aggression can be stimulated by high levels of action even without high violence content. Furthermore, the report emphasized that emotional arousal created by television stimuli that were not necessarily violent had a relationship to aggressive behavior. Increased levels of arousal can lead to excitement that may be channeled into aggression; thus, television content that is exciting could also possibly induce aggressive behavior. In many respects, the report asked more questions than it answered.

Recent Findings on Television and Aggressive Behavior

Dubow and Miller (cited in MacBeth, 1996) reviewed the evidence on experimental studies in laboratory settings and concluded, "Findings in the laboratory enable us to conclude that television viewing can cause viewers to behave more aggressively. But these studies do not allow us to draw conclusions about the effects of television violence viewing in natural settings" (p. 121). Their review of observational studies of children in natural settings ended with the following:

Overall, the majority of observational studies suggest that the relation between TV violence viewing and the development of aggressive behavior is small compared to the relation between other salient environmental variables (e.g., parenting practices) and child aggression. Nevertheless, the significant effect has been repeatedly replicated and is large enough to be considered socially significant. In contrast, by adulthood, relations between violence viewing and aggressive behavior are rarely significant. (p. 122)

Dubow and Miller studied how aggression is learned, and they pointed out that children commit to memory scripts for behavior that are learned from observation and from their own behavior. They speculated that if a child has more violent scripts than nonviolent ones, she or he may access a violent script to use in a social interaction. They also recognized that other environmental, familial, and individual personality traits are potential contributors to behavior as well.

Potter (2003) cites studies ranging from 1977 to 1994 that substantiate that exposure to media violence increases the probability of negative effects such as fear, desensitization, and disinhibition. He concludes, "The body of research clearly shows that when people are exposed to violent portrayals in the media, they are more likely to behave in an aggressive manner when given an opportunity immediately following the exposure" (p. 27). Specifically, the 300 empirical studies that he reviewed have been broken down into three categories of effects: 70% confirm a disinhibition effect, 10% a fear effect, 10% a desensitization effect, and the remaining 10% a variety of other negative effects (p. 29).

Cultivation Studies

Watching violence on television seems to have caused many Americans to be fearful, insecure, and dependent on authority, according to *cultivation studies* by George Gerbner and his associates (Gerbner, Gross, Signorelli, Morgan, & Jackson-Beeck, 1979). The most significant and recurring conclusion of their long-range study of heavy television viewing was that "one correlate of television viewing is a heightened and unequal sense of danger and risk in a mean and selfish world" (p. 194). The researchers thought this would lead people to demand protection and even welcome repression in the name of security. A study of students in junior and senior high schools revealed that those who were heavy viewers of crime shows were more likely to have anti–civil libertarian attitudes (Carlson, 1983). Potter (2003) cites a 1996 study by Chiricos that found a correlation between reports of high-profile crimes on American television news and a significant increase in public belief that crime and violence are the nation's foremost problem. These studies indicate that television influences political learning and, in the case of televised violence, may produce an increasing dependence on the exercise of authoritarian power in society. Weimann (2000, pp. 247–277) cites several international studies that indicate that people in other nations form stereotypical perceptions of Americans and American cities based on exported U.S. media. One general criticism of cultivation research is that it does not demonstrate causality between heavy television viewing and estimates of violence. Comstock (1980) viewed television as a reinforcer of the status quo in society. He thought television portrayals, particularly violent ones, assign roles of authority, power, success, failure, dependence, and vulnerability in a manner that matches the real-life social hierarchy.

Prosocial Behaviors and Television

Other researchers have found that some television programming creates the learning of *prosocial behaviors*. Liebert, Neale, and Davidson (1973) found that children learned altruism, self-control, and generosity from television viewing. Stein and Friedrich (1972) demonstrated that children learn prosocial behaviors such as cooperation, nurturing, and expressing feelings after watching such television programs as *Mr. Rogers*. A review of laboratory and field studies in *Television and Behavior* (Pearl et al., 1982) showed that behaviors such as friendliness, cooperation, delay of gratification, and generosity could be enhanced by exposure to relevant television content. Bandura (in Bryant & Zillmann, 2002, p. 143) cites evidence that serials on television and radio have been positively applied to the most urgent global problems, such as family planning, women's equality, environmental conservation, AIDS prevention, and a variety of beneficial life skills. Lowery and DeFleur (1988) stated that people learn from television and that it can no longer be regarded as mere entertainment: "It is a major source of observational learning for millions of people. In that role it may be one of the most important agencies of socialization in our society" (p. 384).

Pornography

As public standards regarding film and television content related to sex and nudity became less rigid, the public began to be concerned about pornography, especially where women were represented as victims of violence. Research on the effects of filmed pornography (Donnerstein & Malamuth, 1984) has suggested a possible link between pornography and violence against women. On one hand, experiments in laboratory settings demonstrated that, after exposure to aggressive pornography, some men showed less sensitivity toward rape victims, an increase in the willingness to say they would commit rape if not caught, an increase in the acceptance of certain myths about rape, and increased aggressive behavior against women in a laboratory experiment. On the other hand, Fenigstein and Heyduk (cited in Zillmann & Bryant, 1985) suggested that individuals who have tendencies toward sexual violence may be more attracted to violent pornography. The overall link between media violence against women and real violence against women is as yet inconclusive, but researchers are actively exploring it in both laboratory and field studies.

Health, Families, and Politics

Other topics reflecting public concern that have been subjects of television research are health, families, and politics. An increasingly health-conscious public may view physically fit men and women in entertainment programs, but they will not necessarily see them behaving in healthful ways. Dramatic characters on television ate or drank or talked about doing so 75% of the time they were on screen. Instead of eating nutritious meals, television adults snacked 39% of the time, and television children snacked 45% of the time. Alcohol is the beverage most frequently consumed on television, twice as much as coffee or tea and 14 times as often as soft drinks. Alcohol is shown or discussed in 80% of prime-time programs, not counting commercials. Although few television characters are seen smoking, in no instances were antismoking sentiments expressed. Lately, actors in movies are seen smoking with greater frequency. Although many cars and trucks are shown on television and film, seldom do their drivers use seat belts (Lowery & DeFleur, 1995).

Concerns voiced about family by politicians, counselors, and clergy have prompted research regarding both the portrayal of families on television and the effect of television on family and social interactions. Glennon and Butsch (cited in Lowery & DeFleur, 1988, pp. 399–403) content-analyzed 218 family series, finding that the middle class was overrepresented, whereas the working class was underrepresented. Working-class fathers were often depicted as inept, dumb, or bumbling, leading the researchers to speculate that working-class children might perceive their fathers as inadequate and inferior. Middle-class families appeared to be economically successful and often able to solve problems easily. The researchers thought the idealized portrayals of these families might lead viewers to question the adequacy of their own families. Another of Glennon and Butsch's findings was that heavy television viewing is linked to poor family communication and tension (see also

Brody & Stoneman in Morley, 1988, p. 29). Kubey and Csikszentmihalyi (1990), however, found, by having their research subjects report through electronic pagers, that heavy television viewing with the family was a more positive experience than viewing alone and possibly increased the time a family spends together. They found that family members talked with each other during programs, thus making television viewing more cheerful and sociable. Their major finding, however, was that families who engaged in television viewing were passive and less alert, whereas families who engaged in non-television activities felt more alert and active. Although family life, daily schedules, and social interaction have been profoundly affected by television, no area has been more reshaped by television than politics.

Politicians have to voice "sound bites" to ensure 15-second coverage on the evening television news, and television commercials account for a major portion of campaign budgets. The television image of a candidate has become crucial to voter decisions. Evidence suggests a growing reliance on issues such as religion and morality to make voting choices. Lowery and DeFleur (1988) predicted that mediated information may play a greater role in elections, whereas "reinforcement and crystallization, in the sense of cultivating prior loyalties, presumably will have a reduced role" (p. 418).

The Agenda-Setting Function of the Media

One powerful feature of mass communication is its *agenda-setting* function. Early research on this concept began when Donald Shaw and Maxwell McCombs (1974) investigated what voters in North Carolina said were the key issues in the 1968 presidential campaign. They compared these data with the key issues presented in television news, newspapers, and news magazines and found a startlingly high relationship. The news media had not told the voters what to think, but they had told them what to think about. Agenda setting emphasized the gatekeeping aspect of the news. Numerous studies have been conducted in this area, yielding sufficient evidence to conclude that media gatekeepers formulate meaning—selecting, screening, interpreting, emphasizing, and distorting information.

There have been more than 350 empirical studies conducted on the agenda-setting influence of the new media, including online newspapers, on the general public. They have dealt with not only political elections but also civil rights issues, energy, defense preparedness, pollution, and unemployment. In general, they tend to support the theory of agenda setting. McCombs and Reynolds point out that "journalists' daily decisions do significantly influence their audience's picture of the world" (in Bryant & Zillmann, 2002, p. 6).

The Spiral of Silence

Another concept, less widely accepted than agenda setting, is the *spiral of silence* (Noelle-Neumann, 1991). This theory describes people supporting popular opinions presented in the media and suppressing unpopular ones to avoid social isolation. Assumptions made by this theory are that (a) society threatens deviant individuals with isolation, (b) individuals fear isolation continuously, (c) this fear of isolation causes people to assess the climate of opinion at all times, and (d) the results of this assessment affect behavior in public, especially the open expression or concealment of opinions. The more people remain silent, the more they feel that their point of view is not being expressed, and they continue to remain silent, losing confidence and withdrawing from public debate. They may not change their minds, but they stop attempting to persuade others. Although perceptions of dominant opinions are shaped by the media, critics of the spiral of silence point out that tolerance of deviant opinions differs from society to society. Indeed, dissent, if valued in a free society, makes social isolation unlikely. When new issues penetrate public discussion, the spiral of silence is broken.

Dependency Theory

Both the agenda-setting and spiral of silence theories focus on the media as instruments for the distribution or withholding of information, giving issues legitimacy and shaping public opinion. Sandra Ball-Rokeach's dependency model (Ball-Rokeach & DeFleur, 1976) explains why people are reliant on the media to set the agenda for public discussion. In a complex society with a proliferation of information, people rely on the media for information about that which they do not have immediate knowledge. An important premise of *dependency theory,* however, is that people do not use the media separately from other social influences in which they and the media exist. How people use and react to the media is influenced by their past learning about society, including what they learned from the media in the past, as well as what is happening in the present. Thus, a certain piece of media information and subsequent conversations about it will have quite different consequences for different people, depending on their previous experiences and social conditions at the moment. Because dependency theory encompasses the interactive nature of media, audience, and society, it is a more comprehensive theory than others that emphasize simple cause and effect. Dependency theory also recognizes that more urban and industrialized societies have more dependency on the media and that as social change and conflict increase, so does public dependency on the media.

Dependency theory also accounts for media effects that can, in turn, affect society as well as the media. Ball-Rokeach delineated three types of effects: cognitive, affective, and behavioral. The *cognitive effects* are (a) ambiguity resolution, (b) attitude formation, (c) agenda setting, (d) expansion of the belief system, and (e) value clarification. *Affective effects* are emotional responses to mediated information that can create strong feelings about parts of society and/or desensitize people to violence because of excessive exposure. *Behavioral effects* may be initiating new behaviors or ceasing old ones. Any or all of these effects are likely to be felt only by people who depend on media information. Look at the following example of the effects of media coverage of a controversial event to see how this may work.

When Anita Hill, professor of law at Oklahoma University, testified during the Senate hearings on the nomination of Clarence Thomas to the U.S. Supreme Court, sexual harassment became a news agenda item. People who watched the hearings on television or followed them in the newspapers may have experienced all three types of effects. The term *sexual harassment* was clarified for some, made ambiguous for others. Whether or not people believed Hill, attitudes about sexual harassment were formed, and sexual harassment became much more of an agenda item than it previously had been. Public discussion regarding appropriate behavior at work and in school intensified, and in the process, belief systems expanded, and some values were clarified. Strong emotions were felt, especially by those who had experienced sexual harassment in the past, and many women came forth to talk about their experiences. Behavior changes have occurred, especially the cessation of practices that were suspect, and numerous charges against offenders have been brought forth. The agenda regarding sexual harassment was prominent in October 1991, until it no longer was a media story, but the effects of it over the long term are still being felt. Even President Bill Clinton was not immune to sexual harassment charges (for alleged conduct years earlier, while he was governor of Arkansas) in the Paula Jones case.

Uses and Gratifications Theory

Most mass communication theories focus on what the media do to the receiver, but *uses and gratifications theory* focuses on what the receiver does with the media. The consumer of media is viewed as an active selector and goal-directed user of it. The assumption is that the user of media is responsible for choosing media to meet psychological and sociological needs. Elihu Katz (cited in F. Williams, 1989) found in his research "overall patterns that suggest that individuals specify different media for fulfilling different kinds of needs" (p. 71). Human needs are the primary consideration of uses and gratifications studies and include the need to be diverted as well as informed. Katz viewed mass communication as "an elaborate system of cultural, social, and psychological 'services'" (p. 71). After three decades of research on this theory, it has been codified with an understanding of attitude formation based on a consumer's expectancy of media and evaluation of it. One would therefore seek gratification of needs based on one's expectancies of the media content. As one's needs get satisfied, expectations are intensified; thus, the effect is cyclical. One criticism of this type of research is the ambiguity surrounding the concept of *need*. A survey of cross-national studies found that four basic clusters of needs emerged: (a) self and personal identity, (b) social contact, (c) diversion and entertainment, and (d) information and knowledge about the world (Roberts & Maccoby, 1985). Most needs can be fit into one of the reduced categories.

Links may exist between uses and gratifications and effects. Most research in this area centers on political campaigns, news, and wars. People tend to turn to the media for information and issue salience in these areas. Gratification, however, may weaken as well as strengthen media effects. People with strong motivation to gain information are not likely to shift their perception of the importance of issues in accordance with the agenda of the media they use. With regard to political campaigns, people receive more than information because the objective of a campaign is to influence prospective voters.

Uses and Dependency Theory

Some researchers argue that dependency theory and uses and gratifications theory are not mutually exclusive, for although individuals make choices about using the media, the media influence individuals as well. Rubin and Windahl (1986) combined both approaches into what they called the *uses and dependency model*. This model shows societal systems and media systems interacting with audiences to create needs in individuals. The needs influence the individual to choose both media and nonmedia sources of gratification, which subsequently leads to dependencies on the sources. Effects are cognitive, affective, and behavioral, as in dependency theory, and the results are then fed back into the societal and media systems. Rubin and Windahl suggested that people will narrow the search for certain need fulfillment to few media and will therefore be more susceptible to influence. A businessperson, for example, may rely on one newspaper for business information, thus becoming dependent on it and more likely to adopt its views.

The multitude of studies on the effects of television on human behavior has underscored society's concerns with effects. It is generally accepted that the media do influence individuals but do so among and through a nexus of mediating factors and influences. The mass media are viewed as a powerful contributory agent but not the sole cause in the process of reinforcing existing conditions or bringing about change.

Limitations of Effects Research

Research on the effects of the mass media continues to thrive, but it has not become the united behavioral science envisioned by its pioneers. Lazarsfeld regarded mass communication research as "administrative research" in 1941, suggesting that research be carried on in the service of some kind of administrative agency and defining it as social science research primarily concerned with effects. Although government-sponsored research yielded important findings about the effects of various media, it has not been as prevalent as marketing and advertising research. The broadcasting industry regards research as vital to decision making. Meanwhile, other forms of research are taking hold. Empirical and experimental research have been criticized because research questions are often limited by laboratory methods and laboratory settings. Roberts and Maccoby (1985, pp. 543–544) pointed out three major criticisms of experimental research on media:

1. An effect that is attributed to a larger unit may derive from one or more of its components, but it may be totally unrelated to other components. For example, stimuli for experiments related to violence in the media range from single scenes to specifically prepared sequences; thus, research subjects view a specific violent act, which is something quite different from an entire program or film.

2. Researchers tend to be more concerned with media content than with media techniques. Furthermore, they categorize media content subjectively—for example, by genre or by topic.

3. What is used as a stimulus to determine effects may not be representative of media content. For example, what may be used as a prosocial stimulus for children as subjects in an experiment may be totally unrepresentative of the children's typical television diet. Also, what is regarded by the researchers as a type of stimulus may not be perceived that way by the research subjects. A researcher's "violence" may be a research subject's "playful competition."

Roberts and Maccoby (1985) stressed an important adage, well known in communication studies: "Meanings are not in messages, but in people."

Finally, as Jesse Delia (1987) pointed out in his comprehensive history of communication research,

The received view constructed the history of communication research . . . [and] privileged a particular model of scientific practice . . . [which] has profoundly affected the assumptions defining the parameters of the field . . . [and] marginated explorations of the relationship between culture and communication. . . . A deep tension was thus built into the mass communication field from its inception. It aimed to organize the whole scope of concern with the mass media under a single, encompassing umbrella, while its focus on scientific research placed historical and critical studies on the margin. (pp. 21, 71)

The dominant paradigm of effects resulting from the transfer of a message from a source to a receiver has been challenged, and questions related to the functions of cultural communication within the total process of society are now being asked.

Cultural Studies

Culture, defined as actual practices and customs, languages, beliefs, forms of representation, and a system of formal and informal rules that tell people how to behave most of the time, enables people to make sense of their world through a certain amount of shared meanings and recognition of differing meanings. People bring to their understanding of cultural artifacts (images, architecture, literature, etc.) other aspects of their culture that link the artifact to a recognizable context. This enables a person to make sense of an expression or a representation (O'Donnell, in Smith, Moriarty, Barbatsis, & Kenney, 2005, pp. 521–538). The most prominent ideas for the *cultural study* of communication initially came from Great Britain. Raymond Williams, a fellow of Jesus College, Cambridge, opposed the study of mass communication because he thought it limited studies to broadcasting and film exclusively and because it conceived of the audience as a mass. Rather, he proposed that communication be studied as a set of practices, conventions, and forms through which a shared culture is created, modified, and transformed. In his works (R. Williams, 1958, 1961, 1966, 1973), he examined how culture reproduces and articulates existing social structures and how media maintain industrial economic societies. Another prominent British researcher is Stuart Hall, who began his work at the Center for Contemporary Cultural Studies at the University of Birmingham and continues it at the Open University in Milton Keynes, England, and University College London. Hall sees communication as encompassing a wide variety of cultural expression and ritual forms of everyday life. Fundamental to Hall's (1977, 1980, 1984, 1997) work is the encoding process or message formulation in the media, together with social and economic conditions that explain why and how viewers decode messages in a variety of ways. Hall said that a message "hails" a person as if it were hailing a taxi. To answer, the person must recognize that it is she or he, and not someone else, being hailed. To respond to the hail, the person recognizes the social position that has been constructed by the message, and if the response is cooperative, the position has been adopted. Thus, television viewers may be hailed as conformists or sexists or patriots. If the viewers accept the position of the program, then they constitute themselves as subjects in an ideological definition that the program proposes.

There are essentially three social positions—dominant, oppositional, and negotiated—although Hall speculated there could be multiple positions. The *dominant* position is produced by a viewer who accepts the dominant ideology in the media. The *oppositional* position is direct opposition to the dominant ideology in the media or acceptance of an oppositional point of view. The *negotiated* position is produced by viewers who fit into the dominant ideology but need to resist certain elements of it. Negotiated positions are popular with various social groups who question their relationship to the dominant ideology. Cultural studies are concerned with culture in relation to issues of power: power relations, whether driven by economics, politics, or other forms of social discrimination, determine who is and is not represented and what issues are or are not important. A power-related term is *hegemony*, the power or dominance that one group holds over another. A person may prefer the dominant position and thus become the subject within the cultural hegemony. However, if a person resists the dominant meaning, then she or he has the power to oppose it and find a meaning contradictory to the intended one. When people have some control over the production of meaning, they are likely to experience pleasure because they have maintained their own social identity even when they resist the intended meaning of a message or representation.

Cultural analysts investigate the production and exchange of meaning between a representation and its recipient, recognizing that many meanings can be made by different viewers. Cultural analysts may examine audience decoding through ethnographic methods, using in-depth interviews, often over time, to determine how people actively use television to make sense of social experience and of themselves. Cultural critics also work in a manner similar to literary critics, but their texts are the mediated messages of television, newspapers, and films, as well as the behavior of people as it has been shaped by the media. They "read" the "text" to construct its meaning.

Essentially, cultural studies are concerned with the generation and circulation of meanings in industrial societies. James W. Carey (1988) said the sources of cultural meanings are in "construable signs and symbols . . .

Figure 4.1   The Korean War Veterans Memorial in Washington, D.C. This
memorial to the "forgotten war" opened on July 27, 1995, the
42nd anniversary of the armistice that ended the Korean War.
Frank Gaylord was the principal sculptor with the mural done by
Louis Nelson. This is a realistic representation of the soldiers who
fought in the "hot" war of the Cold War. (Note the Lincoln
Memorial in the upper right hand corner of the photograph.)

embedded in things; some relatively durable such as artifacts and practices,
some relatively transitory like fashions and follies" (p. 11). In a later work,
Carey (1989) stressed that human needs and motives must be studied within
the context of history and culture. John Fiske (1987) saw television as "a
bearer/provoker of meanings and pleasures" (p. 1) and thus as a cultural
agent. The view of media as a cultural agent, as well as the construction of
meaning by the users of the media, tries to understand human behavior
rather than to explain it. Rather than attempt to predict human behavior as
social scientists do, cultural analysts attempt to diagnose human meanings.

In addition to the works cited on cultural studies, the journal *Critical
Studies in Mass Communication* is a major source for cultural studies of the
media. We believe that the student of propaganda needs to be conversant
with both social science and cultural studies. Our model of the process of
propaganda in Chapter 8 represents a broad conceptualization based on
both approaches. The nature of research in propaganda and persuasion is
and always has been interdisciplinary.

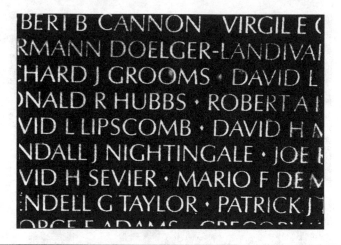

Figure 4.2   A portion of the Vietnam Veterans Memorial in Washington, D.C. The "wall" with the names of 58,209 men and women who died or were missing in action inscribed on black granite was designed by Maya Ying Lin and dedicated on November 13, 1982. Because the wall slopes downward into the point of its "V" shape, some thought it symbolized defeat. Most people, however, found its symbolism an important expression of sadness and loss that helped bring closure to a war that generated such cultural controversy. Another memorial, Frederick Hart's representative sculpture of 3 male infantrymen in Vietnam, was authorized by Congress and erected in 1984. This sculpture represented the more conventional form of memorial and helped placate those who objected to the "wall."

Collective Memory Studies

An area of academic study that has elements of propaganda and persuasion is *collective memory,* defined as "the ways group, institutional, and cultural recollections of the past shape people's actions in the present" (Schudson, 1992, p. 65). Collective memory is formed by folklore, holidays, stories, songs, rituals, ceremonies, museum displays, monuments, paintings, cartoons, films, and television programs. Often white propaganda, collective memory is used to promote patriotism and nationalism. Monuments and memorials reflect nations' ideologies, their beliefs, values, and attitudes. In Washington, D.C., the memorials to Washington, Jefferson, Lincoln, and F. D. Roosevelt symbolize that the history of the United States is based on the efforts of great individual leaders, and the strength of the country is greater still than individuals, as impressive and indestructible as the monuments that represent its past. The war memorials to World War II, the Korean War, and the Vietnam War evoke a sense of sadness, honor, and closure rather than a celebration of victory, and thus they express the nation's reluctance to go to war unless necessary. The Memorial to the Murdered Jews of Europe, unveiled in Berlin, Germany, on May 10, 2005, is a mammoth group of 2,711 steles, carved stone slabs, in heights ranging from 2 to 15 feet high, in a huge field the size of two football stadiums. They appear like "a rippling tide of floating gravestones that are at once a public appeal for redemption and a stunning vision of abstract architecture that forces remembrance" (Fleishman, 2005, p. A3). The memorial's architect, Peter Eisenman, said that the intent of his design was to "establish a permanent memory so future generations would study and debate the atrocities of the Third Reich. . . . [He wanted] to articulate how Jews felt trapped by a Nazi regime that permeated a continent" (Fleishman, 2005, p. A3). Timothy Garton Ash, professor of European Studies at Oxford University, said, "Tuesday's opening of the Holocaust memorial in the heart of Berlin spoke for the great majority of today's Germans. They are struggling to find a just balance between a sense of collective historical responsibility for Nazism and a proper respect for the sufferings of their own compatriots" (http://www.latimes.com, May 12, 2005).

Collective memory displays can also be gray or even black propaganda. Consider the case of the horse Comanche, the only survivor of the U.S. Cavalry in the Battle of Little Bighorn. After his death, Comanche was stuffed and put on display in various places but ended up at the University of Kansas Natural History Museum with a placard that said, "The only surviving horse of the Custer massacre." Until several Native Americans protested, no one gave any thought to the fact that many Indian horses as well as Indians survived because they had been victorious at the battle. The placard was removed, and in its place is a long text that says, in part,

> The horse stands as a symbol of the conflict between the United States Army and the Indian tribes of the Great Plains that resulted from the government's policy of confinement of Indians on reservations and extermination of those Indians who refused to be confined. (Hall, 1997, pp. 212–213)

Thus, the collective memory of General George Armstrong Custer's defeat as a "massacre" was changed, at least in the case of the horse display at the university, to a memory of maltreatment of American Plains Indians.

Zelizer (1995) pointed out that collective memory is partial because an event is never reproduced in its entirety, but rather what is "remembered" is what is useful in social, political, and cultural ways. Kammen (1993) reminded us that some memories are "suspiciously self-serving rationalizations that sustain the political or economic superiority of one group or

Figure 4.3   Diane Evans, an Army nurse during the Vietnam War, campaigned for
ten years to have a monument built to honor the women who served in
the military. The Vietnam Women's Memorial is a sculpture by Glenna
Goodacre that depicts three American nurses and a wounded soldier.
One of the women cradles the soldier's head; one is seated on
sandbags; while the other, an African-American, looks into the
distance as if for help. The statue stands about 300 feet from the
Vietnam Veterans Memorial.

the value system of another" (p. 4). How we remember the Vietnam War is
very much influenced by the films of the 1970s and 1980s, such as *Apocalypse
Now, Coming Home, Full Metal Jacket,* and certain photographs—the
napalm strike on Trang Bang Village and Eddie Adams's photograph of
General Nguyen Ngoc Loan shooting a Viet Cong suspect in the head.
Our collective memory of World War II has undergone some alteration

because of Stephen Spielberg's film *Saving Private Ryan*. As a newer area of study, we suggest that the connection of collective memory to propaganda may be significant and plays an important role in the study of propaganda.

Summary

Research on the nature and effects of propaganda flourished during the World War II years. After the war, research moved into persuasion and communication studies of effects. Research questions were concerned with the variables of communication interaction, especially with regard to attitudes and attitude change. Later, attempts were made to predict behavior and behavior change. With regard to the focus of the book, it would be useful to have a catalog of practices relevant to propaganda that produce effects, but it is not possible to develop such a catalog. The most pertinent conclusion that one can draw after such a review of 85 years of research is that individual differences and contexts determine the nature of effects. It is also important to pay attention to the historical and cultural contexts in which propaganda and persuasion occur and especially to recognize that people construct different meanings according to their social experiences.

Generalizations About Propaganda and Persuasion Effects

When we attempt to make generalizations, we are confronted by the ever-changing nature of what is under study. The media undergo continuous changes, and those changes are primarily related to technology. Social, political, and cultural changes in society are not only continuous but also dramatic, as we have witnessed in the aftermath of the fall of communism in Europe, the breakup of the former Soviet Union, and the terrorists' attack on the World Trade Center and the Pentagon. What may be a valid generalization today may become obsolete a short time later. Nevertheless, a few generalizations can be made regarding propaganda and persuasion.

First, it seems safe to say that communication effects are the greatest when the message is in line with relevance, existing opinions, beliefs, and dispositions of the receivers. Selectivity in the perception of messages is generally guided by preexisting interests and behavior patterns of the receivers. The result is that most messages are more likely to be supportive of, than discrepant from, existing views. Furthermore, mass communication effects tend to take the form of reinforcement rather than change.

Second, when change does occur, it does so as the result of a multitude of factors, including the mass media, socially contextual conditions, group interaction, the presence and influence of opinion leaders, and the perceived credibility of the source or sources of the message. Topics most likely to be influential are on unfamiliar, lightly felt, peripheral issues that do not matter much or are not tied to audience predispositions. Issues deeply rooted and based on values and past behavior patterns are not as likely to change. Ideas related to political loyalty, race, and religion tend to remain stable over time and resistant to influence. As John Naisbitt (1982) said in *Megatrends,* "When people really care about an issue, it doesn't matter how much is spent to influence their vote; they will go with their beliefs. When an issue is inconsequential to the voters, buying their vote is a snap" (p. 191).

Third, the way we maintain consistency of attitudes and behaviors has an economical aspect that gives a propagandist the advantage. As Karlins and Abelson (1970) pointed out, a propagandist does not have to win people over on every issue to get their support. If the propagandist can get people to agree on one or two issues, then their opinion toward her or him may become favorable. Once that has happened, and the mention of the person's name evokes a favorable response in the people, they may find themselves inventing reasons for agreeing with other issues advocated by her or him.

Fourth, people can appear to accept an idea publicly without private acceptance. Behavior can be guided by a system of rewards and punishments that do not require attitude change. Furthermore, public compliance will continue under conditions of surveillance by authority but not necessarily under conditions of nonsurveillance.

Finally, the greater the monopoly of the communication source over the receivers, the greater the effect in the direction favored by the source. Wherever a dominant definition of the situation is accompanied by a consistent, repetitive, and unchallenged message, the influence of the message is greater.

5

Propaganda and Psychological Warfare

Propaganda is an essential element in warfare, going back to the prebiblical period. During World War I, however, sophisticated techniques of propaganda eventually created negative attitudes in the 20th century toward both propaganda and the potential dangers of mass media influence. In the interwar period, radio broadcasting became important and was increasingly used by European nations in the political conflicts that led up to World War II. Propaganda played a significant role in the rise of both communism and fascism and reached a new level of scientific sophistication during the war. In the period after 1945, propaganda became a major weapon in the ideological struggle between East and West. With the end of the Cold War, propaganda activities on the international scene have continued but are now a much more complex mixture of political, religious, and economic ideologies.

The use of propaganda as an integral part of waging war has been a basic part of human history. War itself can be considered a violent means of attaining a specific objective, but there has always been a continuous flow of carefully directed propaganda messages that seek to bring about much the same result but in a nonviolent manner. In a book devoted to the subject, Paul M. A. Linebarger (1954) defined *psychological warfare* as "comprising the use of propaganda against an enemy, together with such other operational measures of a military, economic, or political nature as may be required to supplement propaganda" (p. 40). Harold D. Lasswell (1951), a pioneer in propaganda studies, pointed out that psychological warfare is a recent name for an old idea about how to wage successful war: "The basic idea is that the best success in war is achieved by the destruction of the enemy's will to resist, and with a minimum annihilation of fighting capacity" (p. 261).

By its very nature, the use of propaganda for such directed purposes commences long before actual hostilities break out or war is declared. It also continues long after peace treaties have been signed and soldiers have gone back to their homes. It is a continuous process, shifting in emphasis as required. It is not hindered by the usual constraints of war, such as terrain, arms, or specific battles, but is free to float as only human minds can. The success or failure of these campaigns cannot always be immediately measured, and the results are often known only years later.

History is replete with recorded instances of psychological warfare. One of the best known is the biblical story of Gideon, who created panic in the numerically superior Midianite camp by equipping 300 of his men with a torch and trumpet each. Conventional warfare of the period called for 1 such equipped soldier for every 100 men, and Gideon was therefore able to create the illusion of an army of more than 30,000. These 300 were strategically placed around the Midianite camp in the dead of night, and on command, they each revealed their torches while blowing on their trumpets. Thinking themselves under attack by a superior force, the enemy became confused and even attacked each other. Eventually, the Midianites gave up and fled the battlefield, with the Israelites in hot pursuit (the Bible, Book of Judges, chap. 7).

Other examples of the successful employment of psychological techniques used in warfare are Cortez's use of horses as instruments of terror, as well as the exploitation of the Indian legends concerning the "Fair God" in his conquest of Mexico; the use of rockets by the ancient Chinese, not as weapons but to intimidate their enemies; the Boers' use of commando units to attack the British far behind their own lines in South Africa during the Boer War and their anti-British appeal for sympathy on a worldwide scale; and the widespread use of a variety of propaganda appeals from both sides during the American Revolution. The American colonists particularly delighted in pointing out the class distinctions between the British officers and their enlisted men. Even in so-called primitive cultures, the beating of drums before battle or the conjuring up of magic spells serves to unnerve the enemy. Thus, the use of psychological techniques of persuasion for war propaganda purposes is not new, but the emergence of new forms of information dissemination and the increased sophistication in the understanding of human behavior greatly increased its application and intensity in the 20th century.

The term *psychological warfare* is distinctively an American one; the British, with greater candor, refer to these activities as *political warfare*. Daniel Lerner (1951a, 1951b) noted that when we speak of psychological warfare, we are talking about the use of symbols to promote policies—that is, politics. Propaganda is, after all, a manipulation of the symbolic environment, and although it can be carried out independently of the physical environment, it can also, under certain circumstances, be shaped by that environment. Thus, the development of new technologies of communication has altered the way propaganda is disseminated, but it would be wrong to suggest that old methods are automatically discarded in favor of new. A considerable overlap of media usage continues, and total propaganda campaigns will encompass all available forms of communication, from the very effective oral tradition still widely used to the most sophisticated modern electronic systems.

Where there is a communication channel, there is also a potential propaganda medium. An excellent example is the increased use in the past 20 years of the technology of xerography to copy large quantities of information for easy distribution. In the United States, copy machines are widely available to all who would wish to use them; in the Soviet Union, however, until the collapse of the communist government, almost all copy machines were under the control of the state, and their use was thus limited. This did not stop Soviet dissidents from producing their material on such machines, but the policies of information control made what was in Western society the common copy machine an exotic and much valued propaganda tool in the Soviet Union. Even in the age of *glasnost*, very few such machines still were available for use by the average Soviet citizen, but in the wake of the collapse of the Communist Party, communication in what is now a commonwealth of independent nations is almost totally open to the point of being chaotic.

Since the collapse of the old Soviet Union, new communication technologies have been extensively used to convey propaganda messages. Videotapes, cassettes, and most recently cell phones (and text messaging) have all been used by groups wishing to bypass the traditional channels of communication under the control of official governments. In the face of such ubiquitous technologies, governments appear to be powerless to control the flow of information as they were able to do when communication media were much more restrictive. With a push of just a single button on a computer or a cell phone, pictures and text can be sent to millions of receivers throughout the world.

The public seems most familiar (and comfortable) with the use of propaganda as a wartime activity, a notion that has contributed to the generally negative connotations associated with the term. In times of political conflict, propaganda becomes most manifest to the public as groups use it to achieve their goals. Propaganda of this sort must be viewed in its specific historical context, for without this context, such symbolic manipulations can later appear to be gross distortions of reality, racist, naive, and essentially silly. "Who would have believed that?" we exclaim, looking at wartime posters showing the Japanese soldier as a barbaric, apelike subhuman. The fact is that, within historical context, such impressions were readily accepted as part of the mythology created by the reality of the conflict (e.g., the sneak attack on Pearl Harbor), and the collective public mentality that develops is eager to believe such stereotypes.

It is often strange to look back with nostalgia on historical artifacts of propaganda, such as wartime posters, leaflets, and especially motion pictures made during the conflict, for they dramatically reveal how context bound certain types of propaganda can be. We no longer think of the Germans or the Japanese as brutal, rapacious enemies, but these anachronistic artifacts remain. The German government has been particularly concerned with the showing of old war movies on American television, claiming that this practice continues to provide new generations of Americans with a distorted view of the current German character. This claim has a certain justification.

Countering the residual power of psychological warfare has proved to be a difficult problem. The German government has debated for decades how much Nazi history to present to German schoolchildren and even to the general public. Recent exhibitions of Nazi art and cultural artifacts have attracted large crowds in Germany because these have been a "hidden" part of official German history since 1945. The Japanese have carefully rewritten their high school history textbooks to downplay their wartime activities or to cast them in a less horrific light. This revision has precipitated angry official reactions from other Asian nations, such as China and Korea, which want the youth of Japan constantly reminded of the "true" history of Japan's Asian conquests. The reason for the unwillingness to let go of these potent propaganda images is that they have become part of the official history of nations. If one nation decides to change its image, then this causes an imbalance in the other nations. Thus, for the foreseeable future, Japan and Germany must always be reminded that they were the enemy in World War II. In December 1991, a series of events commemorating the 50th anniversary of the Japanese attack on Pearl Harbor made this painfully obvious. President George Bush stated that the United States did not need to apologize for the dropping of the two atomic bombs on Japan, and the

Japanese parliament, in turn, reacted by refusing to ratify a resolution calling for an apology for Japanese aggression during World War II (Weisman, 1991).

The use of atomic weapons on Japan in 1945 has increasingly been used in Japan to justify an image of Japan as the victim of atrocities far out-weighing the attack on Pearl Harbor. Continued sensitivities surrounding the dropping of the atomic bombs were made very obvious in 1995, when the Smithsonian Institution attempted to mount a 50th-anniversary com-memoration exhibition of the event. This exhibition, in keeping with the mission of the Smithsonian, examined all facets of the event, which included questioning both the necessity and the aftermath of dropping atomic bombs on Japan. This "revisionist" perspective so aroused members of Congress, veterans groups, the Pentagon, and significant segments of the public that the exhibition was canceled, and several senior officials of the Smithsonian resigned in protest. (For more information on the enormous lobbying and propaganda effort that resulted in this failed exhibition, see Martin Harwit's book *An Exhibit Denied: Lobbying the History of Enola Gay* [1996]. Harwit was the then-director of the Smithsonian National Air and Space Museum.)

In the past two decades, we have been forced to deal with the ever-evolving image of the former USSR. Since the collapse of communism, the rest of the world has watched developments in the group of new states that emerged from the breakup of the old Soviet Union. Whereas throughout the Cold War, the "communists" had proved to be a potent enemy in the propaganda war of words, the West no longer has a clear perspective of who this "enemy" now is. But the artifacts of the Cold War remain, and we still view old spy or war movies and read books that cast the communists as the pro-tagonists. Even a recent movie such as *Miracle on Ice* (2004)—which tells the story of the ice hockey game in the 1980 Olympic Winter Games, in which a team of amateur and collegiate players from the United States beats the Soviet Union against near-impossible odds on February 22, 1980, in Lake Placid, New York—is turned into an artifact of the Cold War. As in the case of Germany and Japan, it is impossible suddenly to destroy 60 years of popular culture that used the tensions of this ideological conflict as a staple plot element for so many years.

World War I and the Fear of Propaganda

In the foreword to a book on the history of propaganda in World War I, Harold Lasswell (1938) noted the following:

There is little exaggeration in saying that the World War led to the discovery of propaganda by both the man in the street and the man in the study. The discovery was far more startling to the former than to the latter, because the man in the study had predecessors who had laid firm foundations for his efforts to understand propaganda. The layman had previously lived in a world where there was no common name for the deliberate forming of attitudes by the manipulation of words (and word substitutes). The scholar had a scientific inheritance which included the recognition of the place of propaganda in society. (p. v)

At the end of World War I, even scholars were surprised by the apparent power that propaganda had exhibited as the conflict raged over almost the entire planet. Nothing in previous historical experience had prepared them for the potent combination of the perfect social, political, and economic conditions with the newly established power of the mass media. By 1914, the nations involved in the war had made the mass media an important part of their social infrastructure, and this allowed propaganda activities to assume a role of greater significance than ever before.

Each nation, with the exception of the Soviet Union (which is a special case that is examined later), was able to call on established systems of communication, such as the press or motion pictures, as well as skills developed during peacetime, to aid in the propaganda effort. By 1914, advertising had developed into a highly sophisticated form of persuasion, as had the skill of press agentry, and both were put to good use in creating propaganda messages or in obtaining press coverage of specific events such as war bond rallies. Linebarger (1954) pointed out that the character of the indigenous communication systems dictated the way each nation approached the use of propaganda. Thus, the British, who had one of the world's finest international news-gathering and distribution systems in 1914, backed by a sophisticated domestic "free" press and extensive experience in international communication for technical and commercial purposes through their ownership of undersea cables, turned this background to excellent advantage. The Germans, in contrast, had a more regimented press system and a much more limited network of international telecommunication connections. The Americans, who only entered the war in late 1917, nevertheless used every available form of communication at hand. This included not only the enormous power of the most extensive mass media system in the world but also the churches, the YMCA, Chautauqua groups, and the many private clubs and organizations found in such a polyglot society. The French, on whose ground the battles were being fought, used their professional skills at diplomacy to ensure that messages emanating from Paris received a very sympathetic hearing. The result of all of this use of existing skills was a barrage of propaganda messages that assaulted the ears of civilians and soldiers at every turn. In no previous conflict had "words" been so important, reflecting as it did the fundamental change in the nature of war in an age of mass communication and mass production—the first global conflict of the emerging mass society. No longer did single battles decide wars; now, whole nations were pitted against other nations, requiring the cooperation of entire populations, both militarily and psychologically. One reason why the Russian army did not play a decisive role in World War I was the confusion and subsequent low morale of the population, which eventually became one direct cause of the Russian Revolution in 1917.

British Propaganda

The British took the lead in propaganda activities because they were forced to think seriously about such activities earlier than any of the other belligerent powers. Britain took this action because, at the outbreak of war in August 1914, only in Britain was there internal disagreement about entering the conflict. Unlike the other major powers on the continent, Britain did not have universal conscription into the army, and thus the decision to mobilize its armed forces was more of a political one than in France or Germany. In Britain, the Liberal Party that had been in power since 1905 was predominantly antiwar, as was the opposition Labour Party, and pressure to remain neutral in what was seen as primarily an Austro-Hungarian dispute in southeastern Europe was widespread. The Germans unwittingly settled this internal dissension when they decided to invade Belgium while marching to attack France, for Belgium's neutrality had been specifically guaranteed by the Great Powers, including Germany. The Germans miscalculated that the British would not go to war over a "mere scrap of paper," but when Belgium actually resisted the "dreaded Huns," the British became united in their resolve to defend "brave little Belgium." By September 1915, more than 2,250,000 volunteers had enlisted in the British army (Roetter, 1974). The circulation of atrocity stories coming out of Belgium signaled the first major propaganda salvo and had an immediate impact on British public sympathies.

The chief agency for developing this successful patriotic campaign in Britain was a private organization, the Central Committee for National Patriotic Associations, which was formed in late August 1914, immediately after the war started, with Prime Minister Herbert Asquith as the honorary president. This group organized lectures, patriotic clubs, and rallies in cities and counties and extended its influence into the far reaches of the British Empire to ensure no opposition to the war among the subjects of the king.

(In Canada, as an example, many French Canadians had long opposed the British Crown, and they saw no reason to fight what was essentially in their eyes a British war.) Of special interest was the Neutral Countries Subcommittee, which used the direct personal approach to enlist sympathy and support from countries not in the war. Distinguished Britons lent their names to this enterprise, and as a result, acquaintances, colleagues, fellow workers, and business associates in neutral countries received a flood of propaganda materials. More than 250,000 pamphlets, booklets, and other publications were distributed in this manner between August 1914 and September 1918 (Bruntz, 1938). Another important organization that was eventually appointed to coordinate all British propaganda activities after March 1918 was the War Aims Committee, founded in June 1917 and formed initially to combat pacifism in Britain. Enough Britons were still against all forms of armed conflict this late in the war to warrant such an organization.

The first official propaganda organization in Britain was the War Propaganda Bureau, which concerned itself initially with the distribution of printed materials inside neutral countries and eventually inside Germany itself, which it did through sympathizers using the mail from Holland and Switzerland. When Lloyd George became prime minister in 1916, dissatisfied with British propaganda efforts and in an attempt to avoid what had become a very confused and decentralized situation, he reorganized the War Propaganda Bureau and created the Department of Information. This agency concentrated on enemy civilian psychological warfare outside Britain, whereas the National War Aims Committee dealt with propaganda efforts inside Britain.

The idea of mobilizing such a massive propaganda effort was so new that it had taken the relatively experienced British nearly 5 years to devise a workable system of propaganda management suitable for a great power at war. In the end, the British became quite adept at coordinating their efforts at external political warfare aimed at the enemy with the internal, morale-building efforts of news propaganda. By the time of World War II in 1939, these lessons had been thoroughly learned.

German Propaganda

The Germans were never able to gain the same degree of control over their propaganda activities as the British, and in the end they had only limited success in making their political ambitions clear to important neutral countries such as the United States. Long after the war, many in Germany attributed their loss to the superiority of British propaganda; foremost among these was Adolf Hitler, who in his book *Mein Kampf* (1939) praised the British efforts and noted that the British had understood that propaganda was so important that it had to be handled by professionals. This belief that Allied propaganda (American efforts were also lauded) had been a major contributor to Germany's defeat became a part of the mythology of the Nazis, which held that the German army could not be defeated on the field and that only a "stab in the back" had betrayed the German people in 1918. Thus, the enemy's successful use of propaganda itself was used as a form of propaganda to make the German people wary of becoming complacent and, therefore, susceptible to information from outside sources. The importance of propaganda as an extension of modern warfare was not lost on the fascist German leaders during the interwar period, as we shall examine later in this chapter.

Initial German international propaganda efforts were amateurish, consisting mainly of using enlisted writers and scholars to explain why the Allies were responsible for starting the war. Unfortunately, they only succeeded in creating antagonism in the targeted countries with their arrogance in the face of the atrocity stories coming out of Belgium and France. The stodginess of the German military communiqués also failed to garner any worldwide sympathy. Essentially, German propaganda lacked both organization and moral drive, and the Germans did not receive the cooperation from the international press for which they had hoped. The British Royal Navy dealt the German efforts a serious blow when, on August 15, 1914, it cut the undersea cable linking Germany and the United States. This action deprived the Germans of the means to communicate and effectively shut off attempts to make their position on the war clear to the neutral American population. Before transatlantic radio service could be established, the European Allies had already created the propaganda agenda for the American public, and stories of German atrocities in Belgium and elsewhere were being widely circulated.

For once, the vaunted German efficiency failed to operate, and the various German propaganda efforts were never really coordinated throughout the war. Even the German Foreign Office seemed to be unaware of the importance of trying to establish goodwill and support for the German cause. Roetter (1974) suggested that most of the German diplomats were so convinced of the "rightness" of Germany's cause that they felt no need to justify it, and in any case, it was always arrogantly stated that "the War would be over by Christmas" (pp. 38–39). Eventually, the Foreign Office did establish a special department to deal with overseas propaganda, but the armed services offered virtually no cooperation. At the outbreak of the war, the army had only one officer in contact with the press. One of the most serious problems was the enormous amount of conflicting information sent out by the various civilian and military authorities, and this conflict became a major source of the internal struggle for political control of Germany as the war continued. As the military invariably won these arguments, it tended to underscore for both the German people and those overseas that Germany was essentially a military state. Most neutral countries found it very difficult to understand the German military argument that it had been forced to defend the decaying Hapsburg Empire by invading Belgium.

The Germans also made the mistake of being much too forthright in their use of German sympathizers in the United States to propagandize on their behalf. Germany had provided the second largest segment of the American immigrant stock, and a residual identification with the culture of "the old country" was still strong in many parts of the United States. The German government immediately attempted to flood these German American societies, or *bunds,* with propaganda materials, but they had failed to take into account the degree of "Americanization" that immigrants, especially those of the second and third generations, had undergone. Being proud of one's German heritage did not necessarily mean becoming a propagandist for German military ambitions. In the long run, this tactic did not work and may, in fact, have been counterproductive in that it forced many Americans of German origin to become even more "pro-British" to avoid any hint of suspicion about their loyalties.

The greatest blow to any German propaganda effort in the United States was the "Zimmerman telegram incident." Through a series of dramatic coincidences, the British had known the German naval codes since 1914. On the morning of January 16, 1917, the British intercepted a telegram from the German foreign minister Arthur Zimmerman to Count Johann-Heinrich Bernstorff, the German ambassador in Washington, D.C. Bernstorff had recommended that unrestricted submarine warfare begin on all transatlantic shipping on February 1 and also suggested that Germany make an alliance with Mexico if the United States intervened militarily. The British were not immediately sure how to handle this sensational propaganda opportunity without revealing that they had possession of the German codes, but eventually, using "deflection" disinformation, they made it appear as if they had obtained the information from a Mexican source. The telegram was made available to Walter Page, the U.S. ambassador to Great Britain, and was published in the United States on March 1, 1917. Americans were incensed to discover that, in exchange for a promise to "invade" the United States, Germany was offering to return to Mexico the lost territories of Texas and Arizona (Taylor, 1990, pp. 167–169)! President Wilson, who only 6 months before had won reelection with a campaign to "Keep America Out of the

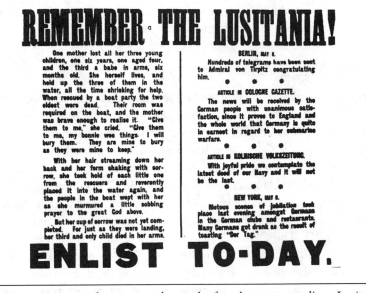

Figure 5.1   A poster that appeared a week after the passenger liner *Lusitania* was sunk by a German U-boat on May 7, 1915, with a loss of 1,198 lives, 128 of them American.

War," had slowly been moving toward intervention before this incident, but he was able to use this startling revelation to bypass the powerful anti-interventionist lobbyists in Congress. The combination of German actions and other factors—the *Lusitania* sinking, the unrestricted submarine warfare, the Bryce report, and the fact that the Allies were becoming more and more dependent on American financial assistance—gave Wilson more than enough reason to declare war on Germany on April 6, 1917. Philip Taylor (1990) noted that although there may have been some suspicion that the Zimmerman telegram was a British propaganda ploy, this was never exploited by the Germans, because on March 3, the foreign minister, "in an astonishing fit of stupidity," himself confirmed that he had sent the telegram (p. 168).

The British also had a much more fundamental propaganda advantage in that the German propaganda efforts were only able to convey the fact that the war was being fought to avenge the country's honor, whereas the British were able to make the war appear to be, as H. G. Wells put it, "the war to end all wars"—that is, the war that would defend humanity everywhere. Germany was never able to claim a moral position to compete with this platitude. What the Germans failed to learn in World War I, they studied and applied with a vengeance in World War II. Hitler did not really care what the rest of the world thought about his policies; he was mainly concerned with domestic propaganda success.

American Propaganda

American propaganda, which the Germans admired so much, was the work of two agencies. The civilian agency was the Committee on Public Information (CPI), which became known as the Creel Committee because of its chairman, George Creel, who had been a newspaper editor. The committee also had as members the secretary of state and the secretaries for the army and the navy. (An excellent history of the CPI is Vaughn, 1980.) The military agency was the Propaganda Section (or Psychologic Section) of the American Expeditionary Forces, under Captain Heber Blakenhorn, also known as G-2D. The CPI had the advantage of having George Creel as its leader: Creel had the confidence of President Wilson and was therefore able to force a coordination of propaganda efforts with other civilian and military agencies. Creel, in his fascinating book about his wartime work, *How We Advertised America* (1920), saw the conflict as "the fight for the minds of men, for the 'conquest of their convictions,' and the battle-line ran through every home in every country" (p. 3). His approach to the problem was to use a technique he thought Americans knew best—sales. He noted, "In all things, from first to last, without halt or change, it was a plain publicity proposition, a vast enterprise in salesmanship, the world's greatest adventure in advertising" (p. 4). Operating with a wide mandate and with a relatively loose organizational structure, the CPI used every available means of communicating with the American public with an intensity never before devoted to a single issue in the United States. Creel congratulated himself on the fact that

> there was no part of the great war machinery that we did not touch, no medium of appeal that we did not employ. The printed word, the spoken word, the motion picture, the telegraph, the cable, the wireless, the poster, the signboard—all these were used in our campaign to make our own people and other peoples understand the causes that compelled America to take arms. All that was fine and ardent in the civilian population came at our call until more than one hundred and fifty thousand men and women were devoting highly specialized abilities to the work of the Committee, as faithful and devoted in their service as though they wore the khaki. (p. 5)

The output of the CPI was intended mainly for domestic consumption, and as Creel stated above, the American public was subjected to an intense barrage of propaganda messages. Of particular interest was the use of the

Figure 5.2   An anti-German poster showing a supposed atrocity. Note that the kaiser is depicted as approving of the nurse's actions, thus linking him directly with such German atrocities.

oral tradition in the form of the "Four-Minute Men," volunteer speakers in local communities who would lecture on the war at a moment's notice to any interested group wishing to acquaint itself with the facts. The growing American film industry was enlisted to make propaganda movies, and the CPI encouraged the showing of these in neutral countries; the fledgling radio medium was used to broadcast messages from the United States to the Eiffel Tower in Paris and, from there, to most of the neutral European countries. The CPI also had commissioners in every foreign neutral and Allied nation, whose job it was to disseminate daily news to the local press.

In the final assessment of the success of the CPI, we must be careful to distinguish between the immediate results and the long-term effects on American society. As an agency of psychological warfare, the CPI was extremely successful, and it created a war psychosis in the United States that went a long way in providing the moral and material support required by the armed services. After the war finally ended, however, and the Wilsonian concept of a war to "make the world safe for democracy" proved to be largely unfounded, the American public and especially the politicians began to question seriously both the tactics and the intensity of the CPI's propaganda activities. The boosterism mentality that accompanied so much of the domestic activities of the CPI, when contrasted with the loss of so many American lives, especially in the face of disillusionment with the settlement of the war, left a bad taste in the mouths of Americans. In turn, this led to a justified suspicion of the power of organized propaganda and ultimately encouraged the pacifist and isolationist tendencies that existed in the United States for the next 20 years. As Linebarger (1954) noted, "A more modest, more calculated national propaganda effort would have helped forestall those attitudes which, in turn, made World War II possible" (p. 68).

American military propaganda activities concentrated on morale and surrender leaflets because radio loudspeaker technology did not exceed the power of the megaphone by much at that time. Therefore, most communication with the enemy had to be in one of the most basic forms of all—the printed leaflet. The British and the French had pioneered in this form of propaganda, but the Americans developed some of their own inventions, and balloons and airplanes were the chief methods of dispersement, but later special leaflet bombs and mortars were also used very effectively. Messages in these leaflets were essentially antimilitaristic and prodemocratic, stressing the class differences between the German leaders and the enlisted men (the same tactic used in the American Revolutionary War!) and reminding German soldiers that American industrial might had now entered the war. The primary mission was to induce an attitude of surrender, and here the Americans really excelled, for they were able to promise the half-starved German infantry first-class American food and care and return to loved ones, all under the rule of international law. It soon became obvious that food was the most popular subject of appeal, for this had become an obsession with the starving German soldiers and civilian population.

Instead of attacking these issues directly by countering the information in the leaflets, the German high command attacked the whole concept of such demoralizing propaganda as being unethical and stressed that German soldiers were expected to do their duty and would not be influenced by such messages. Of course, this tactic failed, and German soldiers surrendered in large numbers to the American and Allied forces in the last months of the war. Once again, the German army's reluctance to get its hands dirty in psychological warfare cost it dearly. One must also point out, however, that the German army had very few propaganda issues with which to counter, for unlike the domestic conditions in Germany, there was very little deprivation and starvation in the Allied countries, especially after America entered the war in 1917. Propaganda is most successful when it has a firm footing in observable reality.

Atrocity Propaganda

Perhaps the most significant feature of World War I propaganda was the wide dissemination of atrocity stories as a means of discrediting the enemy. Often called "hate propaganda," most atrocity stories concentrated on three types of alleged cruelties: (a) massacre, such as the slaughter of the Armenians by the Ottoman Empire, supposedly under the encouragement of the Germans; (b) mutilation, such as the gouging out of the eyes of German soldiers; and (c) the mistreatment of both soldiers and civilian populations by starvation or actual torture. Such forms of propaganda are designed to stiffen the fighting spirit of entire nations, to create fear of defeat, and, as a more practical means, to raise funds and encourage enlistment to halt these inhuman acts. Ultimately, it also served to prolong the fighting and create more severe conditions for surrender.

Literally hundreds of books and pamphlets were devoted to the most graphic details of supposed atrocities committed by both sides. Stories emanating from Belgium had a particularly strong influence in the Allied countries because of the many Belgian refugees who fled to neutral nations in 1914. The popular notion comparing the German soldier to "the Hun" of old (the Huns were actually Mongols from Central Asia), inspired by a careless remark made by the kaiser in 1899 when he admonished the German contingent off to fight the Boxer Rebellion in China to "behave like Huns," became a central theme of propaganda attacks against the Germans. These atrocity stories—a few based on real incidents, but most without foundation—formed the core of the anti-German propaganda aimed at the United States in the years before America entered the war.

Many atrocity stories were widely circulated in the United States and other neutral countries; two have special significance. (Other atrocity propaganda stories are discussed in Chapter 4.) On October 9, 1915, Edith Cavell, a Red Cross nurse working in Brussels, was found guilty by a German court martial of helping British and French soldiers escape into neutral Holland. She was sentenced to death and executed by a firing squad on October 12. She could have saved herself by professing ignorance of the law, but instead she openly admitted that many of the escapees had gone back to join their units; thus, she was manifestly guilty of having committed a capital offense according to the German military code. This daughter of an English clergyman stated at her execution, "Standing before God and eternity, I realize this—patriotism is not enough. I must be free from hate and bitterness!" These words were carved on the monument to Edith Cavell in central London (Read, 1941). Edith Cavell became an instant martyr to the cause of propaganda, and her "cold-blooded murder" was used to give credibility to other atrocity stories coming out of Belgium. Even the supposedly neutral American press printed full accounts of the 50-year-old nurse's courage in the face of her executioners. In Britain, even to this day, Edith Cavell remains a symbol of courage and loyalty.

An interesting sidelight to this story demonstrates the failure of the Germans to understand the value of propaganda. The French had shot several women spies, one of them as early as August 1914 and at least two after Edith Cavell's execution, but the Germans failed to use these events to their advantage, and they were not even reported in the American press. A later attempt by the Germans to make a propaganda event of the execution by the French of the Dutch-Javanese entertainer and professional spy Mata Hari seemed to lack appeal when compared with the death of the English nurse. (Of course, the Mata Hari story later achieved immortality through the efforts of Hollywood, which, in 1931, produced a movie about her exploits featuring the extremely popular actress Greta Garbo.) In the United States and other neutral nations, the Germans were hard-pressed to counter their constant portrayal as a barbaric nation that readily executed women.

The other propaganda event of significance was the furor that surrounded the sinking of the luxury liner *Lusitania* on May 7, 1915, by a German U-boat—without any prior warning and with a loss of 1,198 lives, 128 of them American. Whether the sinking of the ship was justified by the fact that the ship was carrying arms did not seem to matter at the time, for the press in both Britain and America used the incident to reinforce increasingly hostile attitudes toward German acts of atrocity. In one of those curious acts of history, just 5 days after the sinking of the *Lusitania,* the British government issued its long-awaited *Bryce Commission Report* on the accuracy of the stories of German atrocities. The Bryce Commission, headed by a prominent British legal expert, had been formed in early 1915 as a result of a public demand to know the truth about the German outrages.

The final report, which found "a compelling mass of evidence" to substantiate the atrocities, was translated into 30 languages and widely circulated and reported in the United States (Read, 1941, pp. 201–204). The findings of the Bryce Commission only served to accentuate the "barbarity" of the ship's sinking, despite the fact that the Germans may have had some justification for their actions during a state of war. Today, considerable doubt is still expressed about the depositions taken by the Bryce Commission from Belgian refugees, and suggestions are made that the commissioners were themselves caught up in the hysteria of war (Roetter, 1974).

Reaction to World War I Propaganda

Propaganda was effective as a weapon of psychological warfare in World War I, but as indicated in Chapter 4, this must be viewed in its historical context. For the first time in history, nations were forced to draw on the collective power of their entire populations by linking the individual to a larger societal need. As DeFleur and Ball-Rokeach (1982) pointed out,

> It became essential to mobilize sentiments and loyalties, to instill in citizens a hatred and fear of the enemy, to maintain their morale in the face of privation, and to capture their energies into an effective contribution to their nation. (p. 159)

As a result, the general public indicated a response to mass media messages as never before, and this reaction reinforced already existing fears about the potentially dangerous role of the mass media in a mass society. At this time, social scientists were beginning to conduct the first research that suggested the acquisition of information from the mass media was a complex process, largely involving individual predispositions, and that questioned the myth of the "mass audience." Nevertheless, the prevailing theories of psychology and the instinctual understanding of the way the mass media worked were still influential; reinforced by the visible success of wartime propaganda efforts, this led to a misinterpretation of how powerful the media really were. There was little appreciation of the specific social and political conditions that had made World War I propaganda so effective, and this incomplete perception colored much of the thinking about the mass media in general and propaganda in particular for the next 20 years.

The Interwar Years, 1920 to 1939

The role of propaganda in the period between the two world wars can be characterized by three political developments: (a) the Russian Revolution and the rise of the communist Soviet Union, (b) the strong isolationist impulse in the United States as a direct result of disillusionment with the outcome of World War I, and (c) the rise of the fascist states, especially Nazi Germany. All three of these historical developments played direct roles in the outbreak of hostilities again in 1939, only this time all the belligerent nations were aware of the necessity of both offering and countering propaganda in the strongest way possible.

The Emergence of Communist Propaganda

The philosophical underpinnings of the Russian Revolution lay in the adoption of an interpretation of the works of Karl Marx by a group of dissident Russian intellectuals, particularly Nikolai Lenin and Leon Trotsky. Ironically, it was German General Erich von Ludendorff who arranged to have Lenin return to Russia from exile in Switzerland in 1917 specifically to sow the seeds of revolution that would end the war on the eastern front, thus making more German troops available to confront the Allies in the West. Lenin finally succeeded in his Bolshevik Revolution in November 1917 when he overthrew the provisional government of Alexander Kerensky, which had in March deposed Czar Nicholas II. The Bolsheviks came to power, determined to create a new social order, but faced the immense task of transforming the thinking of a largely rural population of more than 170 million, many of whom were illiterate and most of whom were hungry.

To achieve their ends, the Soviet rulers erected an immense network of propaganda that included massive programs of political as well as practical education. Lenin mobilized every available form of communication (and entertainment) to meet this goal: The press, educational institutions, the arts, and even science all became part of the intensive internal propaganda system designed to play the central role in the creation of a communist state. Controlled from the top, the arms of the Soviet propaganda machine reached into every aspect of Russian life, down to the local level where clubs and other quasi-social organizations received political education from trained propagandists. The establishment of reading rooms in even the smallest villages encouraged guided discussions, and films were accompanied by question-and-answer sessions. All this was under the control and tight supervision of the Agitational-Propaganda Section of the Central Committee of the Communist Party, known as Agitprop, which was attached to every division of the Communist Party down to the smallest local cell (Maxwell, 1936). While the internal political convulsions continued in Russia until the late 1950s, this intensive propaganda infrastructure was absolutely crucial to the establishment of the new communist state. It was the most extensive and long-lasting propaganda campaign in modern

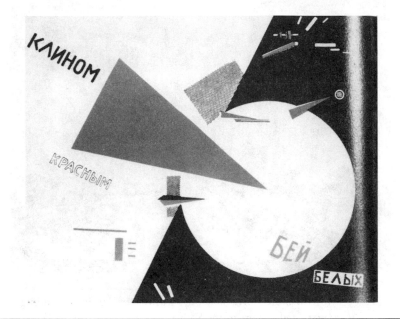

Figure 5.3   Controversial Russian artist El Lissitzky's famous propaganda poster, "Beat the Whites With the Red Wedge," was printed in 1919. In this poster, there is no reference to concrete events or people; the image is the entire idea, conveyed in purely abstract terms, with the "red wedge" driving into the white circle. Such abstract concepts, while well received in the world of avant-garde art, were considered to be too inaccessible for the Russian public and were eventually banned in favor of "social realism."

history, finally coming to an end with the momentous events in the Soviet Union in 1990–1991, which witnessed the end of the Communist Party's hold on that country.

The communists used a variety of symbolic and political devices to enhance their propaganda program. Foremost among the political devices was the idea of the imminent threat or plot, much as had been used in the French Revolution, which allowed the threat of brutality or retaliation to be used against political enemies or those who questioned party actions. The hammer and sickle was a strong visual symbol, and it received wide international recognition, but for many years, the Soviet Union was restricted from lavish spectacle because of spartan internal conditions. Even the "Internationale" was not played in the October uprising because the band did not know it; the stirring French national anthem, "La Marseillaise," was played instead! For many years, until the recent events that destroyed the

Figure 5.4   Moscow State University. This was one of the finest buildings
constructed as part of the Soviet government's attempt to create a
communist architectural style that would reflect "the sense of pride
of the Soviet people in their Socialist state." Unfortunately, many
of the ambitious plans of the Soviets, including the Palace of the
Soviets, which was to be taller than the Empire State Building,
were never completed.

power of the Communist Party, the Soviet Union engaged in massive spectacles of military might and of civilian solidarity. These symbolic displays
became a staple of worldwide communist propaganda, symbolizing the
importance of collectivity over the individual. Until very recently, the Soviets
still held massive May Day parades of military equipment, but the dire economic position of the USSR and the widespread dissatisfaction of the public
gave a hollow ring to such events. The Russian people are now quite capable of seeing the difference between the propaganda inherent in such displays
of military might and the reality of a failed consumer economy. Such osten-
tatious displays have also lost their international propaganda power for all
but the generals in the U.S. Pentagon, who continue to monitor the potential
of Russian militarism.

The breakup of the Soviet Union into a series of smaller states is now a
reality. Events have moved so fast in such a short period of time, however,
that it would be foolish to predict the exact shape and political affiliations
that will emerge from the ruins of the enormous communist state. The massive propaganda military parades and other shows of collective solidarity

have now, with minor exceptions, all but disappeared. For the average citizen of Russia and the other former communist states, such displays at a time of serious economic difficulties tend to have a negative propaganda value. It should be noted, however, that reports from the various states of the former Soviet Union indicate that a substantial segment of the population regrets the demise of the communist system and wishes to restore it. Despite the fact that communism ultimately failed to meet its economic promises, so great was its totalitarian "paternalism" that many people miss this form of government protection in their lives. For many citizens of these countries, the free enterprise, market-based economy that is slowly emerging has proved to be a financial and social disaster. This continued sentiment is, in many respects, a testament to the residual power of 50 years of communist propaganda.

Because an articulated part of the Bolshevik program was to export communism to all parts of the world—"the World Revolution"—Soviet propaganda activities took on a worldwide dimension in the interwar period. In every country, national Communist Parties sprang up, which, in the period before the Stalinist purges of the mid-1930s, were directly under the control of the Soviet Union, all aimed at establishing the international solidarity of the working class. Such sentiments had enormous appeal during the Depression, when unemployment, hunger, and general disillusionment with capitalism all contributed to a rise in the interest in communism in the Western democracies, especially inflation-wrought and war-weary Germany. Even in the United States, the Communist Party and the "Popular Front" of pro-Soviet organizations attracted millions of members in the period from 1935 to 1939, before the ill-fated Stalin-Hitler pact of August 1939 shattered their unity and created a schism with Moscow (O'Neill, 1982).

American Isolationism

As a direct result of their unsatisfactory experiences with the outcome of World War I, and led by their politicians, the American people turned inward during the period from 1920 to 1941. The "America First" movement gained in popularity as people seemed to want to turn away from the turmoil in Europe, and the severe effects of the Depression created a further impetus to concentrate on domestic issues. The reaction against government propaganda was particularly virulent, as those responsible for creating the successful campaigns during the war seemed to be only too eager to explain how it was all done. George Creel had published his book *How We Advertised America* in 1920, and this precipitated a lengthy and somewhat justified suspicion of propaganda. This suspicion was enhanced by the obvious role played by propaganda in the rise to power of Hitler and by the increased use of propaganda by the Nazi Reich and other fascist states such as Italy. Despite the lingering suspicion of propaganda, the social and political conditions of the Depression made the American public highly susceptible to the messages of those who promised them salvation from their economic problems. Many such saviors appeared during this period, but the two most prominent and successful demagogues were the populist governor of Louisiana, Huey Long, and the ultraconservative Roman Catholic priest from the suburbs of Detroit, Fr. Charles E. Coughlin.

Huey Long, who went on to become a U.S. senator, ran Louisiana like a dictatorship between 1928 and the time of his assassination in 1935. Known as "the Kingfish" (after a character on the *Amos 'n' Andy* radio show), he had serious aspirations to become president. Long had courted the press outrageously by playing the country bumpkin (he once received a German naval commander on an official visit to the State House in his green silk pajamas), and he was able to use this publicity to further his "share-the-wealth" philosophy. In April 1932, he rose on the Senate floor to make a major speech, in which he said,

> Unless we provide for redistribution of wealth in this country, the country is doomed. . . . I tell you that if in any country I live in . . . I should see my children starving and my wife starving, its laws against robbing and against stealing and against bootlegging would not amount to any more to me than they would to any other man when it came to a matter of facing the time of starvation. (Brinkley, 1982, p. 44)

Long was saying, as Brinkley (1982) noted, that "the nation faced a choice. It could act to limit large fortunes and guarantee a decent life to its citizens, or it could wait for the otherwise inevitable revolution" (p. 44). This rhetoric won for Long an immediate reputation as a radical and the champion of the "little people." After Franklin Roosevelt was elected president in 1932, Long tried to force his share-the-wealth philosophy on the Democratic president through a series of radio speeches. Roosevelt rejected his views and privately thought of Long as a dangerous nuisance. Rejected by the bulk of the Democratic Party, Long then formed the Share Our Wealth Society in February 1934, which he hoped would encompass a nationwide system of local clubs of people who shared this philosophy.

To get his message across to the public, Long developed a strong propaganda strategy that allowed him to bypass the normal media channels. His publication *American Progress* (1933) had only a small paid subscription list but was mailed free to 300,000 people, which on occasion increased to

1.5 million. His autobiography, *Every Man a King* (published in October 1933), though not a best seller, was given away free to anyone who wanted it. He also had a staff of 60 stenographers (this was in the days before copy machines) who sent out letters, circulars, and pamphlets proclaiming his activities and programs to this enormous mailing list. Radio was most important to Long, and by 1935, he was a regular and, by all accounts, very popular speaker on the NBC radio network. He used a highly effective, personal, and folksy style in his broadcasts. He usually began as follows:

> Hello friends, this is Huey Long speaking. And I have some important things to tell you. Before I begin I want you to do me a favor. I am going to talk along for four or five minutes, just to keep things going. While I'm doing it I want you to go to the telephone and call up five of your friends, and tell them that Huey is on the air. (Barnouw, 1968, p. 49)

According to Barnouw (1968), this device produced steadily mounting audiences. Brinkley (1982) noted,

> Long's national reputation grew at an astounding rate through the spring and summer of 1935, and the size and distribution of his Share the Wealth Clubs grew with it. . . . Long seemed to many to be on the verge of creating a genuine new force in American politics, one whose ultimate power nobody could yet predict. (p. 80)

Some genuinely feared that Long, if elected, would create a political structure similar to the European fascist states, although he had never identified himself with the fascist cause. All that became moot, however, when he was shot and killed in the Louisiana capitol building on September 10, 1935. It is one of history's little ironies that President Roosevelt heard the news of Long's death while entertaining two guests at his home in Hyde Park; Joseph P. Kennedy had brought Father Coughlin along to try to heal the breach between the president and the priest (Barnouw, 1968).

Fr. Charles Coughlin, S.J.

Father Charles Coughlin was born in Hamilton, Ontario, in 1891 and rose from relative obscurity to become a major public figure during the years of the Depression, almost solely through his extraordinary command of the new medium of radio. He had begun to use radio in 1926 when he was a priest at the Shrine of the Little Flower in Royal Oak, Michigan. By the late 1920s, he discovered that the listeners to his modest weekly Sunday radio broadcast were interested in more than just his religious sermons, and after 1930, he switched almost exclusively to political topics. He addressed himself to the issues of the day, the hopes and fears of his largely working-class audience, and found that this created a strong response during this time of great uncertainty. Barnouw (1968) noted,

> His subject matter involved a diversity of political strands, stemming from varied sources. Sometimes he spoke of the perils of Communism, the "red serpent." Sometimes he pleaded for the remonetization of silver, and sounded like a Populist leader of the turn of the century. More often he castigated those of wealth and power, "dulled by the opiate of their own contentedness." (p. 45)

Brinkley (1982), who studied Coughlin's technique as a radio performer, noted,

> Most important was the warm, inviting sound of his voice, a sound that could make even the tritest statements sound richer and more meaningful than they actually were. And there was, too, the ability to make the sermons accessible, interesting, and provocative to his audience. . . .
>   Coughlin used a wide variety of rhetorical techniques: maudlin sentimentality, anger and invective, sober reasonableness, religious or patriotic fervor. Rarely did successive broadcasts strike precisely the same tone, and in this unpredictability lay much of Coughlin's appeal. (p. 97)

Coughlin was able to exploit radio at a time when the medium was just beginning to become an important and integral part of American culture. Although it was difficult to estimate the exact size and demographic composition of his audience, it was extremely large and seemed to consist of people from all strata of society, but with one common denominator: They were all disaffected in some way with American society. Financial contributions poured in from across the country, allowing him to purchase radio time. At the height of his popularity, he received more mail than anyone else in America. His Sunday sermons were widely reported in the Monday newspapers, and "national magazines carried feature articles about the phenomenal success of the 'Radio Priest'" (Brinkley, 1982, p. 101).

Coughlin became more politicized as the Depression wore on, aiming his wrath at Wall Street and the international bankers who he thought controlled the world's economy and precipitated the Depression. Coughlin started his own quasi-political party, the National Union for Social Justice, in 1934 and set out on a speaking tour across the country to attract voters. Everywhere he went, he attracted large audiences, and the National Union had an estimated 8.5 million members in 1936. The problem was that the organization had no real structure beyond being a member of Coughlin's radio audience—really nothing more than names on a mailing list.

At a time when economic uncertainties had created a potentially volatile public open to suggestions on how American society should respond to the crisis, some were concerned about the growing power of the protesting voices of both Long and Coughlin. Things came to a head on March 4, 1935, when Roosevelt's friend and former director of the National Recovery Administration, General Hugh S. Johnson, made a famous speech at the Waldorf Astoria, attacking both Long and Coughlin. In the speech, broadcast by the NBC radio network, he said,

> You can laugh at Huey Long—you can snort at Father Coughlin—but this country was never under greater menace. . . . Added to the fol-de-rol of Senator Long, there comes burring over the air the dripping brogue of the Irish-Canadian priest . . . musical, blatant bunk from the very nostrum of religion, it goes straight home to simple souls weary in distress. . . . Between the team of Huey Long and the priest we have the whole bag of crazy and crafty tricks . . . possessed by Peter the Hermit, Napoléon Bonaparte, Sitting Bull, William Hohenzollern [the kaiser], Hitler, Lenin . . . boiled down to two with the radio and the newsreel to make them effective. If you don't think Long and Coughlin are dangerous, you don't know the temper of the country in this distress! (Barnouw, 1968, p. 48)

Johnson's hour-long speech was enthusiastically applauded at the Waldorf Astoria, but the White House remained silent because the administration was concerned that Johnson had focused unwanted media attention on the two demagogues. Newspapers were already calling this "the battle of the century" (Brinkley, 1982, p. 6), and NBC provided free airtime to both for replies. The biggest fear was that they would join their forces to forge a formidable challenge to Roosevelt's reelection in 1936. Despite the size of both Huey Long's Share the Wealth Clubs and Fr. Coughlin's National Union for Social Justice, however, neither was able to mount a serious threat to Roosevelt in the 1936 elections, although evidence indicates that the president did not take either of them lightly. The death of Long seemed to have an effect on Coughlin, and he went into a decline after his political party obtained less than 2% of the total vote in the 1936 election. Coughlin finally moved over the edge when he attacked international bankers by taking a blatant anti-Semitic stance in 1938, and he also favored neutrality when war began in Europe in 1939. In 1942, his publication *Social Justice* was banned from the U.S. mail, and he was threatened with formal charges of sedition. In May 1942, Coughlin quietly announced that he was severing all political ties "on orders from Church superiors." This did not stop his followers (known as The Christian Front) from continuing to pursue their anti-Semitic beliefs and actions throughout the war. However, despite many requests from his ardent followers to return to the radio after the war, he refused to do so and remained in Detroit the rest of his life, where he died in 1979 (Warren, 1996, p. 282).

As Brinkley (1982) noted,

> Huey Long and Father Coughlin faded so quickly from public prominence that it was easy in the ensuing years to forget how powerful and ominous they once had seemed. . . . [They] seized upon vague anxieties that had afflicted their society for many decades—the animosity toward concentrated power, the concern about the erosion of community and personal autonomy. (p. 261)

Both had instinctual abilities to communicate their ideas to sympathetic audiences, demonstrating that the new medium of radio, with its inherent capacity to become "personal," was a potent force for propagandizing in modern society.

The Institute for Propaganda Analysis

The Institute for Propaganda Analysis (IPA) was started in October 1937 by Columbia University professor Clyde R. Miller, who became its chief executive. (The best history of the IPA is Sproule, 1997, pp. 129–177.) Miller, who, as a reporter during World War I, was convinced that he had been hoodwinked by propaganda, was one of a group concerned that the renewed interwar propaganda battles would once again draw the United States into a futile European conflict. The opinion leaders and educators who established the institute were concerned not only with war propaganda but also with such domestic propaganda issues as the Ku Klux Klan, communists, domestic fascism, and the role of advertising, all as possible threats to the democratic way of life. The overarching concern was that the increasing volume of propaganda from numerous sources was inhibiting people's ability to think clearly and straight. Miller received a $10,000 grant from Edward A. Filene, a wealthy Boston merchant and liberal-minded philanthropist who was "afraid that America was becoming the victim of propaganda (the year was 1936), that Americans had lost their capacity to think things through" (Sproule, 1983, p. 488). Miller had no difficulty recruiting a distinguished group of academicians to serve as officers and also on the advisory board of the institute.

The institute immediately started a monthly bulletin, *Propaganda Analysis*. In the second issue, in the article "How to Detect Propaganda" (1937), it published the famous seven common "devices" or "ABCs of propaganda analysis":

- *Name-Calling.* Giving an idea a bad label and therefore rejecting and condemning it without examining the evidence.
- *Glittering Generality.* Associating something with a "virtue word" and creating acceptance and approval without examination of the evidence.
- *Transfer.* Carries the respect and authority of something respected to something else to make the latter accepted. Also works with something that is disrespected to make the latter rejected.
- *Testimonial.* Consists in having some respected or hated person say that a given idea or program, product, or person is good or bad.
- *Plain Folks.* The method by which a speaker attempts to convince the audience that he or she and his or her ideas are good because they are "of the people," the "plain folks."
- *Card Stacking.* Involves the selection and use of facts or falsehoods, illustrations or distractions, and logical or illogical statements to give the best or the worst possible case for an idea, program, person, or product.
- *Bandwagon.* Has as its theme "everybody—at least all of us—is doing it!" and thereby tries to convince the members of a group that their peers are accepting the program and that we should all jump on the bandwagon rather than be left out (Lee & Lee, 1979).

After discussing how these propaganda devices were used, the bulletin noted the following:

Observe that in all of these devices our emotion is the stuff with which propagandists work. Without it they are helpless; with it, harnessing it to their purposes, they can make us glow with pride or burn with hatred, they can make us zealots in behalf of the program they espouse ("How to Detect Propaganda," 1937, p. 7). In the 1930s, these seven common devices became the cornerstone of the institute's applied studies of contemporary propaganda. In one of the best examples, in the May 1938 issue of *Propaganda Analysis,* they served as the basis for an incisive analysis, "Propaganda Techniques of German Fascism." Thus, under the category Plain Folks, the analysis pointed out that at the same time that the Führer is canonized, an attempt is made to transform him into a "man of the people." In this, the propagandists are greatly assisted by his habits; for he affects ordinary clothes, wears no medals other than his simple Iron Cross, eats plain food and that sparingly, and leads a quiet, secluded life. He is pictured as a man of the people meeting plain folks in their ordinary walks of life, enjoying with them their simple work and pleasures. . . . Jesus, a carpenter, is the Messiah of the Christian world; Hitler, a house painter, is the savior of Germany. ("Propaganda Techniques of German Fascism," 1938, pp. 46–47)

This simple technique of analyzing propaganda was open to criticism, especially in that it can be very subjective in evaluation; however, this 7-point analysis remains with us today and is still widely quoted in textbooks on persuasion and propaganda.

The IPA also conducted a highly successful education program that encouraged the readers of its bulletin to gather materials to conduct their own propaganda analyses. *A Group Leader's Guide to Propaganda Analysis* was developed to promote critical thinking and informed discussion about current issues. This publication also discussed how propaganda analysis could be used to scrutinize advertising, as well as academic subjects such as English literature, music, art, and social science. By September 1939, the IPA's materials were being used in more than 550 high schools and colleges, as well as numerous adult civic groups (Sproule, 1997). According to Alfred and Elizabeth Lee (1979), among the founding members of the institute, propaganda analysis caught on so readily because "it provided a badly needed perspective for current affairs" (p. viii). The institute suspended its operations in late October 1941 when it appeared that the United States was going to enter the war. In the last issue of *Propaganda Analysis* in January 1939, under the title "We Say Au Revoir," the editorial explained the reasons for the institute's decision:

> The Institute's Board of Directors has concluded that to attempt to continue publication during the war period would probably result in weakening the confidence which the Institute has won, and impair its usefulness later. . . . The publication of dispassionate analyses of all kinds of propaganda, "good" and "bad," is easily misunderstood during a war emergency, and more important, the analyses could be misused for undesirable purposes by persons opposing the government's efforts. . . . If it were to continue it would have to analyze all propaganda—of this country and of Britain and Russia as well as that of Germany, Italy and Japan. (p. 1)

The IPA was never to return. The end of World War II was immediately followed by the tensions of the ideological Cold War between the communist and capitalist forces and then the Korean and Vietnam Wars. In this highly politicized and militarized atmosphere, the Institute for Propaganda Analysis would not have been able to function as a constructive critic of American institutions without incurring the wrath of various factions. Sproule (1983) had another view on why the IPA was never revived and why propaganda analysis declined in the postwar years: "Sharing the relatively complacent public mood of the 1940s and 1950s, and implicitly or explicitly aware of the more powerful dampers on social criticism, the academicians embraced the new terminology and technology of academic social science" (p. 496). Thus, the relatively simplistic forms of propaganda analysis developed and employed by the IPA became obsolete in the face of more sophisticated forms of communications research being undertaken in universities. Despite its demise, the IPA continues to serve as an ongoing symbol of the concern for the increased and sometimes subtle role of propaganda in our lives.

American isolationism remained fairly strong even after war broke out in Europe in 1939; however, clear evidence through opinion polls indicates that the American public was increasingly becoming pro-Allies while at the same time they remained antiwar. Congress was reluctant at times to give President Roosevelt approval to supply Britain with arms but gradually relented. The United States officially entered the war against Germany on December 11, 1941—4 days after the Japanese attacked Pearl Harbor. Once committed in this fashion, the American public again became the target of massive propaganda campaigns both on the home front and in the armed services. (Some of these propaganda activities are examined in Chapter 3.) Since the end of World War II, the isolationist impulse has periodically risen, but the realities of the atomic age have effectively prevented total withdrawal from the world political arena, although many Americans still wish that isolationism were possible.

Hitler and Nazi Propaganda

One unexpected consequence of the somewhat hysterical anti-German propaganda of World War I was that it made many people, particularly politicians, suspicious of alleged atrocity stories emanating from Germany during the 1930s. The very success of the British propaganda efforts in 1914–1918 proved to be a serious handicap in getting the world to accept the reality of what was happening in Nazi Germany, and this created a disastrous delay in the public's awareness of the horrors of the concentration camps and other Nazi atrocities.

Adolph Hitler's place in the history of propaganda is ensured, for as Thomson (1977) noted, "Hitler shares with Julius Caesar and Napoleon Bonaparte, the distinction of not only making massive use of new methods of propaganda but also, of quite consciously and deliberately basing his entire career on planned propaganda" (p. 111). Joseph Goebbels, who became Hitler's propaganda minister and the mastermind behind the Nazi propaganda machine, described Hitler's propaganda principles, which he extracted from Hitler's (1939) book *Mein Kampf,* as a carefully built up erection of statements, which whether true or false can be made to undermine quite rigidly held ideas and to construct new ones that will take their place. It would not be impossible to prove with sufficient repetition and psychological understanding of the people concerned that a square is in fact a circle. What after all are a square and a circle? They are mere words and words can be molded until they clothe ideas in disguise. (Thomson, 1977, p. 111)

In *Mein Kampf,* Hitler established several cardinal rules for successful propaganda: (a) Avoid abstract ideas and appeal instead to the emotions, which was the opposite of the Marxist concept; (b) employ constant repetition of just a few ideas, using stereotyped phrases and avoiding objectivity; (c) put forth only one side of the argument; (d) constantly criticize enemies of the state; and (e) identify one special enemy for special vilification. Throughout the Nazi period, Hitler and Goebbels stuck rigidly to these principles, and the world witnessed a mature, cultured people—the Germans—accepting one of the most onerous dictatorships in history, which precipitated a prolonged war and eventually instituted as policy the most heinous of all crimes, genocide.

Hitler had admired the propaganda efforts of the British in World War I; the work of the poet-politician Gabriele D'Annunzio, the short-lived dictator of Fiume in Italy; and the extroverted style and anti-Semitism of Karl Lueger, the mayor of Vienna. A key to Hitler's thinking was that he saw the masses as "malleable, corrupt and corruptible" and open to emotional appeals, but especially he realized that propaganda could become much more effective if a large dose of intimidation and terror stiffened it (Zeman, 1973). Calling his political program National Socialism, Hitler immediately established an image that appealed to a wide section of the confused and demoralized German public. He promised to restore Germany to its former glory and to rid the country of the shackles imposed by the Versailles Peace Treaty, and thus he rose to power with a skillful combination of power, spectacle, and propaganda.

Together, Hitler and Goebbels probably understood the propaganda potential of the mass media better than anyone else alive, and they were in a perfect position to put their theories to the test. Their greatest advantage was the psychological condition of their audience, for the German Weimar government had failed to provide the leadership that would have restored German confidence and morale after 1918, and the German people were desperately searching for answers to their political nightmare. Many of them turned to socialism and communism; National Socialism, with its emphasis on restoring the mythical Germany of the past and the perverse charismatic

„Das deutsche Volk weiß: Je größer die Not, besto stärker immer der Führer!"
(Ministerpräsident Göring aus dem Reichstag am 13. Juli 1934.)

Figure 5.5   "Hitler: Savior of the Fatherland," an illustration from the magazine *Kladderadatsch*, 1934. Here, Hitler is depicted as the man who is responsible for Germany's recovery in the period immediately after his accession to power. The illustration shows Hitler wearing all of the Nazi regalia—the brown shirt, the swastika, and the iron cross medal defending the very Aryan maiden (the country). The words on the flag—*Treue, Ehre, Ordnung* (faithfulness, honor, order)—are quite banal but reflect the totalitarian preoccupation with associating political action with traditional values.

leadership provided by Adolf Hitler, offered an even more palatable alternative. Germany in the late 1920s and early 1930s supplied the perfect setting for the implementation of Hitler's schemes. (An excellent detailed overview of Nazi propaganda is found in Welsch, 1993.)

Figure 5.6   The "Eternal Watch" memorial in Munich, designed by architect
Paul Troost in 1934 to commemorate "the fallen" in Hitler's failed
Beer Hall *Putsch* in 1923. This neoclassical design, monolithic and
imposing, was typical of Nazi architecture, with its harkening
back to the grandeur of the past.

The Weimar Republic had an ineffective press that was so diffused with
small partisan newspapers that the Nazis were easily able to gain control of
the newspapers in the period after 1925. Using the simple, nondoctrinaire
approach, the Nazi newspapers *Volkische Beobachter* (*Racist Observer*) and
later *Das Reich* preached the Nazi philosophy, especially anti-Semitism and
anticommunism, as well as provided information about the Nazi Party itself.
But newspapers were not the main vehicle for Nazi propaganda, for the
emotional appeals stressed by Hitler did not easily translate into written
words. Few journalists in Germany at this time had enough skill to compete
with the fiery speeches from Nazi podiums.

With radio, the Nazis achieved their greatest success, and this medium
was used extensively as the primary medium of official propaganda. The
importance of radio was stressed when the Nazi government produced a
cheap, one-channel radio set for the masses (the *Volksempfänger*) and eventually introduced compulsory installation of radios with loudspeakers in
restaurants, factories, and most public places. During the war, "radio war-
dens" even checked that people were listening to the right stations! As we
have seen in Chapter 3, radio also became the primary medium for overseas
propaganda activities, and Hitler used directed broadcasts to those European
countries in which he was trying to establish contact with German-speaking

Figure 5.7   "All Germany hears their Führer with the people's receiver." This
poster extols the popularity of the specially priced "People's
Receiver" that appeared about a year after the Nazis took power
in 1933 and cost about $24 at the time. By the outbreak of the
war, 70% of all German households owned radios, the highest
percentage anywhere in the world.

populations. Austria, particularly, suffered from a "radio war" in 1933 as
Hitler attempted to incite the Austrians to overthrow their government.
Radio was also extensively used to win the Saar Plebiscite in 1936, when
Goebbels smuggled large numbers of cheap radios into the disputed territory
to gain German support and to smear the anti-Nazi leader Max Braun. On
the day before the secret vote, German radio broadcast that Braun had fled,

and it was too late to counter this move so that even as Braun was driven through the streets, he was called an impostor. Radio was also the perfect medium for communicating the almost religious fervor of Nazi spectacles, with the rhythmic chants of "Sieg Heil," the enthusiastic applause, and the power of Hitler's or Goebbels's speaking style.

Historians and other scholars studying Nazi propaganda differ in their assessments of the relative success of the Nazi film program. In his detailed examination of German film propaganda, Hilmar Hoffman (1996) suggested, "Film was doubtless the most influential among the mass media in the Third Reich. It was also the means of artistic communication that Hitler used to greatest effect in bringing his political ideas to a mass audience" (p. vi). The problem in making any such evaluation is, as has been noted in Chapter 3, that film audiences were more attuned to escapist entertainment, and film propaganda, even when skillfully done, has a tendency to look too heavy-handed. This is especially true if the audience is aware that "this is a propaganda film." Some German propaganda feature and documentary films were memorable, however, such as director Leni Riefenstahl's use of the Odin myth in the making of *Triumph of the Will* (1935); Hans Steinhoff's film about the Boer War, *Ohm Kruger* (*Uncle Kruger,* 1941), which allowed the Germans to attack British colonialism; and Veit Harlan's *Jud Süss* (*Jew Süss,* 1940), which was a subtle anti-Semitic examination of the influence of Jews on German life. Even more violent and obvious in its anti-Semitic attack was *Der Ewige Jude* (*The Eternal Jew*), a documentary film made in 1940 by Fritz Hippler, head of Nazi film production (the *Reichsfilmintendant*), which depicted the worst racial stereotypes and compared Jews to a plague of rats that needed to be exterminated.

Richard Taylor (1979) reported,

The [Eternal] Jew was shown at 66 cinemas in Berlin alone but Security Service reports on its reception suggest that audiences, after *Jew Süss,* were already tiring of anti-Semitic propaganda: "Statements like 'We've seen *Jew Süss* and we've enough of Jewish filth' have been heard." . . . Nevertheless, in August 1941 the German authorities in the occupied Netherlands decreed that every Dutch cinema should include *The [Eternal] Jew* in its programme during the following six-month period. And so the film became at the same time a prelude to the holocaust, a propagandist's excuse for it, and a perverted documentary-format record of its early stages. [Note: Taylor used the title *The Wandering Jew* for this film.] (pp. 204–205)

Hoffman (1996) laid the blame for this film squarely at the feet of Fritz Hippler: "It was he who put together the morally most perfidious, intellectually

Figure 5.8   A poster for *The Eternal Jew* exhibition held in the German
Museum in Munich in late 1937. This is an archetypal caricature
of a Jew showing off shekels in the right hand, as well as a map of
the Soviet Union and a whip in the left. It did not seem to concern
the German propagandists that these were contradictory symbols.
A vicious film based on this exhibition was also released in 1940.

most underhanded, and ideologically most perverse mishmash that has
ever been produced . . . only human scum could bring out such a diabolical
work" (p. 172). The film was undoubtedly one of the most "effective" of all
the Nazi propaganda films, and the actions that followed are a matter of historical record. When the film was first shown in the Casino Cinema in Lodz,
Poland, in January 1941, some 200,000 Jews were crammed into the local

ghetto by Nazi decree. Shortly thereafter, almost the total Jewish population was deported and liquidated in the concentration camps. (A significant part of the film was actually shot on the streets of the Lodz ghetto; thus, much of the miserable living conditions ascribed to Jews was actually the result of Nazi policies.) The key point in the film was the indoctrinating commentary: "Where rats appear, they spread disease and carry destruction into the land. They are wily, cowardly, and cruel and appear mostly in large numbers— just like the Jews among the humans." Such directive dialogue was to have an inevitable result, for as Hoffman noted, "It is no coincidence that the machinery of genocide was set in motion at the same time that this 'documentary' justification of mass murder was released" (p. 176). This film remains highly controversial even today. In recent years, distribution of this film in the United States for supposedly "historic or academic" purposes has been questioned when it was discovered that many neo-Nazi, white supremacist groups were screening it for their members as being a "factual" account of Jewish life in prewar Europe.

It is not surprising that, in the face of these rather dour documentary films, the biggest box office attraction during this period was the purely escapist *Grosse Liebe* (*The Great Love*), the story of a soldier's love, and although the film did glorify death in battle, the emotional theme underscored the audience's rejection of blatant propaganda. Commercial Nazi propaganda films, with rare exceptions, failed to find strong overseas markets and therefore were limited in their influence.

In their use of documentary films for propaganda purposes, however, the Nazis were very successful, and they shifted their direct indoctrination efforts from feature films to documentaries and newsreels. Hoffman (1996) suggested, "The clear differentiation of propagandistic function by film genre showed the Nazis' surprising sensitivity to the various means for effectively influencing the masses" (p. viii). Some war documentaries, as indicated in Chapter 3, did create a fear of the German army in many neutral countries, but they also had the opposite effect of reinforcing opposition to German aggression in countries such as Britain and the United States. The ultimate irony is that extracts from captured copies of these documentaries were used by Hollywood director Frank Capra as a central part of his powerful series of *Why We Fight* orientation films for the U.S. Army.

Posters were also used extensively throughout the Nazi Reich; these usually featured bold colors, especially red, and used large, simplistic illustrations and heavy, dominating slogans. Hitler wanted to be an architect in his youth, and he always had an appreciation for the visual; he understood the importance of strong visual symbols. Even in the period before the Nazis were able to dominate newspapers and radio, the poster became the primary source of propaganda, displaying especially the Nazi symbol of the swastika,

Figure 5.9   This is just part of a crowd of 151,000 who attended the Party Day celebrations in Nuremberg in 1933 to listen to Hitler's speech. Note the massive display of flags in the background and Hitler, thrust out on the podium by himself. Such massive displays were an essential part of Nazi propaganda, designed to demonstrate public solidarity with the policies of the Nazi Party.

the square-jawed pure Aryan Nazi storm trooper, or anti-Semitic images of large-nosed Jews. These propaganda images became commonplace after Hitler came to power in 1933, and they contributed in no small measure to Nazi success (Zeman, 1978).

The Nazis used many propaganda devices, but one they brought to the peak of perfection in the modern era was the spectacle. Under the supervision of Hitler's official architect, Albert Speer, these lavish public displays moved from being mere exhibitions of Nazi might to becoming propagandistic works of art designed to evoke an outpouring of emotional fervor and support. These gigantic rallies also allowed the people of Germany to perceive Hitler in the context of a restored Germany, with strong overtones harking back to the Aryan myths of the past. The annual Nazi Party rallies in Nuremberg were special centerpieces for the public affirmation of Nazi mythology. The Nuremberg rallies lasted up to 8 days and featured dramatic lighting, controlled sound effects, and martial music. With a cast of hundreds of thousands, these annual events were calculated to create a strong emotional resonance of patriotic hysteria in the German people. The enormous size of the rallies, encompassing participants from all parts of Germany, was specifically orchestrated to provide a sense of a pan-German community, visibly communicating that all Germans accepted the single ideology of Nazism. Ward Rutherford (1978) pointed out that Goebbels regarded these rallies as important because they were an effective substitute for actual participation in policymaking by the populace. In several speeches, Goebbels made the point that taking part in such a rally was regarded as superior to voting in a democracy!

Finally, Nazi propaganda made extensive use of a wide variety of carefully designed symbols to emphasize Nazi power and authority. These included the eagle, the Nazi "martyr's" blood, marching (especially the goose step), the Heil salute, the carrying of swords and daggers, the use of fire, the swastika, and the flag (Delia, 1971). Some symbols were more blatant than others, such as the skull and crossbones insignia worn by members of the Gestapo. The Nazis were particularly adept at using architecture and sculpture as propaganda media, and Speer masterminded the massive restructuring of Berlin and other large-scale construction projects ordered by Hitler to reflect his "Thousand Year Reich." Hitler apparently wanted to leave a monument to himself that would have dwarfed all such monuments from the past, including a triumphal arch that would have been 550 feet wide, 392 feet deep, and 386 feet high. Recanting after the war, Speer (1970) called this "architectural megalomania."

One major advantage the Nazis had in ensuring the success of their domestic propaganda campaigns was their total control over Germany. By 1933, there were no competing propaganda messages of any consequence to distract the German public. The educational system, like the Russian, was an instrument of state policy and geared to provide an ideological justification of anti-Semitism and Nazi values. In fact, anti-Semitism became the underpinning of the Nazi propaganda campaign, as the Jews were blamed for everything that was wrong with Germany and the West. Jews were called decadent capitalists or godless Bolsheviks at the same time; it did not "matter that much" if the rhetoric was clearly contradictory, for Hitler's principles of propaganda required that a scapegoat be found, and anti-Semitism served both political and social ends. Through the persistent reinforcement of these messages, Hitler was able to achieve a fiery nationalism by convincing the German people that ridding themselves of Jews would create an undefiled, uncorrupted, pure Aryan nation. Socially, anti-Semitism was evoked to provide a rationale for German failure, as well as a reason to hope for a better future "once the problem had been taken care of." This was a classic propaganda ploy; Hitler was able to both demoralize the Jews and mobilize hatred against them, thus providing a justification for his political and social policies.

In the long run, Hitler's domestic propaganda campaigns were successful, and only defeat on the battlefield finally ended the terror within Germany.

Figure 5.10 The exterior of the House of German Art in Munich. Another example of Nazi architecture designed by Paul Troost. Hitler had a particular interest in and fondness for this building, because it was used to exhibit only artwork that had been officially approved by the Nazis as meeting the ideals of "Aryan culture."

In his study of German propaganda, *The War That Hitler Won,* Robert Herzstein (1978) made a strong case for considering the overwhelming success of Hitler's propaganda efforts in the context of their times. Since 1945, we have concentrated on the loss of the war by the Nazis while ignoring their incredible propaganda victories in Germany and elsewhere. Even after the Allies had liberated a few concentration camps, German leaders were still advocating the extermination of Jews and Bolsheviks and were blaming the loss of the war on these groups. Ultimately, Nazism and its abhorrent racial philosophies could only be defeated on the battlefield. Unfortunately, many of Nazism's worst aspects, particularly anti-Semitism, continue to manifest themselves in modern society. It is fascinating to note the continued, some would say increased, interest that exists in all things pertaining to the Nazis. Every year, hundreds of books, both fiction and nonfiction, are published on the subject; movies and television shows on Nazis, both past and present, continue to occupy our screens; Nazi paraphernalia, such as badges, medals, daggers, and flags (most of them fake copies), are sold at flea markets to collectors; and so-called neo-Nazi groups such as the skinheads continue to claim inspiration from the racial ideologies of Hitler. A search of the Internet

Figure 5.11   The German Pavilion at the Paris World Exhibition in 1937. This international exhibition, held at a time when fascism was rising in Europe, provided an opportunity for the Germans and the Soviets to use their pavilion architecture as propaganda symbolizing the power of their respective countries. Designed by Albert Speer, the German pavilion stood opposite the Soviet pavilion and featured a 500-foot tower, crowned with the symbol of state—the eagle with a swastika. Built of "German iron and stone," it was intended to be left standing after the exhibition was over as a "sacred piece of German earth." It is not clear how the French authorities felt about this. The magazine *Art Digest* commented at the time that this building "can only be seen as an expression of Fascist brutality."

soon turns up many Web sites devoted to aspects of Nazism, both pro and con. Sadly, the symbology and racist ideologies of the Nazis are evoked with regularity by so-called white supremacist groups who see in this philosophy a justification of their own views.

Why all this interest after more than 50 years? Clearly, the material symbology of the Nazis has left a powerful memory in our culture. We are perversely fascinated by a society and its culture that could have had such high aspirations and intellect on the surface but committed such unspeakable cruelties to achieve those ends. How could a society that gave us Bach, Beethoven, and Goethe have also given us Buchenwald? We all recognize the popular culture image of the cultured Nazi officer, in his well-cut military uniform, listening to the music of Wagner while at the same time ordering the deaths of hundreds of Jewish prisoners. Robert Herzstein (1978) was right: The historical persistence of these images is a testament to the strength of Nazi propaganda. (For an interesting examination of how the image of Hitler has become part of modern popular culture, see Alvin Rosenfeld, *Imagining Hitler*, 1985.)

World War II

In many ways, the propaganda efforts of the belligerent nations in World War II were predictable, following the discovery of the potential of psychological warfare in World War I. The major difference, as we have already noted in Chapter 3, is that radio became the principal means of sending propaganda messages to foreign countries. The traditional propaganda media of pamphlets, posters, and motion pictures were again used but with an increased awareness of the psychology of human behavior. On all sides, psychologists were put to work on devising the best methods of appeal, taking into consideration specific cultural and social factors relative to the intended target audience. This was a far cry from the rather "buckshot" approach taken earlier and indicated the seriousness with which psychological warfare was being waged. On both fronts—the European and the Pacific—American propaganda experts from the various agencies created to coordinate domestic and overseas propaganda activities were careful to use scientific methods where possible in devising their campaigns. In particular, emphasis on atrocity propaganda was to be downplayed, except where this served a deliberate purpose, such as President Roosevelt's delayed announcement of the Japanese execution of the American flyers shot down over Tokyo.

One of the most controversial problems facing historians examining World War II is why the issue of the treatment of German concentration camp victims received such little public acknowledgment until almost the end of the war. The showing of the startling black-and-white newsreel footage of the liberation of these camps was the first time that most Americans had a clear idea of what really happened. Would the earlier revelation of the

Figure 5.12   The Russian Pavilion at the Paris World Exhibition in 1937.
The Russian Pavilion provided a slightly different propaganda
perspective on the "power of the state," as symbolized by
architecture. Designed by Boris Iofan, it was planned to be a
combination of architecture, sculpture, and the other arts. The
sculpture on top, titled "Worker and Collective Farm Woman,"
was claimed in the special pavilion brochure as bearing "the
definite imprint of the artistic method we call Socialist Realism."
Again, *Art Digest* suggested that this building "was in the same
spirit" of brutality as the German one.

treatment of the Jews and others in the camps have made a difference in when the United States entered the war? How much of this indifference can be blamed on a reaction to World War I atrocity propaganda? Was there a strain of anti-Semitism in the U.S. Department of State during the early years of the war that deliberately underplayed the plight of the Jews? These questions have not yet been fully answered.

Both sides made much more extensive use of white, black, and gray propaganda through the medium of radio, as the new medium provided the ideal opportunity to establish contact over long distances without necessarily revealing the source of the message. Clandestine radio stations were established that broadcast both true and false information to the enemy, and special commentators were used to create the illusion of broadcasts coming from within their own countries. (The most detailed histories of this interesting subject are Soley, 1989, and Soley & Nichols, 1987.) The British, through the services of the British Broadcasting Corporation (BBC), were particularly adept at this, establishing several black propaganda stations aimed at both German domestic and military targets. These stations, by essentially broadcasting the truth about wartime conditions, were able to make a considerable impact on the German people and often caused confusion on the military front (Roetter, 1974). This emphasis on truth, which became the basic philosophy for the BBC, proved to be an extremely powerful propaganda weapon, and by the end of the war, the German civilian population was listening to these broadcasts to find out about conditions in their own country.

On the domestic front, in both Britain and the United States, extensive campaigns were devised to boost home front morale. Particularly in Britain, where the German Luftwaffe had created chaos with its bombing raids, it was essential that the population be kept from panic. Again, the Ministry of Information, which was charged with this task, realized that truth was their greatest propaganda device, but their experts had a difficult time persuading the government to adopt this tactic. Eventually, the ministry won its argument that, in fighting totalitarianism, Britain should not borrow its weapons of lies and censorship but instead should rely on the sensibility and toughness of the British people, taking them into the government's confidence. Although the entire truth was not always revealed, in the long run, such propaganda tactics played an important part in maintaining the high morale of the British public, even during the darkest periods early in the war (McLaine, 1979).

In the United States, the problems were different, and the major emphasis was placed on providing a clear rationale to the American people about why they were fighting the war in Europe. (There was no equivocation about

Figure 5.13   One of the most popular series of propaganda posters in Britain was that drawn by Fougasse (Cyril Kenneth Bird), which showed, in a whimsical style, the danger of talking carelessly. Here two ladies on the upper-deck of a bus are unaware that Hitler and General Goering are sitting behind them.

why the Pacific War was necessary.) As mentioned in Chapter 4, it was deemed necessary to provide the American fighting man with an orientation to the reasons why he was being asked to risk his life. The *Why We Fight* films, discussed in Chapter 4, were compulsory viewing for enlisted men, and the first of these, *Prelude to War,* was also shown to civilian audiences throughout the nation in 1943. As discussed in Chapter 4, these films were the subject of important research into the effects of propaganda messages on specific audiences. Using all the mass media, the Office of War Information (OWI), the organization charged with handling domestic propaganda before 1943, created immediate antagonism with what had always been a "free press." The American mass media were not used to being told what they could or could not do, and full cooperation with the government came only after a series of delicate negotiations. OWI officials were eager to have the domestic entertainment media use their considerable power to propagandize to the American public in a more blatant fashion than the media executives thought necessary. In the long run, the OWI reduced its demands in the face of congressional disapproval and suspicion that it was being used by President Roosevelt to further his own personal domestic policies. Allan Winkler (1978), in his history of the OWI, suggested that the eventual success of the American propaganda campaigns, both domestic and abroad, was that they "sketched the war as a struggle for the American way of life and stressed the components—both spiritual and material—that . . . made America great" (pp. 156–157).

Post–World War II Conflicts

Four major wars have involved the United States since 1945. In the first two conflicts, Korea and Vietnam, the ideological battle between communism and capitalism was the underlying factor; in the case of the Persian Gulf, the United States and its allies decided that Iraq's invasion of Kuwait could not be tolerated within the context of shifting world power, particularly the collapse of the Soviet Union as a protective force for Iraq, and emphasized the need to "protect" the world's oil supply from falling into Saddam Hussein's hands. In the fourth and most recent conflict, the invasion of Iraq, the U.S. administration decided that the threat posed by Saddam Hussein, 10 years after his initial defeat, required a full-scale military operation to effect a regime change and to prevent the use of "weapons of mass destruction" that he supposedly was holding. Each of these conflicts involved using very different propagandistic strategies because of the international political alliances then in effect and the nature of the public response on the home front. The varied success of these strategies underlined the need to understand the culture of those to whom the propaganda was being directed.

The Korean War, 1950 to 1953

The Korean conflict began on June 25, 1950, when the Soviet-backed government of North Korea invaded South Korea. Even this issue is still in dispute, and some evidence suggests that South Korea may have been the initial aggressor. The United Nations (UN) Security Council met in an emergency session and passed a resolution that demanded withdrawal of the North Korean troops and also authorized UN members to assist in the execution of the resolution. The Soviet Union had been boycotting the UN and was therefore not present to cast a veto in the Security Council. Eventually, the UN Security Council authorized a UN military force "police action" to repel the armed attack, with troops from several nations under the command of U.S. General Douglas MacArthur. American troops eventually composed about half of the fighting forces. During the next 3 years, the opposing armies fought each other up and down the Korean peninsula. On December 31, 1950, about 400,000 Chinese troops entered the war to supplement the 100,000 North Korean soldiers. In a blatant piece of international propaganda, the communist Chinese government disavowed official participation in the war, claiming that all the Chinese troops were volunteers who had decided to help their beleaguered North Korean comrades. Eventually, largely through the use of superior air power, the UN forces were able to drive the North Koreans and the Chinese back across the 38th parallel by June 1951. Truce talks then began that continued until an armistice was signed on July 27, 1953. (These peace talks were, without doubt, the most contentious in the history of warfare.) Negotiations on the exact conditions of the truce and other issues between the opposing forces, however, continue even today, nearly 40 years after the event, and technically the conflict has never really ended.

The propaganda aspects of the Korean conflict were very disturbing for the Americans. Coming out of the propaganda successes of World War II, the U.S. military was suddenly confronted with a very different type of propaganda from the communists. This time, the propaganda battle was being fought in the arena of world opinion, and the vast international audience was divided between the opposing ideological forces of communism and capitalism. The United States, which for most of the 20th century had been on the side of "good," suddenly found itself on the defensive after being accused of being the "bad guy." Early in 1952, the communists charged the UN forces with using germ warfare as a means of explaining the series of epidemics then sweeping the civilian and military populations of North Korea. Pictures of insects supposedly dropped by UN planes were shown to the world's press. The North Koreans tried to force captured UN pilots to admit their complicity, and in May 1952, two American pilots "confessed" their guilt. These confessions came after 4 months of intensive physical and psychological torture. Of the 78 pilots subjected to such pressures, 30 succumbed, whereas the other 48 resisted all forms of torture. At the end of the

Figure 5.14   An American civilian poster, ca. 1943. This poster, produced and
distributed by the Texaco Company, was posted on factory and
office bulletin boards as a reminder that civilians were also
important in the war effort. The caricature of the Japanese soldier
is typical of the period.

war, the germ warfare charges were proven groundless, and all repatriated
pilots repudiated their confessions. These reports were widely circulated
throughout the world, however, and even today continue to be part of the
communist mythology about the Korean conflict. Such accusations, once
made, are very difficult to eradicate totally from the historical record, particularly when the audience may be predisposed to accept the veracity of the
information.

The issue of prisoner exchanges also proved to be a major propaganda
ploy for both sides. The UN troops captured 171,000 communist prisoners,
of whom slightly more than 20,000 were Chinese. It soon became obvious

Figure 5.15   The availability of propaganda images such as this, taken out of
their wartime context, continues to be a problem. This cartoon
by Edwin Marcus portrays the Japanese enemy as an ape-like
barbarian, a familiar device used by both sides. After the Japanese
executed captured American airmen, who had bombed Tokyo on
April 18, 1942, President Roosevelt referred to the "barbarous
execution by the Japanese government," inspiring this caricature.

that more than one half of the North Korean prisoners and two thirds of the
Chinese prisoners were violently opposed to being repatriated to their communist homelands. The North Korean armistice negotiators did not wish to
acknowledge this, demanding that all prisoners be repatriated. The communists even arranged to have trained political agitators deliberately taken
prisoner to maintain ideological control among their prisoners and to
foment trouble in the POW camps. The result was that several violent riots
took place in the camps in early 1952. In many cases, prisoners were forcibly
tattooed with either pro- or anticommunist slogans that turned them into
living political billboards, thus making them unacceptable to the other side.

Figure 5.16   Here again, cartoonist Sy Moyer portrays the Japanese General Tojo as a murderous beast, dripping with blood. The Japanese never fully understood how much their atrocities inflamed the American public and worked against them in the propaganda war.

Eventually, those prisoners who wanted to return home were allowed to do so after the armistice in July 1953, and nearly 100,000 formerly communist troops elected not to return to their home countries. About 15,000 Chinese prisoners decided to go to Formosa (Taiwan). This issue provided the U.S. Information Agency (USIA) with a choice propaganda plum, and motion pictures, broadcast interviews, and press features about the defecting prisoners were sent all over the world (Sorensen, 1968).

The Korean War must be seen as an integral part of the Cold War. As such, it represented a major opportunity for both sides to propagandize on a worldwide scale. In the end, the West may have won the battle, but the prolonged, contentious peace talks and the strong feelings on both sides engendered by the POW issue did not bring about a cessation of ideological hostilities. The escalated levels and viciousness of the propaganda battles of the Korean War forced the U.S. government to reexamine its own propaganda techniques and activities and did much to strengthen the role of the USIA and other agencies charged with shaping America's image at home and abroad.

The Korean War and the "Brainwashing" Issue

In the aftermath of the Korean War, a new word entered our language to describe a disturbing type of coercion that was soon added to the many lists of synonyms for *propaganda*. This word was *brainwashing*, taken from the Chinese term *hse nao*—"wash brain." Chinese communist leader Mao Tse-tung had used the term *ssu-hsiang tou-cheng*, or "thought struggle," as early as 1929 to denote what is now called "mind control" or "thought control." The term has acquired a very sinister connotation and, in recent years, has been widely associated with the type of thought control associated with cults groups, although scientific evidence that "brainwashing" is a viable psychological concept is conflicting (Singer & Lalich, 1995).

The most disturbing aspect of the Korean propaganda war for Americans and Britons was that, after the prisoners returned home from their ordeals, it was revealed that a substantial portion—perhaps 15% among Americans—had actively collaborated with the enemy and that only a few—about 5%—had resisted all communist efforts to indoctrinate them or to use them for propaganda purposes. The remainder, generally apathetic, had not been collaborators but had given in to some degree to communist pressures (Dupuy, 1965). The extensive and expert brainwashing encountered by Korean War prisoners was an entirely new form of coercive propaganda and caused much discussion within the U.S. military and among academicians interested in propaganda techniques. This led to both a general belief that the men had not been adequately prepared to withstand the psychological and physical tortures they would encounter and a reassessment of what ideological training they should have received.

After the former POWs returned home, many of them were subjected to courts of inquiry investigating their cooperation with the enemy; this was especially so for the pilots who had "confessed" to having participated in germ warfare bombings. In one famous case, renowned Dutch psychiatrist Joost Meerlo gave evidence on behalf of U.S. Marine Corps Colonel Frank H. Schwable, who had been so charged. After his repatriation, Colonel

Schwable had signed a repudiation of his confession and described the horrors of his long months of imprisonment. Of his confession, he said, "The words were mine, but the thoughts were theirs. This is the hardest thing I have to explain: how a man can sit down and write something he knows is false, and yet, to sense it, to feel it, to make it seem real" (Meerlo, 1956, pp. 3–4). Meerlo noted that after the colonel was captured, he was not treated as a prisoner of war but rather as a victim who could be used for propaganda purposes. As such, he was subjected to a range of physical and emotional torture aimed at breaking him down mentally. Meerlo outlined for the court the exact process whereby this was done. He told the court,

> In my opinion hardly anyone can resist such treatment. It all depends on the ego strength of the person and the exhaustive technique of the inquisitor. Each man has his own limit of endurance, but that this limit can nearly always be reached and even surpassed is supported by clinical evidence. (p. 14)

Meerlo (1956) called this process "mentacide"—from the Latin *mens*, "the mind," and *caedere*, "to kill," and noted,

> It is an organized system of psychological intervention and judicial perversion through which a powerful dictator can imprint his own opportunistic thoughts upon the minds of those he plans to use and destroy. The terrorized victims finally find themselves compelled to express complete conformity to the tyrant's wishes . . . his confession can be used for propaganda, for the old war, to instill fear and terror, to accuse the enemy falsely, or to exercise a constant mental pressure on others. (p. 10)

In a dramatic moment in the inquiry, Meerlo (1956) told the court that "nearly anybody subjected to the treatment meted out to Colonel Schwable could be forced to write and sign a similar confession." The colonel's attorney asked, "Anyone in this room, for instance?" and Meerlo, looking in turn at each of the officers sitting in judgment, replied firmly, "Anyone in this room" (p. 16). The Schwable case was ultimately decided in the colonel's favor, but the legacy of the brainwashing scare remained.

One bizarre reaction to the brainwashing scare was that the Central Intelligence Agency (CIA) started its own program of "behavior control" experimentation. This program, named MK-ULTRA, was authorized in April 1953 by CIA Director Allen Dulles. The unusual and sometimes inhumane tests conducted by the MK-ULTRA program were revealed in the few remaining documents made public in the early 1970s, although the program had apparently ceased in 1963, and most of the documents relating to MK-ULTRA were destroyed by the CIA in 1972. The most notorious of these experiments involved the use of lysergic acid diethylamide, or LSD. The CIA was intrigued by this drug and hoped it could be used to disorient and manipulate target foreign leaders, as well as loosen tongues during interrogations. These experiments were part of a frantic attempt to give the United States an advantage in the "mind wars" precipitated by the international tensions of the Cold War, and they did not stop there. The CIA research program included many other unusual investigations relating to the science of mind control, including the potential of numerous parapsychological phenomena such as hypnosis, telepathy, precognition, photokinesis, and "remote viewing"— being able to see remote places in the mind (Marks, 1979).

This disconcerting legacy of the Korean War, together with the increasing power of world communism, called into question the ideological and moral strength of the United States. This apparent weakness was a major plank in the anticommunist platform from which Senator Joseph McCarthy and his followers were able to create their national hysteria about the depth of communist influence in the United States. Among the many far-reaching results of this renewed nationalism was the requirement that teachers and professors sign oaths of loyalty and the revamping of school and university curricula to emphasize American history and culture (Schrecker, 1986). In the military, the Uniform Code of Military Justice was also rewritten to outline the behavior expected from prisoners subjected to brainwashing by their captors.

The Vietnam War

In Vietnam in 1965, the United States launched what is probably the largest propaganda campaign in the history of warfare. The history of the Vietnam conflict is a complex one, having its origins in the almost 2,000-year struggle of the Vietnamese people against outside invaders. First the Chinese and Mongols, and then, in the 19th century, the French tried to turn Vietnam into a colony, but each time the largely peasant armies were eventually able to defeat the intruders. Starting in the 1930s and continuing throughout the Japanese occupation during World War II, the Vietnamese Communist Party (many of whose members had been trained in Moscow in the 1920s) were adroitly able to fashion a program of nationalism that fused anticolonialism and anticapitalism and that blamed the French colonial system for all the country's ills. At the conclusion of the war in 1945, the country was split by many competing political factions, but all were opposed to French colonial rule. The communists took a leading role in the struggle, which culminated in the expulsion of the French from Indochina in 1954. This led to a divided Vietnam—the communists in the North, with their capitol Hanoi, and the noncommunists in the South, with their capitol Saigon. When many diplomatic efforts failed to reunite the country, the National Liberation Front (Viet Cong) was formed to hasten the collapse of the southern republic and lay the groundwork for reunification. The United States provided "advisers," as well as financial and military aid, to bolster the democratic Saigon government, but by 1964, the fighting had escalated to the point that it appeared certain the communists would win. At this point, the United States decided to send increased numbers of American soldiers to fight with the South Vietnamese.

The Gulf of Tonkin Incident

The immediate pretext used by the U.S. government to justify its entry into the Vietnam conflict was the Gulf of Tonkin incident. On August 2, 1964, the USS Maddox, an intelligence-gathering vessel, was involved in an "incident" in the Gulf of Tonkin, 30 miles off the coast of Vietnam, when it was the subject of an "unprovoked attack" from North Vietnamese gunboats. During the "battle," one North Vietnamese patrol boat was severely damaged, and the rest were chased off by U.S. air support from the carrier USS Ticonderoga. Another attack took place on August 4 on the Maddox and USS C. Turner Joy; this time, it was claimed that the North Vietnamese had fired torpedoes. Secretary of Defense Robert S. McNamara wasted no time in informing Congress of these events, telling the lawmakers that he had "unequivocal proof" of the second "unprovoked attack" on U.S. ships. Within hours of McNamara's revelations, on August 7, 1964, Congress passed support for Tonkin Gulf Resolution 88–2, with only Senators Wayne Morse (D–Oregon) and Ernest Gruening (D–Alaska) voting nay; the House voted 416 to 0 in support, and the United States was plunged into the only war it has ever lost. McNamara's account, backed by the Johnson administration, did not go unchallenged in Congress. Senator Morse dubbed the conflict "McNamara's War" and noted that U.S. vessels were "conveniently standing by" when these incidents allegedly took place. Morse prophetically closed his argument by saying, "I believe that within the next century, future generations will look with dismay and great disappointment upon a Congress which is now about to make such a historic mistake" (Ford, 1997, p. 3). Since 1964, a series of "official" revelations has made it clear that the entire Gulf of Tonkin incident was deliberately staged to provoke the North Vietnamese into an attack and then to exaggerate the nature and extent of this attack (see the summary of such revelations in Ford, 1997).

The propaganda surrounding the Gulf of Tonkin incident, precipitating the escalation of a U.S. military presence, became symbolic of the entire strategy of the propaganda effort in the Vietnam War. President Lyndon Johnson, eager to be reelected in 1964, resorted to an elaborate form of black propaganda to justify the wider use of the U.S. military. Once begun in this fashion, a significant portion of the propaganda associated with the war was deliberate distortion (the "body count" reports from U.S. military press briefings—the "five o'clock follies," as the press dubbed them) or outright lies (the total number of troops involved and exactly where they were fighting). Even after Richard Nixon succeeded Johnson as president, this policy continued, with Nixon's infamous duplicity regarding the nature and extent of U.S. military operations in the neighboring country of Cambodia. This widespread practice of black and sometimes gray propaganda by the administration took its toll in terms of public credibility and trust. As has been noted several times, this is the dilemma of propaganda in democracies: Eventually, most "secrets" become public, and the inability to "control" the competing information sources undermines the "official" propaganda efforts.

"Hearts and Minds": The Propaganda Campaign

The direct intervention of U.S. forces certainly ensured the survival of the South Vietnamese government for the short run, but it also allowed the propaganda of the communists, both from the North and from inside South Vietnam itself, to claim that once again the country was being invaded by foreigners and colonial oppressors. The long-term communist propaganda appeal to all the Vietnamese people was to "save Vietnam from American imperialism" (Chandler, 1981, pp. 7–9). This nationalistic, anticolonial appeal, combined with other military factors, eventually triumphed in the face of the far superior firepower of the combined American and South Vietnamese forces.

Official U.S. government propaganda efforts (termed *psychological operations*) began in Vietnam in 1954, during the period of transition from French rule, when anticommunist rumor campaigns were conducted in both North and South Vietnam. As the insurgency escalated, so did the propaganda efforts, and by the early 1960s, three special agencies were assisting the South Vietnamese propaganda and psychological warfare programs: the U.S. Information Service (USIS—the overseas arm of the USIA), the U.S. Department of State's Agency for International Development (USAID), and the Joint Chiefs of Staff's Military Assistance Command (MACV). Although they were supposed to coordinate their efforts, the activities of these three agencies were marked by duplication and inefficiency. To many observers, the "hearts and minds" battle being waged from South Vietnam was simply not working. As a result, on July 1, 1965, the Joint U.S. Public Affairs Office (JUSPAO) became the delegated authority for all propaganda activities. The MACV was to continue to operate as the military psychological warfare branch, but under the control of the JUSPAO. This organization was under the supervision of the USIA but operationally subordinate to the U.S. ambassador to the Republic of South Vietnam (Chandler, 1981). The JUSPAO was invited to become an active participant in the U.S. Mission Council, the ambassador's highest policymaking body. Chandler (1981) noted that "it was the first meaningful American attempt to integrate the psychological aspect of foreign policy with the political, economic, and military instruments" (p. 27).

The JUSPAO had two major propaganda objectives: The first was to undermine and eventually abolish support for the communist regime in North Vietnam; the second was to win the "hearts and minds" of the South Vietnamese and solid support for a prodemocratic and nationalistic South Vietnam. To achieve these goals, three audiences were targeted: The first were the communist soldiers (the Viet Cong) and their supporters within South Vietnam, the second were the masses and elites of North Vietnam, and the third were the noncommunists in South Vietnam.

The propaganda campaign aimed at the Viet Cong was known as *Chieu Hoi,* meaning "open arms." The basic message was "Give up the fight and return to the folds of the government of Vietnam!" Under this program, Viet Cong surrendering to the Republic of Vietnam were guaranteed protection, medication, and rehabilitation with new jobs in the south. The media used to convey these messages were mainly surrender leaflets and broadcasts from low-flying aircraft. It is estimated that, during the 7 years it operated in Vietnam, the USIA, supported by the armed forces, dropped nearly 50 billion leaflets—nearly "1,500 for every person in both parts of the country" (Chandler, 1981, p. 3). Five specific propaganda appeals were used in the *Chieu Hoi* program:

1. *The "fear of death" appeal.* The leaflets depicted dead soldiers, including decapitations and severe maimings, under headlines reading "Continue your struggle against the National Cause, and you will surely die a mournful death like this."

2. *The hardships endured by the Viet Cong.* The soldiers were reminded of their poor living conditions and their desires to be with their families.

3. *The loss of faith in a communist victory.* Combined with the fear of death, this appeal gave the numbers of communist dead and suggested that the Viet Cong were being betrayed by their leaders.

4. *The soldier's concern for his family and the hardships they faced without him.* This appeal was aimed at the central role the family played in

Vietnamese culture and was one of the most successful. Leaflets typically depicted a worried family or a father playing with his son. The captions stated, "*Chieu Hoi* means to be reunited with your loved ones. It means escape from your loneliness."

5. The last appeal was in reality a combination of all of the others and coalesced around the theme of *disillusionment with the war*. This focused on the soldier's insecurities and was supposed to make him question the decisions of the authorities. A typical leaflet read, "Your leaders have deceived you to a lonely death far from your home, your family and your ancestors."

The net effect of these campaigns is difficult to assess. Ernest and Edith Bairdain, of Human Sciences Research, conducted a special study of the *Chieu Hoi* propaganda campaign and found that in terms of numbers of defectors, the campaign was quite successful but that these were mainly lower ranking and the least ideologically motivated individuals (Chandler, 1981). Between 1963 and 1972, more than 200,000 people came over to the South Vietnamese side. Most of these were simply people who had been swept up into communist service. They included relatively fewer teachers, physicians, division commanders, and so forth. Most important, very few North Vietnamese soldiers defected because they were far from their families and believed in the justness of the communist goal of liberating the south from the American "colonialists." The northern soldiers were also very resistant to surrender proposals and other propaganda appeals and were expected to uphold their honor by fighting until they died. In an assessment made of the Vietnam propaganda efforts by the Rand Corporation in 1970, specialist Konrad Kellen noted that "neither our military actions nor our political or psywar efforts seem to have made an appreciable dent on the enemy's overall motivation and morale structure" (Chandler, 1981, p. 96).

Several other factors mitigated against a successful propaganda effort to capture the hearts and minds of the North Vietnamese; foremost among these was the decision to try to bomb the north into submission. This bombing destroyed the internal transportation systems and agriculture of the north, but sustained by heavy support from the Soviet Union and communist China, the people showed a remarkable ability to withstand these attacks and carry on the war. Chandler (1981) suggested that the bombing had a boomerang effect, resulting in a "burst of patriotism" rather than the despair it was intended to create. "The [Communist] Party adroitly fanned the fires of anger from these attacks and channeled the people's ire toward hatred of the United States and dedication to driving the 'foreign invaders' from Vietnam" (p. 147). Americans had failed to learn the lesson from the blitz on Britain and the saturation bombing of Germany during World War II—namely, that a direct, frontal attack on a society tends to strengthen the will of the people to fight back even under the most trying of circumstances. It also has the effect of increasing the capacity of the society to better prepare itself for future attacks and to adopt measures that allow it to restore vital functions and effect repairs much more quickly. The end result was that the "Hate the U.S." propaganda campaign became a very powerful motivating force for the North Vietnamese and is generally credited with helping bring about the final victory. The North Vietnamese were too dedicated to their cause to be influenced otherwise, and many of the large peasant class in the south simply wanted to be left in peace. In the final assessment, the massive propaganda efforts of the United States and the South Vietnamese proved to be ineffective in penetrating the "ideological shield" that surrounded the north's population and armed forces.

The propaganda strategies of the Vietnam War have only received systematic study in the past decade. During the conflict itself, the intense domestic politicization of the conflict mitigated against objective evaluation of what American propaganda was trying to accomplish. In her extensive analysis of "official propaganda" in the Vietnam War, Caroline Page (1996) noted that the war "required explanation and justification" and that "the presentation of a government's position in the best possible light, to both its home audience and foreign observers, is an important feature of [government] policy" (p. 1). The difficulties the U.S. government had with this "presentation" resulted in the enormous internal discontent that doomed massive public support for the military effort, as well as set off worldwide opposition.

Page (1996) broke down the presentation problem into two groups of factors—the first dealing with the problems of the war itself and the second focusing on the significant impact of new communication technologies on the mass media.

The War

- The remoteness of Vietnam from the American continent made it difficult to justify fully the "dangers" of the conflict for Americans.
- The lengthy period of the conflict made it difficult to sustain any propaganda strategies. For Page (1996), the key question was, "For how long can a democratic government keep the supportive interest of its people and allies when that nation is not directly threatened?" (p. 2).
- The type of government in South Vietnam (ever-changing military juntas lacking popular support and seen as corrupt) "contradicted all the political and human ideals that the American Administration professed to be

preserving . . . and was also seen as making a mockery of America's own allegiance to these ideals" (Page, 1996, p. 2).

- The initial secrecy surrounding the level of U.S. military involvement in South Vietnam resulted in a suspicious public who "became aware of the extent of the American commitment only when the war was escalating." Against this background, "the American Administration was caught in a trap of its own making" (Page, 1996, p. 2).

The Media

- The spread of modern-day communication networks created an "enlargement" of the administration's scope of media activity, but this also enlarged the potential number of "rival viewpoints" that had to be countered. The worldwide arena of this communications network "limited the possibilities for the successful promotion of distinctive propaganda campaigns in different parts of the world" (Page, 1996, p. 2).
- The speed of communications ensured that it would be difficult to control the nature of the "official" propaganda and, importantly, to correct mistakes once they were made (which happened often in this complex conflict).

What lessons can we learn from the propaganda efforts in the Vietnam War? Chandler (1981) pointed out interesting parallels between the Vietnam War and the American Revolutionary War, in that both conflicts saw a relatively small group of backward farmers bring a world superpower to its knees by protracted and unconventional warfare. In both cases, the odds for success were minimal, but "psychologically with both patriotism and a vision of the future, the weak prevailed over the mighty—a common denominator in both revolutions was love of country and an uncompromising desire to achieve freedom from foreign rule" (p. 256).

Of course, one of the most interesting aspects of the propaganda efforts in the Vietnam War were the intense propaganda battles waged on the American home front between those who supported the war and those who opposed it. As disenchantment with the war grew, it became the central focus around which a variety of issues—political, social, and cultural—revolved. The Vietnam War provided a focus for a younger generation seeking to break away from the materialistic values of their parents; for many young men, it also raised the issue of being drafted to fight an "immoral war"; and eventually, it brought about a major shift in American culture and left a legacy of disillusionment and suspicion of government. Soldiers returning from Vietnam found that the nation had turned its back on them, and they would have to wait until the morally uplifting victory of the Gulf War more than 20 years later before they received their just recognition.

The Gulf War, 1990 to 1991

The war in the Persian Gulf that pitted U.S.-led coalition forces against the vaunted army of Iraq under President Saddam Hussein provided an opportunity for reestablishing the United States as a major world power following the collapse of the Soviet Union. In the minds of the American people, the cause was just, for our ally, the tiny and somewhat helpless Kuwait, had been illegally invaded by the brutal forces of the dictator Hussein and subjected to atrocities. Besides, this action posed a serious threat to U.S. domestic security by threatening the flow of oil from the Middle East. The war, though of short duration, offered an interesting challenge to propaganda agencies on both sides as they battled to place their respective positions before the court of world public opinion. At the conclusion of the Gulf War in 1991, the United States and the other members of the international coalition formed to defeat the Iraqis celebrated a victory of "the new World Order."

This victory proved to be illusory, and for the next decade, there was increasing tensions between a defiant Iraq administration led by Saddam Hussein, who openly defied many UN resolutions, especially those requiring him to reveal the nature of his supposed "weapons of mass destruction." After his second defeat in 2003, and no weapons of such destructive force were found inside of Iraq, it was suggested that Saddam Hussein had succeeded in fooling the West through the use of a massive propaganda campaign to exaggerate the nature and extent of his power. If this is true, it backfired against him, because it was the stated cause for the decision to go to war to remove him for once and for all.

The Balkans Conflict: Propaganda and Ethnic Cleansing

The consequences of the collapse of the communist states in Eastern Europe continues to resonate throughout the world as new nations are formed, are contested, and undergo the laborious process of establishing viable governments. The long, tortured history of the Balkan peninsula presented perhaps the most difficult of these problems in the postcommunist world. For more than 1,000 years, this region has been beset by religious and ethnic differences, which manifest themselves in a continued struggle for control of blocs of territory and brutal extermination of whole populations. In the aftermath of World War II, this volatile region, composed of the states Bosnia-Herzegovina, Croatia, Macedonia, Montenegro, Serbia, Slovenia, and Vojvodina, was united by the personal strength and personality cult of Josip Broz Tito. Tito was able to impose arbitrary internal ethnic boundaries, and his national military and police forces kept some semblance of peace among the various competing factions, all under the titular nation of Yugoslavia.

After Tito died in 1980, the power that held Yugoslavia together as one nation began to disintegrate. The collapse of European communism provided the opportunity for these competing ethnic and religious factions to revert back to their ancient animosities. Violence erupted over the boundaries between mainly Muslim Bosnia and Eastern Orthodox Catholic Croatia and Serbia, as well as the other, smaller states. New alliances have been made and broken, large populations have been forced to migrate from one region to another, soldiers on both sides have brutally raped women and children, and the practice of "ethnic cleansing" (a ruthless combination of genocide and forced expulsion) suddenly became the focus of the international community.

In this ongoing volatile situation, the use of propaganda, in all its forms, has become a major factor. Through the control of all radio, television, and newspapers, the competing governments have blatantly propagandized to exhort their populations to violence and nationalistic fervor. In terms of the definition of propaganda used in this book, the practice of propaganda in the Balkans has been a classic example of shaping perceptions, manipulating cognitions, and directing behavior to achieve a response that furthers the desired intent of the propagandist. The end result has been a chaotic and violent civil war that has resulted in the deaths and disappearance of tens of thousands of civilians and in which the media have played an important role.

This propaganda battle itself became a major focal point in the world's press when charges were made that the press was biased against one group or another. In a major analysis of this issue in the influential publication *Foreign Policy,* Peter Brock (1993–1994) noted that, between 1991 and 1993, "readers and viewers received the most vivid reports of cruelty, tragedy, and barbarism since World War II. It was an unprecedented and unrelenting onslaught, combining modern media techniques and advocacy journalism" (p. 153). He continued,

> In the process, the [Western] media became a movement, co-belligerent no longer disguised as noncombatant and nonpartisan. News was outfitted in all its full battle dress of bold head-lines, multipage spreads of gory photographs, and gruesome video footage. The clear purpose was to force [outside] governments to intervene militarily. The effect was compelling, but was the picture complete? (p. 152)

Brock (1993–1994) then listed a series of mistakes made by the press in misidentifying scenes of combat: deliberate use on the cover of *Time* magazine of an emaciated, "tubercular" patient to underscore the treatment of prisoners in detention camps (in essence, the journalists photographed the "skinniest" person they could find); mislabeling of the ethnic origins of the dead, with Serbs being identified as Muslims and vice versa; a clear anti-Serb bias in the Western press; and blatant advocating of U.S. military intervention. As Brock pointed out,

> By late 1992, the majority of the media had become so mesmerized by their focus on Serb aggression and atrocities that many became incapable of studying or following up numerous episodes of horror and hostility against Serbs in Croatia and later in Bosnia-Herzegovina. (p. 157)

Although we may never know the "truth" behind all the charges and countercharges in this brutal conflict, there is little doubt that, in the race for headlines, the reporting of this conflict has been colored and shaped by the propaganda strategies of the various combatants.

More than 8 years after the conflict ended, "war crimes" trials are currently being held in the Hague in which some of the atrocities on both sides are being described. The Balkan conflict is by no means over, and all sides still use their media to propagandize their positions, while the international press is still experiencing difficulties in trying to give its audience an "accurate" picture of what is happening in that troubled region of the world.

The Cold War, 1945 to 1998

Once World War II was over, the world entered a new age; people no longer entertained the naive idea that global conflict could be won or lost by conventional means, for the frightening power of nuclear destruction loomed menacingly over the international scene. Even though wars of physical destruction continued, other types of wars were to be fought as the world moved beyond its imperialist-colonial period and many new nations fought for their rights in the global arena. This generated increased demands for more extensive propaganda activities, particularly as the two great world powers, Russia and the United States, sought to establish their political and cultural hegemony in the rest of the world.

In the struggle for international power, which has become a feature of modern politics, all nations have been forced to adopt new and permanent propaganda strategies as an integral part of their foreign policies. In fact, the use of international propaganda in its many forms is so ubiquitous that the foreign policy of most nations is geared toward both its generation and its refutation on a continuous basis. In an age when instantaneous communication is the norm, nations have become conscious of creating and maintaining specific images they hope to project to the rest of the world. A vast amount of time, money, and human energy is spent on such activities. The astonishing growth of new communication technologies, such as television satellites and transistor radios, has created a worldwide audience for what were previously small-scale international activities. Increasingly, world leaders are becoming astutely aware that their every action is being critically examined within this new electronic arena, and like the good actors that most politicians are, they are adjusting their postures and policies to make the most of their exposure. Since the end of World War II, there has been a tremendous increase in the growth of new forms of propaganda activities, ranging from the traditional foreign policy pronouncements to more subtle but no less effective activities such as travel bureaus, sporting events, international trade exhibitions and world expositions, achievements in space and other technologies, and cultural phenomena such as art, fashion, and music. In fact, it would not be inaccurate to say that almost every aspect of human activity can be propagandized in the international arena. The Russians claim to have the oldest people in the world, the Scandinavians the lowest infant mortality rate, and the Americans the most automobiles per capita. All of these claims are used in one form or another as propaganda.

As was discussed previously in Chapter 1, the Olympic Games, in particular, have become a major propaganda event ever since Adolf Hitler used the 1936 Berlin Games to showcase his Aryan Reich. (A fine history of the 1936 Olympics is found in Hart-Davis, 1986.) In recent years, both the United States in 1980 (Moscow) and then the Soviets in 1984 (Los Angeles) boycotted the Olympic Games as a means of propagandizing their displeasure over each other's foreign policies. The Soviets went even further, claiming that "criminal elements" would make Los Angeles unsafe for their athletes, hoping to score international propaganda points by drawing attention to the state of domestic and racial conditions in the United States. Ultimately, the Los Angeles Games not only proved to be the safest in recent years but also generated a profit for the International Olympic Committee (IOC)! At this point, the Soviets, having been proved wrong, objected that the Americans had subverted the Olympic ideals into a "capitalist sideshow"—and thus are modern propaganda battles waged.

In 1988, the Games were held in Seoul, South Korea, and became a deliberate and carefully orchestrated international showcase for the economic development of that Pacific nation. In 1992, the Olympic Games in Barcelona, Spain, proved to be a showcase for that country and for the emerging European

Union. Much was made in the world press about the "artistic and architectural aesthetics" of Barcelona and the overall "humaneness" ("noncommercialization") of the European "lifestyle."

In 1996, the Olympic Games were held in Atlanta, Georgia, and were marred by the detonation of a bomb at a park during evening festivities. The Atlanta Games, in marked contrast with those of Barcelona, were universally criticized by the international press (including the U.S. press) for being the most crassly commercialized yet. It has become obvious that the cost of hosting the Olympics is now so high that corporate sponsorship has become an economic necessity, but this comes at the risk of having to feature such products as the "official chewing gum of the Olympic Games" or "the official beer of the Olympic Games."

In 1998, the Winter Olympic Games at Nagano, Japan, were a good example of how the best propaganda efforts of the host nation can, in fact, be subverted by the control and bias of media coverage. Unexpectedly heavy snowfalls forced cancellation or postponement of several key events, leaving the American television network CBS with "gaps" in its prime time coverage. The American commentators virtually ignored the displays of the rich culture of Japan that the Olympic organizers had provided and instead focused on repeating coverage of the exploits of U.S. athletes such as the skier Picabo Street and the ice skater Tara Lipinski. Thus, this "gatekeeping" function of CBS meant that the American television audience was not given the same opportunity to learn about Japanese culture as were audiences in other parts of the world. The propagandist does not always have control of the medium used to disseminate the information. In the 2004 Games in Athens, Greece, the swimming events were the big feature for U.S. television coverage, with the focus being on whether Michael Phelps could win seven gold medals. (He subsequently won six golds and two bronze medals when he relinquished his place on a relay team so that his teammate, Ian Crocker, could earn a gold medal.) While this was a genuine newsworthy story, so intense was the focus on Phelps that much else that happened in the pool was of secondary importance. (It should be noted that, at every recent Olympic Games, a minority of the American audience has complained strongly that U.S. network coverage is too narrow and focuses too much on U.S. athletes while ignoring those from other countries.)

Despite the ethnocentric problems with press coverage, the vast international television audience possible through the use of satellites has greatly enhanced the propaganda potential for the host country, so despite the enormous costs involved, countries continue to lobby for decades, using expensive campaigns, to influence the IOC to award the Olympic Games to them. This is especially true of countries such as the new multiracial Republic of

South Africa, eager after decades of being an international pariah to show to the rest of the world that it has now become "the Rainbow Nation." Even though South Africa has serious financial problems in all sectors of its economy, the government was prepared to underwrite holding the games in Cape Town in 2004 to underscore the country's emergence as a regional power in Africa. (The Olympic Games have never been held on the African continent.) Such is the perceived propaganda power of the Olympic Games. While that campaign was defeated, South Africa did successfully bid to host the Football World Cup Tournament in 2010.

With the development of powerful communication satellites, the televising of the World Cup (soccer) now attracts a worldwide audience equal to, and often exceeding, that for the Olympic Games. Because of the team nature of this sport, the World Cup takes on an even more "nationalistic" fervor, and the winning nation is afforded a definite propaganda advantage on the world stage. The international sense of "superiority" that winning the World Cup brings may be basically irrational when examined closely, but it is real nonetheless, allowing the winner to bask in the diplomatic sun for the next 4 years. Winning countries often use such victories to underscore or initiate internal political achievements or programs.

The emergence of new communication technologies has often made it possible for those wishing to propagandize to make direct contact with their target audiences, and thus governments have much less control over the flow of information than was possible in the age of print. The consequences of this important historical shift are already noticeable as world public opinion gains influence. Evidence is increasing that the populace in less developed countries is exhibiting the "frustration of rising expectations." This is caused by a comparison of their own standards of living with those in the images of the relatively luxurious lifestyles in Western democracies, as shown daily on worldwide television networks such as CNN and FNN. This frustration often manifests itself in hostile acts and bellicose propagandizing against the capitalist nations.

The world is also witnessing the emergence of new networks of common interest that cross international boundaries, such as terrorist organizations composed of members of the Irish Republican Army, the Palestine Liberation Organization, Al Qaeda and other Middle East factions, the Italian Red Brigade, and Japanese radicals, often funded by Libya, Syria, or Iran with the oil revenues obtained largely from European countries. (It was hoped that the defeat of Iraq in the Gulf War would end this type of support, but that was not the case.) The 1995 bombing of the World Trade Center in New York, as well as the 1998 bombing attacks on U.S. embassies in Kenya and Tanzania, underscored the international scope of such activities, but this was just the forerunner for what occurred on September 11, 2001, with the destruction of the Twin Towers in New York. The acts of terror these various groups engage in are, in fact, their specific forms of propaganda for their differing causes. Capturing an American airplane or an Italian cruise ship can guarantee extensive media coverage that these groups could otherwise not afford. Clearly, in cases such as these, the terrorists often misjudge the extent of worldwide sympathy for their cause, but these propaganda acts serve an important morale-building function for the groups themselves (Wright, 1990). In the case of the destruction of the World Trade Center, the gains made by the terrorists in terms of propaganda prestige among their followers was more than offset by the level of retribution meted out by the U.S. military that essentially led to a "regime change" in both Afghanistan and Iraq.

This new development in international propaganda activities creates a problem for open societies such as the United States and Great Britain. In recent years, the issue of the rights of the free press have been questioned when these rights have run up against the necessity for the government to maintain some sort of secrecy. This is particularly true in the wake of the terrorist attack on the World Trade Center in September 2001. The U.S. Congress, after some vigorous debate, passed what was known as the "Patriot Act," which restricted certain rights related to privacy, freedom of travel, and freedom of speech, albeit in a very specific way aimed at thwarting would-be terrorists from any future attacks on the United States. This legislation caused great concern for civil libertarians who feared that abrogating such powers to the U.S. government was just a slippery slope leading to less freedom for all U.S. citizens. So far, their fears have not been realized on a major scale, but cases have arisen where application of the legislation has restricted the rights of speech or travel for individuals. The Patriot Act, while necessary for "the defense of the realm," runs very close to damaging the thin line of protection provided by the Constitution.

In 1971, the Supreme Court decided by a 6 to 3 vote that the *New York Times* had the right to publish the Pentagon Papers, even though their exposure would result in an embarrassment for the government and its Vietnam policies. In a closed society, as the Soviet Union was at that time, no such public admission of government subterfuge could have been made, the press having been under total control of the political system.

Open societies are constantly faced with negative disclosures in the press that provide ammunition for propagandistic attacks. This is one tribute that living in a free society exacts, and despite the apparent disadvantages, it seems as if public confidence is greater in open societies in which the public has some, albeit often skeptical, confidence in their news media. Although the tendency is to "kill the messenger" who brings the bad news, this is preferable to receiving managed news or no news at all. As an example, the Soviets were often reluctant to report major catastrophes such as earthquakes, airplane crashes, atomic accidents, or natural disasters such as floods or tornadoes. For reasons known only to the communist psyche, such events were seen as a weakening of their image and a possible source of negative propaganda against communism as a political and social system.

The events at the power station in Chernobyl, Ukraine, on Saturday, April 26, 1986, proved to be a turning point in this policy of official secrecy. (An excellent account of the propaganda aspects of this event is Luke, 1989.) It took more than 3 days to announce publicly what had taken place, and in the meantime, the world's press, in the absence of the official "facts" from the Soviet government, made enormous propaganda gains by reporting that more than 2,000 people were dead or dying from radiation poisoning. (The *New York Post* ran a headline, borrowed from a New Jersey Ukrainian-language weekly, that clearly had its own propaganda agenda and screamed, "MASS GRAVE:—15,000 reported buried in Nuke Disposal Site.") Not until May 4 did the Soviet government broadcast any convincing television images of the accident on the evening news program *Vremya,* and a full overview did not occur until May 14, when President Mikhail Gorbachev spoke to the nation on this same program. By the time it was officially announced that 2 people had died "promptly," that 29 others had died more slowly, and that another 300 were suffering from radiation sickness, the world's press had become skeptical and accused the Soviets of lying and being untrustworthy. This event, perhaps more than any other, forced the Soviet Union to become more forthcoming about natural and humanmade disasters within its borders. It would be almost impossible in the West to "hide" such events from the media for lengthy periods of time.

One of the most difficult issues that the U.S. military had to handle after the successful invasion of Iraq and the toppling of Saddam Hussein was that of the prisoner abuse scandal at Abu Ghraib prison. The revelation, as well as the subsequent wide dissemination of photographs of Muslim prisoners being tortured and humiliated, was a major blow to the propaganda efforts to win over the Iraqi population and seriously hampered the efforts of the forces on the ground to stabilize Iraq. Most significantly, it also provided an ideal opportunity for those propagandizing against the actions of the occupying forces. These images, now available through the Internet and featured with dramatic commentary by the Al Jazeera cable news network, have done incalculable damage to the image of the West in the minds of millions of Arabs living in the region. Many people in the United States sought to minimize the actual extent of such brutal and humiliating treatment as being the work of just a few undisciplined "loose cannons" who were not sufficiently trained for their duties as jailers. However, in the Arab world, these photographs and the evidence presented at subsequent courts martials of the individuals responsible were seen as clearly representing the values and behavior that one would expect from the West. This is a classic example where in a propaganda war, the same evidence can be used by either side to make its point.

In May 2005, *Newsweek* magazine published accounts that guards stuffed pages from the Koran into toilets to demoralize Muslim prisoners being held at the camp at the U.S. naval prison at Guantanamo Bay, Cuba, causing a major outbreak of rage in the Arab world and resulting in more than 15 deaths. Despite a later retraction of this story by the magazine, the damage was already done, and the propaganda damage done to the U.S. reputation was incalculable. The U.S. government was forced to instruct all of its embassies throughout the world to spread the word that America respects all faiths (Los Angeles Times.com, May 17, 2005). It did not matter really if the Koran desecration story was true or not; in the eyes of the Arabs, after the revelations about the Abu Ghraib abuse, such atrocities were perfectly within the frame of how the United States is perceived as being anti-Arab and anti-Muslim.

Here again, a new challenge to the control of international propaganda is presented by the emergence of the Internet. For all the reasons outlined in Chapter 2, the Internet provides a remarkably potent conduit for the dissemination of accurate information, unknowing misinformation, and deliberate disinformation. A quick perusal of the World Wide Web will turn up literally thousands of pages of material on an incredible number of topics, including many Web sites that purport to contain "secret" or "classified" government documents. The wildest rumors are swiftly circulated, enhanced, and enshrined as truth. Apparently, no topic is off-limits to the millions of "netizens" who now search and post their thoughts in cyberspace. For anyone needing fuel to fan the flames of propaganda, the Internet is proving to be an invaluable and inexhaustible supply depot.

The emergence of this international media culture places a great deal of importance on the shaping and channeling of information to gain the maximum advantage; in some ways, it has become more important to say what a nation is doing than to do it. At least we can be thankful that mass propaganda is now largely practiced through trade, travel, and exchange of culture and scientific and sporting achievements and not through warfare. Despite the "flare-ups" between nations (usually new or developing nations trying to secure their territorial or cultural rights) that occur with disappointing regularity, in the war of words that we are all subjected to, the large superpowers have, thankfully, taken to trying to "outpeace" each other.

6

How to Analyze Propaganda

A 10-step plan of propaganda analysis is identification of ideology and purpose, identification of context, identification of the propagandist, investigation of the structure of the propaganda organization, identification of the target audience, understanding of media utilization techniques, analysis of special techniques to maximize effect, analysis of audience reaction, identification and analysis of counterpropaganda, and completion of an assessment and evaluation.

Analysis of propaganda is a complex undertaking that requires historical research, examination of propaganda messages and media, sensitivity to audience responses, and critical scrutiny of the entire propaganda process. One may be tempted to examine the short-term aspects of propaganda campaigns, but a true understanding of propaganda requires analysis of the long-term effects. Propaganda includes the reinforcement of cultural myths and stereotypes that are so deeply embedded in a culture that recognizing a message as propaganda is often difficult.

As we said in Chapter 1, *propaganda* is a deliberate and systematic attempt to shape perceptions, manipulate cognitions, and direct behavior to achieve a response that furthers the desired intent of the propagandist. Its systematic nature requires longitudinal study of its progress. Because the essence of propaganda is its deliberateness of purpose, considerable investigation is required to find out what the purpose is.

We have designed a 10-step plan of analysis that incorporates the major elements of propaganda. On one hand, this schema makes it difficult to study propaganda in progress because the outcome may not be known for a long time. On the other hand, to study propaganda in progress enables the analyst to observe media utilization and audience response directly in actual settings. Long-range effects may not be known for some time in a contemporary study. Chapter 7 contains four case studies of propaganda, two ("Women and War: Work, Housing, and Child Care" and "The 1991 Gulf War: Mobilization of World Public Opinion") of which are from the past; the others are ongoing ("Smoking and Health: Corporate Propaganda Versus Public Safety" and "Premarin: A Bitter Pill to Swallow"). We believe that contemporary propaganda techniques differ from past techniques mainly in the use of new media. New technologies must be taken into account, for the forms of media and how they are used have always been significant in propaganda.

The 10 divisions for propaganda analysis are as follows:

1. The ideology and purpose of the propaganda campaign

2. The context in which the propaganda occurs

3. Identification of the propagandist

4. The structure of the propaganda organization

5. The target audience

6. Media utilization techniques

7. Special techniques to maximize effect

8. Audience reaction to various techniques

9. Counterpropaganda, if present

10. Effects and evaluation

These 10 divisions take into account the following questions: To what ends, in the context of the times, does a propaganda agent, working through an organization, reach an audience through the media while using special symbols to get a desired reaction? Furthermore, if there is opposition to the propaganda, what form does it take? Finally, how successful is the propaganda in achieving its purpose?

The Ideology and Purpose
of the Propaganda Campaign

The ideology of propaganda provides, according to Kecskemeti (1973), "the audience with a comprehensive conceptual framework for dealing with social and political reality" (pp. 849–850). In locating the ideology, the analyst looks for a set of beliefs, values, attitudes, and behaviors, as well as for ways of perceiving and thinking that are agreed on to the point that they constitute a set of norms for a society that dictate what is desirable and what should be done. Martha Cooper (1989) described *ideology* as a coherent "world view that determines how arguments will be received and interpreted. The common sense of the world view provides the basis for determining what is good, bad, right, wrong, and so forth" (p. 162). Ideology accordingly contains concepts about what the society in which it exists is actually like. It states or denies, for example, that there are classes and that certain conditions are desirable or more desirable than others. An ideology is also a form of consent to a particular kind of social order and conformity to the rules within a specific set of social, economic, and political structures. It often assigns roles to gender, racial, religious, and social groups.

The propaganda analyst looks for ideology in both verbal and visual representations that may reflect preexisting struggles and past situations, current frames of reference to value systems, and future goals and objectives. Resonance of symbols of the past encourages people to apply previously agreed-on ideas to the current and future goals of the propagandist. Cooper (1989) cited the example of the ideology of the Old South plantation myth from Civil War days being invoked as white supremacy during the civil rights movement of the 1960s. White supremacists, such as skinheads, in the present day invoke the Nazi ideology of the Aryan myth.

The purpose of propaganda may be to influence people to adopt beliefs and attitudes that correspond to those of the propagandist or to engage in certain patterns of behavior—for example, to contribute money, join groups, or demonstrate for a cause. Propaganda also has as its purpose to maintain the legitimacy of the institution or organization it represents and thereby to ensure the legitimacy of its activities. *Integration* propaganda attempts to maintain the positions and interests represented by "officials" who sponsor and sanction the propaganda messages. *Agitation* propaganda seeks to arouse people to participate in or support a cause. It attempts to arouse people from apathy by giving them feasible actions to carry out. Kecskemeti (1973, p. 849) said that agitation consists of stimulating mass action by hammering home one salient feature of the situation that is threatening, iniquitous, or outrageous.

Mainly, the purpose of propaganda is to achieve acceptance of the propagandist's ideology by the people. Nazi propagandist Joseph Goebbels said that propaganda had no fundamental method, only purpose—the conquest of the masses.

2 The Context in Which the Propaganda Occurs

Successful propaganda relates to the prevailing mood of the times; therefore, it is essential to understand the climate of the times. The propaganda analyst needs to be aware of the events that have occurred and of the interpretation of the events that the propagandists have made. What are the expected states of the world social system (e.g., war, peace, human rights, healthy people)? What is the prevailing public mood? What specific issues are identifiable? How widely are the issues felt? What constraints exist that keep these issues from being resolved? Is there a struggle over power? What parties are involved, and what is at stake? It has been said that propaganda is like a packet of seeds dropped on fertile soil; to understand how the seeds can grow and spread, analysis of the soil—that is, the times and events—is necessary.

It is also important to know and understand the historical background. What has happened to lead up to this point in time? What deeply-held beliefs and values have been important for a long time? What myths are related to the current propaganda? What is the source of these myths? A myth is not merely a fantasy or a lie but rather is a model for social action. For example, the mythology of American populism was based on a classic and good hero such as Abraham Lincoln, who rose from humble birth to self-made lawyer to the White House. This hero is a Christ-like figure because he not only rose from humble beginnings but also was martyred. The *model for social action* is that a person can rise above difficult circumstances to become a leader who can make significant differences in people's lives. A *myth* is a story in which meaning is embodied in recurrent symbols and events, but it is also an idea to which people already subscribe; therefore, it is a predisposition to act. It can be used by a propagandist as a mythical representation of an audience's experiences, feelings, and thoughts. Western movies provided a myth not only about the Old West but also of American character. The idea of the yellow ribbons displayed to support the troops in the two wars in Iraq may have come from John Ford's 1949 film *She Wore a Yellow Ribbon,* but the myth of the Western hero (John Wayne) fighting the villain was symbolized in the yellow ribbons as well.

3

Identification of the Propagandist

The source of propaganda is likely to be an institution or organization, with the propagandist as its leader or agent. Sometimes, there will be complete openness about the identity of the organization behind the propaganda; sometimes it is necessary to conceal the identity to achieve the goals set by the institution. When identity is concealed, the task of the analyst is a demanding one. It is quite difficult to detect black propaganda until after all the facts are known. In black propaganda, not only is the distortion deliberate, but the identity of the source is usually inaccurate.

Some guidelines for determining the identity of the propagandist are found in the apparent ideology, purpose, and context of the propaganda message. The analyst can then ask, Who or what has the most to gain from this? Historical perspective is also very valuable in making such a determination. The analyst can also look at the broader picture, for generally propaganda that conceals its source has a larger purpose than is readily discernible.

When the propagandist is a person, it is easier to identify that person because propagandists usually have what Doob (1966) called "verbal compulsions" (p. 274). Look for the person who speaks frequently and with authority. It is possible, however, for the person to be an agent or "front" for the actual propagandist, concealing the true identity of the leader or institution.

4 The Structure of the Propaganda Organization

whose in charge of the campaign.

Successful propaganda campaigns tend to originate from a strong, centralized, decision-making authority that produces a consistent message throughout its structure. For this reason, leadership will be strong and centralized, with a hierarchy built into the organization. The apparent leader may not be the actual leader, but the apparent leader espouses the ideology of the actual leader. The analyst can investigate how the leader got the position and try to determine how the leader inspires loyalty and support. The leader will have a certain style that enables her or him to attract, maintain, and mold the members into organizational units. The leadership style may include the mythic elements of the ideology, a charismatic personality, and/or identification with the audience.

what are their methods

Structure also includes the articulation of specific goals and the means by which to achieve them. Furthermore, in relationship with goals, there may be specific objectives and means to achieve them. Goals are usually long range and broader than objectives, which are short range and more easily met. For example, a goal could be to stop the deforestation of old-growth forests, whereas an objective could be to enlist the support of key figures in the community and government.

The selection of media used to send the propaganda message is another structural consideration. The analyst needs to look into the means of selecting the media. Often, where propaganda is distributed, the organization owns and controls its own media. Whoever owns the media exercises control over the communication of messages.

The analyst has to determine the makeup of the membership of the propaganda organization. There is a difference between being a follower and being a member of an organization. Hitler (1939) wrote in *Mein Kampf,*

> The task of propaganda is to attract followers; the task of party organization is to win members. A follower of a movement is one who declares himself in agreement with its aims; a member is one who fights for it. (pp. 474–475)

The analyst might then ask, How is entry into membership gained? Is there evidence of conversion and apparent symbols of membership? Does new membership require the adoption of new symbols, such as special clothing or uniforms, language, in-group references, and/or activities that create new identities for the membership? Do rituals provide mechanisms for conversion or transformation to new identities? Are special strategies designed to increase (or decrease) membership? What rewards or punishments are used to enhance membership in the organization?

The organization can be examined to find out whether it has an apparent culture within itself. A *culture* is a system of informal rules that spell out how people are to behave most of the time. Hall (1997) used the word *culture* "to refer to whatever is distinctive about the 'way of life' of a people, community, nation, or social group" (p. 2). Wilson (1998) said, "Culture is created by the communal mind . . . culture is reconstructed each generation collectively in the minds of individuals" (p. 127). Culture is equal to the set of social practices that incorporates and forms the shared values that arise among social groups on the basis of their historical conditions and relationships. Values are the bedrock of a culture; thus, the propaganda of an organization is based on a complex system of values in its ideology that will be instrumental in achieving and maintaining all elements of its structure. According to Hall, "Culture is concerned with the production and exchange of meanings between [and among] the members of a society or group" (p. 2). Beliefs will be talked about; slogans will be used; everyone in the organization will agree with and consistently use these meanings in many ways, for they assist in organizing and regulating social practices. A culture also has heroes and heroines who personify the culture's values. *Rituals* are the systematic and programmed day-to-day routines in the organization, or they may be anniversary rituals that take place on a grand scale—for example, the parade of athletes at the Olympics opening ceremonies or the inauguration of a president in Washington, D.C. Rituals provide visible and potent examples of what the ideology is.

The organization will also have a set of formal rules. The analyst should determine not only what the rules are but also how they are sanctioned. Is there a system of reward and punishment? How are the rules made known? Who oversees enforcement of the rules?

An organization network becomes apparent through message distribution. How is the network used to foster communication? How is information disseminated from the leader to the membership? How is information transmitted to the public? Is there evidence that the public is denied access to information that is made available only to the membership or the organization elite?

To obtain the data necessary to analyze the structure of a propaganda organization, the analyst should have access to sources that penetrate the organization. Previous investigators (Altheide & Johnson, 1980; Bogart, 1976; Conway & Siegelman, 1982) have either used assistants to feign conversion or been members of the organization at one time themselves. Often, verbal compulsions of the propagandists result in autobiographical treatment of their roles in the organization (Armstrong, 1979).

The structure of propaganda organizations also varies according to whether the communication is within the organization or directed to the public. The analyst may discern two different and separate structures—one for the hierarchy and the membership and one for the audience and potential members.

5

The Target Audience

A target audience is selected by a propagandist for its potential effectiveness. The propaganda message is aimed at the audience most likely to be useful to the propagandist if it responds favorably. Modern marketing research enhanced by new technologies enables an audience to be targeted easily. Many facets of an audience are easily determined. Mailing lists can be purchased and coordinated with audience responses to media appeals. For example, if a person responds to a television pledge drive with a contribution, her or his name is put on a mailing list for future mail appeals from the same organization or from other organizations that buy the list. Grocery stores give customers "free" discount cards that identify them at the cash register when they buy certain products. When people buy books on the Web, they get recommendations for similar books and discount coupons. Pop-up advertisements on the Web are geared toward interests reflected in other viewed Web pages.

The traditional propaganda audience is a mass audience, but that is not always the case with modern propaganda. To be sure, mass communication in some form will be used, but it may be used in conjunction with other audience forms such as small groups, interest groups, a group of the politically or culturally elite, a special segment of the population, opinion leaders, and individuals. Bogart (1995, pp. 55–56) pointed out that the U.S. Information Agency (USIA, now known as the Bureau of International Information Programs) addressed itself to those in a position to influence others—that is, to opinion leaders—rather than to the masses directly. He quoted a USIA report that stated, "We should think of our audiences as channels rather than as receptacles" and "It is more important to reach one journalist than ten housewives or five doctors." Opinion leaders are a target for American propaganda abroad. In the Middle East, for example, the masses can be reached indirectly through the culturally elite 10% of the population. In America, opinion leaders are usually professionals who are respected by the public (e.g., doctors, outstanding athletes, celebrities).

A distribution system for media may generate its own audience. A television program, film, or Web page may attract a supportive audience. Once that audience is identified, however, it, too, can be targeted for receipt of propaganda messages.

Some organizations prefer a "buckshot" approach to a mass audience. Kecskemeti (1973) claimed that a strong propagandist could work the message media in a homogeneous way with a consistent message. Some audience members accept the message more eagerly than others; some reject it.

There are many variations of audience selection, and none should be overlooked by the analyst. It is useful to examine the propagandist's approach to audience selection, noting any correlation between selection practices and success rate.

Media Utilization Techniques

At first, it may not seem difficult to determine how propaganda uses the media. The analyst examines which media are being used by the propagandist. Modern propaganda uses all the media available—press, radio, television, film, the Internet, e-mail, telephone, fax machines, direct mail, posters, meetings, door-to-door canvassing, handbills, buttons, billboards, speeches, flags, street names, monuments, coins, stamps, books, plays, comic strips, poetry, music, rituals, museum displays, sporting events, cultural events, company reports, libraries, and awards and prizes. Kepel (2004) emphasized that with the U.S. occupation of Iraq, "the war for Muslim minds entered the global jungle of the Internet. Photos of Iraqi prisoners being tortured or humiliated circulated freely along with videos of hostages being mistreated by their terrorist captors" (p. 7). Some well-established awards function as propaganda—for example, the Rhodes Scholarship, the Fulbright Scholars Program, and the Presidential Medal of Freedom. Rhodes scholars from the United States are expected to represent their country and return to the states as eventual leaders. Likewise, American Fulbright scholars are often asked to give guest lectures about issues in their own country. The ceremony for the Presidential Medal of Freedom emphasizes American patriotism and heroism.

Also, tone and sound may have a conditioning effect. In 1950, Dobrogaev, a Russian psychologist, began working with speech tones and sounds for conditioning. When the Soviets took power, they chose to broadcast ideology over loud speakers (Starr, 2004). In 1954, China also began using loud speakers that broadcast official "truths" in city squares and gathering places; this is still being done in China today. A French fable reminds us, "Man is like a rabbit; you catch him by the ears." Musical anthems and patriotic songs are forms of conditioning, for people walk around whistling these melodies and even sing their children to sleep with them. Musical slogans can become detached from the original composition, as were the four opening notes of Beethoven's Fifth Symphony during World War II, which came to signify the V for victory, the sounds of the Morse code for V, dot-dot-dot-dash.

The various messages coming from the same source via the media need to be compared to determine any consistency of apparent purpose. All output will be tied to ideology in one way or another. Describing the media usage alone is insufficient in drawing a picture of media utilization, for the analyst must examine the flow of communication from one medium to another and from media to groups and individuals. Evidence of multistep flow and diffusion of ideas should be sought. The relationship among the media themselves and the relationship between the media and the people should be explored.

The main focus should be on how the media are used. The propagandist might show a film and hand out leaflets afterward. This type of practice maximizes the potential of the media. When an audience perceives the media, what expectation is it likely to have? What is the audience asked to do to respond to the message in the media? Does it seem that the audience is asked to react without thinking? Are the media used in such a way as to conceal the true purpose, identity, or both of the propagandist?

Propaganda is associated with the control of information flow. Those who control public opinion and behavior make maximum and intelligent use of the forms of communication available to them. Certain information will be released in sequence or together with other information. This is a way of distorting information because it may set up a false association. Propaganda may appear in the medium that has a monopoly in a contained area. There may or may not be an opportunity for counterpropaganda within or on competing media. The media should have the capability to reach target audiences, or new technologies may have to be designed and constructed to do so.

The analyst should see what visual images are presented through pictures, symbols, graphics, colors, filmed and televised representations, books, pamphlets, and newspapers. Also, verbal innovations need to be examined for information, slogans, and emotional arousal techniques. The analyst should go beyond interpretation of the message to a closer scrutiny of the ways the message is presented in the media. What is the overall impression left with the audience? Essentially, how are the visual and verbal messages consistent with the ideology? The book, *Representation* (Hall, 1997), is an excellent resource for understanding the codes and systems of representation and interpreting their meanings.

Selection of the media may be related to economics, as well as to the most effective access to the audience. An audience located in a remote region without access to major media will have to be reached in appropriate ways. Sometimes, the ways that messages are distributed require acceptance of innovations on the part of the audience. It may be asked to try new technologies or to participate in novel activities.

For analysis of media utilization, every possibility should be examined. Bogart (1995) told of the faculty members in engineering and medicine at Cairo University who were so intensely sympathetic to communism that they would not come to the American library or read American material. They would, however, come to see a film about a new surgical procedure developed by an American physician or a film about an application of engineering to industry. The overt purpose of the film was to transmit valuable information, but the covert purpose was to get the faculty to observe superior information, compared with information from other sources in their professional specialties. They were not expecting propaganda, but they absorbed a good impression of American science. Eventually, they started coming to the American library.

The analyst needs to be aware of unusual and unsavory media utilization as well. In 1954, for example, China began to send opium to Thailand to promote addiction, dependency, passivity, and lethargy, thus rendering a group of people susceptible to takeover.

7

Special Techniques to Maximize Effect

We have deliberately chosen not to make a comprehensive list of propaganda techniques in the manner of the Institute for Propaganda Analysis (see Chapter 5). Propaganda is too complex to limit its techniques to a short list. Certain principles, however, can be elaborated to assist the analyst in examining techniques. Aristotle, in discussing rhetoric, advised the persuader to use "all of the available means of persuasion." Goebbels, in discussing propaganda, advised the propagandist that every means that serves the purpose of the conquest of the masses is good. Qualter (1962), in discussing the techniques of propaganda, said that the common slogan of the four basic criteria of successful propaganda should be considered: It must be seen, understood, remembered, and acted on.

We believe that propaganda must be evaluated according to its ends. Ends may be desired attitude states, but they are more likely to be desired behavior states such as donating, joining, and voting. They may also be aroused enthusiasm manifested in behavior states such as cheering and yelling.

Predispositions of the Audience: Creating Resonance

Messages have greater impact when they are in line with existing opinions, beliefs, and dispositions. Jacques Ellul (1965) said, "The propagandist builds his techniques on the basis of his knowledge of man, his tendencies, his desires, his needs, his psychic mechanisms, his conditioning" (p. 4). The propagandist uses belief to create belief by linking or reinforcing audience predispositions to reinforce propagandistic ideology or, in some cases, to create new attitudes or behaviors or both. Rather than try to change political loyalties, racial and religious attitudes, and other deeply held beliefs, the propagandist voices the propagandee's feelings about these things. Messages appear to be resonant, for they seem to be coming from within the audience rather than from without. Lawrence Weschler (1983), writing about martial law in Warsaw in 1982, quoted John Berger, the British art critic, who said, "Propaganda preserves within people outdated structures of feeling and thinking whilst forcing new experiences upon them. It transforms them into puppets—whilst most of the strain brought about by the transformation remains politically harmless as inevitably incoherent frustration" (p. 69). Some obvious techniques to look for when analyzing propaganda are links to values, beliefs, attitudes, and past behavior patterns of the target audience.

Messages that are supportive of, rather than discrepant from, commonly held views of the people are more likely to be effective. Yet, the propagandist uses canalization to direct preexisting behavior patterns and attitudes. Once a pattern has been established among a target audience, the propagandist can try to canalize it in one direction or another.

When change does take place, it does so because of a multitude of factors related to the source of the message, the impact of opinion leaders, group interaction, the context in which the message is sent and received, and media utilization.

Source Credibility

Source credibility is one contributing factor that seems to influence change. People have a tendency to look up to authority figures for knowledge and direction. Expert opinion is effective in establishing the legitimacy of change and is tied to information control. Once a source is accepted on one issue, another issue may be established as well on the basis of prior acceptance of the source.

The analyst looks for an audience's perceived image of the source. How does the audience regard the source? Are the people deferential, and do they accept the message on the basis of leadership alone? Is the propaganda agent a hero? Does the audience model its behavior after the propagandist's? How does the propagandist establish identification with the audience? Does she or he establish familiarity with the audience's locality, use local incidents, and share interests, hopes, hatreds, and so on? During the Vietnam conflict, the Viet Cong would move into a hamlet and establish rapport with the local citizenry, taking their time to become integrated into the life of the hamlet. Soon, they would enlist help from the villagers; for example, some would prepare bandages, and boys would carry messages. Seeing that they were helping the Viet Cong, the villagers would experience cognitive dissonance and have to justify their own behavior by accepting the Viet Cong's view of the world. American soldiers in Afghanistan and Iraq help communities by building schools and restoring facilities.

Opinion Leaders

Another technique is to work through those who have credibility in a community—the opinion leaders. Bogart (1995, p. 102) told how the USIA warned its agents not to offend the opinion leaders in other cultures. They were ordered to avoid taboos, curb criticism of respected leaders, and observe national pride. He said that Americans should sit down when being photographed with Asians in order not to emphasize the Asians' shorter stature. Above all, the agents were warned not to patronize opinion leaders in other cultures. The analyst should identify the opinion leaders and examine the ways the propagandist appeals to their status and influence.

Face-to-Face Contact

The analyst should look for face-to-face contact as a separate activity or following an event or the screening of a film. For example, does the propaganda institution provide local organizations or places to go for "information"? Is the environment of the place symbolically manipulated? Traditionally, propagandists have provided listening stations, "reading huts," "red corners," libraries, and cultural events. Bogart (1995) said the USIA provided cultural events that were free of political content but that had secondary effects on the people. USIA (now the Bureau of International Information Programs) libraries are used as "bait" to get people to go in and hear lectures, see films, and listen to tapes. The USIA made special efforts to create a "pretty, inviting place" with flowers and comfortable furniture. The coauthor of this book, Victoria O'Donnell, lived in Europe at one time and remembers the American centers and libraries as places to meet important American authors, read American books and magazines, drink good bourbon, and eat American food. At the time, these centers were a bit plusher and symbolized a "good life" more than native places did.

Group Norms

Group norms are both beliefs, values, and behaviors derived from membership in groups. They may be culturally derived norms or social and professional norms. Research on group behavior has shown that people will go along with the group even when the group makes a decision contrary to privately held beliefs and values (Karlins & Abelson, 1970, pp. 41–67; Pratkanis & Aronson, 2001, pp. 167–173). The propagandist exploits people's conforming tendencies, and the analyst should look for examples of this. Conforming tendencies are also used to create a "herd instinct" in crowds. The propagandist may manipulate the environment to create crowded conditions to achieve a more homogeneous effect. It is common practice to hold large meetings in halls too small to accommodate the crowd in order to create the impression of a groundswell of support.

Reward and Punishment

Another way to get people to accept an idea "publicly" is through a system of rewards and punishments. A propagandist may even use threats and physical inducements toward compliance. *Propaganda of the deed* is when a nonsymbolic act is presented for its symbolic effect on an audience. For example, public torture of a criminal has been practiced for its presumable effect on others. When the Taliban was in power in Afghanistan, women accused of adultery were stoned to death before large crowds of people. Giving "foreign aid" with more of an eye to influencing a recipient's attitudes than to building the economy of a country is an example of symbolic reward.

Monopoly of the Communication Source

Whenever a communication source is a monopoly, such as a single newspaper or television network, and the message is consistent and repetitious, people are unlikely to challenge the message. Weschler (1983) said that, in Poland prior to the victory of Solidarity, people heard the same thing over and over again. "After a while," he said, "it does get through, and they find themselves thinking. Those Solidarity extremists really were bastards. But the strange thing is that this in no way affects their hatred of the government" (p. 69).

Visual Symbols of Power

The analyst should look at the media messages to examine the visual symbolization of power. Do visual representations have an iconographic denotation of power and ubiquity? For example, when a speaker stands in front of a huge flag, an emotional association is transferred to the speaker. Sometimes, a speaker will stand in front of a huge poster of herself or himself. This symbolizes a larger-than-life feeling and creates a sense of potency. Hitler, represented as a Teutonic knight, and Mussolini, a state prince, were symbolized in pictures and posters as the new emperors of Europe. Soviet socialist realism art featured paintings of tireless laborers, courageous Red Army soldiers, diligent schoolchildren, and dedicated Communist Party activists, symbolizing Soviet political ideals. Stalin was depicted in paintings as a tall, handsome man, although he was short, bandy-legged, and had a pockmarked face and withered left arm (T. Clark, 1997, pp. 87–101).

Corporate lobbies often have marble floors; guards at the elevators; tall, live trees and plants; and a large, imposing reception desk. Executive offices are usually on the top floors where the luxurious custom-detailed doors are made of fine wood and taller than average, hallway walls are paneled, and from inside their offices, the executives have panoramic views that extend the office out into the city skyline. The desk puts 7 feet between the executive and a visitor, and walking toward the desk is akin to approaching a throne. In fact, the executive's chair is like a throne, sitting higher than the visitor's. Franklin Becker, in his book *The Successful Office* (1982), said that these and other forms of control and power in an office are meant to be intimidating. Expensive art on the walls and rare objects of art are additional visual symbols of power. Major monumental complexes, such as the Acropolis of Athens and the Forbidden City of Imperial China, created a sense of power by the planned approaches to them. The Acropolis stood at the highest point of Athens, with individual buildings forming a processional path to it. The Forbidden City in Peking created a cumulative effect as it symmetrically aligned many buildings, gateways, plazas, and terraces that led visitors to the center, creating awe and respect. Whether a complex of buildings, an office, a photograph, or a logo, a visual symbol is a key to a propagandist's desired image.

Language Usage

Verbal symbolization can also create a sense of power. The use of language associated with authority figures such as parents, teachers, heroes, and gods renders authority to that which the language describes—"the fatherland," "Mother Church," "Uncle Sam." The propaganda agent who can manipulate sacred and authority symbols but avoid detection can define a public view of the social order. Propaganda uses language that tends to deify a cause and satanize opponents. Symbolization affects receivers according to associations they make with the symbols. According to Noam Chomsky (1992), Western intervention against the Soviet Union during the Cold War was warranted by language: "Language that was used in the West was that 'the rot may spread' and the 'virus' may 'infect' others" (p. 141).

Positive terms may mask the actual intent of government bills and laws. Environmentalists decry the "Clean Air Act" that softened controls on air pollution and the "Healthy Forests Initiative" that increased timber cutting.

In wartime, the enemy is often symbolized as subhuman or animal-like to soften the killing process linguistically. Metaphors of hunting down animals or exterminating vermin were common in the rhetoric of both sides during World War II. Symbols of sex and death are also common in war.

Exaggeration is often associated with propaganda. Goebbels said that outrageous charges evoked more belief than milder statements. A great deal of exaggeration is associated with the language of advertising. Everything is the "best there is," and "satisfaction is guaranteed." During the Cold War, the Soviets called Americans "imperialists" but referred to the Soviet Union as the "camp of peace and democracy."

Innuendo is also associated with propaganda, implying an accusation without risking refutation by saying it causes people to draw conclusions. If one says, "The captain was sober today," an audience might draw the conclusion that she or he is usually drunk.

Music as Propaganda

From stirring patriotic anthems to protest songs, music and lyrics are important propaganda techniques. Whether the exhilarating melodies and words of "La Marseillaise" or a commercial jingle advertising Tums, music is effective because it combines sound and language and is repeated until it becomes familiar. "Yankee Doodle Dandy," sung in the American Revolutionary War, was an American adaptation of an English satire against themselves. Arlo Guthrie's "Alice's Restaurant," written in 1968, was both a protest against "an officious and petty village police department, as well the Viet Nam War draft" (Perris, 1985, p. 5). The national anthems played for the Gold Medal winners at the Olympic Games signify nationalist pride. The "Star Spangled Banner" is sung at the opening of baseball and football games. Music is an effective propaganda technique because it touches the emotions easily, suggests associations and past experiences, invites us to sing along, and embraces ideology in the lyrics.

Arousal of Emotions

Propaganda is also associated with emotional language and presentations. Although this is sometimes true, many agents believe that dispassionate reporting is more effective. The British Broadcasting Corporation (BBC) for years has been known for its objective and accurate reporting. Outrage was expressed when the British government invoked for the first time a little-known clause in the BBC licensing agreement that gives the government the right to take over the BBC transmitters in times of crisis. In 1982 during the Falklands invasion, a BBC-originated program came on the air in the guise of an Argentine radio program. On the program was "Ascension Alice," a sultry-voiced announcer who attempted to demoralize Argentine troops on the Falkland Islands. Alice reported that Argentine President General Leopoldo Galtieri said in a television interview that he was prepared to lose 40,000 men to defend the Falklands. She also played sentimental Latin ballads and a rock song by Queen called "Under Pressure." The Associated Press (AP) said that the BBC also broadcast "clearly fake requests from Argentine mothers for their boys at the front" ("British Enlist 'Alice,'" 1982, p. 10A). Without explaining how it received the requests, the BBC played messages such as a request from Ernesto's mother, who said, "Look after yourself son and please come home safely soon." Conservative M.P. Peter Mills said, "We have to win the propaganda war. It's just as important as firing bullets and so far not enough ammunition has been made available" ("British Enlist 'Alice,'" 1982, p. 10A).

Bogart (1995) said that emotional propaganda may be appropriate for semiliterate people, but as previously noted, the USIA tried not to offend opinion leaders. He thought reporting should not be heavy-handed. Instead of saying, "The Soviet premier was lying again today when he said ' . . . ,'" Voice of America would report, "Comment on this subject points out. . . ."

8

Audience Reaction to Various Techniques

The analyst looks for evidence of the target audience's response to propaganda. If the propaganda campaign is open and public, the journalists will offer critical reaction to it. This should not be mistaken for the target audience's attitudes in opinion polls and surveys reported in the media.

The most important thing to look for is the behavior of the target audience. This can be in the form of voting, joining organizations, making contributions, purchasing the propagandist's merchandise, forming local groups that are suborganizations for the main institution, or acting in crowds. The analyst also looks for the audience's adoption of the propagandist's language, slogans, and attire. Does the target audience take on a new symbolic identity? If so, how does it talk about the identity? Over time, does the propaganda purpose become realized and part of the social scene?

9

Counterpropaganda

Counterpropaganda is likely in a free society where media are competitive. Where the media are completely controlled, counterpropaganda can be found underground. Underground counterpropaganda may take as many media forms as the propaganda itself. Some forms of underground counterpropaganda, such as handbills and graffiti, are obvious, but other important forms of counterpropaganda are theater, literature, television, film, and poetry. Alternative ideology is presented in the form of entertainment. A. P. Foulkes (1983) presented many examples of both counterpropaganda and propaganda in various literary forms. Examples of counterpropaganda to McCarthyism in the 1950s include especially Arthur Miller's play *The Crucible*. Films such as *High Noon* were also thought to be counterpropaganda to McCarthyism.

Satellite transmission of video counterpropaganda was widely used in Czechoslovakia and Poland to resist the communist governments. Home video cameras and rented satellite dishes enabled the resistance movement to broadcast its messages widely.

NORML   Counterpropaganda may become as active as propaganda itself. The analyst should attempt to determine whether it is clear to the public that counterpropaganda exists to oppose propaganda. Very often, both propaganda and counterpropaganda exist apart from mainstream ideology and the beliefs and behaviors of the general public.

If a counterpropaganda campaign is well organized and carried out, the analyst can apply some or all of the 10 divisions of propaganda analysis to it as well.

10 Effects and Evaluation

The most important effect is whether the purpose of the propaganda has been fulfilled. If not the overall purpose, then perhaps some specific goals have been achieved. If the propaganda has failed to achieve goals, the propaganda analyst should try to account for the failure in her or his analysis.

Questions related to growth in membership should be examined as effects. The analyst must be careful about sources in making a determination of membership. Propaganda agents traditionally inflate numbers regarding membership, contributions, and other goals.

Sometimes, effects can be detected as adjustments in mainstream society. The analyst looks for the adoption of the propagandist's language and behaviors in other contexts. Legislation may be enacted to fulfill a propagandist's goal, but it may be sponsored by a more legitimate source.

Evaluation is directed to the achievement of goals but also to the means through which the goals were adopted. How did the selection of media and various message techniques seem to affect the outcome? Would a different set of choices have altered the outcome? How did the propagandist manipulate the context and the environment? Would the outcome have been inevitable had there been no propaganda? If the public-at-large changed directions, what seems to account for the swing?

If the analyst can answer the many questions contained within these 10 categories, a thorough picture and understanding of propaganda will emerge. It is not always possible, however, to find all the information one needs to make a complete analysis. Years later, a memoir or set of papers will appear to fill in missing links and sometimes alter conclusions.

7

Propaganda in Action

Four Case Studies

> The four case studies in this chapter were selected to provide examples of how propaganda has been and is being used in our society. The subjects are (a) the U.S. government's and industry's unusual efforts to promote productivity by easing the lives of women shipyard workers in Vanport, Oregon, during World War II; (b) propaganda efforts during the two U.S. invasions of Iraq; (c) the propaganda of the tobacco industry in the wake of attempts by government and private health organizations to protect the public from the dangers of smoking; and (d) an attempt by a pharmaceutical company to maintain a monopoly in its production of estrogen sold under the brand name Premarin while fending off charges of animal cruelty. Applying the 10-step analysis suggested in Chapter 6, each case study examines the propagandists, the audience, the various techniques employed, and counterpropaganda. These case studies demonstrate that propaganda can be used in a variety of ways in modern society.

In this chapter, the 10 steps of propaganda analysis are applied in various ways to what we consider to be four important examples of propaganda in our time. The case studies were chosen for the intensity of their propaganda, as well as for their relevancy in today's society. The only case study that can be said to be truly over is that of Vanport, although the issue of government support of child care for working women continues. Although the first Gulf War is over, the full effects of the propaganda efforts during that conflict are still being resolved, and the second war in Iraq continues. The antismoking campaign reached new heights as attorneys general from numerous states sued or prepared to sue the American Tobacco Company for misleading the public about the effects of cigarette smoking while tobacco legislation failed in Congress in 1998. Nine million women who purchased and used Premarin were targeted by animal rights activists and sympathizers in an extensive counterpropaganda campaign. When medical evidence connected hormone replacement therapy to heart disease, breast cancer, and other life-threatening illnesses, millions of women stopped using Premarin and other estrogen products, but the pharmaceutical company changed its advertising strategies in an attempt to get them back.

Women and War: Work, Housing, and Child Care

In 1943, the wartime housing project, Vanport City, Oregon, opened. *Vanport* was a contraction of *Van*couver, Washington, and *Port*land, Oregon, for it lay in the lowlands along the Columbia River between the two cities. Forty thousand people from all parts of the United States came there to work for the Kaiser shipyards, where the famous Liberty and Victory ships as well as tankers, troop transports, and aircraft carriers were built, and moved into specially built apartment houses paid for by the Federal Housing Authority (FHA). Public bus transportation was set up to run on a straight line from the housing, past the schools and the Kaiser Child Service Centers, to the job sites for convenience to parents and children.

The Kaiser Child Service Centers, specifically designed to assist working mothers in every possible way, had picture windows facing the shipyards so that the children could look out and "see where Mommy is working" (see Figure 7.2), and the centers were open 24 hours a day, 7 days a week, 12 months a year. Infirmaries staffed by physicians and nurses were available so that mothers could work when their children were sick. Child-sized bathtubs, elevated so that the Child Service Center staff did not have to strain their backs, were used for bathing the children before their mothers picked them up to go home at the end of the workday (see Figure 7.3). Dieticians and cooks in large professional kitchens prepared nutritious meals not only for the children to eat at the centers but also for the mothers to pick up at the end of the workday to take home, heat, and feed the whole family (see Figures 7.4 and 7.5).

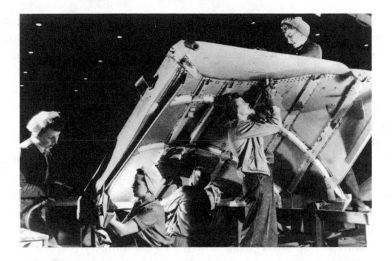

Figure 7.1   Women riveters at Vanport City, Kaiser shipyards, 1943

SOURCE: Used by permission of the Oregon Historical Society, #OrHi86502.

Figure 7.2   Vanport Child Service Center, facing the ship-launching site

SOURCE: Used by permission of the Oregon Historical Society, #OrHi78700 (cropped).

Between 1943 and 1945, more than 7,000 women worked for Kaiser in Oregon as shipfitters, machinists, painters, pipefitters, plumbers, sheet metal workers, tank scalers, draftspersons, boilermakers, blacksmiths, slab and flangepersons, electricians, welders, burners, and laborers (see Figure 7.1).

Each woman went to work knowing that her children were receiving excellent care and that she could spend quality time with them after work because she was not burdened with household chores. The schools adapted their classes to the women's work shifts; thus, children could arrive as early as 5:45 a.m. for early classes or attend afternoon classes and stay until 6:30 p.m. and participate in activities such as dancing lessons, basketball, and crafts. All meals were provided at appropriate hours. Whatever a mother's shift, the school accommodated her children.

After World War II ended, the shipyards closed, the women lost their jobs, and Vanport City, for the most part, was dismantled. A flood in 1948 destroyed what was left, so it no longer exists. Some of the many wartime communities built and supported by government and industry for the massive wartime effort had child care facilities. This case study analyzes the propaganda of the U.S. government and American industry for one of them, Vanport City. It is unusual in that the housing and child care facilities were part of the propaganda techniques.

The Context, Ideology, and Purpose of the Propaganda Campaign

December 7, 1941, when Japanese planes attacked Pearl Harbor, marked the U.S. entry into global war. This military crisis stimulated the government to take extraordinary efforts to maximize industrial production for equipping the military and its allies. At this time, prevailing attitudes about women's capabilities and proper roles fixed them as wives and mothers whose primary concerns were their families and homes. Women, for the most part, were sharply limited in their opportunities to work or to earn decent wages if they held jobs. During the Depression, women were denied the government relief and participation in recovery programs that were granted to men. Married women who worked during the Depression were viewed as taking jobs away from male breadwinners. "Women's place" was considered to be in the home, although recent studies indicate that many female wartime workers had prewar work experience (Golden, 1991).

When World War II began, at first defense employers were reluctant to hire women. The federal government's largest training program, Vocational Training for War Production, created no programs for women. As millions of men withdrew from jobs to go into military service, however, a different ideology was born of necessity, and the possibilities for women to receive government training and defense employment increased. By 1942, industry and the government began an intense courtship of women that lasted until 1944. The War Manpower Commission and the Office of War Information

Figure 7.3   Kaiser Child Service Center staff worker bathing a child in a special tub

SOURCE: Used by permission of the Oregon Historical Society, #OrHi80376.

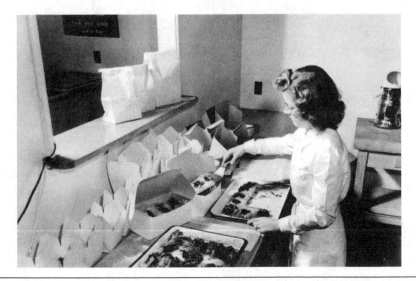

Figure 7.4   Kaiser Child Service Center employee packs meals for mothers to take home when they pick up their children, 1944

SOURCE: Used by permission of the Oregon Historical Society, #OrHi80373.

Figure 7.5   All you do is " heat and eat" the food from the Child Service
Center, 1944

SOURCE: Used by permission of the Oregon Historical Society, #OrHi86503 (cropped).

launched national media appeals to women in an effort to get them to go to
work. The ideology of government and industry was that women should
fulfill their patriotic duty and hasten victory by joining the workforce.
Margaret Hickey, chairperson of the Women's Advisory Committee to the
War Manpower Commission, coined the slogan "The day of the lady loafer
is almost over" (Renov, 1988, p. 34). Women working, however, was considered to be a temporary, emergency situation, for they were not regarded
as a permanent part of the workforce.

The propaganda purpose was to achieve maximum production of wartime materials and recruit women to the workplace; the related purpose was
to get women to perceive civilian defense work as glamorous, exciting, and

a patriotic duty. This was based on the myth that women could assume men's roles in a time of crisis, although their true mission in life was to be wives and mothers. An advertisement for vitamins depicted a soldier writing his last letter to his wife that said his life would be endangered unless civilians pitched in to do work for the war. The slogan in the ad was, "The more women at war . . . the sooner we win." The most controversial aspect of this view was created by the deeply held belief that mothers should stay at home to care for their small children. Many attempts were made to alter that belief for the duration of the war, and child care programs were hastily organized. Most were inadequate and poorly staffed (Anderson, 1981), with the exception of Vanport City and the Kaiser Child Care Service Centers.

Identification of the Propagandist and the Structure of the Propaganda Organization

The U.S. government openly conducted a propaganda campaign to alter perceptions of women in the workplace. The government as propagandist was assisted by industry, the media, and local groups; thus, there was an amazing consistency in the tone of the campaign. The Signal Corps film *The Hidden Army* depicts fictional German leaders calling American women "decadent playgirls" because they would not work like German women. American women are dramatized as resenting work because it interferes with shopping until they receive telegrams telling them of the deaths of their loved ones. Then the women are shown leaving their children in day nurseries and going to work as welders. A woman says, "This is why women know this is a women's war." Nazi leaders are then shown lamenting their underestimation of American women while a woman says, "This is the greatest woman of all," as the image of the Statue of Liberty is shown. *Glamour Girls of 1943* is an Office of War Information film that reassured women they could do the work in the factories. A woman is shown operating a lathe "as easy as a juicer in her kitchen," and another uses a drill press "as if it were a sewing machine." An African American woman is learning how to weld while the voice-over says, "This woman is taking to welding as if it were a washing machine in her own home." These metaphors sound silly today, but they were important in emphasizing women's domestic role, as well as their abilities to do wartime work. An RKO Pathé News newsreel titled *The Homefront* (1943) presents a soldier on furlough who sees children being well cared for in nurseries while their mothers work in factories. Popular movie stars were also featured in newsreels with messages, such as Loretta Young's, "It is your duty to go to work," and Helen Hayes assuring women that children are happy and learn good values in child care centers.

Katherine Hepburn told "what mothers did in the war in the battle of production."

Henry J. Kaiser had agreed to build 60 freighters for Great Britain in early 1941 and then contracted with the U.S. government to build 200 Liberty ships. He owned the Oregon Shipyard Corporation, which had three huge shipyards, and his son Edgar was the general manager. There, they built the famous Liberty ships, the first of which was launched on September 27, 1941. The production rate for these ships was so great that 76 ships had been built by September 1942. In fact, the *Joseph N. Teal* was built in a record 10 days. President Franklin D. Roosevelt attended the launching, where his daughter christened the ship before 14,000 spectators (*President Visits Vanport, Oregon,* 1943). Speedy production was necessary to supply the military with ships to fight the war; therefore, the government and the shipbuilding industry worked hand in hand. By the end of 1942, 75,000 workers were employed in the shipyards, with expectations of 100,000 within months. The workers came from all over America, creating a housing shortage of enormous proportions in Portland, Oregon. People slept in cars and tents. Movie theaters started feature films at 2:15 a.m. to accommodate the homeless. Appeals were made to retirees to move to other cities to make room for the workers.

To relieve the situation, Kaiser bought 650 acres along the Oregon side of the Columbia River to build a wartime housing project. Funds for wartime housing projects generally came from Lanham Act appropriations, which were funneled through the National Housing Authority and its subsidiary, the Federal Public Housing Administration (FPHA), but these funds were already expended. Kaiser went to the U.S. Maritime Commission (USMC) with his plan. The USMC approved it and advanced $26 million to Kaiser, who would build the project that would be supervised by the FPHA. Kaiser signed a cost-plus $2 contract to build his city. This differed from other wartime housing projects because two different government agencies were involved in addition to the Kaiser company. Kaiser was in charge of architectural planning, but the FPHA had to approve the design. A 1943 article titled "Vanport City" in *Architectural Forum* articulated his goal and called Kaiser "the 'miracle man' of World War II production and the most effective crusader for housing the United States has ever seen. But not for philanthropic reasons" (p. 53). The article quoted Michael Miller, manager of Kaiser's Vancouver shipyard:

> The way people live and the way their families are cared for is bound to be reflected in production. If members of his family are sick, the worker worries on the job or stays home to take care of them. (p. 54)

Thus, the propaganda goal to be achieved by building the facilities at Vanport City was optimum production.

The Portland architectural firm Wolff and Phillips was hired to design Vanport City, with the following design objectives: (a) to house as many people as possible with the least amount of building materials, (b) to include nursery schools and bus shelters, and (c) to facilitate women's entry into the war (Maben, 1987; "Vanport City," 1943). These design objectives were propaganda objectives as well, for the housing facilitated women's work that supported the propagandist's purpose. The city, now dubbed "Kaiserville," for 40,000 new residents, including 9,000 children, was constructed in 10 months and officially completed on September 26, 1943, although people had begun moving from their tourist cabins, trailer camps, and rented rooms into completed units 10 months earlier. In addition to 10,000 housing units, five grade schools, six nursery schools, five social halls, a post office, three fire halls, a library, a theater, stores, and a hospital were built—the largest housing project in the world.

The Housing Authority of Portland (HAP) was the last link in the structure of the propaganda organization, for it administered the project locally, although neither the city of Portland, the county of Multnomah, nor the state of Oregon was consulted on any phase of the planning (Maben, 1987). Vanport City had no municipal government, and the residents had no voice in its operation. The propaganda organization functioned as a strong partnership between government and industry.

The Target Audience

Men and women were recruited to work in the Kaiser shipyards. The first full-page advertisements appeared in the Portland *Oregonian,* exhorting people in the name of patriotism to work in the shipyards. Recruiters went to New York City to recruit 20,000 workers there and provided a 17-car train to transport them to Portland. Workers were brought in from so many states that only four states were not represented—Rhode Island, New Hampshire, Maine, and Delaware (Maben, 1987). Basically, the recruits were young, married, and had young children. Shipyard work had been strictly a male bastion, but Kaiser, a pioneer in hiring women to work in shipyards, hired them without discrimination in position or wages. Although other defense industries recruited women in door-to-door solicitation drives in Baltimore, Seattle, and Detroit (Anderson, 1981), there is no evidence that Kaiser did anything but advertise in the newspapers.

Certainly, the national media campaign to encourage women to make home front sacrifices comparable to those of men in the battle zones must have affected the women who decided to work in the shipyards. Some women workers came with their husbands who subsequently went to war; thus, the women stayed and worked in their husbands' places. Other factors were economic necessity, a desire for independence, and loneliness. Many women had to leave their children with friends and relatives to go to work in other shipyards. Those who went to Vanport City took their children with them. This and the prospect of good wages, no doubt, were major incentives.

Media Utilization Techniques

One form of media utilization is the control of information flow. Vanport City closely resembled the corporation company town of an earlier era. In cooperation with the U.S. government, HAP was the town's operator, and it imposed heavy restrictions and regulations on the occupants. Efforts to change the regulations were effectively squelched. One Vanport couple submitted an article to the *Saturday Evening Post,* complaining about the regimentation and bureaucracy. HAP got the *Post* to suspend publication of the article on the grounds that it interfered with the war effort (Maben, 1987). Another regulation required the schools to be operated on a double-shift basis, 12 months of the year. Superintendent James T. Hamilton tried from 1943 to end the double shift for the sake of the children. Not until 1945 did federal officials, with private knowledge of how well the war in the Pacific was going and that ship production would be phased out, withdraw their objections.

Special Techniques to Maximize Effect

To get the workers to give their best energies to production, Kaiser provided the workers' needs for affordable housing, on-site services, and extensive child care services. Dolores Hayden (1986), in her book about architecture, *Redesigning the American Dream,* said that Vanport City "was the most ambitious attempt ever made in the United States to shape space for employed women and their families" (p. 8). Vanport City offered a dazzling array of inducements for mothers with children to take on wartime jobs. James L. Hymes, who was in charge of the child care centers at the shipyards, which were initially suggested by First Lady Eleanor Roosevelt, said,

> In the past good nursery schools have been a luxury for the wealthy. The Kaiser Child service centers are among the first places where working people, people of average means, have been able to afford good nursery education for their children. (Hayden, 1986, p. 161)

Every woman who was a mother was interviewed by Kaiser-employed counselors to determine how she planned to care for her children while working. The majority of mothers were reluctant at first to leave their children in the child care centers and made other, less satisfactory arrangements for their care. The administrative staff of the Kaiser Child Care Service Centers conducted an intensive campaign to convince the mothers to bring their children to the centers. Every mother who worked at the shipyards received direct mail with a registration form complete with return postage. Posters about the child care centers were prominently displayed in the shipyards. Announcements about the child care centers were made over the public address systems during lunchtime. Conducted tours of the centers were held on Sundays (*Publicizing the Centers to Workers,* 1944). The Kaiser company newspaper, *Bos 'n' Whistle,* featured pictures of happy children at play and families bringing their babies and toddlers to the center ("Service Byword," 1944). Eventually, both child care centers filled to their capacity of 2,400 children ("(2400 Families," 1944). The cost for child care in the state-of-the-art centers with all amenities was 75 cents a day for the first child and 50 cents a day for each additional child. Parents and children went through initial interviews together so that each child could be given special attention and appropriate placement. The children were cared for and taught by highly qualified professionals directed by Lois Meek Stoltz, former head of the Institute of Child Development at Columbia University, and the student-teacher ratio was about 30 to 1. Every effort was made to reassure parents that their children were well cared for, and it was convenient to take the children to the center because the buses traveled on a straight line from Vanport City to the shipyards via the Child Service Center.

The child care centers offered other services to the mothers as well. Clothing that needed mending could be dropped off at no charge. Shoppers picked up groceries and other staples "to save the mother's strength," according to a Kaiser pamphlet (*Meeting Needs,* 1944).

The apartment complexes maximized the living quarters and minimized the cooking areas because hot meals could be brought home from the child care centers. Most workers purchased the meals-to-go four times a week. These mothers could spend time with their children instead of cooking and doing dishes. The design and the support activities symbolized cultural attitudes toward women's work. It was valued, and it was assisted with strong regard for the welfare of the children. The women also gained a strong identity as workers who did not have to perform major domestic chores.

Audience Reaction to Various Techniques

People came in droves to Vanport City. They complained about the restrictions related to maintenance and recreation, but the housing units were always filled, and the schools and the Kaiser Child Service Centers were huge successes. In the video *Women, War, and Work* (O'Donnell, 1994, 1998),[1] women who worked in the shipyards and their family members are interviewed. They express strong satisfaction with the living and working conditions and the Vanport schools and child care centers.

Effects and Evaluation

Occupancy of Vanport City reached its highest peak during January 1945. When layoffs began, they were severe: 3,000 were terminated in the first week. By July 1945, the population had dropped from 40,000 to 26,000. By November, the housing projects were half full. Stabilized by July 1946 at 15,000, demolition paid for by Lanham Act funds began. Twelve hundred housing units were moved to Bremerton, Washington, for the naval yard. Additional units were used for salvage. At the end, 6,396 units remained (Maben, 1987). This was consistent with the rest of the nation as war contracts were canceled, men returned from war, and women lost their jobs.

The housing project at Vanport City met working mothers' needs in a sensitive and helpful way. Never again have American working women been treated as carefully as they were when women's work was needed for a national emergency.

Between June and September 1945, one of every four women in the United States lost their jobs in the factories, the automobile and steel industries, and the shipyards. Those who remained in the labor force shifted to clerical, service, and sales positions, with reduced earnings (Hartmann, 1982). Another propaganda campaign to remind women of their "proper" roles was on the horizon.

The 1991 Gulf War: Mobilization of World Public Opinion

The fighting war in the Persian Gulf lasted for 43 days, from the first attacks by allied jets on Iraq on the evening of January 17 to the suspension of hostilities on February 28, 1991. These 43 days of dramatic modern warfare were the focus of intense analysis by military hardware and strategic experts, public opinion analysts, and media scholars. The war actually began, however, on August 2, 1990, when Iraqi troops stormed the border of Kuwait and took control of that country. In the next 5 months leading up to the start of actual combat, the world audience was subjected to a barrage of propaganda from all sides in this conflict. This case study is an analysis of the propaganda that helped shape and give definition to the events of the Gulf War. Also, although the war was a coalition of countries arrayed against the Iraqis, the emphasis here is essentially on the propaganda strategies of the U.S. forces. Other countries, such as Britain, for example, had a quite different set of sociohistorical contexts and circumstances shaping its propaganda strategies.

The Ideology and Purpose
of the Propaganda Campaign

One main objective of propaganda is to achieve acceptance of the propagandist's ideology by both its own and the other side. In the Gulf War, any analysis of the propaganda must start with an analysis of the ideological objectives of both sides. Only against this ideological background do these propaganda strategies make sense. The dominant ideology of the United States is firmly based on the idea of a participatory democratic political structure and a free enterprise capitalist economic structure. These are the ideological tenets of faith that underlie all U.S. perspectives on other countries and cultures. The key ideological term is *freedom*. Although the United States does not actively seek to impose its ideology in a militaristic sense, it tends to judge the relative merits of other countries by posing two key questions: How far do other countries deviate from the normative democratic ideology of the United States, and how "free" are their citizenry to express their views without fear of official retribution? The farther a country is from the U.S. ideal, the more likely the United States will view it as politically and culturally immature.

Thus, the dominant ideological approach that governed all propaganda aimed at the Iraqis and its allies was that the United States was dealing with an enemy that denied basic democratic rights to its own citizens, especially to those it had conquered. In the Gulf War, the United States was able to claim that the "totalitarian Iraqi dictatorship" had invaded and was attempting to destroy the "freely elected democratic" nation of Kuwait. Official U.S. sources said little about the actual lack of democracy (or women's rights) in Kuwait, although this was a key issue for those who opposed the war. In the aftermath of the victory in the desert, the failure to restore any semblance of democracy in Kuwait only serves to underscore this propaganda ploy. It was also a form of ideological propaganda for the United States to (a) appeal directly to the Iraqi people to overthrow their tyrant ruler and restore democracy and (b) emphasize that the fight was with Saddam Hussein and not the Iraqi people. A strong ideological belief in democracy always emphasizes that the people are inherently good; it is

Figure 7.6   The "Victory Arch" in Baghdad, constructed in 1989. This monument, built from the melted metal remnants of weapons from the battle between Iran and Iraq, was designed at the special request of President Saddam Hussein to commemorate the Iraqi dead. It features giant casts of Hussein's hands and forearms holding crossed swords. Higher than the Arc de Triomphe in Paris, there are two such arches at each end of the avenue. An amalgam of pop art, militarism, and religious symbology, these arches have come to symbolize Hussein's total power in Iraq.

government institutions that can go bad. Witness our newfound respect for the Russian people but continued suspicion about the motives of their armed forces and new government structures.

The Iraqis were much more direct in their ideological propaganda, developing themes that struck deep into the roots of modern history of the Middle East and that centered around the desire for pan-Arabic unity and the need to remove all Western influence from the region. Saddam Hussein's propaganda campaign had few rules, as he used every ploy he could to gain media attention. First, he claimed that Kuwait had wronged his country by deliberately stealing Iraqi oil; then, he claimed that Kuwait was historically part of Iraq; and finally, he sought a *jihad*—a holy war against the infidel because the American forces were foreign invaders who were "drinking alcohol, eating pork, and practicing prostitution" on the holy soil of Islam. These themes played quite well with a small group of Arabic countries, particularly Jordan, where the dislocated Palestinians were eager to back anyone who opposed Israel, but it failed to ignite the Arabic world as Saddam had hoped.

In the long run, although each side used its own dominant ideology as a basis for its propaganda efforts, there is little evidence so far that it has had

Figure 7.7   A cartoon by Morin in the *Miami Herald,* showing Saddam Hussein as a vicious spider holding captive the world's oil supply and the American people. Such images help to reinforce the public's image of the "enemy" as a dangerous beast, devoid of human qualities.

SOURCE: Reprinted with special permission of King Features Syndicate.

any permanent effect on the Persian Gulf region as a whole. The key victory was on the domestic fronts of the Coalition forces, with the emphasis on the belief that democracy will triumph over totalitarianism.

Even this victory, however, proved to be brief. Seven years later, Saddam Hussein was still in power and continued to defy the United Nations (UN) arms inspections teams. The embargo placed on Iraq after the war has come under widespread criticism for "denying essential medicines to Iraqi children," and the former Coalition forces are no longer unified in their opposition to Saddam Hussein. The victory in the Gulf War was the result of an unprecedented coming-together of nations and overwhelming armed might to meet a specific threat at a specific time. Once that immediate threat was negated, there was no further need to retain the military coalition and the expedient ideological coherence that was forged to meet that threat.

The Context in Which the Propaganda Occurs

Successful propaganda takes into account the prevailing mood of the times and is conducted within a very specific sociohistorical context. This part of the analysis takes into account the historical events (and its various interpretations) that led up to the propaganda campaign and includes an

Figure 7.8   In this cartoon from the *Miami Herald,* Morin captures the image
of the press as being "managed" by the military. Most polls
indicated that there was strong public approval of the tight
military control of the press in the Gulf War. This was a legacy
left over from the Vietnam War, from which it was believed that
the way the American press reported the war was responsible for
the eventual communist victory in that country.

SOURCE: Reprinted with special permission of King Features Syndicate.

analysis of the beliefs and myths that shape historical interpretations. It is
also of great importance to understand as fully as possible the various predispositions of the target audiences. Behind the Gulf War is a vast and com-
plicated history of Arabic relations with the West that overarches the entire
conflict.

A key factor in examining the sociohistorical contexts of the propaganda
for both sides is their previous experiences in warfare. The Iraqis saw their
invasion of Kuwait as an extension of the 10-year bitter war with Iran. In
this context, the propaganda image of the battle-hardened Iraqi army as
a formidable foe for the Coalition forces was deliberately developed. This
image was also used by the Coalition forces to prepare their own soldiers
and their home front publics that this was a "real" war and not another
minor incursion such as Grenada or Panama. Thus, the publics were prepared for a battle involving what was widely called "the fourth largest standing army in the world," making the eventual victory even more significant
and prestigious even if it was something of an anticlimax after all the
propaganda buildup.

In the United States, the issue of Vietnam was central to understanding the propaganda effort, especially that aimed at the home front. The scars of Vietnam are deeply etched into the American mind, and the Gulf War was clearly fought against this gestalt. In a fascinating bibliometric study (Lamay, 1991a) by the Freedom Forum of about 66,000 news stories in major newspapers, evening television news programs, and news services between August 1, 1990, and February 28, 1991, it was found that the word *Vietnam* appeared 7,299 times overall, "more than any other word or term, and nearly three times as often as the runner-up, 'human shields,'" which had 2,588 mentions (p. 41). Of course, many of these mentions of Vietnam referred to the previous military experience of the officers, but the specific term *another Vietnam* was "strikingly prevalent" and was nearly two thirds of the total. The fear of *another* Vietnam was initially a negative metaphor, but it also set the groundwork for developing a strong propaganda campaign aimed at creating a mood in the American public that those experiences would never be repeated. Largely against the background of the Vietnam experience, such propagandistic messages as "This time we'll fight to win," "Support the troops in the field even if you don't support the war," and "Let's show our gratitude by welcoming home the troops" were successful in marshaling the bulk of American public opinion to support the war.

Also, of course, the Vietnam syndrome has played a major role in the structuring of the current relationship between the U.S. military and the press. In the belief that the press was responsible for the erosion of public support for the earlier conflict, the U.S. (and British) military devised a very restrictive set of rules for war coverage. Through the use of supervised "pool" coverage, the military was able to control the information flow to fulfill its own propaganda objectives. It was hoped that, with the thoroughness of the victory in the desert, demonstrating the obvious superiority of U.S. armed forces on a world scale, the demoralization of the Vietnam syndrome would abate and be replaced with a more positive public attitude.

An important aspect of context is the actual cultural practices of a group. Experience has shown that to be successful, those who use propaganda must take into account the culture of their audience. Although much analysis of this issue remains to be done, an initial reaction is that both sides in the Gulf War, deliberately or otherwise, failed to take into account the cultural practices of the other. This was particularly true during the period leading up to the start of the actual fighting, when both sides seemed reluctant to engage in the normal tradition of quiet diplomatic negotiation. The Iraqis felt insulted at the tone of the letter that President George H. W. Bush sent to Saddam Hussein, and the Americans resented the ill treatment of prisoners and the violent rhetoric emanating from Baghdad. We also need to consider how much of this palaver was due to Bush's determination to exorcise publicly the "wimp factor" with which he had been saddled in his first 2 years as president.

The predispositions of the public on both sides appeared to incorporate the propaganda strategy that suggested a potential for improvement of their current economic, social, and even cultural situations "after the war." The propaganda on both sides promised more than it could actually deliver in terms of a solution to the region's problems, however, far more so for the Iraqis. Much work remains to be done to evaluate the prewar moods of the Iraqis and their Arabic supporters to estimate how much of the propaganda they were offered they believed. Ultimately, both the Americans and the Arabs turned out to be disappointed in the immediate aftermath. In his article in the *London Review of Books,* the noted Arab American scholar Edward Said (1991) lamented,

> It does no one in it [the Gulf War] any credit, and it will not produce any of the great results which have been predicted, however ostensibly victorious either side may prove to be, and whatever the results may prove to be for the other. It will not solve the problems of the Middle East, or those of America, now in deep recession, plagued by poverty, joblessness, and an urban, education and health crisis of gigantic proportions. (p. 7)

Said's comments, written on the eve of the fighting, have proved to be sadly true. (In the United States after 1992, a series of factors not associated with the Gulf War combined to propel the country into a period of major economic growth. In contrast, the Iraqis have suffered enormous economic hardships in the same period almost entirely as a result of having "lost the war.") Evaluating the current mood of public opinion against the prewar hopes and aspirations promises to be a rich source for the diligent propaganda analyst. As an example, the buoyant economic mood of the American public clearly "colors" the perspective of the outcome of the Gulf War and may be a major factor in accounting for the lack of concern about the nature of the propaganda effort mounted by the U.S. government. If the economy had gone into a downturn during the same period, there is little doubt that the war would have been blamed in some fashion.

Identification of the Propagandist

The source of propaganda is likely to be an institution or organization with the propagandist as its leader or agent. Sometimes, the identity of the organization behind the propaganda will be completely open; sometimes, it will be necessary to conceal the identity to achieve the goals set by the institution. Identification of the propaganda institutions is one of the most difficult tasks that await the propaganda analyst. In the Gulf War, each side had many organizations, both official and unofficial, engaged in formulating and spreading propaganda. Some of these propaganda organizations are quite obvious, such as the various offices of the U.S. armed forces, but many others working behind the scenes are, as yet, unknown. For example, many clandestine operations in the Middle East were fomenting opposition on both sides, and most of these remain secret. (Both the United States and Britain still have not revealed the full extent of their secret operations in World War II!) This is one area where much research remains to be done, and it may be many more years before most of this information is publicly revealed.

The Structure of the Propaganda Organization

The most successful propaganda campaigns tend to originate from a strong, centralized, and decision-making authority that produces consistent messages throughout its structure. An examination of the structure of the propaganda organization also includes an articulation of the specific goals of that organization and the selection of communication media used to further those objectives. This is also a very difficult category to research because it requires the analyst to have access to information that penetrates the structure of government organizations that may not be readily available.

In the Gulf War, the roles of the official propaganda agencies, such as the Voice of America or Radio Baghdad, are known, but even here the actual policies formulated for these organizations in the conflict will await further research. On the Iraqi side, the structure of the propaganda agencies remains rather sketchy, and the exact day-to-day role of Saddam Hussein remains a matter of speculation. Who, for instance, decided to put the captured airmen on display? Who allowed CNN to stay in Baghdad? (There is some indication that, in this latter instance, it was more the result of confused "non-decision" rather than a deliberate propaganda ploy.) Solving these mysteries provides a very rich area for propaganda analysis but requires perseverance and diligence on the part of the researcher.

The Target Audience

A clear vision of the target audience is an essential part of a successful propaganda campaign. The traditional propaganda audience was essentially a mass audience, with little differentiation between groups. The availability of new technologies and market segmentation research has made a greater selectivity possible. In the Gulf War, propaganda was aimed at both the mass audience and specific audiences. For example, what specific target audiences did the Coalition forces define for external propaganda in the Arabic world? Such an analysis would show how specific audiences were targeted and the comparative success rate for each group at specific points in time.

Differences in securing the credence of the various audiences, particularly as the war progressed, are clear. Initially, those who supported the Iraqi position, especially in other Arabic countries, gave strong credibility to the Iraqi propaganda about Iraq's potential military strength. Such propaganda lost its credibility, however, once the fighting itself began, and the Iraqi supporters were forced to adopt other justifications, such as, "Saddam may be losing, but he has held up under Coalition pressure far longer than anyone anticipated. This is a moral victory for the Arabs." These justifications continued long after the fighting ceased, especially after Saddam Hussein was allowed to continue in office.

The ideological environment for the Coalition audience in this particular case appeared to be much more conducive to the implementation of the ultimate propaganda objectives for, after all, the Coalition won the war. We need to examine the structure of Iraqi society in prewar Iraq, however, to see whether the prevailing environment at that time allowed the Iraqi people to take their leader's propaganda seriously. This requires an understanding of Iraqi and Arabic history, as well as of the political history of the region. As indicated above, the infrastructure of American society and culture, complete with the accepted ideological tenets of freedom in its many manifestations, clearly provided an ideal environment from which to launch a propaganda campaign against a tyrant such as Saddam Hussein.

One target audience that was not well served by the Coalition side was the large numbers of Palestinians living in various Arabic countries. From all accounts, a deliberate attempt was made to isolate and even ignore this group because of their support for Saddam Hussein. We will never know whether this represented a lost opportunity to deal with the vexing Palestinian problem by failing to offer a viable alternative to their support of the Iraqis. Postwar efforts made by the Bush administration to deal with the Palestinian issue suggest that more could have been done during the actual conflict to capture their "hearts and minds." In the years since the conclusion of the war, relations between the United States and the Palestinians have deteriorated even further, but this is largely because of American support for Israel. Nonetheless, Saddam Hussein's continued defiance of the United Nations provided a measure of propaganda value for Palestinian pride.

Media Utilization Techniques

The category "media utilization techniques" determines how propaganda uses the media available to it. This would also compare the differences or consistencies between the messages carried by various media. Propaganda is associated with the control of information flow, and this analysis would also examine the sequence of such message flow. In the Gulf War, for example, did newspapers have a different series of propaganda messages because they came later than television, for example, in the sequence of information flow? Were specific media used to carry specific propaganda messages? Was television used for emotion and print media for ideological justification? These are the types of questions the analyst would ask (for a detailed analysis of this subject see, Taylor, 1992).

Obviously, given that the conflict was fought out daily in the newspapers and on the television and radio sets of the world, this ensured that the attention of the audience was secured. Reactions of this audience to the variety of propaganda messages, however, were varied within each separate culture (reaction to the CNN broadcasts of civilian bombings in Iraq was different in Jordan than in the United States) and even within individual cultures themselves (not all Americans agreed with the administration's position).

One very obvious media technique used to maximum effect by the Coalition was the press briefing that appeared on U.S. television every afternoon. Reporters were immediately reminded of the "five o'clock follies" of the Vietnam War (see Chapter 5). This became the focal point of the flow of information for a substantial number of Americans and therefore was one of the most effective sources of propaganda. Through these briefings, the public was given a specific structure to the events leading up to the war and then to the conduct of the war itself. For example, the issue was posed in the Canadian press that the press briefings often provided deliberate disinformation to deceive Saddam Hussein about the relative strengths of the two sides, leading him to think he could win a ground war (Gwyn, 1991). Kellner (1992) described the content and propaganda value of these briefings:

Technowar measures its successes and its ability to control the situation through numbers by means of quantitative measurement. The numbers game in the Gulf War focused on the number of sorties, planes shot down, and equipment destroyed. During the last days of the war there was a daily count of remaining Iraqi tanks, artillery, and ground vehicles rather than body counts. . . . The total number of U.S. casualties was never really a part of the discourse of the war. (pp. 196–197)

Another interesting by-product of the press briefings was the public's perception that the reporters were ill-mannered at these briefings. This perception did much to coalesce public support for the military's position on the need to control the press in the combat zone. A key event was a *Saturday Night Live* sketch lampooning the press's behavior at the briefings that convinced White House officials and the president not to ease restrictions on the coverage of the war (DeParles, 1991). Of such events are great administrative decisions made!

Special Techniques to Maximize Effect

Although propaganda is too complex to limit all of its techniques to a short list, certain techniques for "maximum effectiveness" are worthy of further analysis.

Understanding the Predispositions of the Audience and Creating a "Resonance" Within the Target Audience

Clearly, both sides in the Gulf War thought they "knew" what issues would best justify their actions. In a totalitarian society such as Iraq, control of the systems of communications allowed the government to set the basic agenda, and the various reasons offered for invading Kuwait over the period of several months went largely unchallenged (or so it appears; we still do not have a complete picture of Iraqi public opinion).

The Bush administration, on analysis, appears to have had the more difficult job of selling the impending conflict to the American public, and several propaganda strategies were tried before the right combination for achieving a public resonance was found. In the first phase, right after the invasion of Kuwait, there was a great deal of confusion and uncertainty about the administration's position. Were we there to protect the sovereignty of Kuwait, or our oil interests, or the borders of Saudi Arabia? All three reasons were offered, either alone or in combination, and the majority of the American public, though supportive of ousting Saddam Hussein from Kuwait, were not exactly sure why we were sending massive numbers of troops to the area. The second phase came after the November 1 speech in which President Bush, escalating the verbal offensive, said that Saddam Hussein was more brutal than Adolf Hitler. This at least provided a context in which the public could assess the need to commit troops, and by November 6, the Pentagon released figures showing that more than 230,000 troops were deployed in Operation Desert Shield.

The third propaganda phase was the most significant. As the conflict escalated toward actual combat, the nature of the news coverage of the Gulf War changed. In a very useful study (Lamay, 1991a) conducted by the Freedom Forum, the findings from the February/March issue of the *Tyndall Report* (which analyzes network television news) were used to demonstrate the emergence of the "yellow ribbon factor." This can be traced to President Bush's strong emphasis in his State of the Union address in early January on the need to support "the boys and the girls" in the Gulf and his avuncular concern for their welfare. This speech was aimed at uniting the defeated supporters of sanctions, the proponents of a continued air war, and those who argued for a ground offensive and attracted by far the most rousing applause. Thus was born "yellow ribbonitis"—the notion of supporting the troops regardless of one's feelings about the war itself. In the 3 weeks prior to January 18, 1991, "controversy" stories dominated yellow ribbon stories on network news by 45 to 8. In the following 6 weeks, yellow ribbon stories came to the fore 36 to 19 (Lamay, 1991b). Here, we have a dramatic quantitative measure of "jumping on the bandwagon" (to use one of the ABCs of propaganda developed by the Institute for Propaganda Analysis) in order not to be left behind as the force of public opinion changed in favor of supporting the troops and going to war. The key questions here are, What issues could the peace movement have used to create its own bandwagon? What predispositions of the American public made support for the war so overwhelming? What other propaganda techniques did the Bush administration use to bring about successfully this strong coalition of public opinion? Finally, one tantalizing question that still needs much examination is why the "success" of the Bush administration's Gulf War propaganda failed to carry over into the 1992 presidential campaign.

Using Metaphor and Imagery

Another important method in maximizing propaganda effectiveness is the selected use of the metaphors and images created to enlist public support for the propagandist's position and to explain events that can shape and manipulate public perceptions. Metaphor is extremely significant in our lives, for as Lakoff and Johnson (1980) pointed out, "We claim that most of our normal conceptual system is metaphorically structured; that is, most concepts are partially understood in terms of other concepts" (p. 56). Thus, the use of specific words and images has a direct bearing on how certain events are structured in the minds of the public. Key images and concepts are evoked by a careful combination of previous experiences with new events. For such metaphorical propaganda to be effective, these images must be readily recognizable to the audience being propagandized.

In the initial phases of the conflict, even before Iraq occupied Kuwait, the Iraqis had massed thousands of troops on the Kuwaiti border while negotiations over the "oil rights" issue were under way. (The misinterpretation of this Iraqi propaganda ploy by the U.S. Department of State has been the cause of much concern about the accuracy of U.S. intelligence gathering.) For reasons that are still unclear, the Kuwaitis did not appear to take this propaganda threat seriously. When the official U.S. response to this specific action seemed to be a vague desire for neutrality in the issue, the Iraqis turned the psychological propaganda threat into the reality of invasion. The question remains, What made Saddam Hussein think that what had clearly started out as a psychological warfare ploy could be implemented with relative impunity? Did the U.S. government and the Kuwaitis misinterpret this as yet another form of posturing, which is so common in the Arabic world (Patai, 1983)? Once the invasion of Kuwait had been accomplished, a similar threat was immediately posed to the Saudi Arabian borders, but this time President Bush, setting the stage for his own psychological propaganda, made it very clear that "the integrity of Saudi Arabia" was vital to U.S. interests. On August 8, President Bush told the nation and the Iraqis that "a line has been drawn in the sand"—a metaphor (and a pun, considering the geographic location of the conflict) that has a very precise symbolic meaning for the American public. Derived from countless uses in popular culture, this "don't step over the boundary" image crystallized the logistics of the conflict for the American public and the rest of the world and provided a clear signal to the Iraqis that there was a specific point beyond which the United States would engage in military action. The message was obviously very clear, for after this statement was made, no further Iraqi expansionist military actions were made.

Once the occupation of Kuwait began, a constant stream of psychological propaganda was aimed at setting up the specific metaphors by which the conflict would be structured for the world audience. (In this particular instance, because of the role of CNN and other international television networks, we can consider that the audience for the theater of war was worldwide.) On August 20, President Bush set aside all diplomatic euphemisms and declared that the 3,000 Americans remaining in Kuwait were, in fact, hostages. The word *hostages* conjured up immediate images of the demoralizing impotency experienced during the Iran hostage crisis of a decade earlier, an experience the American public was in no mood to repeat. In the interim, the word had also become synonymous with *terrorism,* and this added to the willingness (even eagerness) of the majority of Americans to accomplish finally something that had frustrated them since Iran—namely, to engage terrorists directly in combat. The positioning of the Iraqis as terrorists was a significant factor in coalescing opposition to their actions and tended to obscure whatever legitimate reasons there might have been for their original disagreement with Kuwait. In addition, the comparison of Saddam Hussein to Hitler was a clear image that had strong public resonance. The ill-advised display of the captured American and Coalition flyers on television for all the world to see simply reinforced the image of the Iraqis as terrorists. The American peace movement, particularly after the appearance of the prisoners, was never able to counter these powerful propaganda images with strong peace metaphors.

The Iraqis had their own metaphors. Saddam Hussein at various times referred to George Bush as "Criminal Bush," "Oppressor Bush," "Satan," "Criminal Tyrant," "Loathsome Criminal," "Evil Butcher," and "America's Satan." He also called Saudi Arabia's King Fahd the "Midget Agent," "Traitor Fahd," "Agent Fahd," "Enemy of God," "Ally of the Forces of Evil and Shame," and, worst of all, "Jewish" (Pletka, 1991, p. 12). Flowery rhetoric is part of the Arabic culture, and when Saddam used phrases such as "Americans will swim in their own blood," it meant simply, "We're going to kick ass" (something that George Bush, using his Texas persona, had no difficulty in clearly articulating), but the imagery had more specific and literal connotations to an American audience: It fed directly into the long-established popular cultural imagery of bloodthirsty, barbaric Arabs committing atrocities.

Limitations of space preclude an extensive analysis of every potential technique for maximizing the effectiveness of propaganda campaigns, and the reader is referred to Chapter 6 for other useful techniques.

Audience Reaction to Various Techniques

The analyst looks for evidence of the target audience's response to propaganda. If the propaganda campaign is open, then very often it will be discussed by journalists and other commentators. This should not be mistaken for audience reaction, which can be better gauged in shifts in public opinion polls and surveys, as well as overt behavior such as parades or even taking up arms. The analyst looks for the audience's adoption of the propagandist's language and slogans. Does the audience take on a new ideological identity? Over time, does the propaganda objective become realized and an integral part of the sociocultural scene?

In the case of the Gulf War, opinion polls were taken literally daily on the public's attitude to every phase of the conflict. The administration and the

Pentagon were able to use these and their own polls to alter propaganda appeals and strategies to counter any trend thought to be harmful to their goals. Future Gulf War propaganda analysts will have the advantage of this having been the most polled war in history. The initial reaction is that the administration's propaganda strategies were enormously successful in gaining the majority of public support; the key mystery is how carefully these strategies were planned ahead of time and who did the planning.

Counterpropaganda

In the Gulf War, various organizations intent on more peaceful solutions to the crisis made serious attempts to counter the propaganda efforts of the U.S. government on the home front. As indicated earlier, these antiwar efforts were dealt a serious blow by the inexplicable actions of the Iraqis—in particular, the parading of "hostages" and then the captured flyers on international television. The nature and extent of the counterpropaganda that developed in Iraq is still not clear at this time.

Effects and Evaluation

The most important effect is whether the objectives of the propaganda campaign have been met. If not all the objectives, then which of the specific goals have been achieved? A wide variety of measures possible are available for assessing the effectiveness of a propaganda campaign, as diverse as detailed surveys of public opinion, the success of legislative action, the increase in contributions, and the growth in the membership of specific organizations. Even if the campaign failed, an evaluation should be able to indicate the reasons for such failure. Also, not all effects of propaganda can be seen immediately; some effects are deliberately designed to have a delayed or long-term influence. In the Gulf War, the short-term propaganda campaigns on the U.S. home front and internationally were quite effective, but translation of the battle victory into realizing peace in the Middle East, solving the Saddam Hussein problem, and dealing with U.S. domestic issues has not been as successful. Of course, the most difficult evaluation is the long-term impact on relationships with all Arabic nations. What new mythologies and images of the West has the war fostered in the minds of Arabs?

By January 1992, some of the propaganda strategies used by the Kuwaiti government to sway American public opinion to their cause were beginning to be revealed. One story in particular, which had caught the imagination of the American public and politicians during the conflict, was revealed to have been a major propaganda ploy. On October 10, 1990, a 15-year-old Kuwaiti girl named "Nayirah" had shocked the Congressional Human Rights Caucus when she tearfully asserted that she had watched as Iraqi soldiers took 15 babies from their incubators in Al-Adan Hospital in Kuwait City and "left the babies on the cold floor to die." Nayirah's true identity was kept a secret to protect her family from reprisals in occupied Kuwait. On January 6, 1992, John R. MacArthur revealed in the *New York Times* that Nayirah was, in fact, the daughter of the Kuwaiti ambassador to the United States, Suad Nasir al-Sabah, a member of the Kuwaiti ruling family. Once the Gulf War ended, all attempts to verify the story by independent groups such as Amnesty International and Middle East Watch failed to turn up any evidence that this incident had actually taken place. A subsequent investigation by Kroll Associates, a U.S. company hired by the Kuwaiti government, found that Nayirah's testimony was based on a single, isolated incident and that, overall, about 6 infants were removed from incubators during the entire occupation (Manheim, 1994, p. 140). No other independent confirmation of this story has been made.

MacArthur (1992b) and later Manheim (1994) also revealed the significant role played by the major public relations firm of Hill and Knowlton in its work for the Citizens for a Free Kuwait organization. Ostensibly a group of concerned private citizens, in reality, Citizens for a Free Kuwait received more than 95% of its funding directly from the Kuwaiti government and lobbied Congress for military intervention, as well as played a major role in swaying American public opinion in favor of such intervention. Hill and Knowlton received more than $6 million for its efforts, which included writing speeches for Kuwaitis and coaching them on their appearances before the media and public. Of special interest was its use of focus group techniques to pinpoint those issues that would have the most resonance for the American public. As Manheim noted, the company also conducted

> daily tracking surveys from early September to late October, then with biweekly surveys until mid-December, when polling ceased as it became clear that the objective of the overall campaign—moving the U.S. to act decisively in Kuwait—was about to be achieved. (p. 141)

These focus groups and tracking surveys conducted by the Werthlin Group, at a cost of $2.6 million, revealed that atrocity stories were very likely to sway public opinion in favor of going to war. MacArthur (1992b) claimed that the "dead babies" story was a defining moment in the propaganda campaign to prepare the American public for the need to go to war. President Bush used the dead babies story more than 10 times in the 40 days following Nayirah's testimony, and in the Senate debate on whether to approve military action, seven senators specifically focused on the story. The final margin of victory in favor of military intervention was five votes.

Despite the obvious manipulation of the emotions of the American public, revelation of the propaganda aspects of the dead babies on both ABC (*20/20*) and CBS (*60 Minutes*), as well as in MacArthur's (1992a) *New York Times* article, failed to elicit a major public outcry. Although this incident is reminiscent of George Creel's (1920) revelations in his book *How We Advertised America: The First Telling of the Amazing Story of the Committee on Public Information, 1917–1919* after World War I, the American public, mired in an economic depression at the time, clearly did not care that they had once again been duped by skillful, professional manipulators.

The pivotal role played by Hill and Knowlton in the creation and dissemination of the dead babies story and the manipulation of American public opinion is of particular concern to the propaganda analyst. Most of the firm's efforts were focused on providing "media training" for its Kuwaiti clients. For instance, the Kuwaitis usually wore Western business attire, but they were instructed to change into Arabic dress when they appeared on television (Manheim, 1994, pp. 141–142). It is also a strange twist of fate that, in the aftermath of the war, the public relations company suffered a downturn in business fortunes, losing major clients and ultimately downsizing its Washington operations. How much of this was a result of the revelations of its efforts on behalf of the Kuwaitis is a matter of considerable speculation (Lee, 1992).

Perhaps the most surprising aspect of the domestic propaganda efforts by the U.S. government was the public's reaction in the years following the Gulf War. Despite the documented revelations by MacArthur (1992b) and others about the way the entire war was "orchestrated" for domestic consumption, the vast majority of Americans were extremely "apathetic" to such propaganda manipulations. It was left to scholars and dedicated members of various "peace movements" to continue to research and present evidence of the extent of the propaganda surrounding the lead-up to, and participation in, the Gulf War. The silence from the general public seemed to indicate a tacit acceptance of the fact that, "in times of crisis, all governments engage in such activities, so why should we expect anything different?" The public indifference to these revelations is an indication of the pervasiveness of propaganda in our society and the widespread acceptance of such activities as "business as usual."

The Gulf War was important politically and militarily, but it was also a major event in the history of propaganda because of the wide-scale application of new communication technologies in the battle for the hearts and minds of the public. Many years will be spent studying this issue before we will have anything approaching an accurate assessment of the role and effectiveness of the various propaganda activities of this conflict.

The Aftermath (2005):
The Invasion of Afghanistan and Iraq

The events of September 11, 2001, shattered forever any potential American illusions that this country was safe from a terrorist attack. But the loss of American innocence was not all that took place, for the geopolitical circumstances that appeared to precipitate the event provided a catalyst for completing the destruction of Saddam Hussein that had not been completed at the end of the Gulf War. It is far too early to fully understand all of the ramifications that led the United States into the Iraqi conflict; we can understand the invasion of Afghanistan and the removal of the Taliban government with greater clarity for, after all, they harbored Osama bin Laden, who had masterminded the attack on the Twin Towers. One can argue, as many have, about the strategy employed in the invasion and pacification of Afghanistan, but the motivations for revenge and to ensure future safety from terrorist attacks are clear. The decision to invade Iraq however, has become a hornet's nest of complexities, ranging from the psychological need for the president to complete the job that his father did not accomplish a decade earlier, to America's insatiable need for oil, to a genuine desire to make the world safe from a "madman possessing weapons of mass destruction." Where lies the truth? It will take many years and the release of millions of documents before we will ever know why this event took place, but what we do know is that the use of propaganda played a key role in bringing it about.

The Iraqi war presented the United States with a different sort of military problem—a preemptive war, one waged in response to a prediction of a forthcoming attack against the United States or its allies. As such, to gain public support, the government had to present the public with a sufficient reason for this presumptive action. To do this, the government had to convince the public to accept the validity of intelligence reports to which it had no direct access. It was incumbent upon the government to present the intelligence findings honestly and without bias if it hoped to retain the confidence of the public throughout the entire action. If a government chooses to present the facts dishonestly, it prevents the public from making an informed choice about one of the most important decision made in a democracy—whether or not to go to war.

From the very beginning of the decision to strike back at the terrorists after September 11, 2001, the government began informing the American public that Saddam Hussein was somehow implicated in this event, and as such, he had to be removed. He was directly linked to the Al Qaeda terrorist network, and it was claimed that he either had or was in the process of constructing nuclear weapons. He was posed as a direct threat to the American homeland and to his neighboring countries. Later evidence from members of the intelligence community, as well as direct inspections of facilities in Iraq, revealed that there was no clear association between Saddam Hussein and Al Qaeda and that he did not have "weapons of mass destruction." Was the American public deliberately propagandized into agreeing to support the government's preemptive invasion of Iraq? Did the president consciously lie to achieve his goal of the destruction of Saddam Hussein? Was the American public seduced into supporting an expensive and deadly conflict because of the long-term fuel needs of this country? These and hundreds of other equally salient questions have yet to be fully answered, but all of the evidence has yet to be collected before the jury of public opinion can make its final decisions.

What we do know is that public support for the rebuilding Iraq has been seriously eroded since the invasion. On May 4, 2005, *USA Today* reported,

> Support for the decision to go to war in Iraq has fallen to its lowest level since the campaign began in March 2003, according to a USA TODAY/CNN/ Gallup Poll released Tuesday.
>
> The findings, made public on the same day that Iraq's first democratically elected government in 50 years was sworn in, show that 41% say the war was worth it; 57% say it wasn't.
>
> "The patience of the American public is beginning to get worn down a little bit by how long this is taking," said Charles Pena, a military affairs analyst at the Cato Institute, a think tank in Washington. "While we have made progress . . . I think people are just tired of this and want it to be over."
>
> The poll conducted Friday through Sunday asked 514 adults the question. The margin of error was +/–5 percentage points.
>
> Public support peaked as Saddam Hussein's regime fell in 2003 when 76% of those polled said the war was worth it.
>
> The latest poll shows a drop in positive feelings sparked by Iraqi elections in January. In a similar poll taken Feb. 7–10, 48% said the war had been worth waging, while 50% said it had not been. Violence declined in the weeks after the election, but insurgents launched a wave of suicide bombings and attacks in recent weeks, raising concerns that violence will continue. (p. A1)

It has become clear that the public has begun to question the rationale that they were given for going to war with Iraq, as well as the potential for an outcome that will ultimately be satisfactory. The enormous cost of the war, with no clear end in sight, is becoming a drain on the economy, and disillusionment with the entire affair is rampant. At some point, the full story of the government's propaganda campaign, devised to gain public support, will be made clear, but until that time, we can only restate what has been pointed out in previous chapters—that in a democracy, a government should not lie to those who have elected it, and in the long run, it does so at its own peril.

Smoking and Health: Corporate Propaganda Versus Public Safety

Sometimes it takes a long time to solve a problem, and often no real progress seems to be made in arriving at a solution. Those who fought the tobacco industry and to make the public aware of the enormous health dangers associated with the consumption of tobacco products endured many years of frustration. The tobacco industry and the many other parties who profited from the sale of tobacco fought one of the longest, costliest propaganda battles in the history of the United States, aimed at fending off any attempts to establish a causal link between tobacco consumption and a myriad of health problems—most notably, lung cancer. The industry rightly feared that if causal links were firmly established, then the industry would be vulnerable to lawsuits for enormous sums of money.

This case study examines specific issues surrounding the campaign to remove cigarette advertising from the broadcast media and the long-running efforts to make the tobacco industry face up to the dangers of smoking. It shows that very often, propaganda from one side is so powerful and well organized that it simply overwhelms the opposing forces. For many years, the tobacco lobby was so powerful in the United States that it appeared virtually untouchable in the halls of Congress; yet, inroads were made, albeit small ones. In the early 1990s, a dramatic combination of events suddenly forced the tobacco industry on the defensive and to begin to negotiate an unprecedented series of costly settlements with national and state health authorities.

Most cities now have legislation that establishes no-smoking areas in both public and work places; many companies, such as Pacific Northwest Bell, have banned smoking from their office buildings; universities have begun to declare themselves "smoke-free environments"; and all over the United States, restaurants are creating smoke-free areas. This case study demonstrates that, over time, constant pressure, often originating with just a small group of individuals and aided by the right combination of economic, political, and social climate, can effect changes even in the face of a massive propaganda structure. This is an examination of how a combination of personal fortitude; legislative, legal, and political maneuvering; and some luck has brought about change. As this case study is being written, the battle among the tobacco industry, a multitude of government health agencies, and states' attorneys general continues. Although the outcome of this battle (massive financial settlements by the industry) is now more predictable than just 10 years ago, the exact nature and extent of this settlement are still being hotly negotiated and debated.

The Ideology and Purpose
of the Propaganda Campaign

Tobacco has been the subject of controversy ever since it was introduced into Europe after Christopher Columbus's visit to the Americas. Columbus had reported that North American natives used its dry leaves for inducing pleasure. The first widely reported medical condemnation of tobacco occurred in 1665, when the great diarist Samuel Pepys witnessed a Royal Society experiment in which a cat "quickly expired" after being fed "a drop of distilled oil of tobacco" (Glantz, 1996, p. 1). Not until the late 1940s, however, did modern scientific experimentation begin to turn up consistent evidence of the harmful nature of tobacco, and the link between smoking and lung cancer began to be accumulated. This resulted in the first U.S. surgeon general's report on smoking and health, in 1964, which contained the conclusion that smoking causes lung cancer. At this point, the tobacco industry began an all-out assault on the increasing body of scientific evidence that threatened its existence. For more than 30 years, the industry mounted massive public relations campaigns backed by costly legal and political strategies to fend off attempts to restrict the sale of tobacco. For most of this time, these strategies were successful in protecting the industry's enormous profits despite the overwhelming scientific and medical evidence that consumption of tobacco products disabled or killed hundreds of thousands of smokers and even nonsmokers every year.

Underscoring this battle are the provisions of the Constitution of the United States. Essentially, as long as tobacco is a consumer product that is legally and openly available on the market (admittedly with certain limitations regarding age), it is protected under a variety of legal guarantees. Thus, because tobacco is not a "banned" substance like marijuana or cocaine, it can openly be sold and advertised (again with certain "negotiated" restrictions). The tobacco industry has constantly resorted to a "First Amendment" defense of its right to continue to sell and advertise its products. Legislators have an obvious reluctance to ban all tobacco products; the dominant economic impact of the industry in the so-called tobacco states, the intensive lobbying efforts at all levels of government, and the enormous contribution that tobacco taxes make to city, state, and national treasuries mitigate against this drastic action. Also, previous attempts to ban outright such "addictive" leisure-inducing products as alcohol in the Prohibition Era (1919–1932) resulted in an extremely damaging flaunting of the law and a flourishing black market in the product. (Many historians have suggested that Prohibition was largely responsible for the rise and solidification of organized crime in the United States.) The campaign to remove tobacco advertising from television and subsequent tobacco health settlements must be evaluated against the background of this complex interplay of the ideology of capitalism and the First Amendment–versus–government intervention for purposes of public protection.

The Context in Which the Propaganda Occurs

This case study concentrates on the period leading up to, and the aftermath of, the attempts to ban cigarette advertising on television and radio. Prior to this development, cigarette and other tobacco product companies had been major sponsors of commercial broadcasting since the early days of radio in the 1920s, and public "brand identification" for such products as Camel, Lucky Strike, and Marlboro was exceptionally high. Smoking was as everyday an activity as drinking a cup of coffee and was widely practiced and accepted in society.

On January 1, 1971, all cigarette advertising disappeared from American radio and television. No longer was the Marlboro Man able to light up and show off his tattoo at the same time, the "cool" world of mentholated cigarettes with smoking couples always carefully depicted in a green pastoral setting ceased to exist, and the recently introduced line of "women's cigarettes"—Virginia Slims—could no longer entertain us with humorous vignettes depicting what happened to women who were caught smoking in the period before the 1930s. In the words of the Virginia Slims slogan, the fight against tobacco advertising on broadcasting had "come a long way, baby!" But to reach this point required a series of actions and reactions involving a complex mixture of groups and individuals, both inside and outside Congress, and the development of propaganda campaigns with literally billions of dollars at stake.

The Broadcasting Ban

The emergence of first radio advertising and then television advertising proved to be of immense significance to the growth of the cigarette industry.

The use of broadcast advertising was a major propaganda weapon in promoting smoking as an acceptable social behavior. Of course, other mass media, most notably the movies, which often depicted cigarette smoking as a glamorous and romantic activity, and magazines, with their colorful full-page advertisements, must also accept major responsibility here. Cigarette brands were widely associated in the public's mind with the sponsorship of many popular radio and then television shows. Brands such as Lucky Strike, Camel, Philip Morris, and Chesterfield became symbols of entertainment as much as commerce during the era of the large radio networks. The emergence of television as a major advertising force in the 1950s brought into prominence such brands as Kent, with its "micronite filter" (later shown to have contained asbestos), and Winston, which "tastes good like a cigarette should," or the Old Gold woman dancing away inside her cigarette box, with only her arms and legs visible. Of all these new television-promoted brands, Marlboro, featuring the clean outdoors and the weathered features of the Marlboro Man in his cowboy hat and tattoo, was most memorable even though the actor involved later contracted lung cancer from cigarette smoking.

Television was used to promote filter cigarettes, with broad hints or often specific claims that these were "healthier" than the unfiltered variety. In the late 1940s, filter cigarettes accounted for 1.5% of the total market; by 1968, this had increased to nearly 75%. During this same period, the number of different brands grew from a half dozen to more than 30, in all shapes and sizes. In the latter part of the 1960s, the heavy promotion given to new brands of longer, 100-millimeter cigarettes was particularly upsetting to those who were beginning to demand government regulation. In 1967, 3 years after the U.S. surgeon general's report linking cigarette smoking to lung cancer and other medical problems, tobacco manufacturers were spending about $217 million on television. In that same year, the U.S. Public Health Service issued a report containing the finding that "cigarette smokers have substantially higher rates of death and disability than their non-smoking counterparts in the population" (Whiteside, 1970, p. 43).

Although the forces opposed to smoking lacked the structural organization to match the industry's propaganda, they were not without friends in the federal bureaucracy, as well as in Congress. After a complex series of legislative steps fought every step of the way by the tobacco industry, the Federal Trade Commission (FTC) finally managed to get President Lyndon Johnson's signature on a bill on July 27, 1965, requiring a health warning on cigarette packages. This bill also prevented the FTC from any further action against the tobacco industry for 4 years. The industry wanted a permanent ban, but nevertheless this action was seen more as a victory for the propaganda efforts of the Tobacco Institute than a positive health measure. The label was not seen as a serious threat to tobacco sales, whereas removing the FTC from the issue was seen as a major blow for the antismoking group. After examining this battle, one lobbyist for the antismoking side characterized the contest between the tobacco industry and the health people as being similar to a match between the Green Bay Packers and a high school football team. The rather unexpected fight to remove cigarette advertising from the broadcast media must be viewed against this background.

The FCC and John Banzhaf III

A young New York lawyer, John Banzhaf III, was concerned about the tactics being used to advertise cigarettes, particularly "about the use of the public airwaves to seduce young people into taking up smoking without any attempt to tell the other side of the story on television and radio" (Whiteside, 1970, p. 46). He wrote a letter to WCBS-TV in New York, asking that free airtime be made available to present the health hazard side of the cigarette story. This request was denied, as Banzhaf had expected, so his next step was to file a petition with the Federal Communications Commission (FCC), pointing out that the U.S. surgeon general's report and other scientific findings had shown a relationship between smoking and health, and furthermore, that because this was a controversial issue of public importance, it was therefore proper for the FCC to order radio and television stations to provide reply time under the Fairness Doctrine. This petition was presented early in January 1967, and on Friday, June 2, of that year, the FCC—to everyone's surprise—ruled that its Fairness Doctrine did indeed apply to cigarette advertising on radio and television. The commission dismissed Banzhaf's appeal for "equal time," offering instead a ratio of one antismoking message to three cigarette commercials. Everyone from the tobacco interests to Congress was caught off guard, but it was clear that the ruling would be appealed.

Once he had achieved this major victory, Banzhaf expected that he could bow out and that major private health organizations, such as the American Cancer Society, the National Tuberculosis Association, and the American Heart Association—all known propagandists against smoking—would step in and take over. He quickly discovered, however, that these groups had serious misgivings about alienating the broadcasters, on whom they relied for free airtime for their own causes and especially for fund-raising activities. The health group support for the FCC decision was quiet, unassertive, and almost nonexistent during the period when the tobacco industry and the broadcasters appealed the FCC's ruling. Even Senator Robert Kennedy tried to intervene with the health groups on behalf of Banzhaf, but without success. To their credit, the health agencies thought the burden of the defense of the original decision lay with the FCC's own legal staff, and eventually they were proved correct. On November 21, 1968, the U.S. Court of Appeals held that the FCC could use its Fairness Doctrine to require free airtime for antismoking commercials because this decision was "a public-health measure addressed to a unique danger authorized by official and congressional action."

The result was that a series of antismoking commercials began to appear on radio and television, and this constituted the first major media propaganda campaign against tobacco interests. Tobacco companies even tried to obtain "right of reply" to the antismoking commercials but were turned down by the courts. The real importance of getting these antismoking commercials on the air was only realized later, when, in February 1969, the FCC issued a public notice that it intended to propose a ruling to ban cigarette advertising from all radio and television broadcasting. This notice was filed 4 months before the end of the 4-year moratorium on the ban that had prevented federal regulatory agencies from taking action against the tobacco industry. The FCC had put Congress on notice that if it did not act by July 1 of that year, the FCC would go ahead with its intentions and tobacco advertising would disappear from the airwaves.

The tobacco lobby quickly swung into preparation, and several long congressional hearings were held to discuss the whole issue of cigarettes and health and the proposed FCC action. The National Association of Broadcasters (NAB) actively joined forces with the Tobacco Institute to combat the FCC's intention with a barrage of propaganda claiming that the broadcast industry should be left to regulate itself. Eventually, however, cracks began to appear in this seemingly impregnable alliance, and on July 8, 1969, the NAB announced a plan to phase out all cigarette advertising from the air over a 3½-year period beginning on January 1, 1970. It is unclear exactly what prompted this decision, but it seems to have been inspired by the fear of having to air both pro and con advertising for tobacco products for the foreseeable future. Moreover, who knew where this might lead with regard to other controversial products? It was far better to bite the bullet and get rid of cigarette advertising lest it contaminate other products. In any case, it was thought that, in the 3½-year interim, the broadcast industry would easily find other customers only too eager to buy into the prime-time programs or sporting events made available by the removal of cigarette advertising. The tobacco industry, stung by what it considered to be betrayal by the broadcasters, went one step further and voluntarily agreed to end all broadcast advertising by September 1970.

Eventually, acting in a statesmanlike, responsible manner, broadcasters moved the date up to January 1, 1970. The broadcast industry, which stood to lose more than $250 million a year for 3 years by this decision, became the injured party. Naturally, the print media were elated at the prospect of all that additional advertising revenue coming their way. Eventually, after much lobbying by all parties, a compromise was reached, and the final date of January 1, 1971, was set to allow the broadcasters one last chance to extract some revenue from the football bowl games on New Year's Day. The tobacco industry had to get Congress to exempt it from antitrust action to act in a concerted manner like this. Congress also managed to extract from the tobacco industry an agreement to strengthen the warning on cigarette packages to read: "Warning: The Surgeon General Has Determined That Cigarette Smoking Is Dangerous to Your Health."

Since 1971, no cigarette advertising has appeared on radio or television; however, as Fritschler (1983) pointed out,

> The cigarette manufacturers were discovering that agreement with the anti-smoking people was not such a bad thing. The advertising budgets of the manufacturers dropped an estimated 30 percent in 1971, the first year of the television and radio ad ban, and gross sales were up 3 percent. (p. 141)

The tobacco industry simply switched its advertising strategy, purchasing more print and billboard space and sponsoring special sporting and other events that gave it clear identification in the media. Kool Mentholated cigarettes sponsored a series of jazz festivals, Virginia Slims supported women's tennis tournaments, and numerous other events suddenly found tobacco sponsors.

This somewhat unexpected victory for the antitobacco forces was really just a starting point in the propaganda war that was to follow. Their decision to remove themselves from broadcast advertising was a calculated strategy on the part of the cigarette manufacturers to remove pressure in an area where the government did have the power to legislate through the FCC. Now, the battle to make the public aware of the health dangers posed by smoking would begin to intensify.

Identification of the Propagandist

In a propaganda battle as massive and long running as this one, many propagandists can be identified on both sides of the controversy. The propagandists are the large international companies that constitute the tobacco industry—for example, R. J. Reynolds, Liggett and Myers, Brown and

Williamson—on one side, and on the other side, there is the array of public and government organizations that oppose the consumption of tobacco products because it constitutes a health hazard and an environmental nuisance.

First, tobacco interests in the United States constitute an impressive part of the nation's economy and have established themselves as an important force in American politics. The so-called tobacco coalition includes the eventual clientele who smoke more than $43 billion worth of tobacco products annually, the 22 states in which tobacco is grown (3 states—Virginia, North Carolina, and South Carolina—currently grow most of the tobacco that supplies the industry), the approximately 2.5 million jobs of varying types with a payroll of $52 billion supported by the tobacco industry, and the $16.5 billion contribution tobacco makes directly to the nationwide tax base. The industry as a whole accounts for about 2.5% of the nation's gross national product. Beneficiaries of this multi-billion-dollar industry include manufacturers, advertising agencies, the mass media, farmers, tax collectors, and shopkeepers (Fritschler, 1983). Clearly, a lot of money and many other issues are involved in any political decisions regarding smoking.

Second, tobacco has an almost mystical role in American history; it was one of the first American crops exported by the early settlers and was once so valuable that it was even used as currency. Third, this ties in with one of the ideological perspectives mentioned above that concerns the traditional historical antagonism that arises between government and business, especially when the regulation of health or environmental matters is the primary issue. In these instances, unless the advantages to the business community involved are very obvious, there is likely to be a great deal of politicking, and the myth of government interference in free enterprise is likely to be raised. Besides, most Americans do not like to be told what to eat, drink, or smoke.

Fourth—and this is a very complex factor indeed—since 1933, tobacco producers have been the beneficiaries of federal assistance through the U.S. Department of Agriculture (USDA), which operates a price support program and market quota rules that enforce a mandatory limit on production. These regulations have driven tobacco prices up and kept the supply down. The contradiction here is obvious, for as Fritschler (1983) noted,

> For the proponents of these tobacco regulations to turn around and fight consumer-health regulation on the grounds that government regulation is unwarranted interference by big brother and bad for the economy is the kind of argument which makes rational people wince. (p. 9)

The tobacco industry tends to slide by this conundrum in its antilegislative philosophy. Perhaps this is best exemplified by the statement by Jesse

Helms, the conservative Republican senator from the major tobacco state of North Carolina and a leader of the industry's fight against regulation: "In North Carolina, tobacco isn't a commodity, it's a religion!" Thus, we have a large, powerful industry, determined to preserve its privileges, facing continuous pressure from an equally determined, increasingly empowered group of individuals, together with various private and government health and legal agencies, all of whom are concerned by the growing and very costly health menace that smoking has become.

The Structure of the Propaganda Organization

Over the years, many organizations have been created to propagandize on both sides of this issue. The tobacco industry has always had one essential goal for its propaganda: reinforcing the consistent viewpoint that, despite the thousands of studies that have established the connection between smoking and various physical ailments, the actual causal link between smoking and these medical problems has not been clearly established. The list of health problems associated with tobacco use is a long one—lung cancer; cancer of the mouth, larynx, esophagus, stomach, pancreas, cervix, kidney, and bladder; and emphysema, chronic bronchitis, cardiovascular disease, stroke, sudden death, ulcers, hypertension, and brain hemorrhage. Although the health hazards of smoking had been pointed out as early as the mid-19th century, it took a series of private and government reports between 1954 and 1964 to bring the matter into the public arena for political debate. After the initial 1954 study reports by a private group, the tobacco industry responded with the creation of the Tobacco Industry Research Committee (now called the Council for Tobacco–USA), which distributed fairly substantial funds for scientific research on the use of tobacco and its effects on health. Although this served as a counterpropaganda move, in that the industry began funding its own health-related research, thereby demonstrating its concern, this organization was not in a position to counter directly the growing propaganda movement demanding some sort of regulation of public smoking. In 1958, the increased pressure was met head-on with the creation of the Tobacco Institute, Inc., a lobbying public relations group supported by large contributions from the various factions making up the tobacco industry. The Tobacco Institute subsequently became the source of most of the industry's propaganda aimed at containing the disorganized array of health groups pushing for the labeling of cigarettes or other regulatory measures.

On the side opposing cigarette advertising (and, of course, indirectly the sale of tobacco products) were arrayed many small, largely ineffective groups mainly interested in health issues. But not until the campaign to restrict the advertising of tobacco on radio and television broadcasting did these small groups begin to coalesce and gain strength.

The Target Audience

For the tobacco industry, the target audience for tobacco products was the entire adolescent and adult population. Current estimates indicate that 26 million men (28.2%) and 23.1 million women (23.1%) are smokers and that 4.4 million teenagers ages 12 through 17 years are smokers. Although studies indicate that smoking has declined by about 40% since 1965, recent data suggest that this decline is leveling off (American Heart Association, 1998, p. 1). For most of the 20th century, smoking was popular among all segments of the population, especially males. Boys as young as 8 or 9 regularly smoked, and although smoking by women was once considered unacceptable, since the 1920s, the number of female smokers has steadily increased to the point where teenage girls are considered to be the fastest growing segment of the cigarette market (Peirce, 1996).

This increase in smoking among females of all age groups is of particular concern as the number of women in the workforce has increased. Despite the best efforts of health advocates, teenage females continue to see smoking as a symbol of sophistication and maturity (University of Michigan, 1995). With this increase in smoking has also come a concomitant rise in tobacco-related illnesses in women.

It is a well-understood dictum in the psychology of advertising that adolescents make an ideal target group for the adoption of new products. At this time, maturing individuals seek to become independent from their parents and, with their increased buying power, are eager to create the own personalities and tastes. Deliberate defiance of adult authority is a common symbol of this growing independence. The tobacco industry has always understood this fact and has used it to its advantage by deliberately targeting the message at adolescents and young adults. The documented revelation of this practice was a major factor in the creation of legislative hostility toward the industry. In an ABC-TV documentary *Never Say Die: How the Cigarette Companies Keep on Winning,* host Peter Jennings (1996) pointed out that "the average age for beginning smokers was 12-and-a-half years old. And, on average, most who smoked had tried to quit by the age of 14. By the time they were 15 or older, nearly half the young smokers said they were hooked" (p. 1).

Ann-Marie Barry (1998) pointed out that "young adult smokers" constitute the "key share" in maintaining tobacco company profits because if youngsters do not start smoking by the time they are 18 or 19, they won't smoke at all; 90% of smokers begin smoking before the age of 18. At the other end, 450,000 older smokers (older than age 50) "leave the market because they either quit or die." Young adult smokers make up 90% of all new smokers and are the only viable source of tobacco consumers.

Internal documents from the R. J. Reynolds Company (RJR) that were released in 1998 by Congressman Henry Waxman (D–CA) indicated that the company deliberately targeted 14- to 24-year-olds. One memo, written in 1975 to an RJR vice president, noted, "The Camel Brand must increase its share of penetration among the 14–24 age group . . . which represents tomorrow's cigarette business." A 1986 memo noted how the Joe Camel advertising campaign would use "peer acceptance/influence" to "motivate the target audience to take up cigarettes." Waxman noted that the documents "show that our worst fears about the tobacco companies were true: They were surveying the kids, targeting them and implementing a successful strategy to get them to smoke" (Mintz & Torry, 1998, p. A1).

Another segment of the population specifically targeted by the tobacco industry was young African Americans. This is a rather cynical strategy because African American men are 30% more likely than white men to die from smoking-related diseases, which cause an estimated 48,000 deaths in African American communities annually. Also, African Americans smoke cigarettes with a higher nicotine and tar content than whites, and these brands are heavily advertised in African American media. In fact, cigarette advertising accounts for 10% of all advertising in *Jet* and *Essence,* two leading African American magazines, and these and other African American publications rarely, if ever, mention the health consequences of smoking. The tobacco industry also specifically targets African Americans through the funding of cultural events, higher education institutions, elected officials, and civil rights organizations; all these activities help build the industry's image and credibility in the African American community (information about African Americans and smoking is taken from the Maryland Department of Health and Physical Hygiene at http://sailor.lib.md.us/docs/tobacco/afriamer.htm).

Overall, the tobacco industry was extremely successful in identifying and targeting segments of the population that were most "vulnerable" to the various appeals of cigarette smoking. For a long time, this strategy served the industry well, but since the industry has been under attack, the nature of these propaganda activities has been closely scrutinized, analyzed, and disclosed to the public. Despite this close scrutiny, the tobacco industry gives every indication of continuing these "targeting" strategies while the tobacco settlement is being worked out.

Media Utilization Techniques

As we have already noted, the tobacco industry had once been a major sponsor of programming on television and radio, and the names of cigarette brands were common everyday words like *Coke* or *Pepsi*. Cigarette advertising was prominent in every form of mass communication, and advertisements for tobacco products could be seen everywhere—from the sides of barns to the most specialized magazines to billboards to buses to major television "spectaculars." When broadcast advertising was no longer available, the tobacco industry simply increased its advertising expenditures in other media. Despite the intensified antismoking campaigns of the past decade, we are still inundated with images of happy people (mostly young and glamorous) enjoying the exciting life that smoking can apparently create.

Tobacco companies have been extremely adept at finding ways to get their brand logos before the public. Cigarette brand names are found plastered on everything from the exciting NASCAR racing automobiles to trendy clothing obtained by redeeming coupons found in cigarette packs. An estimated 30% of children aged 12 to 17, both smokers and nonsmokers, own at least one tobacco promotional item. Cigarette companies' annual spending for promotional items quadrupled, from $184 million to $756 million, in just 2 years, 1991 to 1993 (*Questions and Answers About the FDA's Regulations*, 1998).

The Food and Drug Administration (FDA) has proposed shutting down some of these tobacco-related promotional activities, such as in Grand Prix auto racing, where during one televised broadcast of the Marlboro Grand Prix, the Marlboro logo or name appeared 5,933 times! The use of tobacco advertising is banned at many European Grand Prix sites. Many cities, such as New York, have restricted tobacco billboard advertising. The New York bill outlaws cigarette advertising within 1,000 feet of schools, playgrounds, and other youth centers. Despite concerns that such laws might be unconstitutional, many cities have adopted or are considering similar laws aimed at curbing the ubiquity of tobacco advertising.

The FDA has also suggested that only black-and-white text-only advertising be allowed for all outdoor tobacco advertising, all point-of-sale advertising, and advertising in publications with significant youth readership.[2] It is thought that eliminating color and image advertisements would reduce tobacco's appeal to youth (*Questions and Answers About the FDA's Regulations*, 1998, p. 2).

For those opposed to smoking, the propaganda battle between the tobacco industry and the health interests did not cease with the groups' Pyrrhic victory in 1971. Those groups concerned with the larger issue of the enormous cost of the damage to public health caused by cigarette smoking initiated propaganda campaigns to depict smoking as being "antisocial" and "unacceptable." This campaign has been aimed mainly at a younger audience, where research has indicated that despite all the anticigarette propaganda, smoking adoption rates have increased slightly in recent years (University of Michigan, 1995). In autumn 1985, then-U.S. Surgeon General C. Everett Koop suggested that, by the end of the century, smokers would find their behavior so socially unacceptable that they would have to smoke in private. In the years since that remark, smoking in public places has indeed become a rarity.

Antismoking groups have an impressive array of data they can use to make their points about the dangers of smoking. An estimated 47 million adults in the United States smoke cigarettes, even though statistics indicate that this behavior will result in death or disability for one 1 of every 2 regular users. Tobacco usage results in more than 430,000 deaths each year, or 1 in every 5 deaths. These deaths cost the country an enormous sum of money—more than $50 billion in medical expenses and another $50 billion in indirect costs each year. Then there are the other health problems associated with the nonsmokers exposed to cigarette smoke, and each year exposure to environmental tobacco smoke (ETS) causes an estimated 3,000 Americans to die from lung cancer and up to 300,000 children to suffer from lower respiratory tract infections (*Targeting Tobacco Use*, 1998, pp. 1–2).

Special Techniques to Maximize Effects

In the fight against the tobacco industry, antismoking groups have used a wide range of media and special techniques. The most direct of these has been legislation aimed at curbing and discouraging the sale of tobacco products. For instance, besides banning cigarette advertising on radio and television, beginning in 1965, Congress passed laws requiring that health warning labels be placed on cigarette packs. These warnings were strengthened in 1970, 1971 (on printed advertisements), and again in 1984 (rotating warnings on packs and advertisements). Congress also required warnings on other tobacco products, such as chewing tobacco and snuff, and banned the broadcast advertising of these products.

Over the years, cigarette manufacturers have adopted several simple themes in their advertising, which, combined with sophisticated artwork and production techniques (when they were on television), have been very effective in conveying the message that "cigarettes can make life fun!" In pursuit of this theme, tobacco companies have often resorted to ideas that have a particular appeal to a young audience.

In late 1991, a major study indicated that the cartoon camel logo (Joe Camel) used for Camel cigarettes had enormous appeal with children. Although R. J. Reynolds, the company that produces this brand, claimed that its advertising was intended for adults, the researchers said the campaign had been "far more successful at marketing Camel cigarettes to children than to adults" (J. E. Brody, 1991, p. A16). As proof for this assertion, the researchers noted that Camel's share of the illegal children's cigarette market had increased from 0.5% to 32.8%, representing sales estimated at $476 million a year. Even without television advertising, the children were as familiar with the Joe Camel symbol as they were with the Mickey Mouse logo for the Disney Cable Channel. An additional factor was the extensive promotional campaign offering T-shirts, caps, and other items with the Joe Camel logo, which enticed children to purchase this brand. Publication of this study in the prestigious *Journal of the American Medical Association* prompted Congressman Waxman to urge a total ban on all cigarette advertising.

Even as the tobacco industry is under attack, a recent report in the *Houston Press* (N. Cooper, 1998) indicated how extensively the tobacco industry continues to promote and merchandise its products in bars, as well as provide bar supplies and pay for bands. In many bars, tobacco money now exceeds alcohol money in terms of financial assistance as dueling cigarette companies fight for position. The article noted,

> Deprived of traditional advertising venues, the tobacco industry has focused on bars and clubs to fill the air with their brand names. The glorification of the connection between music, bar patrons and smoking has been encapsulated in tobacco advertising aimed at club customers. (p. 6)

As one bartender noted, "They're [the tobacco industry] not going into a market where the people are 30 years old; they're going where the kids are 18 or 19 and dumping free cigarettes in their lap" (p. 6).

In recent years, determined efforts have been made to eradicate smoking by making both the usual health claims and by presenting smoking as being socially unacceptable. Antismoking advertisements have gone so far as to depict smokers as ugly, smelly individuals and also to suggest to teenagers that smoking is "uncool." The tobacco industry's attempts to maintain public recognition by the sponsorship of sports or cultural events have also been criticized. The association between Virginia Slims and professional women's tennis, as well as Philip Morris's sponsorship of the touring show celebrating the 200th anniversary of the Bill of Rights, came under fire as a form of surreptitious advertising. The Philip Morris sponsorship was particularly interesting in that questions were raised concerning whether the tobacco company was trying to make a point that smokers have rights too.

Audience Reaction to Various Techniques

As indicated earlier, some small victories have been achieved, and the number of adults who smoke has declined since the advertising ban went into force. There is still a real concern, however, that the propaganda efforts of tobacco companies continue to attract large numbers of younger smokers. The various promotional campaigns that offer merchandise featuring the logos of cigarette brands and the ready availability of "samples" at public events are particularly effective in attracting young adults. Also, the "defiance effect" cannot be discounted, as many adolescents willfully disregard health messages on the dangers of smoking as not applying to them. The tobacco industry's stance that smoking is an act of "free choice" made by individuals contributes to this attitude.

On the other side, the combined efforts of health agencies, legal suits, and massive media coverage of the issue have led to an increased public awareness of the dangers of smoking. Despite the basic resistance that individuals have to deliberate propaganda messages, the antismoking campaigns, through persistence and increasing revelations of insidious industry practices, eventually made a real breakthrough in the public's consciousness. No longer is the tobacco industry able to dominate and shape this discussion, and the result is a definite shift in public attitudes against smoking in public. The majority of the public now favors severe restrictions on tobacco use and supports the efforts of different levels of government to make the tobacco industry pay for the enormous health costs associated with cigarette smoking.

Counterpropaganda

The counterpropaganda to the tobacco industry came from those groups outlined above in the section "Identification of the Propagandist." The objectives of this counterpropaganda campaign were aimed at countering the massive and decades-long propaganda from the tobacco industry that defiantly denied any connection between smoking and health problems while continuing to profitably market cigarettes and other tobacco products. For many years, antismoking groups worked with definite disadvantages and were relatively poorly funded in comparison with the hundreds of millions of dollars spent on tobacco advertising and public relations campaigns aimed at protecting the industry from criticism. Gradually, however, the counterpropaganda began to take hold, and eventually, the combination of increasingly sound scientific evidence linking smoking with a myriad of health problems, together with the new strategy of legal challenges to the tobacco industry in court, culminated in what has become known as "the tobacco settlement." Although still far from being "settled," this series of legal decisions has signaled the increasing success of the counterpropaganda efforts.

Effects and Evaluation

The effects and evaluation of the tobacco industry's propaganda efforts and the counterpropaganda from the antismoking side are ultimately judged by developments leading up to "the tobacco settlement."

The Tobacco Industry Under Attack: The Tobacco Settlement

In 1993, the attorney general of Mississippi, Michael Moore, contacted lawyer Dick Scruggs, who had won a historic case for the state against several asbestos companies. This victory had forced the asbestos companies to pay for the removal of asbestos from public buildings and to compensate workers for lung disease they had contracted as a result of exposure to this product. Moore had determined that the state could sue the tobacco companies to recover the Medicaid expenses associated with smoking-related health problems. The tobacco companies had been sued many times before, but by individuals, and the companies had always won because they were able to establish that smoking was a matter of individual choice. A state suing for recovery of smoking-related medical expenses, however, was another matter entirely, and this proved to be the major blow to the tobacco industry's long run of legal victories.

Not only did Mississippi eventually win a substantial settlement ($3 billion), but other states immediately mounted their own lawsuits for the recovery of medical costs related to smoking. Since 1994, 41 states and Puerto Rico have sued the tobacco industry. So far, Florida, Minnesota, and Texas have all won massive settlements, although these are still in various stages of appeal or legal dispute (mostly involving the fees to be paid to the states' lawyers). Faced with a never-ending series of costly lawsuits, the tobacco industry agreed to try to settle on a national level. On June 20, 1997, a group of state attorneys general and industry lawyers announced that they had reached a settlement for $368.5 billion over 25 years to reimburse states for their tobacco-related medical costs and also to pay for tobacco control programs to reduce tobacco use among teenagers. This settlement also called for giving the FDA the authority to regulate nicotine-containing tobacco products as restricted devices. In return, the settlement proposed changes to the civil justice system that would provide the tobacco companies with broad protection from future civil litigation.

What made this dramatic shift in the industry's position possible? It was the public disclosure of a vast number of private industry documents that clearly indicate the deliberate attempt to hide the many years of research that signaled the dangers associated with cigarette smoking and the addictiveness of nicotine. On April 14, 1994, executives from seven of the leading tobacco companies had stood before Congress and declared that they believed that nicotine was not an addictive substance. John Scanlon, a long-time public relations official for the tobacco industry, said the following of this testimony: "The presentation was so incredible and unbelievable that the industry's traditional arguments—about the whole issue of choice—were tainted even in the eyes of people who wanted to be rational about cigarette companies" (*The Tobacco Settlement,* 1998). Just 2 years later, these same companies were eager to make an unprecedented financial settlement to avoid catastrophic litigation.

Unfortunately, a final national settlement was not reached during the initial congressional debate in June 1998, when the Republicans in Congress defeated the McCain Tobacco Bill, which would have mandated broad federal regulation of tobacco and imposed the largest price increase ever on cigarettes. Many issues were involved in this defeat, including an unprecedented $40 million, 8-week radio and television advertising barrage by the tobacco industry that sought to portray the bill as a "tax and spend" measure. Since then, Congress has moved slowly, and although several alternative measures have been suggested, the final "settlement" has yet to be agreed on. As former U.S. Surgeon General C. Everett Koop told the National Press Club in Washington in September 1998,

> Having used their money and lying advertising campaign to defeat the best tobacco legislation in the history of this country, the industry can now sit back and watch its profits grow, as Medicare, Medicaid, Veterans Affairs, private health insurance and public hospitals pay the real price of their products. (Koop, 1998, pp. 3–4)

On November 13, 1998, the four biggest cigarette makers and officials of eight states announced the outline of a settlement designed to resolve all remaining state claims over health costs related to smoking (Meier, 1998). This plan, which was drafted to cover all the remaining states that had not yet settled with the tobacco industry, would cost the tobacco companies $206 billion spread out over 25 years and would restrict cigarette advertising and marketing. This plan would not shield tobacco companies from personal and class-action liabilities.

This plan specifically targeted certain marketing practices and would ban billboard and transit advertising, as well as the sale of clothing and merchandise with brand-name logos. The cigarette companies also agreed to pay an additional $1.45 billion over the next 5 years to finance smoking cessation programs and advertisements to counter underage tobacco use. Finally, the companies also agreed to pay $25 million a year over the next decade to underwrite a foundation that will research ways to reduce youth smoking and legally pledged that they will not market to those younger than 18. (As this edition of this book is being finished, the plan was still being evaluated by the antitobacco forces, many of whom thought it did not go far enough . . . and so the saga continues.)

It is certain that the tobacco industry still is capable of wielding significant lobbying power, especially among Republicans. Nonetheless, the handwriting is clearly on the wall: The tobacco industry is being held responsible for billions of dollars in smoking-related health costs; smoking is increasingly becoming an "antisocial" activity; more and more public places do not allow smoking; for those who still wish to continue smoking, the cost of this activity will steadily increase; and the attacks on the tobacco industry will continue from several fronts.

The continued public awareness of the nature of tobacco industry propaganda activities and legislative lobbying strategies is of vital importance. C. Everett Koop, in his September 1998 speech to the National Press Club, summed it up best, when he noted,

> I believe that the press was quite effective in its reporting on the tobacco wars. Ironically, the paid ads [of the tobacco industry's attack on the McCain Bill] in print on radio and on television undermined much of what the message was that you were reporting, but the reporting was generally comprehensive and very thoughtful. . . .
>
> This country and the public health community in particular need you now as never before. Please continue to be advocates for the public health. The public health folks do not have the resources to counter the sheer volume of industry propaganda, and we must rely on you for the so-called free media to make the system honest. . . .
>
> And never underestimate the tobacco industry. It is a social disease as dangerous as any malignancy and it metastasizes more rapidly. . . .
>
> The tobacco industry perhaps could have once been controlled by surgery. But after waiting 200 years, such therapy is out of the question for now. It might gradually respond to such other therapies such as radiating light on its misdeeds and holding the industry responsible for its actions. (p. 4)

The Aftermath (2005): The Controversy Continues

One only has to search the Internet to discover that not a day goes by when there is a not another controversy surrounding the tobacco industry somewhere in the world. It may be a report of yet another city banning smoking in public places, it may be a serious lawsuit dealing with health issues, or it may be related to deceptive advertising practices or advertising aimed at youth; the list is continuous. Let's look at just five such cases taken from the Web site of the Tobacco Public Policy Center at Capitol University Law School in Columbus, Ohio (http://www.law.capital.edu/Tobacco/ News).

Case 1

May 11, 2005

Forty state attorneys general signed a notice sent to R. J. Reynolds Tobacco Co. on March 28, warning the company that one or more states plan to file lawsuits based on claims that the company has "engaged in unfair and deceptive acts and practices by publishing false or misleading claims about its Eclipse brand cigarettes." The cigarettes are advertised as "reduced-risk," based on company claims that cigarettes reduce second-hand smoke. The attorney generals claim that such advertisements are a violation of the 1998 Master Settlement Agreement (MSA), which placed restrictions on marketing and advertising by tobacco companies. Among other provisions, the MSA prohibits "material misrepresentation[s] of fact regarding the health consequences of using any Tobacco Product."

Case 2

May 11, 2005

The Canadian Journal of Public Health reports that the results of a recent study demonstrate that cigarettes labeled "light" or "mild" are just as harmful as regular brands and, in fact, may contain nicotine levels 5% higher. Researchers found that the perforations in the filters of light cigarettes, which are supposed to allow for more air to pass through and dilute the ingested smoke, are often blocked by people's fingers, saliva, or lips and rendered useless . . .

Although research studies have shown that cigarettes marketed as low-nicotine or "light" are just as harmful as the regular brands, a state judge in Minneapolis recently dismissed a lawsuit related to such cigarettes. The lawsuit, filed against RJ Reynolds Tobacco Company, claimed that consumers are misled by advertising and cigarette labels that promote light cigarettes as less dangerous than those containing higher levels of tar. As the basis for her opinion, the judge cited the Federal Cigarette Labeling and Advertising Act, which defines what language must be on packages and prohibits a "state, by positive enactment or a finding of liability for an omission, from imposing further requirements." If allowed to proceed, the case could have meant a multi-billion dollar verdict for the plaintiffs who, on behalf of Minnesota smokers, sought a refund of the money spent on cigarettes labeled as "light."

Case 3

May 9, 2005

Georgia Governor Sonny Perdue signed a bill into law today that prohibits smoking in most public indoor places, ending weeks of spec- ulation over whether he would approve the measure. The law permits smoking in restaurants and bars that do not employ workers 18 years old and younger. Beginning July 1, violators will face fines between $100 and $500. Georgia becomes the twelfth state with some form of statewide smoke-free law.

Case 4

August 23, 2005

The Delaware Chancery Court issued a judgment yesterday that the **truth** advertising campaign, which is run by the American Legacy

Foundation, does not vilify or personally attack the tobacco industry or its employees. The Lorillard Tobacco Company had filed suit against the American Legacy Foundation, claiming that the truth ads violated the vilification clause of the Master Settlement Agreement. The American Legacy Foundation was established in 1999, following the Master Settlement Agreement reached between the major tobacco companies and 46 state attorneys general. In March 2005, the *American Journal of Public Health* published a study crediting the **truth** campaign with accelerating the decline in youth smoking rates by 22 percent, or almost 300,000 fewer smokers, in its first 2 years

Case 5

September 1, 2005

The six public health groups allowed to intervene in the Department of Justice's racketeering suit against the tobacco industry filed a brief Wednesday asking Judge Gladys Kessler to strengthen the remedies proposed by the government. The brief was filed by the American Cancer Society, American Heart Association, American Lung Association, Americans for Nonsmokers' Rights, the National African American Tobacco Prevention Network and the Tobacco-Free Kids Action Fund. The remedies proposed by the intervening health groups include:

- A $4.8 billion a year smoking cessation program that will continue until less than 10 percent of smokers say they want to quit (instead of the five-year, $2 billion a year program suggested by the government).
- A requirement that the tobacco companies pay $600 million a year for ten years (instead of the $400 million a year proposed by the DOJ [Department of Justice]) to fund a public education and countermarketing campaign in three areas: youth smoking, low-tar and light cigarettes, and secondhand smoke. The youth smoking program would remain in effect until youth smoking rates are less than five percent, and the other programs would continue until more than 90 percent of smokers are informed of the risks of low-tar and light cigarettes as well as secondhand smoke.
- Limiting tobacco advertisements to black text on a white background in publications with large youth readership or in any retail stores open to youth, prohibiting tobacco companies from collecting any data or records on youth, and prohibiting all brand name sponsorships that result in exposure to children.

- Financial penalties if youth smoking rates do not fall 42% from 2003 levels by 2010 (rather than 2013, as proposed the DOJ), with levels based on monthly rather than daily smoking rates in order to account for experimentation as well as regular smokers.
- Expanded authority and jurisdiction for the Independent Investigations Officer appointed by the Court to monitor compliance by the tobacco companies.

These and thousands of other cases of a similar nature indicate that the battle to eliminate or at least control the consumption of tobacco still has a long way to go. In the meantime, more than 440,000 Americans die every year of cigarette-attributable illnesses (http://www.cdc.gov/mmwr/preview/mmwrhtml/mm5235a4.htm). On the positive side, there is every indication that smoking by teens is declining. This trend is constantly being put to the test by another trend showing an increase in the depiction of smoking by characters in movies or on television to a greater extent than presettlement days. Despite pleas from health authorities, the film and television industries show no signs of relenting from this practice, which is viewed as a free speech issue. Considering the many years that the tobacco industry had to wield its considerable propaganda power to promote smoking as contributing positively to one's lifestyle, as well as the fact that smoking is still seen as a "glamorous" activity by many, especially the young, the battle to eliminate the continued harmful effects of tobacco is far from over.

Premarin: A Bitter Pill to Swallow

Most people take their doctors' prescriptions without asking many questions. They probably assume that pharmaceuticals are produced in laboratories from chemicals or plant derivatives. Menopausal and postmenopausal women were regularly put on hormone replacement therapy (HRT) or estrogen replacement therapy (ERT), which means taking a daily estrogen supplement together with progesterone or taking estrogen alone for approximately 25 days each month. The predicted benefits of ERT are reduced menopausal symptoms and possible prevention of osteoporosis, heart disease, colon cancer, and Alzheimer's disease, whereas the risks may include uterine and possibly breast cancer, blood clots, and gallbladder disease (J. Brody, 1997a, 1997b, 1997c, 1997d; Nash, 1997). Until 2002, about one third of the more than 30 million postmenopausal women in the United States took estrogen, and almost 90% use the brand known as Premarin, which is manufactured by Wyeth-Ayerst Laboratories in the form of pills, creams, injections, and patches. Wyeth-Ayerst also manufactures Prempro, a single tablet that combines Premarin and a progestin, PrempPhase, and Prempac-C.

In 2002, the National Institute of Health announced that it was halting the Women's Health Initiative HRT study due to a suspected link between hormone replacement therapy and an increase in incidence of breast cancer and other serious health risks occurring in the control group. This announcement caused millions of women to stop taking Premarin and Premro. Sales revenues for these products plummeted, and, for a while, advertising for the drugs ceased.

Premarin, however, was at the center of an intense controversy before 2002. Not only did the pharmaceutical companies that manufacture synthetic and generic estrogens and related drugs want to compete with Wyeth-Ayerst's best-selling product, but the process of acquiring the estrogens that make up Premarin created revulsion and hostility among many physicians, animal protection organizations, and a growing portion of the public. Then, as now, others believe that estrogen in the form of a drug is not necessary at all and advocate alternate natural methods. All of this has created a very strong counterpropaganda campaign, thus making this case study a difficult one in which to determine the primary propagandist. An analyst could say that the animal rights organizations, the other pharmaceutical companies, and alternative medical groups are the primary propagandists; however, because Premarin appeared first and because there are several different counterpropaganda groups, we have decided to focus on Wyeth-Ayerst as the primary propagandist and the opponents as the counterpropagandists.

The Ideology and Purpose of the Propaganda Campaign

Before 2002, Wyeth-Ayerst Laboratories dominated the world estrogen market for more than 50 years. Wyeth-Ayerst holds 80% of the estrogen supplement market worldwide, Premarin was Canada's most lucrative pharmaceutical export, and Premarin was the most prescribed drug in the United States. Clearly, the ideology for Wyeth-Ayerst was to maintain its monopoly over the estrogen market while making huge profits, and the purpose was to prevent government approval of a generic Premarin, to have consumers believe that Premarin is a superior product, and to defend itself against animal cruelty charges. Before 2002, production of Premarin generated $860 to $930 million yearly for Wyeth-Ayerst, and in 1995, sales were over $1 billion. As the women of the baby boom generation matured into their 40s and 50s, Wyeth-Ayerst expected to double or even triple earnings from the production of Premarin. If a generic Premarin were approved, the financial loss for Wyeth-Ayerst would have been enormous because most prescription benefit plans, health maintenance organizations (HMOs), and Medicare and Medicaid are required to use the lower cost generic versions of a drug.

The Context in Which the Propaganda Occurs

The name *Premarin* is a contraction of "*pre*gnant *ma*re u*rine*" (PMU) because it is made from urine extracted from pregnant mares kept on horse farms that contract independently with Wyeth-Ayerst Laboratories, which have been manufacturing the prescription drug with the same well-ordered system since 1942. To produce the level of urine necessary for Premarin, female horses must be impregnated, often through artificial insemination, and kept tied up indoors for at least 6 of the 11 months' gestation period in stalls that are 8 by 3½ by 5 feet. The horses are fitted with a urine collection device (UCD) and are unable to lie down. Any exercise outside the stall is at the discretion of the farm manager. Drinking water is limited so that the urine will yield more concentrated estrogens. Because they are tied in front and strapped in behind, these horses cannot turn around or take more than two or three steps forward or backward (Eke, 1996). The foals that are born are seriously endangered, for there is a 67% mortality rate in the first week after foaling, followed by a 45% mortality rate the following week (Hass, Bristol, & Card, 1996). Those that survive are sold, mostly for human consumption. Foals are slaughtered in Canada and the frozen meat sent to Europe, or the live foals are shipped to Japan, where tender foal meat is in demand (Paulhus, 1996). This process violates the USDA's "no live export for slaughter" rule, but no one has enforced it. Within 2 weeks of giving birth, the mares are impregnated again and returned to the PMU production line.

Owners of the PMU farms are paid according to a prescribed quantity of concentrated horse urine, but they also sell the foals when they are only 3 to 4 months old to feedlots and slaughterhouses. The PMU mares are regarded as producers of urine, whereas the foals are regarded as "by-products." One Wyeth-Ayerst representative said, "See, the foals—and the mares which can't get pregnant any more—they are the by-product of the PMU industry. We crush 'em and recycle 'em, just like cans" (D. Jones, 1995, p. 3).

There were approximately 600 PMU farms in Canada, mostly in Manitoba, Alberta, and Saskatchewan, and about 40 in the United States, mainly in North Dakota. PMU farms had been in Ontario, but the government there has strict regulations regarding them, and allegations of horses living in squalor and of mistreated foals resulted in citations and revoked permits. For many years, with the exception of Ontario, little notice had been taken of the PMU farms. In 1995, however, after receiving repeated allegations of abuse to mares on PMU farms, the Canadian Farm Animal

Care Trust arranged to have 12 equine experts inspect 32 of the PMU farms selected by Wyeth-Ayerst in Saskatchewan, Alberta, and Manitoba. Wyeth-Ayerst representatives were present during each inspection. The 12 experts found mares in stalls that were too small, improper bedding, inadequate sanitation, untreated illnesses, lower limb abnormalities, skin abrasions from the urine-collecting harnesses, and an overall lack of water, grooming, and exercise (Russell, 1995a, 1995b; Salter, 1995).

Although Wyeth-Ayerst indicated it would take constructive action, its only response was that it would study the watering situation. Carrie Smith Cox, vice president for women's health care at Wyeth-Ayerst, wrote in response to the report, "Our goal is to implement continuous watering for the horses in the 1996–97 season as long as it does not affect the health of the horses or the quality of our product" (Black, 1996, p. 12). Wyeth-Ayerst denied subsequent requests for further inspections (Salter, 1995).

Another problem related to the PMU farms has been water pollution, for once the urine is collected, it is brought to a plant in Brandon, Manitoba, where the estrogen is extracted by a process that produces waste urine and ammonia. In 1996, the plant generated 4 million gallons of waste urine (Black, 1996). Canadian legislators and environmentalists expressed concern about the taxed sewage system and the potential for an overflow of millions of gallons of waste urine into the Assiniboine River, a water source for much of Manitoba (International Generic Horse Association [IGHA], 1998).

Critics of Wyeth-Ayerst and the PMU farms claim the farms use an antiquated method of producing estrogen and therefore urge women who take estrogen to switch to alternatives. At least a dozen synthetic and plant-derived estrogens have been approved by the FDA—for example, Climara, Estrace, Estraderm, Estradiol, Neo-Estrone, Menest, and Ogen—but these are not generic Premarin.

Duramed Pharmaceuticals of Cincinnati developed Cenestin, a generic, vegetable-based synthetic version of Premarin. Barr Laboratories has developed a generic Premarin, but Duramed became the test case. In 1991, Duramed applied to the FDA for approval of Cenestin, but Wyeth-Ayerst alleged that the generic estrogen did not mimic Premarin identically because it entered the bloodstream faster than Premarin. Wyeth-Ayerst also "issued dire warnings that this alleged discrepancy could increase the incidence of cancer in users" (Schatz & Paige, 1997, p. A22), and the FDA dropped Duramed's application. Meanwhile, Wyeth-Ayerst's Canadian version of Premarin was found to be as fast acting as the generics. Canada's regulatory agency rejected Wyeth-Ayerst's objection to a generic Premarin produced by ICN Canada Ltd. and left it on the market. A Canadian drug advisory committee concluded in a 1991 report, "If Wyeth's position were correct, then Premarin had been producing unsafe plasma levels in Canadian women for years" (J. Carey, 1997, p. 130). This statement apparently went unnoticed by the FDA. Meanwhile, Duramed solved the absorption problem by 1994, but this time Wyeth-Ayerst contested FDA approval of Cenestin on the grounds that the generic drug lacked one of the estrogens, called delta 8,9 (dehydroestrone sulfate), that is present in Premarin. The FDA gave a unanimous ruling in 1994 that delta 8,9 was an impurity and not a required ingredient of any generic.[3] Duramed applied for FDA approval of Cenestin in September 1995, and Barr followed the next July (J. Carey, 1997). "The FDA led Duramed and Barr to believe that approval of their generic versions was imminent" (Schatz & Paige, 1997, p. A22), but the conflict moved into the political arena.

Identification of the Propagandist and the Structure of the Propaganda Organization

The propagandist is Wyeth-Ayerst Laboratories, a major division of American Home Products Corporation and Whithall Laboratories, a *Fortune* 150 global pharmaceutical company, makers of Advil, Aleve, Anacin, Black Flag, Chef Boyardee, Dristan, Easy Off, Jiffy Pop, Neet, Pam, Preparation H, Quick and Easy, Sani-Flush, Woolite, and various other products, with headquarters in Philadelphia, Pennsylvania. Wyeth-Ayerst is also the manufacturer of phen-fen and Redux, the diet drugs banned for causing heart damage. Wyeth-Ayerst executives and spokespersons speak for the company. Wyeth-Ayerst also has several lobbyists in Washington, and it hired Burston-Marstellar, the largest public relations firm in the United States, to respond to the negative publicity generated by the controversy.

The Target Audience

The target audience for the sale of Premarin was the millions of menopausal and postmenopausal women and their physicians. As stated earlier, Wyeth-Ayerst will earn $1 billion annually from Premarin sales alone. Women who used Premarin were targeted to stay with the brand, and potential new users were encouraged to use the product to protect themselves from heart disease, osteoporosis, and other health problems. Other audiences were targeted in the controversy as well—women's organizations concerned about issues related to women's health and key Washington politicians. Each of these groups is discussed in the section "Special Techniques to Maximize Effect."

Media Utilization Techniques

Wyeth-Ayerst employed numerous media techniques, both offensive and defensive, to maintain the credibility of its product and its activities. It had a massive advertising campaign with full-page spreads in news, special interest, and "women's" magazines, as well as five-page advertisements in health magazines. The February 9, 1997, issue of *Time* had a full-page advertisement, "The Body of Evidence," that also appeared in news, history, health, and women's magazines with increasing frequency. It not only said that estrogen combats "uncomfortable symptoms" of menopause but also suggested that it aids sexuality, the brain (memory, cognitive functioning, and the consequences of Alzheimer's disease), the eyes (cataracts), teeth, the heart, bones, and the colon. The advertisement said, "So-called 'selective' or 'designer' estrogens may not impact a number of health issues associated with menopause." The terms *selective* and *designer* are not used in any other literature about synthetic or plant-derived estrogens examined in this study; thus, it is clear that they are intended to have negative connotations. An advertisement for Prempro, the combination of Premarin and a progestin, in *Smithsonian* magazine said, "Today, more than 8,000,000 American women take Premarin. Premarin, the most studied of all estrogens, has been earning women's confidence generation after generation." Physicians who prescribed Premarin gave patients a complimentary video and brochure about the drug. In the video, an actress portrayed Dr. Hughes, a woman who appears to be older than 50 and wears a white lab coat. She discussed the problems of menopause with a group of women and then said, "There are, however, other problems related to estrogen loss that you don't feel, and these problems won't go away. . . . But don't get discouraged because treatment is available. . . . If taking estrogen is right for you, there is a product your doctor can confidently prescribe . . . the Premarin regimen is the one I prescribe." She ended by holding up a Premarin tablet and stating, "This is what Premarin looks like. There is no other." The brochure, titled *Quality, Commitment, and Caring*, stated, "No synthetic components have ever been introduced to the unique combination of natural estrogens." The brochure not only praises Premarin and its "unique" qualities but also featured color photographs of beautiful horses grazing in fields. The captions with these photographs stated, "The mares are highly prized and well cared for" and "Providing for the care and well-being of horses is crucial to the production of Premarin." The text stated, "No other type of livestock ranching has as many checks and balances for animal care and welfare."

The coauthor of this book, Victoria O'Donnell, called the Wyeth-Ayerst's toll-free number to discuss the treatment of the PMU farm horses, and the woman who answered asked whether she could send out materials. A letter of thanks for the "opportunity to correct the misinformation you received about the care of the horses in PMU production and about the importance of Premarin to millions of women" arrived a few days later. The letter said that the horse farms are run by families, many of them third- and fourth-generation ranchers. It also included a statement by an equine veterinarian, Dr. Shauna L. Spurlock: "In my opinion, the aspect that sets these ranchers apart and makes me, as an equine practitioner, somewhat envious is the fine standard of care that exists and their determination to improve the quality of the care of the horses." The five-page letter ended with a warning that "the conjugated estrogens in Premarin are the only approved hormone replacement therapies available to women with an intact uterus." Included with the letter was a copy of Dr. Spurlock's 10-page report, *Care and Management of Horses at PMU Ranches*.

PMU ranchers have their own association, the North American Equine Ranching Information Council (NAERIC), which has its own Web page (http://www.naeric.org). The page discussed the care of the PMU horses, assuring the reader that PMU ranching has "more checks and balances to ensure animal care and welfare than any other livestock sector, making it one of the most regulated and closely inspected equine-related activities in the world." The inspections are done by NAERIC members and selected veterinarians. Today there is no mention of the PMU horses on NAERIC's home page on the Web, but the slogan at the top of the page states, "Promoting the unique partnership between Agriculture and Women's Health Care." There is also a promotion for the Wyeth Equine Ranching Scholarship for children and grandchildren of equine ranchers. This is the only time Wyeth is mentioned.

Special Techniques to Maximize Effect

According to Tom Schatz and Leslie Paige in the *Wall Street Journal* (1997),

> American Home Products CEO John Stafford attended one of President Clinton's now-famous White House kaffeeklatsches. Shortly thereafter, American Home Products bestowed $50,000 on the Democratic National Committee, the company's only soft-money contribution to the Democratic Party on record at the Federal Election Commission. (p. A22)

Wyeth-Ayerst's lobbyists recruited Senators Barbara Boxer, Bill Bradley, Olympia Snowe, Barbara Mikulski, and Patty Murray to write letters urging the FDA to halt the Duramed generic drug's progress (Schatz & Paige, 1997). Senators Mikulski and Murray coauthored a letter that said, "[We seek] the FDA's assurance that it has no intention of approving a generic version of Premarin that lacks the same active ingredient as the innovator" (Mann, 1997, p. E13). Eddie Bernice Johnson, a representative from Texas and a former nurse, originally supported the generic drug because it would have enabled women with low incomes to start and stick with a program of the low-cost generic drug, but the company's lobbyists talked her into switching sides. She said, "I just have a strong feeling that an inferior generic is no bargain" (J. Carey, 1997, p. 130).

Women's groups were enlisted to join the cause, such as the Business and Professional Women's Association, the American Medical Women's Association, the Women's Health Research Institute, and the National Osteoporosis Foundation. "All of these groups received thousands of dollars in funding from Wyeth-Ayerst" (Schatz & Paige, 1997, p. A22). Jane Tobler, a communications officer for the Business and Professional Women's Association, acknowledged that its foundation had received $65,000 from Wyeth-Ayerst (Mann, 1997). The Women's Health Research Institute is a subdivision of Wyeth-Ayerst working to determine the effect of HRT on postmenopausal women with heart disease (D. Shaw, 1997).

In the House, Representatives John Dingell and Ron Wyden, and in the Senate, Senator John Glenn, demanded that the FDA explain the delays in decision making and noted that consumers would save money should the generic drug be approved (D. Shaw, 1997). Senator Mike DeWine asked Commissioner David Kessler to investigate whether key regulators, including those who had final approval authority on a generic Premarin, "may have been removed or transferred from the review process." Senator DeWine received no response but said the scientists and medical community should be making this decision. "If not, that's certainly very troubling" (D. Shaw, 1997, p. 3).

According to D. Shaw (1997), Roger Williams, director of the FDA Office of Generic Drugs, had repeatedly rejected the notion of reclassifying delta 8,9 as an essential ingredient. Since then, a divisional reorganization occurred in the FDA, and Williams was no longer directly involved in the Premarin matter. The new top official making these decisions was now physician Janet Woodcock, director of the FDA Center for Drug Evaluation and Research. Wyeth officials said they had nothing to do with any changes at FDA. In March 1997, Dr. Woodcock testified before a Senate subcommittee that a scientific decision had been made, although she would not say what the decision was. On May 6, 1997, the FDA released its decision—a denial of the approval of a generic drug, citing as its reason the absence of delta 8,9 in the

Premarin alternative. Schatz and Paige (1997) cited an internal document released by the FDA's Office of Pharmaceutical Science, dated May 3, 1997, that disputed Wyeth-Ayerst's scientific claims about delta 8,9 because 25 other inactive impurities are also in Premarin. Schatz and Paige deduced from the memo that the FDA's decision on generic alternatives to Premarin "was based more on politics than science" (p. A22). On May 14, the inspector general of the U.S. Department of Health and Human Services contested the lack of documentation supporting Wyeth-Ayerst's own changes to Premarin (Schatz & Paige, 1997). Judy Mann (1997) wrote in the *Washington Post*, "Approval for drugs should be based strictly on science—not on politics, lobbying pressure or money" (p. E13). John Carey (1997) wrote in *Business Week*, "In a growing trend, brand-name companies such as Wyeth-Ayerst are using regulatory and legal tactics to delay the approval of cheaper generics" (p. 128). Schatz and Paige criticized the FDA: "In making this important decision, the agency appears to have sacrificed science and the public health to political considerations" (p. A22). Wyeth-Ayerst's executives, however, have stood by their actions. Michael Dey, president of the Wyeth-Ayerst unit ESI Lederle Inc., said, "We make no apologies for defending our product and its earnings" (J. Carey, 1997, p. 131).

In addition to giving physicians Premarin videos and elaborate brochures, Wyeth-Ayerst sponsored and funded symposia for the opinion leaders, the physicians, such as the one held in Laguna Niguel, California, in 1987—*The Long-Term Effects of Estrogen Deprivation*. The proceedings of these symposia are published and sent to physicians. The usual "gifts" are also given to physicians by the pharmaceutical salespersons—Post-it notes, pens, calculators, and samples.

Audience Reaction to Various Techniques

Washington politicians, women's organizations, and FDA decision makers reacted favorably to Wyeth-Ayerst's propaganda campaign despite knowing that approval of the generic Cenestin would have saved the government, hospitals, and managed care organizations almost $300 million per year because Cenestin would have cost $3 per month, compared with Premarin's $12 to $16 per month (Mann, 1997, p. E13; Schatz & Paige, 1997, p. A22). Certain physicians, however, stopped prescribing Premarin for their patients in favor of synthetic estrogens. It is interesting to note how many have either given public testimony or written articles to state their position. Ray M. Kellosalmi is a physician at Peachtree Medical Center in Peachland, British Columbia. He used to prescribe Premarin until he learned of the conditions on the PMU farms. Dr. Kellosalmi writes articles for publications such as *Family Practice* and encourages his patients to write letters to the editor to inform others about the PMU farms. He wrote the following in the May 8, 1995, article "Inhumanity by Prescription" in *Family Practice:*

> During the last several months, I have discussed the issue of conjugated equine estrogen with postmenopausal patients asking about ERT. Fully 100% of those patients have chosen another option. Unfortunately, for physicians it is easy and comfortable to prescribe drugs that have been around for a long time. It is also easy to not think about our contribution to the cruel chain of events that our prescriptions may allow, and thus the PMU industry is supported by our ho-hum acquiescence. (p. 9)

Phillip Warner, an Orinda, California, gynecologist who is the director of the Menopause Clinic of Northern California, stopped prescribing Premarin in 1994. Warner, who writes letters to the *New York Times* criticizing Premarin, spoke at a press conference in Fargo, North Dakota, where some PMU farms are located. He said,

> Premarin is no longer the most appropriate technology—if we were starting from scratch today to replace the human hormone that women lose at menopause, we would not be looking to the horse. Premarin is helpful, certainly, but it is no longer the most useful hormone-replacement-drug. (IGHA, 1998, p. 5)

People for the Ethical Treatment of Animals (PETA, http://envirolink .org/arrs/peta/index.html) sent literature about PMU farms to a group of physicians representing a cross section of the United States and asked for a response from them. Of those who responded, 63% said they were more likely to prescribe synthetic estrogen after being made aware of the conditions of the horses on the PMU farms. Nine comments from these physicians are posted on a Web page (athena.athenet.net/nrspntg/ PRNnewsmag.html). Five female and four male physicians attested to the fact that they no longer prescribed Premarin and that synthetic estrogens such as Estradiol or Estrace were their drugs of choice. No conclusions can be drawn from a sample this small; however, physicians were important opinion leaders of persuasion in this controversy.

Other audiences did not openly oppose Premarin but rather supported alternative drugs or a lifestyle that includes a healthful diet and exercise. New drugs have been developed to combat osteoporosis and other postmenopausal disorders. Raloxifene and Fosamax are among several new drugs that can help women at risk of developing osteoporosis, as well as those who have it. They may be acceptable substitutes for estrogen (J. Brody, 1997d). Eli Lilly and Company applied to the FDA to market Raloxifene under the trade name Evista (Mestel, 1997).

Some physicians and pharmaceutical company advertisements are advocating a healthy lifestyle of diet and exercise instead of drugs for post-menopausal conditions. The most prominent physician who makes this case is Susan Love, a breast cancer specialist at the University of California at Los Angeles. Dr. Love forecasted that scientists do not know enough about the risks and benefits of estrogen to be prescribing it so widely (Nemecek, 1997). Although she believes that estrogen therapies are helpful for women who have had hysterectomies, she only advocates short-term use of hormones—3 to 5 years. Her main concern was that estrogens may cause breast and uterine cancer, blood clots, and gallbladder disease. Her position is this:

> Menopause is not a disease; it is a normal part of life. . . . Women must redefine menopause as something natural. We need to make sure that we have accurate information and not wishful thinking. And we must be on our guard lest vested interests sell us a bill of goods. (Love, 1997, p. A25)

She has written two best-selling books—*Dr. Susan Love's Hormone Book* and, with Karen Lindsey, *Making Informed Choices About Menopause*—and she regularly appears on talk shows and has been interviewed in *Ms* (Felner, 1997), the *New Yorker,* and *U.S. News & World Report* (Shute, 1997). Love and others support a natural diet of soy foods, fiber, vegetables, and fruits plus a regimen of exercise (J. Brody, 1997a; Gleason, 1994).

Lilly ran nine-page advertising supplements in health magazines (e.g., *Prevention,* October 1997), claiming, "Of course there's life after menopause." Interestingly, this pharmaceutical company was not advertising a drug, although it stated, "Scientists are continuously studying new treatments that may help prevent or treat the diseases associated with menopause. You should check with your doctor about the availability of these new treatments." In fact, one section of the advertisement is under the heading "Really *Talk* with Your Doctor." It says, "Communicating openly with him or her is a critical part of protecting your health after menopause." The last part of the advertisement was a full-page spread in deep red with the beginning of a question in white letters: "If estrogen is the answer." The next page (in white with black letters) has a continuation of the question in red letters: "Why are there so many questions?" The advertisement ended with a reminder that Lilly was conducting research to find new alternatives to estrogen and offers a toll-free number to call for information.

Counterpropaganda

The most vocal counterpropagandists were nearly all the major animal protection organizations that oppose the PMU farms via major articles in their magazines and newsletters. The American Society for the Prevention of Cruelty to Animals (ASPCA), one of the oldest and most traditional animal protection societies, featured cover stories in its magazine *Animal Watch* about the PMU mares since 1995. These articles not only discussed the inhumane conditions of the horses but also summarized health studies about the hazards of estrogen or recommended alternative drugs and lifestyles. Wyeth-Ayerst was prominently mentioned in these articles, and readers were advised to write to Robert Essner, president of Wyeth-Ayerst, and to John Stafford, CEO of American Home Products, in protest. An article titled "Canada's Foals" (P. Clark, 1997), in the fall 1997 *Animal Watch,* included a plea to readers to adopt one of what the organization calls the "Premarin foals" to save them from slaughter, but it also cited a June 15, 1997, article in the *New England Journal of Medicine* that had a study whose researchers concluded that "women who use hormone therapy are thirty to forty percent more likely to develop breast cancer than women who have never taken menopausal hormones" (P. Clark, 1997, p. 26). The article ends with a motivational appeal:

> Is there any hope for ending the holocaust for horses written into every prescription for Premarin? . . . It is estimated that for every 150 patients who change their prescriptions from Premarin to a plant-derived or synthetic estrogen product, one mare is taken out of production. . . . The struggle to free the Premarin mares and prevent thousands of foal deaths each season will ultimately be won quietly, without fanfare, at the prescription counter. (P. Clark, 1997, p. 27)

The Humane Society of the United States (HSUS) also featured articles about the PMU mares in its attractive magazine, *HSUS News*. The HSUS also took direct aim at Wyeth-Ayerst for giving the horses "lives of misery" and for sending young foals to slaughter. An insert in one article, "What Women Should Know," gave advice about whether to take estrogen and suggested synthetic or plant-derived drugs. *Humane Review,* a newsletter from the New York State Humane Association, discussed "the cruelty of Premarin" and gave the names of alternative drugs "that produce fewer side effects" (Cheever, 1995, p. 3). The article "Premarin: Prescribed Cruelty" (1997) in the International Society for Animal Rights (ISAR) report also offered alternatives to Premarin. This article urged its readers, "Spread the Word: We must keep informing physicians and patients on the facts regarding

Premarin." The article concluded with offers of reprints of the article to leave in physicians' waiting rooms (ISAR, 1997, p. 10).

Several horse organizations and horse magazines have also joined the counterpropaganda protest. The International Generic Horse Association (IGHA) had an extensive Web page devoted to the PMU mare situation. This group, which does not solicit donations, included much information about Wyeth-Ayerst and Premarin. It said the following under the heading "The solution is really quite simple . . .":

> There are currently 9 million women taking Premarin. Educating those 9 million women (and their doctors) as to how Premarin is actually produced, and having them use one of the many synthetics now available as a substitute, will eventually dry up all the profits from Premarin production.

It ended with the slogans "ZERO women taking Premarin equals ZERO Premarin produced!" and "Just say NEIGH (to Premarin)" (home.earthlink .net/ighahorseaid/pmu_link). The IGHA urges horse lovers to wear purple ribbons (similar to the AIDS red ribbons) to let their protest be known. Actor Billy Bob Thornton wore one when he accepted his Oscar at the 1997 Academy Awards. The IGHA Web page as of March 5, 2005, continues to include petitions that one can download and addresses for sending letters of protest regarding the mistreatment of horses on PMU farms. The IGHA Web page in 1998 expressed gratitude to Chris Carter and the *Millennium* television series, episode 119, which depicted the character Frank Black, played by Lance Henriksen, being shocked when a veterinarian tells him about the PMU farms and about shipping the foals off to slaughter. The killer of women and horses in the episode, it turned out, was raised on a PMU farm. Carter was alleged to have used the IGHA Web site as a reference for writing this episode. Readers of the Web page were asked to contact Fox Broadcasting to ask that the episode be aired again (www.igha.org/pmu_ new).

The most active group has been PETA, which uses direct mail, brochures, celebrity testimonials, letters to government officials, demonstrations, and a Web page to protest Wyeth-Ayerst and the conditions of the PMU farms. This organization claims 500,000 members and says it is the largest animal rights organization in the world. If you called its Premarin number (800-KNOW-PMU), you would hear Dr. Susan Clay tell you, "Crush a Premarin pill, and you can smell the odor of horse urine." For several years every issue of PETA's *Animal Times* had articles about Premarin, featuring many movie actresses, including Hayley Mills, Lesley Anne Down, Gates McFadden, and Dame Judi Dench, holding a sign that proclaims, "I'll never take Premarin!" If a woman writes to PETA, she can get her own sign, have her picture taken with it, and have her picture added to the hundreds of pictures of ordinary women holding the same sign with their names on it in a huge photo album on display at the Virginia headquarters of PETA.

Comedian Tracy Ulmann's face appeared on a PETA brochure with yellow around her lips and a shocked look on her face with the question, "What's in your estrogen drug?" at the top and the answer as a caption *ew!* under her face, "URINE?!"

Actress Mary Tyler Moore made a video in which she proclaims, "I'll never take Premarin! No horses will suffer and die for me."

British television actress Ronnie Townsend, with her long hair covering her breasts, rode nude on horseback through the streets of Coventry, England, with a sign stating, "This lady says NEIGH to Premarin," as did Carrie Kramer in front of the FDA's offices in Washington, D.C. Animal protection activists threw horse manure on the steps of the agency in protest of the treatment of PMU horses.

PETA offers advice to women about managing menopause with natural foods or synthetic estrogen and suggests various strategies for protesting against Wyeth-Ayerst, including writing letters to local newspapers, members of Congress, the USDA, and various offices in the FDA; signing petitions; and making toll-free calls to Wyeth-Ayerst. PETA has filed a legal complaint with the FDA, asking that it require Wyeth-Ayerst to label Premarin to let consumers know its main ingredient is horse urine. The current label says "conjugated estrogens." The complaint is still pending.

Effects and Evaluation

Clearly, the powerful corporation American Home Products and Whithall Laboratories, as well as its major division Wyeth-Ayerst, won the battle to keep the generic Cenestin off the market. Wyeth-Ayerst plants had planned to triple the current processing of Premarin to more than 9 million gallons a year, according to the company's 1997 annual report. As the women of the baby boom generation mature, Wyeth-Ayerst expected earnings to reach nearly $2 billion annually by the year 2000, when more than 50 million women reached menopause.

Another company, Natural Biologics, Inc. of Minneapolis, Minnesota, planned to establish 100 PMU farms in the United States in 1998. This company had issued several promotional brochures that list the "positive" aspects of urine production and was selling franchise licenses in 1998 (IGHA, 1998).

After the announcement by the National Institutes of Health that HRT could possibly be linked to serious diseases, the demand for Premarin declined. Sales plummeted by 30% in 2003 and continue to do so as more studies link the drug to serious health consequences. Wyeth Organics, the arm of the company that coordinates the horse farms, began to cut its PMU contracts by notifying PMU farmers in Alberta, Saskatchewan, and Manitoba that they would be reducing the number of ranchers who produce the urine by one third. They also reduced production at their own plant in Brandon, Manitoba, downsizing by 50% the number of horses required for urine production. Premarin, once the most prescribed drug in America, is now the fourth most prescribed drug in the United States and Canada. Wyeth-Ayerst is attempting to increase its sales in foreign markets to compensate. In March 2005, a Florida judge said that as many as 300,000 women could sue Wyeth as a group over claims that they were injured by Wyeth's Prempro. Shares of Wyeth fell 22 cents to $41 on the New York Stock Exchange (*Los Angeles Times,* March 8, 2005, p. C3).

In July 2003, federal regulators approved a lower dose version of the hormone therapy treatment. Almost immediately, Wyeth-Ayerst started a new advertising campaign on television and in magazines such as *Ladies Home Journal, Redbook,* and *Time,* with the slogan, "Go Low with Premarin" and "Go Low with Prempro." Celebrities such as Lauren Hutton and Patti LaBelle are spokeswomen for the campaign. The cost of Premarin with its low dose of 0.3 mg is 26% higher than before (*Orange County Register,* April 13, 2005, p. 4). The Wyeth Web page (http://www.premarin.com, May 14, 2005) has warnings about possible links to health risks, but it also cites clinical trials that downplay such risks.

Animal rights organizations continue to protest the PMU farms and to support alternatives to Premarin. "HorseAid filed a petition with the FDA Advisory Committee in 2004 asking for a clarification on why the FDA had not removed their approval of PMU based medications from the U.S. marketplace in light of the many studies showing a link between the Premarin family of medications and several severe health risks associated with their use" (HorseAid, 2005).

The Pew Charitable Trusts sponsored a review of animal rights activism for Tufts University School of Veterinary Medicine (1995), titled *The Animal Research Controversy,* whose authors concluded that PETA "has done well in obtaining [media] coverage . . . but the animal protection groups have, for the most part, not been that skilled at disseminating their message nor have they had particularly good media contacts" (p. 131).

Ultimately, as in other propaganda campaigns, it is up to the audience to become educated about the issues. Instead of blindly accepting brand-name drugs from their physicians, patients must ask questions and seek alternatives.

These case studies examined four very different topics. Each case entailed much more information than we could possibly include in one chapter. We wanted not only to illustrate the 10-part method of analysis of propaganda but also to emphasize how propaganda operates in our time in our society, whether in war or in peace.

Notes

1. *Women, War, and Work: Shaping Space for Productivity in the Shipyards During World War II*, a film by Victoria O'Donnell, is available in 40- and 57-minute versions from KUSM-TV, Montana State University, Bozeman, MT 59717–3340.

2. Interestingly, this proposal has a precedent. In the 1930s, Congress responded to the aggressive and seductive advertising of investment securities vendors by banning pictures and images in all advertisements for stocks and bonds. The resulting advertisements contained only lists of the brokers making the offering.

3. The Drug Price Competition and Patent Term Restoration Act of 1984 requires that generics have the same active ingredients and that they act at the same rate, strength, and concentration as the brand name (Mann, 1997).

8

How Propaganda
Works in Modern Society

Propaganda is a form of communication and therefore can be depicted as a process. A model of the propaganda process includes the social-historical context, a cultural rim made up of government, economy, events, ideology, and myths of society; the institution; propaganda agents; media methods; the social network; and the public. Generalizations about propaganda in modern society are based on the events and concepts discussed throughout this book.

T his chapter presents a model of propaganda and several generalizations that have evolved from the events, ideas, and concepts discussed in previous chapters. This chapter also reaffirms our position that propaganda is a form of communication that can be depicted as a process.

A Model of the Process of Propaganda

Looking at the model of propaganda in Figure 8.1, one can see that it depicts the development of propagandistic communication as a process within a social system. The model is complex because, as we have seen in the preceding chapters, propaganda itself is complex. The process of propaganda takes the

357

form of a message flow through a network system that includes propaganda agents, various media, and a social network, originating with an institution and ending with the possibility of response from the public or a target audience within the public. The message flow is contained within a cultural rim that is itself placed within a social-historical context. The model therefore depicts the necessity of examining the process of propagandistic communication within the multitude of features contained within a social-historical-cultural framework. The flow of propaganda from institution to public has several canals that feed into, or are fed by, the elements of the cultural rim, to and from the institution itself, to and from the media, and to and from the public. This flow indicates that, as propaganda occurs, it has a potential impact on the culture at any point during the process, and of course the culture has, in turn, an impact on the process of propaganda.

Social-Historical Context

Propaganda as a process is socially determined. The social-historical context provides a heritage that gives a propagandist motivation and even a "style" of communication. To understand how propaganda works, we must consider how the existing social-historical context allows it to work. The propaganda that emerges is the product of forces established long before the activity originated and is controlled by those forces. That is why the uses and methods by which propaganda emerges differ from society to society.

The propagandist is influenced by past models through allusions to historical figures, methods, and impulses for current propagandistic activity. For example, the idea that freedom is worth dying for was the basis for Patrick Henry's "Give me liberty or give me death" speech in the time of the American Revolution. The same idea provided the impulse for the anticommunist slogan "Better dead than Red" almost 200 years later. In another culture, the Middle East, present-day propaganda can be traced back to the social-historical context of the origins of Muhammadanism in the seventh century and the subsequent spread of the Islamic religion. Thirteen centuries later, Mohammed's charge to his disciples to convert the infidels and to be willing to die fighting for the faith still shapes the content that takes form through modern technologies. When the Palestinians commit what Americans may think are "suicidal" acts, they do so believing that a death for the cause will ensure them a place on the right hand of God. Each incident of propaganda is thus historically based; yet, each act of propaganda also takes place at a specific time in history and is a product of its time. It is highly unlikely that the propaganda of Adolf Hitler would have worked in Germany during a time of prosperity. Time, both past and present, shapes the internal dynamics of the model.

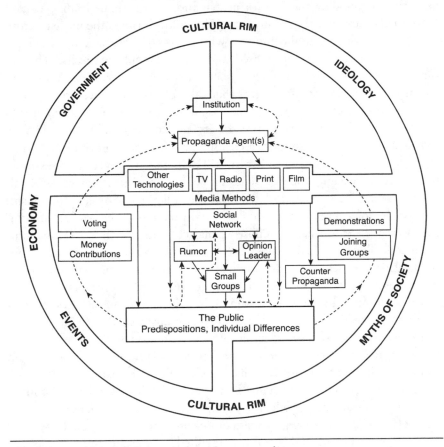

Figure 8.1   Model of the process of propaganda

The flow of propaganda to and from an institution depends on the conditions of the times and the availability of the media. For example, conditions in the United States in the 1950s tended to be more restrictive than in the 1960s because of the "Red scare" and McCarthyism. In the 16th century, Martin Luther's ability to reach his audience was made possible by the development of the printing press. If the times and conditions are right, to paraphrase Nietzsche, the propagandist is a hero who does nothing but shake the tree when the fruit is ripe.

Cultural Rim

Culture includes the social-historical context. We have depicted culture within the social-historical context only for purposes of clarifying the concepts presented here. In the model, the elements of culture are depicted as a rim surrounding the flow of propaganda, with canals leading to and from the process and the cultural rim. The cultural rim is the infrastructure that provides the material context in which messages are sent and received. How propaganda is developed, used, and received is culture specific. The elements of a culture—its ideologies, societal myths, government, economy, social practices, and specific events that take place—influence propaganda. Take, for example, whether a society is open or closed. Even though it is increasingly difficult for an entire society to remain totally "closed" in a world inundated with sophisticated and prolific communication systems, some countries, such as North Korea, still deliberately prevent outside information from reaching their citizens. The communist government of North Korea, feeling increasingly isolated after the collapse of Soviet communism, has for ideological reasons turned its back on the rest of the world, suffering the consequences of its self-imposed isolation. The North Korean government controls all media and maintains very strict access to information from the outside. Consequently, government propaganda dominates and shapes most aspects of North Korean life. Since 1996, North Korea has suffered a terrible famine, subsequently allowing relief agencies from the West past its borders to provide assistance. The Korean administration's unwillingness to share even the most basic demographic information with these agencies, however, has hampered efforts to deal with the problems of hunger and starvation. In addition, the West has labeled North Korea a "rogue state" because it is suspected of engaging in a wide variety of international crimes, including nuclear arms production, drug smuggling, and counterfeiting of U.S. $100 bills (www.mwgastories.com/nkorea/glossary/rogue). How long North Korea will remain this tightly controlled is uncertain, but it is a society with a closed cultural infrastructure that prevents messages from the "outside" from coming into the system.

An open society, in contrast, tends to have more flexible, accessible media systems that accept or reject messages without having to refer to higher authorities. In the autumn of 1985, the American Broadcasting Company (ABC) and the producers of the television program 20/20 chose to reject a program segment about the death of Marilyn Monroe and a connection with Robert Kennedy because of the producer's personal friendship with the Kennedy family. The British Broadcasting Corporation (BBC), however, chose to broadcast the story. In open systems, the variety of channels in the media, competing images, and easy access to them tend to make audiences less suspicious but also more discerning and concerned about the potential for propaganda.

The economy dictates the flow of propaganda relative to the sale or consumption of goods. Advertising certainly dictates the structure of the commercial mass media system in the United States. In the 19th century, the economy even dictated the attainment of literacy. If a nation needed laborers, it was less likely to support education of the masses.

Culture is a system of formal and informal rules that tell people how to behave most of the time. People's behavior, in turn, can alter the culture by creating new societal myths or changing ideologies. As James Carey (1988) pointed out,

> Culture as a system of construed meanings changes in relation to other cultural objects such as technologies and economic practices or other social processes such as conflict and accommodation; such changes are transformations on a given cultural tradition, a tradition that insists on reasserting itself. (p. 11)

The Process of Propaganda

The Institution

An institution generally initiates and fosters propaganda because of its organizational and financial powers. The propaganda may be to maintain the institution's legitimacy, its position in society, and its activities. An institution outside the established order may also initiate propaganda to agitate to show support for a counterideology or concern over an issue. Institutional affiliation may not be revealed by the propagandists, who may act as "fronts," or agents, for the source. This is often the case during wartime or for espionage activity.

Propaganda Agents

Propaganda agents are the people who facilitate messages directly and through the media for an institution. Sometimes, they are powerful and charismatic figures; at other times, they are bureaucrats or low-key disseminators of information. Their purpose is to send out ideology with a specific objective to a target audience for the benefit of the institution but not necessarily for the good of the receivers. A hierarchy of agents with a chain of command is likely; this is to ensure that the message will be homogeneous.

Media Methods

Propaganda agents select and use the available media to send the message to the target audience. The development of new technologies affects the nature of propaganda and has been seen to be the major factor in the use of propaganda. Starting in the 1930s, shortwave radio enabled the major governments of the world to broadcast ideology to remote places. This medium, now less strident in its propagandistic function, nevertheless continues to be an important method of disseminating information across international boundaries. The development of powerful communication satellites has greatly increased the international range and impact of television. Cable television viewers from Australia to New York to Cape Town can regularly watch the BBC evening news broadcast. The Atlanta-based Cable News Network (CNN) has become regular viewing in hotel rooms throughout the world. For a short period of time, fax machines became so commonplace that they, too, were used to deliver propaganda messages. Fax machines were soon overshadowed by an even more significant development—the Internet.

Since the early 1990s, the amazingly swift development of the World Wide Web (the Internet) has produced an unprecedented level of international communication among all levels of society—government, business, and private individuals. The Internet's increasingly important role as a disseminator of propaganda messages has caught most governments unprepared to deal with this new communication medium. Also, the inherent characteristic of the Internet that allows one individual to send the same message to hundreds, thousands, even millions of others almost instantaneously makes it an extremely potent and potentially dangerous propaganda vehicle. It is with apprehension that we note we have only begun to explore the full propagandistic potential of this technology.

Media utilization is vital to a propaganda campaign. Access to and control of the media literally mean access to and potential control of public opinion. The type of medium selected by the propagandist is appropriate to the audience that needs to be reached. Media are used to disseminate information to the membership of a propaganda organization, as well as to those whose support is solicited. Where the media are not owned, the propagandist runs the risk of the information being filtered through the media or released in an inappropriate fashion. The media message should be homogeneous, with a consistency of purpose, for the propaganda to be effective. Less control over the media means less control over the homogeneity of the message.

The mass media have become so extensive and influential that they affect culture. Although the propagandist's intent is to reach a target audience, media utilization can influence culture along the way to the target audience. Likewise, the culture influences the media. An open society allows competing messages to come from the media; thus, the propagandist's message, when mediated by unsympathetic or critical people, can be diffused. In contrast, the worldwide media are avaricious for sensational news. This enables propagandists to receive worldwide exposure at no cost. Certainly, terrorist hijackings of airplanes and ships and the subsequent media coverage have promulgated messages that otherwise would have remained unheard or unseen. The terrorist attack on the World Trade Center in New York City on September 11, 2001, was seen all over the world, almost as it occurred. Conversely, media coverage of a competing event can completely diffuse the impact of a propaganda event, such as on September 21, 1998, when at the same time that President Bill Clinton was addressing the United Nations (UN) on important foreign policy issues, all the major commercial networks were airing the 4-hour videotape of the president's deposition before the grand jury investigating his affair with White House intern Monica Lewinsky. Only C-Span covered the president's UN speech.

The media also affect propaganda agents and the institution. Too much exposure may be harmful, causing the propagandist to have to change strategies. Unwanted publicity can lessen the credibility of an agent or institution. The peculiarities of the medium itself may not be understood well enough. Presidential candidate Richard M. Nixon discovered that television caused him to appear unshaven and unattractive in the 1960 debates with fellow presidential candidate John F. Kennedy because he wore improper makeup and the wrong color of suit. Before his 1969 campaign appearances on television, Nixon hired Johnny Carson's makeup man to ensure that his appearance was appropriate for the televised image.

Sometimes, the target audience receives the message directly from a medium or combination of media; sometimes, selected audiences function as channels of communication to broader audiences through a social network.

The Social Network

A *social network* is made up of the following: (a) opinion leaders who may influence an audience because of their position with the social network; (b) small groups of people that may include opinion leaders, propaganda agents, or both; and (c) people who facilitate rumors innocently or deliberately throughout a social network. In the multistep flow of communication, a social network receives information from the media that is, in turn, disseminated throughout a community by leaders within it. Likewise, the public may receive information from the media and carry it back to the opinion leaders for explanation or confirmation.

As we have seen, in institutions such as the U.S. Information Agency, information may be sent directly from the propaganda agent to opinion leaders, sidestepping the media altogether. Although the process model of propaganda depicts the flow of information from the propaganda agent through the media to the social network, it is possible that the message will bypass the media and go directly to opinion leaders or small groups. For the most part, however, the media are used heavily by propaganda agents, with the social network coming into play as a mediating influence.

The Public

The propagandist's audience may be the general public or a segment of the public targeted for a specific set of responses. As we have seen in Chapter 6, the predispositions of the audience are canalized by the propaganda message, having the effect of resonance. Media experiences create shared experiences; thus, the public may form "communities" related to the propaganda message. For example, the abortion controversy has created moral communities among those who oppose abortion.

The public response to propaganda messages takes many forms. The public may fail to receive a message, it may choose to ignore it, it may be skeptical and suspicious, it may take sides for and against, or it may respond in desired ways. Examples of desired behavioral responses are voting, contributing money, purchasing products, joining groups, engaging in demonstrations, and putting pressure on elected officials through e-mail, petitions, letters, telegrams, and telephone calls. Such responses can be observed and measured, enhancing the propagandist's effectiveness. The same responses can also be fed back into the cultural rim, creating new events, affecting the economy, creating new myths, electing new government officials, and altering ideology over time.

The model of the process of propaganda is interactive and cyclical, with each segment having the potential of interacting with another. Propaganda is a communicative form with the potential to create change. This book has demonstrated changes throughout history, but more important, it should equip the reader with the ability to recognize and evaluate propaganda in modern society. We have learned more about propaganda in writing and revising this book, and the following generalizations, though few in number, may constitute new ways of looking at a very old subject.

Generalizations

JBO? your strange

1. Propaganda creates and is created by strange and powerful (bedfellows.) Special interests cause groups that are usually diverse to unite in a common cause. The abortion controversy brought the far Right and Roman Catholics

together. The anti-pornography movement united the Moral Majority and
some feminists.

2. Propaganda serves an informative function in that it tells people what to
    think about and how to behave. Because people turn to the media for help in
    understanding events and for finding out what to do about them, they unwit-
    tingly expose themselves to propaganda and may become willing or naive
    supporters of an invisible institution.

3. Even when it is obvious that a message is propaganda, people will respond
    favorably to it. Knowledge that communication is propagandistic does not
    necessarily neutralize people's reaction to it, especially when a message pro-
    duces resonance in an audience. Sometimes, it is a matter of repetition and
    familiarity of a message, particularly when in the form of a clever slogan
    or jingle. The best examples of this can be found in advertising slogans and
    jingles that have worked their way into our colloquial speech—for example,
    Nike's "Just Do It!"

4. People tend to divide into opposing camps in response to propaganda, and
    public "communities" are formed that create powerful "armies" to fight for
    and support a cause. The media can instantly transmit information, and the
    community responds with instantaneous reactions.

5. New technologies are powerful allies of propagandists. Satellite dishes and
    home video cameras have assisted the transmission of counterpropaganda in
    societies where the media have been controlled. Twenty-four-hour worldwide
    television broadcasts reach nearly all areas of the world. Instant information
    is readily available at all times. The Internet offers an important channel
    for propaganda, as well as easy access to information often enhanced by
    moving images and sounds. Unsolicited e-mail messages and advertisements
    ("spam") clutter our electronic mailboxes. "Spam" has become so proliferate
    that California recently passed legislation to make it illegal. People's predis-
    positions are easily identifiable through market research, making them easy
    targets for propaganda.

6. External propaganda may be created for internal consumption. Displays of
    aggression toward an enemy may not phase the enemy, but they can bolster
    morale at home.

7. Propaganda is not necessarily an evil thing. It can only be evaluated within
    its own context according to the players, the played upon, and its purpose.

This examination of propaganda has, we hope, made you more aware of
how much this activity has shaped our lives and helped form the attitudes
we have on so many subjects. Propaganda by itself is a natural outgrowth of
the development of sophisticated media of communication; it will always be

with us in one form or another, and we as individuals can accept or reject it as we wish. We should not fear propaganda, for in a free society, somewhere, somehow, alternative message systems always appear. As this book was being revised for the second edition in 1991, the world witnessed a series of remarkable events—the fall of the Berlin Wall and the reunification of Germany, the demise of communism in most of Eastern Europe, and the breakup of the Soviet Union into a myriad of smaller nationalistic states. In September 1998, 7 years after the end of the Cold War, the U.S. Department of Defense began to change the purpose of the agencies that dealt with the former Soviet Union during the cold war. Defense budgets will remain the same, but the agencies will now have as their purpose to cope with "weapons of mass destruction" ("Morning Edition," National Public Radio broadcast, October 1, 1998).

As we prepared this third edition, we viewed these events with a new perspective. The reunification of Germany has not been a total economic success, and the former East Germany has gone through a period of unprecedented economic difficulties while attempting to become a "market economy." Just a few days before this last paragraph was being written, a new, more socialist government was elected in Germany, with tremendous support from the former East German part of the country. What this new government can do to alleviate these difficulties remains to be seen. The emergence of a "new" Russia has also had enormous economic and social difficulties. Many Russians have begun to question the quality of life in a capitalist system and find it difficult to cope without the assistance of the paternalistic communist system under which they lived for so many years. Many of the states, once rigidly controlled by the central communist government, that split away from the Soviet Union have remained politically unstable and fraught with ethnic conflicts.

"Ethnic cleansing" in the Balkans has brought new horrors to the world as Serbian security forces pursue a deadly dismantling of the ethnic-Albanian rebellion and, in turn, the Kosovo Liberation Army establishes new guerrilla strongholds. Hundreds of thousands of Albanians have been forced to flee their homes as the harsh winter begins. Separatist propaganda fans the fires of disarray in attempts at establishing government and some sense of peace. Overall, the sudden collapse of communism in central Europe has left an economic and political vacuum that has not been successfully filled. It will take many years of struggle before these countries will be able to establish successfully a market economy and democratic political system.

At home in the United States, the threat of domestic terrorism reached dreadful proportions when the Alfred P. Murrah Federal Building in Oklahoma City was bombed in 1995, killing not only adult government and office workers and people conducting business there but also young children in a day care center. The bomb was not planted by foreign terrorists but by two discontented American men loosely associated with groups that oppose the federal government. American embassies in Kenya and Tanzania were blown up by bombers suspected of being part of a worldwide network of Muslim militants.

As we prepare this fourth edition, we are faced with a new series of challenges that now dominate the international stage. The attack on the World Trade Center and the Pentagon on 9/11 changed the world forever. Three thousand people were killed, and their deaths affected everyone as if the loss had been personal. America lost its innocence; thus, optimism was replaced by fear. The Bush administration went to war in Afghanistan and once more in Iraq. Terrorists effectively used the Internet not only to communicate within their own membership but also to cause the world to witness graphic torture and beheadings of their hostages. As we prepared this fourth edition, the realization that the study of propaganda is more important than ever became more and more obvious.

Thus, the world continues to change, and new challenges emerge. In response, new propagandistic strategies and campaigns will develop. As propaganda strategies become more sophisticated and more urgent in their application as current world conditions dictate, we sincerely believe that their impact can be ameliorated by understanding how such strategies work. In the late 1930s, the Institute for Propaganda Analysis (see Chapter 3) believed the same thing, and for the short while that it was allowed to exist, it was tantalizingly successful in educating its supporters on "how to analyze propaganda." The institute's demise was brought about precisely because it was able to neutralize propaganda messages by demystifying them, and it did not pick sides, analyzing propaganda regardless of its source. The time has come to push for more such "demystification" programs, starting in the elementary schools and going all the way through college. We are surrounded by propaganda of all kinds; therefore, it only behooves us to study, analyze, and ultimately understand how it works. If there is one thing we have learned in the 20 years we have been researching and writing the four editions of this book, it is that we only fear those things we do not understand.

References

Advisory Board for Cuba Broadcasting. (1989). *Report for 1989*. Washington, DC: Author.

Advisory Council for Cuba Broadcasting on TV Marti. (1991). *Special report.* Washington, DC: Author.

Ajemian, R., Goodgame, D., & Kane, J. J. (1991, February 18). Can the pro-war consensus survive? *Time,* pp. 32–34.

Ajzen, I., & Fishbein, M. (1980). *Understanding attitudes and predicting social behavior.* Englewood Cliffs, NJ: Prentice Hall.

Alexandre, L. (1988). *The Voice of America from detente to the Reagan doctrine.* Norwood, NJ: Ablex.

Allport, G. W. (1935). Attitudes. In C. Murchison (Ed.), *The handbook of social psychology* (pp. 798–884). Worcester, MA: Clark University Press.

Altheide, D. L., & Johnson J. M. (1980). *Bureaucratic propaganda.* Boston: Allyn & Bacon.

American Heart Association. (1998). *Cigarette smoking statistics.* Retrieved from http://www.americanheart.org/presenter.jhtml?identifier=4559

Anderson, K. (1981). *Wartime women: Sex roles, family relations, and the status of women during World War II.* Westport, CT: Greenwood.

Angell, M. (2004a). *The truth about drug companies: How they deceive us and what to do about it.* New York: Random House.

Angell, M. (2004b, July 15). The truth about drug companies. *New York Review of Books,* pp. 52–58.

Armstrong, B. (1979). *The electronic church.* Nashville, TN: Thomas Nelson.

Aronson, E. (1980). *The social animal.* San Francisco: Freeman.

Associated Press (2001, October 18). Troops ready for action. *Bozeman Chronicle,* pp. A1, A8.

Bailey, D. (Ed.). (1965). Phaedrus. In *Essays on rhetoric.* New York: Oxford University Press.

Bailyn, B. (1967). *The ideological origins of the American Revolution.* Cambridge, MA: Harvard University Press.

Ball-Rokeach, S. J., & DeFleur, M. L. (1976). A dependency model of mass-media effects. *Communication Research, 3,* 3–21.

Bandura, A. (1977). *Social learning theory.* Englewood Cliffs, NJ: Prentice Hall.

Bandura, A. (1986). *Social foundations of thought and action: A social cognitive theory.* Englewood Cliffs, NJ: Prentice Hall.

Bandura, A. (2002). Social cognitive theory of mass communication. In J. Bryant & D. Zillmann (Eds.), *Media effects: advances in theory and research* (2nd ed., pp. 121–154). Mahwah, NJ: Lawrence Erlbaum.

Bandura, A., Grusec, J. E., & Menlove, F. L. (1966). Observational learning as a function of symbolization and incentive set. *Child Development, 37,* 499–530.

Barnouw, E. (1968). *The golden web: A history of broadcasting in the United States, 1933–1953.* New York: Oxford University Press.

Barnouw, E. (1978). *The sponsor: Notes on a modern potentate.* Oxford, UK: Oxford University Press.

Barry, A. M. (1998, June). *The Joe Camel story: Tobacco industry manipulation and the necessity for visual intelligence.* Paper presented at the annual meeting of the Visual Communication Association, Winter Park, CO.

Becker, F. (1982). *The successful office: How to create a workspace that's right for you.* Reading, MA: Addison-Wesley.

Bem, D. J. (1970). *Beliefs, attitudes and human affairs.* Belmont, CA: Brooks/Cole.

Bennett, W. (1994). *The book of virtues.* New York: Simon & Schuster.

Benson, T. W., & Prosser, M. H. (1969). *Readings in classical rhetoric.* Boston: Allyn & Bacon.

Berkowitz, L., Corwin, R., & Heironimus, M. (1963). Film violence and subsequent tendencies. *Public Opinion Quarterly, 27,* 229.

Berkowitz, L., & Rawlings, E. (1963). Effects of film violence on inhibitions against subsequent aggression. *Journal of Abnormal and Social Psychology, 66,* 405–412.

Bernays, E. (2005). *Propaganda.* New York: IG Publishers. (Original work published 1928)

Biddle, P. R. (1966). *An experimental study of ethos and appeal for overt behavior in persuasion.* Unpublished doctoral dissertation, University of Illinois, Urbana.

Bin, Z. (1999). Mouthpiece or money-spinner? The double life of Chinese television in the late 1990s. *International Journal of Cultural Studies, 2*(3), 291–305.

Black, J. (1995, Winter). Another season of suffering. *Animal Watch,* pp. 15, 18–20.

Black, J. (1996, January/February). A bitter pill. *Animals,* pp. 11–13.

Bloom, A. (1987). *The closing of the American mind.* New York: Simon & Schuster.

Blumer, H. (1933). *Movies and conduct.* New York: Macmillan.

Bogardus, E. S. (1925). Measuring social distance. *Journal of Applied Sociology, 9,* 299–308.

Bogart, L. (1976). *Premises for propaganda: The U.S. Information Agency's operating assumptions in the Cold War.* New York: Free Press.

Bogart, L. (1995). *Cool words, cold war: A new look at USIA's premises for propaganda*. Washington, DC: American University Press.

Bonner, R. J. (1933). *Aspects of Athenian democracy*. Berkeley: University of California Press.

Book sales on the decline. (2005, May 17). *Los Angeles Times*, p. E8.

Boster, R. J., & Mongeau, P. (1984). Fear-arousing persuasive messages. In R. N. Bostrum & B. H. Westley (Eds.), *Communication yearbook 8* (pp. 330–375). Beverly Hills, CA: Sage.

Bramson, L. (1961). *The political context of sociology*. Princeton, NJ: Princeton University Press.

Brinkley, A. (1982). *Voices of protests: Huey Long, Father Coughlin and the Great Depression*. New York: Vintage.

British enlist Alice in propaganda war. (1982, May 23). *Dallas Morning News*, p. 10A.

A British guide to dirty tricks: How a covert campaign helped steer America into World War II. (1989). *Washington Post National Weekly Edition, 6,* 10–11.

Brock, P. (1993–1994). Dateline Yugoslavia: The partisan press. *Foreign Affairs, 93,* 152–172.

Brock, T. C., & Green, M. C. (Eds.). (2005). *Persuasion: Psychological insights and perspectives*. Thousand Oaks, CA: Sage.

Brody, J. (1997a, August 27). Diet may be one reason complaints about menopause are rare in Asia. *New York Times*, p. C8.

Brody, J. (1997b, August 20). Estrogen after menopause? A tough dilemma. *New York Times*, p. C8.

Brody, J. (1997c, June 19). Hormone use helps women, a study finds. *New York Times*, p. A1.

Brody, J. (1997d, September 30). When bones are weakening, several treatments can help save them. *New York Times*, p. F9.

Brody, J. E. (1991, December 11). Smoking among children is found linked to cartoon advertisements. *New York Times*, p. A16.

Brown, J. A. C. (1963). *Techniques of persuasion: From propaganda to brainwashing*. Baltimore: Penguin.

Browne, R. W. (1850). *The Nichomachean ethics of Aristotle* (Vol. 2). London: H. G. Bohn.

Brownfield, A. C. (1984, May 4). *Washington Inquirer*, p. 6.

Brownstein, R. (1990). *The power and the glitter: The Hollywood-Washington connection*. New York: Pantheon.

Bruntz, G. G. (1938). *Allied propaganda and the collapse of the German empire in 1918*. Stanford, CA: Stanford University Press.

Bryant, D. C. (1953, December). Rhetoric: Its function and scope. *Quarterly Journal of Speech, 39,* 401–424.

Bryant, J., & Zillmann, D. (2002). *Media effects: Advances in theory and research*. Mahwah, NJ: Lawrence Erlbaum.

Bumpus, B., & Skelt, B. (1985). *Seventy years of international broadcasting*. Paris: UNESCO.

Burke, K. (1973). *The philosophy of literary form*. Berkeley: University of California Press.

Burnett, N. F. S. (1989). Ideology and propaganda: Toward an integrative approach. In T. Smith III (Ed.), *Propaganda: A pluralistic perspective* (pp.127–137). New York: Praeger.

Cameron, K. S., Ireland, R. D., Lussier, R. N., New, J. R., & Robbins, S. P. (2003, December). Management textbooks as propaganda. *Journal of Management Education, 27*(6), 711–729.

Campbell, C. W. (1985). *Reel America and World War I*. Jefferson, NC: McFarland.

Cantor, J. (1998) *Mommy, I'm scared: How TV and movies frighten children and what we can do to protect them*. Orlando, FL: Harvest Books.

Carey, A. (1997). *Taking the risk out of democracy: Corporate propaganda versus freedom and liberty* (A. Lohrey, Ed.). Urbana: University of Illinois Press.

Carey, J. (1997, February 3). The politics of generics. *Business Week*, pp. 128–131.

Carey, J. W. (Ed.). (1988). *Media, myths, and narratives: Television and the press*. Newbury Park, CA: Sage.

Carey, J. W. (1989). *Communication as culture: Essays on media and society*. Boston: Unwin Hyman.

Carlson, J. (1983, October). Crime-show viewing by pre-adults: The impact on attitudes toward civil liberties. *Communication Research, 10*, 529–552.

Cary, H. (1854). *Plato: Works of Plato* (Vol. 1). London: H. G. Bohn.

CBS spreads disinformation on AIDS. (1987, April 13). *AIM Report*, pp. xvi–8.

Chandler, R. W. (1981). *War of ideas: The U.S. propaganda campaign in Vietnam*. Boulder, CO: Westview.

Cheever, H. (1995, Spring). The cruelty of *premarin*. *Humane Review*, p. 3.

Chomsky, N. (1992). A view from below. In M. J. Hogan (Ed.), *The end of the Cold War: Its meanings and implications* (pp. 137–150). Cambridge, UK: Cambridge University Press.

Choukas, M. (1965). *Propaganda comes of age*. Washington, DC: Public Affairs Press.

Cialdini, R. B., Trost, M. R., & Newsom, J. T. (1995). Preference for consistency: The development of a valid measure and the discovery of surprising behavioral implications. *Journal of Personality and Social Psychology, 69*, 318–328.

Clark, P. (1997, Fall). Canada's foals. *Animal Watch*, pp. 18, 26–27.

Clark, T. (1997). *Art and propaganda in the twentieth century*. New York: Harry N. Abrams.

Cohn, J. (1989). *Creating America: George Horace Lorimer and the Saturday Evening Post*. Pittsburgh: University of Pittsburgh Press.

Coles, R. (1986). *The political life of children*. Boston: Houghton Mifflin.

Coll, S. (2004). *Ghost wars: The secret history of the CIA, Afghanistan, and bin Laden, from the Soviet invasion to September 10, 2001*. New York: Penguin.

Comstock, G. (1980). *Television in America*. Beverly Hills, CA: Sage.

Constable, P. (2002, December 16–22). A campaign for hearts and minds. *Washington Post National Weekly Edition*, p. 15.

Conway, F. & Siegelman, J. (1982). *Holy terror: The fundamentalist war on America's freedoms in religion, politics, and our private lives.* Garden City, NY: Doubleday.

Coombs, J. E., & Nimmo, D. (1993). *The new propaganda: The dictatorship of palaver in contemporary politics.* New York: Longman.

Cooper, L. (1932). *The rhetoric of Aristotle.* New York: Appleton-Century-Crofts.

Cooper, M. (1989). *Analyzing public discourse.* Prospect Heights, IL: Waveland.

Cooper, N. (1998, October 17). Bar patrons: Warning tobacco companies' advertising money may be addictive in Houston's club scene. *Houston Press,* pp. 6, 8.

Costello, J. (1985). *Love, sex and war: 1939–1945.* London: Pan Books.

Creel, G. (1920). *How we advertised America: The first telling of the amazing story of the Committee on Public Information, 1917–1919.* New York: Harper & Row.

Critchlow, J. (1995). *Radio hole-in-the-head: Radio liberty—an insider's story of Cold War broadcasting.* Washington, DC: American University Press.

Crouthamel, J. L. (1989). *Bennett's New York Herald and the rise of the popular press.* Syracuse, NY: University of Syracuse Press.

Cull, N. (1996). *Selling war: The British propaganda campaign against American "neutrality" in World War II.* New York: Oxford University Press

Cull, N., Culbert, D., & Welch, D. (2003). *Propaganda and mass persuasion: A historical encyclopedia, 1500 to the present.* New York: ABC-Clio.

Cunningham, S. B. (2002). *The idea of propaganda: A reconstruction.* Westport, CT: Praeger.

Czitrom, D. J. (1982). *Media and the American mind.* Chapel Hill: University of North Carolina Press.

Darwin, C. (1982). *The origin of species by means of natural selection: The preservation of favored races in the struggle for life.* London: Penguin Classics. (Original work published 1859)

Davison, W. P. (1971, November). Some trends in international propaganda. *Annals of the American Academy of Political and Social Science, 398,* 1–13.

Davison Hunter, J. D. (1991). *Culture wars: The struggle to define America.* New York: Basic Books.

DeFleur, M., & Ball-Rokeach, S. (1982). *Theories of mass communication.* New York: Longman.

Delia, J. (1971). Rhetoric in the Nazi mind: Hitler's theory of persuasion. *Southern Speech Communication Journal, 37*(2), 136–149.

Delia, J. G. (1987). Communication research: A history. In C. R. Berger & H. Chaffee (Eds.), *Handbook of communication science* (pp. 20–98). Newbury Park, CA: Sage.

DeParles, J. (1991, May 5). Long series of military decisions led to Gulf War news censorship. *New York Times,* p. A1.

DeVito, J. A. (1986). *The communication handbook: A dictionary.* New York: Harper & Row.

Dewey, J. (1927). *The public and its problems.* Chicago: Swallow Press.

Dewey, J. (1935). *Liberalism and social action*. New York: Putnam.

Dickens, A. G. (1968). *Reformation and society in sixteenth century Europe*. New York: Harcourt Brace Jovanovich.

Doherty, T. P. (1993). *Projections of war: Hollywood, American Culture, and World War II*. New York: Columbia University Press.

Dondis, D. (1981). Signs and symbols. In R. Williams (Ed.), *Contact: Human communication and its history* (pp. 71–86). New York: Thomas & Hudson.

Donnerstein, E., & Malamuth, N. (Eds.). (1984). *Pornography and sexual aggression*. New York: Academic Press.

Doob, L. W. (1948). *Public opinion and propaganda*. New York: Henry Holt & Co.

Doob, L. W. (1966). *Public opinion and propaganda* (2nd ed.). Hamden, CT: Archon.

Doob, L. W. (1989). Propaganda. In E. Barnouw, G. Gerbner, W. Schramm, T. L. Worth, & L. Gross (Eds.), *International encyclopedia of communications* (Vol. 3, pp. 374–378). New York: Oxford University Press.

Dowe, T. (1997, January). The netizen: News you can abuse. *Wired*, pp. 53–56, 184–185.

Downing, J. D. H., McQuail, D., Schlesinger, P., & Wartella, E. (Eds.). (2004). *The handbook of media studies*. Thousand Oaks, CA: Sage.

Duffey, B., & Walsh, K. T. (1991, March 4). The Gulf War's final curtain. *U.S. News & World Report*, pp. 24–34.

Dupuy, T. N. (1965). Korean War. In *Encyclopedia Britannica* (Vol. 13, pp. 467–475). Chicago: Encyclopedia Britannica.

Ebon, M. (1987). *The Soviet propaganda machine*. New York: McGraw-Hill.

Editorial foreword. (1937, January). *Public Opinion Quarterly, 1,* 3.

Edwards, M. U. (1994). *Printing, propaganda, and Martin Luther*. Berkeley: University of California Press.

Edwards, W. (1954). The theory of decision making. *Psychological Bulletin, 51,* 390–417.

Eke, R. (1996, March 26). A mare's worst nightmare. *Great Falls Tribune*, pp. 1D, 4D.

Ellul, J. (1965). *Propaganda: The formation of men's attitudes*. New York: Knopf.

Emery, E., & Emery, M. (1984). *The press and America*. Englewood Cliffs, NJ: Prentice Hall.

Fazio, R. H. (1986). How do attitudes guide behavior? In R. M. Sorrentino & E. T. Higgins (Eds.), *The handbook of motivation and cognition: Foundations of social behavior* (pp. 204–243). New York: Guilford.

Felner, J. (1997, July/August). Dr. Susan Love cuts through the hype on women's health. *MS, 8,* 37–43.

Festinger, L. (1957). *A theory of cognitive dissonance*. Stanford, CA: Stanford University Press.

Fielding, R. (1972). *The American newsreel*. Norman: University of Oklahoma Press.

Fishbein, M., & Ajzen, I. (1975). *Beliefs, attitudes, intentions, and behavior: An introduction to theory and research*. Reading, MA: Addison-Wesley.

Fiske, J. (1987). *Television culture*. London: Methuen.

Fleishman, J. (2005, May 11). Permanent memory of Holocaust opens in Berlin. *Los Angeles Times*, p. A3.

Fleming, D., & Bailyn, B. (Eds.). (1969). *The intellectual migration, Europe and America, 1930–1960*. Cambridge, MA: Harvard University Press.

Ford, R. E. (1997). New light on Gulf of Tonkin. Retrieved from http://www.thehistorynet.com/Vietnam/articles/1997/08972 text.htm

Forman, C. W. (1979). Christian missions in the ancient world. In H. D. Lasswell, D. Lerner, & H. Speier (Eds.), *Propaganda and communication in world history: Vol. 1. The symbolic instrument in early times* (pp. 330–347). Honolulu: University Press of Hawaii.

Foulkes, A. P. (1983). *Literature and propaganda*. London: Methuen.

Fowles, J. (1997). *Advertising and popular culture*. Thousand Oaks, CA: Sage.

Freemantle, A. (1965). *The age of faith*. New York: Time-Life Books.

Fritschler, A. L. (1983). *Smoking and politics*. Englewood Cliffs, NJ: Prentice Hall.

Furhammer, L., & Isaksson, F. (1971). *Politics and film*. New York: Praeger.

Galbraith, P. W. (2004, September 24). Iraq: The bungled transition. *New York Review of Books*, pp. 70–74.

Galimore, T. (1991, May). *Radio Marti: A study of U.S. international broadcasting policy and the ban on domestic dissemination of government information.* Paper presented at the ICA, Chicago.

Gallatin National Forest thinning plan moves ahead. (2005, January 9). *Bozeman Daily Chronicle*, pp. 1, 8.

Gerbner, G., Gross, L., Signorelli, N., Morgan, M., & Jackson-Beeck, M. (1979, Summer). The demonstration of power: Violence profile no. 10. *Journal of Communication, 29*, 177–196.

Gilmore, A. B. (1998). *You can't fight tanks with bayonets: Psychological warfare against the Japanese army in the southwest Pacific*. Lincoln: University of Nebraska Press.

Ginsberg, B. (1986). *The captive public: How mass opinion promotes state power*. New York: Basic Books.

Glantz, S. E. (1996). *The cigarette papers*. Berkeley: University of California Press.

Gleason, S. (1994, Spring). Menopause: It's not a disease: Natural approaches to a change in life. *Good Medicine, 17*, 12–14.

Golden, C. D. (1991, September). The Palmer Survey. *American Economic Review*, pp. 3–5.

Goodman, E. (2003, June 22). Jessica Lynch a human, not a symbolic hero. *Missoulian*, p. B4.

Graff, H. J. (Ed.). (1981). *Literary and social development in the West*. Cambridge, UK: Cambridge University Press.

Grandin, T. (1939). *The political uses of radio*. Geneva, Switzerland: Geneva Research Center.

Gruening, E. (1931). *The public pays: A study of power propaganda*. New York: Vanguard.

Gustainis, J. (1989). Propaganda and the law: The case of three Canadian films. In T. Smith III (Ed.), *Propaganda: A pluralistic perspective* (pp. 115–126). New York: Praeger.

Gwyn, R. (1991, February 26). Saddam tricked into thinking that he could win. *Toronto Star,* p. A1.

Hale, J. (1975). *Radio power.* Philadelphia: Temple University Press.

Hall, S. (1977). *The hinterland of science: Ideology and the sociology of knowledge* (Working Papers in Cultural Studies No. 10). London: Hutchinson.

Hall, S. (1980). Cultural studies: Two paradigms. *Media, Culture, and Society, 2*(1), 57–72.

Hall, S. (1984, January). The culture gap. *Marxism Today,* pp. 18–22.

Hall, S. (Ed.). (1997). *Representation: Cultural representations and signifying practices.* Thousand Oaks, CA: Sage.

Hanke, H. (1990). Media culture in the GDR: Characteristics, processes and problems. *Media Culture and Society, 12*(2), 175–193.

Hardt, H. (1989). The return of the critical and the challenge of radical dissent: Critical theory, cultural studies, and American mass communication research. In J. A. Anderson (Ed.), *Communication yearbook 12* (pp. 558–600). Newbury Park, CA: Sage.

Hart, J. D. (1965). Paul Revere's ride. In *The Oxford companion to American literature* (p. 639). New York: Oxford University Press.

Hart-Davis, D. (1986). *Hitler's games: The 1936 Olympics.* New York: Harper & Row.

Hartmann, S. M. (1982). *The home front and beyond: American women in the 1940s.* Boston: Twayne.

Harwit, M. (1996). *An exhibit denied: Lobbying the history of Enola Gay.* New York: Copernicus/Springer-Verlag.

Hass, S. D., Bristol, F., & Card, C. E. (1996, February). Risk factors associated with the incidence of foal mortality in an extensively managed mare herd. *Canadian Veterinarian, 37,* 31.

Hayden, D. (1986). *Redesigning the American dream: The future of housing, work, and family life.* New York: Norton.

Hayward, J. W. (1997). *Letters to Vanessa: On love, science, and awareness in an enchanted world.* Boston: Shambhala.

Heider, F. (1946). Attitudes and cognitive organization. *Journal of Psychology, 21,* 107–112.

Heilbroner, R. L. (1985, January). Advertising as agitprop. *Harper's,* pp. 71–76.

Herzstein, R. (1978). *The war that Hitler won.* New York: Putnam.

Hess, S., & Kaplan, M. (1975). *The ungentlemanly art.* New York: Macmillan.

Hitler, A. (1939). *Mein Kampf.* New York: Reynal & Hitchcock.

Hoffman, H. (1996). *The triumph of propaganda: Film and national socialism, 1936–1945.* Providence, RI: Berghahn.

Honey, M. (1984). *Creating Rosie the Riveter: Class, gender, and propaganda during World War II.* Boston: University of Massachusetts Press.

HorseAid. (2005, May 14). Premarin.org: A part of the Equine Rescue dot net. Retrieved from http://www.premarin.org

Hovland, C. I., Janis, I. L., & Kelly, H. H. (1953). *Communication and persuasion: Psychological studies of opinion change.* New Haven, CT: Yale University Press.

Hovland, C. I., Lumsdaine, A. A., & Sheffield, F. D. (1949). *Experiments on mass communication: Vol. 3. Studies in social psychology in World War II.* Princeton, NJ: Princeton University Press.

Hovland, C. I., & Mandell, W. (1952). An experimental comparison of conclusion drawing by the communicator and by the audience. *Journal of Abnormal and Social Psychology, 47,* 581–588.

How to detect propaganda. (1937). *Propaganda Analysis, 1*(2), 5–8.

Hunt, E. L. (1925). Plato and Aristotle on rhetoric and rhetoricians. In E. L. Hunt (Ed.), *Studies in rhetoric and public speaking* (pp. 3–60). New York: Century.

Ignatius, D. (1989, October 2–8). A British guide to dirty tricks. *Washington Post National Edition,* pp. 9–11.

International Generic Horse Association (IGHA). (1998, March 27). Retrieved March 27, 1998, from http://www.igha.org

International Society for Animal Rights (ISAR). (1997). *Premarin: Prescribed cruelty.* Retrieved August 21, 2005, from http://www.isaronline.org/pn_1997_autumn_02.htm#premarin

Jennings, P. (1996). ABC proves cigarette companies target kids. Retrieved from http://www./globa12000.net/yph/document/abc.html

Johnson, G. (1991). *In the palaces of memory.* New York: Vintage.

Jones, D. (1995, January 17). The price of a "wonder drug": What happens when the medical men have got what they came for? *Today* [Television broadcast]. New York: NBC.

Jones, D. B. (1945). Hollywood war films. *Hollywood Quarterly, 1*(1), 1–19.

Jones, M. (1990). *Fake? The art of deception.* London: British Museum Publications.

Jowett, G. S. (1976). *Film: The democratic art.* Boston: Little, Brown.

Jowett, G. S. (1982). They taught it at the movies: Films on models for learned sexual behavior. In S. Thomas (Ed.), *Film/culture* (pp. 209–221). Metuchen, NY: Scarecrow.

Jowett, G. S., Jarvie, I., & Fuller, K. H. (1996). *Children and the movies: Media influence and the Payne Fund studies.* New York: Cambridge University Press.

Kammen, M. (1993). *Mystic chords of memory: The transformation of tradition in American culture.* New York: Vintage.

Kapferer, J. N. (1990). *Rumors: Uses, interpretations, and images.* New Brunswick, NJ: Transaction Press.

Karlins, M., & Abelson, H. I. (1970). *Persuasion: How opinions and attitudes are changed.* New York: Springer.

Kecskemeti, P. (1973). Propaganda. In I. D. Pool, F. W. Frey, W. Schramm, N. Maccoby, & E. B. Parker (Eds.), *Handbook of communication* (pp. 844–870). Chicago: Rand McNally.

Kellner, D. (1992). *The Persian Gulf TV war.* Boulder, CO: Westview.

Kellosalmi, R. (1995, May 8). Inhumanity by prescription. *Family Practice,* p. 9.

Kelman, H. C., & Hovland, C. I. (1953). Reinstatement of the communicator in delayed measurement of opinion change. *Journal of Abnormal and Social Psychology, 48,* 3.

Kepel, G. (2004). *The war for Muslim minds: Islam and the West* (P. Ghazaleh, Trans.). Cambridge, MA: Belknap Press of Howard University Press.

Key, W. R. (1973). *Subliminal seduction.* New York: Signet.

Kim, M. S., & Hunter, J. E. (1993). Attitude-behavior relations: A meta-analysis of attitudinal relevance and topic. *Journal of Communication, 43*(1), 101–142.

Kneitel, T. (1982, December). Secrets of propaganda broadcasting. *Popular Communication: The Monitoring Magazine,* pp. 8–21.

Koop, C. E. (1998, September 14). Speech before National Press Club. Retrieved from www.ash.org/sept98/09-14-98-1.html

Kubey, R., & Csikszentmihalyi, M. (1990). *Television and the quality of life: How viewing shapes everyday experience.* Hillsdale, NJ: Lawrence Erlbaum.

Kurtz, H. (1998). *Spin cycle: Inside the Clinton propaganda machine.* New York: Free Press.

Lakoff, G., & Johnson, M. (1980). *Metaphors we live by.* Chicago: University of Chicago Press.

Lamay, C. (1991a). By the numbers I: The bibliometrics of war. In C. Lamay & E. Dennis (Eds.), *The media at war: The press and the Persian Gulf conflict* (pp. 41–44). New York: Freedom Forum.

Lamay, C. (1991b). By the numbers II: Measuring the coverage. In C. Lamay & E. Dennis (Eds.), *The media at war: The press and the Persian Gulf conflict* (pp. 45–50). New York: Freedom Forum.

Land, R. E., & Sears, D. O. (1964). *Public opinion.* Englewood Cliffs, NJ: Prentice Hall.

Lang, K. (1989). Communications research: Origins and development. In E. Barnouw, G. Gerbner, W. Schramm, T. L. Worth, & L. Gross (Eds.), *International encyclopedia of communications* (Vol. I, pp. 369–374). New York: Oxford University Press.

Lapiere, R. T. (1934). Attitude versus actions. In M. Fishbein (Ed.), *Readings in attitude theory and measurement* (pp. 26–31). New York: John Wiley.

Lasswell, H. (1927). *Propaganda technique in the world war.* New York: Knopf.

Lasswell, H. (1938). Foreword. In G. G. Bruntz (Ed.), *Allied propaganda and the collapse of the German empire in 1918* (pp. v–viii). Stanford, CA: Stanford University Press.

Lasswell, H., & Blumsenstock, D. (1939). *World revolutionary propaganda: A Chicago study.* New York: Knopf.

Lasswell, H. D. (1951). Political and psychological warfare. In D. Lerner (Ed.), *Propaganda in war and crisis* (pp. 261–277). New York: G. W. Stewart.

Lasswell, H. D., Lerner, D., & Speier, H. (Eds.). (1979). *Propaganda and communication in world history: Vol. 1. The symbolic instrument in early times.* Honolulu: University Press of Hawaii.

Lasswell, H. D., Lerner, D., & Speier, H. (Eds.). (1980). *Propaganda and commu-nication in world history: Vol. 2. The emergence of public opinion in the West.* Honolulu: University of Hawaii Press.

Laurie, C. D. (1996). *The propaganda warriors: America's crusade against Nazi Germany.* Lawrence: University Press of Kansas.

Lazarsfeld, P. L. (1941). Remarks on administrative and critical communications research. *Studies in Philosophy and Social Science, 9*(1), 2–16.

Lazarsfeld, P. L., Berelson, D., & Gaudet, H. (1948). *The people's choice: How the voter makes up his mind in a presidential campaign.* New York: Duell, Sloan, & Pearce.

Lazarsfeld, P. L., & Stanton, F. N. (Eds.). (1944). *Radio research, 1942–43.* New York: Duell, Sloan, & Pearce.

Lears, J. (1994). *Fables of abundance: A cultural history of advertising in America.* New York: Basic Books.

Lee, A. M., & Lee, E. B. (1979). *The fine art of propaganda.* San Francisco: International Society for General Semantics.

Lee, C. (1980). *Media imperialism reconsidered: The homogenization of television culture.* Beverly Hills, CA: Sage.

Lee, G. (1992, September 25). PR firm loses bid to curb ex-employees. *Washington Post,* pp. F1–F2.

Lerner, D. (1951a). Effective propaganda: Conditions and evaluation. In D. Lerner (Ed.), *Propaganda in war and crisis: Materials for American policy* (pp. 344–354). New York: G. W. Stewart.

Lerner, D. (Ed.). (1951b). *Propaganda in war and crisis: Materials for American policy.* New York: G. W. Stewart.

Liebert, R. M., Neale, J. M., & Davidson, E. S. (1973). *The early window: Effects of television on children and youth.* New York: Pergamon.

Likert, R. (1932). A technique for the measurement of attitudes. *Archives of Psychology,* p. 140, 55.

Limbaugh, R. H., III. (1993). *See, I told you so.* New York: Simon & Schuster, 1993.

Linebarger, P. M. A. (1954). *Psychological warfare.* New York: Duell, Sloan, & Pearce.

Lippmann, W. (1925). *The phantom public.* New York: Harcourt Brace.

Lippmann, W. (1960). *Public opinion.* New York: Macmillan. (Original work published 1922)

Lipstadt, D. (1993). *Denying the Holocaust: The growing assault on truth and memory.* New York: Plume.

Long, H. P. (1933). *Every man a king: An autobiography of Huey P. Long.* New Orleans, LA: National Book Company

Love, S. (1997, March 20). Sometimes Mother Nature knows best. *New York Times,* p. A25.

Lowery, S. A., & DeFleur, M. L. (1988). *Milestones in mass communication research.* New York: Longman.

Lowery, S. A., & DeFleur, M. L. (1995). *Milestones in mass communication research* (2nd ed.). New York: Longman.

Luke, T. W. (1989). *Screens of power: Ideology, domination and resistance in informational society*. Urbana: University of Illinois Press.

Maben, M. (1987). *Vanport*. Portland: Oregon Historical Society Press.

MacArthur, J. R. (1992a, January 6). *New York Times*, p. A11.

MacArthur, J. R. (1992b). *Second front: Censorship and propaganda in the Gulf War*. New York: Hill & Wang.

MacBeth, T. M. (1996). *Tuning in to young viewers: Social science perspectives on television*. Thousand Oaks, CA: Sage.

MacCunn, J. (1906). The ethical doctrine of Aristotle. *International Journal of Ethics, 16*, 301.

Machiavelli, N. (1961). *The prince* (G. Bull, Trans.). London: Penguin. (Original work published 1513)

Mann, J. (1997, April 2). The politics of pharmaceuticals. *Washington Post*, p. E13.

Manheim, K. (1943). *Diagnosis of our time*. London: Routledge Kegan Paul.

Manheim, J. B. (1994). Strategic public diplomacy: Managing Kuwait's image during the Gulf conflict. In W. L. Bennett & D. Paletz (Eds.), *Taken by storm: The media , public opinion, and U.S. foreign policy in the Gulf War* (pp. 131–148). Chicago: University of Chicago Press.

Marks, J. (1979). *The search for the "Manchurian candidate": The CIA and mind control*. New York: Times Books.

Martin, L. J. (1971, November). Effectiveness of international propaganda. *Annals of the American Academy of Political and Social Science, 398,* 61–70.

Marwell, G., & Schmitt, D. R. (1967). Dimensions of compliance gaining behavior: An empirical analysis. *Sociometry, 30*(3), 340–364.

Maxwell, B. W. (1936). Political propaganda in Soviet Russia. In H. L. Childs (Ed.), *Propaganda and dictatorship* (pp. 61–79). Princeton, NJ: Princeton University Press.

McBride, S. (1980). *Many voices, one world*. New York: Unipub.

McCroskey, J. C. (1969). A summary of the effects of evidence in persuasive communication. *Quarterly Journal of Speech, 55*(1), 169–176.

McGuire, W. J. (1964). Inducing resistance to persuasion: Some contemporary approaches. In L. Berkowitz (Ed.), *Advances in experimental social psychology* (Vol. 1, pp. 124–139). New York: Academic Press.

McGuire, W. J. (1968). Personality and attitude change. In A. G. Greenwald, T. C. Brock, & T. M. Ostrom (Eds.), *Psychological foundations of attitudes* (pp. 171–196). New York: Academic Press.

McGuire, W. J. (1985). Attitudes and attitude change. In G. Lindzey & E. Aronson (Eds.), *The handbook of social psychology* (Vol. 2, pp. 233–346). New York: Random House.

McLaine, I. (1979). *Ministry of morale: Home front morale and the Ministry of Information in World War II*. London: Allen & Unwin.

McQuail, D. (1994). *Mass communication theory: An introduction* (3rd ed.). Thousand Oaks, CA: Sage.

Meerlo, J. (1956). *The rape of the mind: The psychology of thought control, menticide, and brainwashing*. New York: World.

Meeting needs: The war nursery approach. (1944). Berkeley: Henry J. Kaiser Mss. Bancroft Library, University of California, Berkeley.

Meier, B. (1998, November 14). Cigarette makers and 8 states reach a tentative accord. *Houston Chronicle,* p. 8A.

Merton, R. (1968). *Social theory and social structure.* New York: Free Press.

Mestel, R. (1997, November/December). A safer estrogen: Would you take it? *Health, 11,* 72–75.

Miller, G. (1980). Afterword. In D. P. Cushman & R. D. McPhee (Eds.), *Message-attitude-behavior relationship: Theory, methodology, and application.* New York: Academic Press.

Mintz, J., & Torry, S. (1998, January 15). Internal RJ Reynolds documents detail cigarette marketing aimed at children. *Washington Post,* p. A1.

Mitchell, M. (1970). *Propaganda, polls, and public opinion: Are the people manipulated?* Englewood Cliffs, NJ: Prentice Hall.

Morley, D. (1988). *Family television: Cultural power and domestic leisure.* London: Comedia.

Mufson, S. (1998, July 13). Riding the Internet wave. *Washington Post National Weekly Edition,* pp. 6–7.

Naisbitt, J. (1982). *Megatrends.* New York: Warner.

Nash, M. (1997, April 21). Early flash points. *Time,* pp. 99–100.

Negrine, R., & Papathanassopoulos, S. (1990). *The internationalization of television.* London: Pinter.

Nelson, M. (1997). *War of the black heavens: The battles of Western broadcasting in the Cold War.* Syracuse, NY: Syracuse University Press.

Nemecek, S. (1997, September). Hold the hormones? *Scientific American, 277,* 38.

Nichols, J. S. (1997). Institutionalization of anti-Castro broadcasting. In N. L. Street & M. J. Matelski (Eds.), *Messages from the underground: Transnational radio in resistance and solidarity* (pp. 102–115). Westport, CT: Praeger.

Noelle-Neumann, E. (1991). The theory of public opinion: The concept of the spiral of silence. In J. A. Anderson (Ed.), *Communication yearbook 14* (pp. 256–287). Newbury Park, CA: Sage.

Nordenstreng, K. (1982, Summer). U.S. policy and the Third World: A critique. *Journal of Communication, 32,* 54–59.

Nordenstreng, K., & Schiller, H. I. (1979). *National sovereignty and international communication.* Norwood, NJ: Ablex.

Norton, M. L., Monin, B., Cooper, J., & Hogg, M. (2003). Vicarious dissonance: Attitude change from the inconsistency of others. *Journal of Personality and Social Psychology, 85,* 47–62.

Nye, G. P. (1941, September 15). Our madness increases as our emergency shrinks. *Vital Speeches, 7,* 722.

O'Donnell, V. (1993). *Introduction to public communication.* Dubuque, IA: Kendall-Hunt.

O'Donnell, V. (1994). *Women, war, and work: Shaping space for productivity in the shipyards during World War II* [Television broadcast, 56:40 minutes]. Bozeman: KUSM-TV of Montana State University.

O'Donnell, V. (1998). *Women, war, and work: Shaping space for productivity in the shipyards during World War II* [Television broadcast, 42:39 minutes]. Bozeman: KUSM-TV of Montana State University.

O'Donnell, V. (2005). Cultural studies theory. In K. Smith, S. Moriarty, G. Barbatis, & K. Kenney (Eds.), *Handbook of visual communication: Theory, methods, and media* (pp. 521–538). Mahwah, NJ: Lawrence Erlbaum.

O'Donnell, V., & Jowett, G. (1989). Propaganda as a form of communication. In T. J. Smith (Ed.), *Propaganda: A pluralistic perspective* (pp. 49–63). New York: Praeger.

O'Donnell, V., & Kable, J. (1982). *Persuasion: An interactive dependency approach*. New York: Random House.

O'Neill, W. L. (1982). *A better world*. New York: Simon & Schuster.

Opinion Works. (2004). Fahrenheit 9–11. Retrieved from www.opinionworks.com

Osgood, C. E., Suci, G. J., & Tannenbaum, P. G. (1957). *The measurement of meaning*. Urbana: University of Illinois Press.

Osgood, C. E., & Tannenbaum, P. G. (1955). The principles of congruity in the production of attitude change. *Psychological Review, 62,* 42–55.

Packard, V. (1957). *The hidden persuaders*. New York: D. McKay.

Page, C. (1996). *U.S. official propaganda during the Vietnam War 1965–1973: The limits of persuasion*. London: Leicester University Press.

Parry-Giles, S. J. (1996). "Camouflaged" propaganda: The Truman and Eisenhower administrations' covert manipulation of news. *Western Journal of Communication, 60,* 146–167.

Parry-Giles, S. J. (2002). *The rhetorical presidency, propaganda, and the Cold War: 1945–1955*. Westport, CT: Praeger.

Patai, R. (1983). *The Arab mind*. New York: Scribner.

Paulhus, M. (1996, Winter). A bitter pill. *Humane Society of the United States News, 41*(1), 36–39.

Pearl, D., Bouthilet, L., & Lazar, J. (Eds.). (1982). *Television and behavior: Ten years of scientific progress and implications for the eighties*. Washington, DC: Government Printing Office.

Peirce, J. P. (1996). Influence of tobacco marketing and exposure to smokers on adult susceptibility to smoking. Retrieved from http://www/global2000.net/ytp/document/habit.html

Perris, A. (1985). *Music as propaganda: Art to persuade, art to control*. Westport, CT: Greenwood.

Petty, R. E. (1995). Attitude change. In A. Tesser (Ed.), *Advanced social psychology* (pp. 195–255). New York: McGraw-Hill.

Petty, R. E., & Cacioppo, J .T. (1986). The elaboration likelihood model of persuasion. *Advanced Experimental Psychology, 19,* 123–205.

Philippe, R. (1980). *Political graphics: Art as a weapon*. New York: Abbeville.

Pletka, D. (1991, March 4). Swimming in blood and other flowery phrases. *Insight*, p. 14.

Pope, D. (1983). *The making of modern advertising*. New York: Basic Books.

Potter, W. J. (2003). *The 11 myths of media violence*. Thousand Oaks, CA: Sage.

Pratkanis, A. R., & Aronson, E. (2001). *Age of propaganda: The everyday use and abuse of persuasion* (2nd ed.). New York: Freeman.

Pratkanis, A. R., & Greenwald, A. G. (1985). A reliable sleeper effect in persuasion: Implications for opinion change theory and research. In L. S. Alwit & A. A. Mitchell (Eds.), *Psychological processes and advertising effects* (pp. 157–73). Hillsdale, NJ: Lawrence Erlbaum.

Pratkanis, A. R., & Turner, M. E. (1996). Persuasion and democracy: Strategies for increasing deliberative participation and social change. *Journal of Social Issues, 52,* 187–205.

Premarin: Prescribed cruelty [pamphlet]. (1997). Clarks Summit, PA: International Society for Animal Rights.

President visits Vanport, Oregon [Paramount newsreel]. (1943). Washington, DC: National Archives.

Propaganda techniques of German fascism. (1938, May). *Propaganda Analysis, 2*(5), 46–47.

Psy-Ops Bonanza, A. (1991, June 17). *Newsweek,* pp. 23–24.

Publicizing the centers to workers. (1944). Berkeley: Henry J. Kaiser Mss. Bancroft Library, University of California, Berkeley.

Puddington, A. (2000). *Broadcasting freedom: The Cold War triumph of Radio Free Europe and Radio Liberty.* Lexington: University of Kentucky Press.

Qualter, T. H. (1962). *Propaganda and psychological warfare.* New York: Random House.

Qualter, T. H. (1985). *Opinion control in democracies.* New York: St. Martin's.

Qualter, T. H. (1991). *Advertising and democracy in the mass age.* New York: St. Martin's.

Questions and answers about the FDA's regulations. (1998). Retrieved from http://www.global2000.net/ytp/document/habit.html

Rampton, S., & Stauber, J. (2003). *Weapons of mass deception: The uses of propaganda in Bush's war on Iraq.* New York: Jeremy P. Tarcher.

Randall, R. S. (1968). *Censorship of the movies.* Madison: University of Wisconsin Press.

Rashid, A. (2004, May 27). The rise of bin Laden. *New York Review of Books,* pp. 19–22.

Read, J. (1941). *Atrocity propaganda, 1914–1919.* New Haven, CT: Yale University Press.

Reeves, N. (1986). *Official British film propaganda during the First World War.* London: Croom Helm.

Reinard, J. C. (1988, Fall). The empirical study of the persuasive effects of evidence: The status after fifty years of research. *Human Communication Research, 15,* 3–59.

Renov, M. (1988). *Hollywood's wartime women: Representation and ideology.* Ann Arbor, MI: UMI Research Press.

Rhoads, K. (2004). *Propaganda tactics and Fahrenheit 9–11.* Retrieved from www.workingpsychologist.com

Rich, F. (2003, March 30). Iraq around the clock. Retrieved March 30, 2003, from http://nytimes.com

Roberts, D. F., & Maccoby, N. (1985). Effects of mass communication. In G. Lindzey & E. Aronson (Eds.), *Handbook of social psychology* (Vol. 2, pp. 539–598). New York: Random House.

Roelker, N. L. (1979). The impact of the reformation era on communication and propaganda. In H. D. Lasswell, D. Lerner, & H. Speier (Eds.), *Propaganda and communication in world history: Vol. 1. The symbolic instrument in early time* (pp. 41–84). Honolulu: University Press of Hawaii.

Roetter, C. (1974). *The art of psychological warfare, 1914–1945.* New York: Stein & Day.

Rogers, E. M. (1982). *Diffusion of innovations.* New York: Free Press.

Rogers, E. M. (1994). *A history of communication study.* New York: Free Press.

Rogers, E. M., & Shoemaker, F. F. F. (1971). *Communication of innovations: A cross-cultural approach.* New York: Free Press.

Roloff, M. E., & Miller, G. R. (Eds.). (1980). *Persuasion: New directions in theory and research.* Beverly Hills, CA: Sage.

Ronalds, F. S., Jr. (1971, November). The future of international broadcasting. *Annals of the American Academy of Political and Social Science, 398,* 31–80.

Rosenberg, H. L. (1983). For your eyes only. *American Film, 8(9),* 40–43.

Rosenfeld, A. (1985). *Imagining Hitler.* Bloomington: Indiana University Press.

Rosenthal, S. P. (1934). Changes of socio-economic attitudes under radical motion picture propaganda. *Archives of Psychology,* no. 166.

Roskos-Ewoldsen, D. R. (1996). Attitude accessibility and persuasion: Review and a transactive model. In *Communication yearbook 20* (pp. 185–225). New Brunswick, NJ: International Communication Association.

Roskos-Ewoldsen, D., Yu, H. J., & Rhodes, N. (2004). Fear appeal messages affect accessibility of attitudes toward the threat and adaptive behaviors. *Communication Monographs, 71,* 49–69.

Rubin, A. M., & Windahl, S. (1986). The uses and dependency model of mass communication. *Critical Studies in Mass Communication, 3(2),* 184–199.

Russell, F. (1995a, September 8). PMU regulations expected. *Winnipeg Free Press,* p. 3.

Russell, F. (1995b, June 24). Wall of silence hides PMU industry. *Winnipeg Free Press,* p. 3.

Rutherford, W. (1978). *Hitler's propaganda machine.* London: Bison Books.

Rutten, T. (2003, June 14). The Blair affair fuels a 70-year-old scandal. *Los Angeles Times,* pp. E1, E18.

Ryan, M. (August 23, 1998). He fights dictators with the Internet. *Parade Magazine,* p. 12.

Said, E. (1991, March 7). Writes on the eve of the Iraqi-Soviet talks. *London Review of Books,* pp. 7–8.

Salter, L (1995, October 20). *Millions of women taking Premarin cautioned* [Press release]. London: World Society for the Protection of Animals (WSPA).

Schatz, T., & Paige, L. (1997, July 21). Politics trumps science at the FDA. *Wall Street Journal,* p. A22.

Schiller, H. I. (1970). *Mass communication and American empire.* New York: Augustus M. Kelly.

Schrecker, E. W. (1986). *No ivory tower: McCarthyism and the universities.* New York: Oxford University Press.

Schreiner, S. A., Jr. (1977). *The condensed world of* Reader's Digest. New York: Stein & Day.

Schudson, M. (1978). *Discovering the news.* New York: Basic Books.

Schudson, M. (1984). *Advertising: The uneasy persuasion.* New York: Basic Books.

Schudson, M. (1992). *Watergate in American memory: How we remember, forget, and reconstruct the past.* New York: Basic Books.

Schwartz, S. H., & Bilsky, W. (1987). Toward a universal psychological structure of human values. *Journal of Personality and Social Psychology, 53,* 550–562.

Seeing isn't believing. (2004, September).*Reader's Digest,* pp. 144–146.

Service byword of child care center. (1944, November 17). *Bos'n' Whistle,* p. 5.

Shannon, C., & Weaver, W. (1949). *The mathematical theory of communication.* Urbana: University of Illinois Press.

Shaw, D. (1997, January 20). A small pill is in the center of a big fight. *Philadelphia Inquirer,* pp. 1–5.

Shaw, D. L., & McCombs, M. E. (1974). *The emergence of American political issues: The agenda-setting function of the press.* St. Paul, MN: West.

Shaw, J. F. (Trans.). (1873). On Christian doctrine. In Rev. M. Dodds (Ed.), *The works of Aurelius Augustine, bishop of Hippo.* Edinburgh, UK: T. & T. Clark.

Sheeran, P., & Orbell, S. (2000). Using implementation intentions to increase attendance for cervical cancer screening. *Health Psychology, 19,* 283–289.

Shibutani, T. (1966). *Improvised news.* Indianapolis, IN: Bobbs-Merrill.

Shulman, H. C. (1990). *The Voice of America: Propaganda and democracy, 1941–1945.* Madison: University of Wisconsin Press.

Shulman, H. C. (1997). The Voice of America, U.S. propaganda and the Holocaust: "I would have remembered." *Historical Journal of Film, Radio, and Television, 17*(1), 91–103.

Shultz, R. H., & Godson, R. (1984). *Dezinformatsia: Active measures in Soviet strategy.* Washington, DC: Pergamon-Brassey's.

Shute, N. (1997, March 24). Menopause is no disease. *U.S. News and World Report, 122,* 71–72.

Simpson, C. (1994). *Science of coercion: Communication research and psychological warfare, 1945–1960.* New York: Oxford University Press.

Singer, M. T., & Lalich, J. (1995). *Cults in our midsts.* San Francisco: Jossey-Bass.

Smith, B. L. (1958). Propaganda. In D. L. Sills (Ed.), *Encyclopedia of the social sciences* (Vol. 12, pp. 579–588). New York: Macmillan.

Smith, K., Moriarty, S., Barbatsis, G., & Kenney, K. (Eds.). (2005). *Handbook of visual communication: Theory, methods, and media* (pp. 521–538). Mahwah, NJ: Lawrence Erlbaum.

Smith, T. J. (1989). *Propaganda: A pluralistic perspective.* New York: Praeger.

Snow, N. (2003). *Information war: American propaganda, free speech and opinion control since 9/11.* New York: Seven Stories Press.

Soley, L. C. (1989). *Radio warfare: OSS and CIA subversive propaganda.* New York: Praeger.

Soley, L. C., & Nichols, J. S. (1987). *Clandestine radio broadcasting.* New York: Praeger.

Sorensen, T. C. (1968). *The word war.* New York: Harper & Row.

Sparks, A. (1990). *The mind of South Africa.* New York: Knopf.

Speer, A. (1970). *Inside the Third Reich.* New York: Macmillan.

Speier, H. (1950, January). The historical development of public opinion. *American Journal of Sociology, 55,* 376–388.

Speier, H., & Otis, M. (1944). German radio propaganda in France during the Battle of France. In P. Lazarsfeld & F. Stanton (Eds.), *Radio research, 1942–1943* (pp. 208–247). New York: Duell, Sloan, & Pearce.

Sproule, J. M. (1983). The institute for propaganda analysis: Public education in argumentation, 1937–1942. In D. Zarefsky, M. O. Sellers, & J. Rhodes (Eds.), *Proceedings of the Third Summer Conference on Argumentation* (pp. 486–499). Annandale, VA: Speech Communication Association.

Sproule, J. M. (1987). Propaganda studies in American social science: The rise and fall of the critical paradigm. *Quarterly Journal of Speech, 73,* 60–78.

Sproule, J. M. (1989). Progressive propaganda critics and the magic bullet theory. *Critical Studies in Mass Communication, 6*(3), 225–246.

Sproule, J. M. (1991). Propaganda and American ideological critique. In J. A. Anderson (Ed.), *Communication yearbook 14* (pp. 211–238). Newbury Park, CA: Sage.

Sproule, J. M. (1994). *Channels of propaganda.* Bloomington, IN: Edinfo.

Sproule, J. M. (1997). *Propaganda and democracy: The American experience of media and mass persuasion.* Cambridge, UK: Cambridge University Press.

Starr, P. (2004). *The creation of the media: The political origins of mass communications.* New York: Basic Books.

St. Hill, T. N. (1974). *Thomas Nast: Cartoons and illustrations.* New York: Dover.

Steele, R. W. (1985). *Propaganda in an open society: The Roosevelt administration and the media, 1933–1941.* Westport, CT: Greenwood.

Stein, A. H., & Friedrich, L. K. (1972). Television content and young children's behavior. In J. P. Murray, E. A. Rubenstein, & G. A. Comstock (Eds.), Television and social behavior: Vol. II. Television and social learning (pp. 67–85). Washington, DC: Government Printing Office.

Stowe, H. B. (1991). *Uncle Tom's cabin, or, Life among the lowly.* Camp Hill, New York: Reader's Digest. (Original work published 1852)

Szanto, G. H. (1978). *Theater and propaganda.* Austin: University of Texas Press.

Taithe, B., & Thornton, T. (Eds.). (2000). *Propaganda: Political rhetoric and identity, 1300–2000.* Oxford, UK: Sutton.

Targeting tobacco use: The nation's leading cause of death at a glance. (1998). Retrieved from http://www.global2000.net.yph/document/sur.htm:1-2

Taylor, P. M. (1990). *Munitions of the mind: War propaganda from the ancient world to the nuclear age.* Manchester, UK: Manchester University Press.

Taylor, P. M. (1992). *War and the media: Propaganda and persuasion in the Gulf War.* Manchester, UK: Patrick Stephens.

Taylor, R. (1979). *Film propaganda: Soviet Russia and Nazi Germany.* London: Croom Helm.

Tebbel, J. (1969). *The American magazine: A compact history.* New York: Hawthorn.

Tesser, A. (1995). *Advanced social psychology.* New York: McGraw-Hill.

Thomas, W. I., & Znaniecki, F. (1918). *The Polish peasant in Europe and America* (Vol. 1). Boston: Badger.

Thomson, O. (1977). *Mass persuasion in history.* Edinburgh, UK: Paul Harris.

Thomson, O. (1999). *Easily led: A history of propaganda.* Phoenix Mill, UK: Sutton.

Thurstone, L. L. (1929). *The measurement of attitudes.* Chicago: University of Chicago Press.

The tobacco settlement. (1998, March 16). Retrieved from http://www.policy.com/issuewk/98/0316/031698a/html

Triandis, H. C. (1977). *Interpersonal behavior.* Monterey, CA: Brooks/Cole.

Tufts University School of Veterinary Medicine, Center for Animals and Public Policy. (1995). *The animal research controversy: Protest, process, and public policy.* Medford, MA: Author.

Turow, J. (1991). *Media systems in society: Understanding industries, strategies and power.* New York: Longman.

2400 families use child care centers. (1944, December 29). *Bos 'n' Whistle,* p. 70.

University of Michigan. (1995). *Monitoring the future study.* Ann Arbor: University of Michigan Press.

Valins, D. (1966). Cognitive effects of false heart-rate feedback. *Journal of Personality and Social Psychology, 4*(4), 400–408.

Vanport City. (1943, August). *Architectural Forum, 9,* 53–62.

Vaughn, S. L. (1980). *Holding fast the inner lines: Democracy, nationalism, and the committee on public information.* Chapel Hill: University of North Carolina Press.

VOA in 1989 and beyond. (1989). Washington, DC: Voice of America.

Wanger, W. (1941, November). The role of movies in morale. *American Journal of Sociology, 47,* 375–383.

Ward, L. N. (1985). *The motion picture goes to war: The U.S. government film effort during World War I.* Ann Arbor: University of Michigan Research Press.

Warren, D. (1996). *Radio priest: Charles Coughlin, the father of hate radio.* New York: Free Press.

We say au revoir. (1939, January). *Propaganda Analysis,* p. 1.

Weimann, G. (2000). *Communicating unreality: Modern media and the reconstruction of reality.* Thousand Oaks, CA: Sage.

Weisman, S. R. (1991, December 5). Japanese regrets over war unlikely after Bush's stand. *New York Times,* pp. A1, 12.

Welsch, D. (1993). *The Third Reich: Politics and propaganda*. New York: Routledge.

Weschler, L. (1983, April 11). A state of war—1. *New Yorker,* pp. 45–102.

Westley, B. H., & MacLean, M. S., Jr. (1977). A conceptual model for communications research. In K. K. Sereno & C. D. Mortensen (Eds.), *Foundations of communication theory* (pp. 73–83). New York: Harper & Row.

Wheeless, L. R., Barraclough, R., & Stewart, R. (1983). Compliance-gaining and power in persuasion. In R. N. Bostrom (Ed.), *Communication yearbook 7* (pp. 105–145). Beverly Hills, CA: Sage.

Whiteside, T. (1970, December). Cutting down. *New Yorker,* pp. 42–95.

Whitfield, S. J. (1991). *The culture of the Cold War*. Baltimore: Johns Hopkins University Press.

Wicker, T. (1991, May). Oh, what a censored war! *Newsletter on Intellectual Freedom, 40*(69), 93–97.

Wilkerson, M. M. (1932). *Public opinion and the Spanish-American War*. Baton Rouge: Louisiana State University Press.

Williams, F. (1989). *The new communications* (2nd ed.). Belmont, CA: Wadsworth.

Williams, R. (1958). *Culture and society: 1780–1950*. New York: Columbia University Press.

Williams, R. (1961). *The long revolution*. New York: Columbia University Press.

Williams, R. (1966). *Communications*. London: Chatto & Windus.

Williams, R. (1973). *The country and the city*. London: Chatto & Windus.

Wilson, E. O. (1998). *Consilience: The unity of knowledge*. New York: Knopf.

Winkler, A. (1978). *The politics of propaganda: The Office of War Information, 1942–1945*. New Haven, CT: Yale University Press.

Wisan, J. E. (1934). *The Cuban crisis as reflected in the New York press*. New York: Columbia University Press.

Wish, H. (1950). *Society and thought in Early America*. New York: David McKay.

Witte, K. (1992). Putting the fear back into fear appeals. *Communication Monographs, 59,* 329–349.

Wright, J. (1990). *Terrorist propaganda*. New York: St. Martin's.

Zajonc, R. B. (1968). Attitude effects of mere exposure. *Journal of Personality and Social Psychology Monograph, 9*(2, Pt. 2).

Zajonc, R. B. (1980). Feeling and thinking: Preferences need no inferences. *American Psychologist, 35,* 151–175.

Zelizer, B. (1995). Reading the past against the grain: The shape of memory studies. *Critical Studies in Mass Communication, 12,* 214–239.

Zeman, Z. A. B. (1973). *Nazi propaganda*. New York: Oxford University Press.

Zeman, Z. A. B. (1978). *Selling the war: Art and propaganda in World War II*. London: Orbis.

Zillmann, D., & Bryant, J. (1985). *Selective exposure to communication*. Hillsdale, NJ: Lawrence Erlbaum.

Zimbardo, P. G., Ebbeson, E., & Maslach, C. (1977). *Influencing attitudes and changing behavior*. Reading, MA: Addison-Wesley.

Zimbardo, P. G., & Leippe, M. R. (1991). *The psychology of attitude change and social influence.* New York: McGraw-Hill.

Additional Resources

Allport, G. W. (1968). The historical background of modern social psychology. In G. Lindzey & E. Aronson (Eds.), *The handbook of social psychology* (Vol. 1, pp. 1–280). Reading, MA: Addison-Wesley.

Anderson, J. A. (1991). *Communication yearbook 14.* Newbury Park, CA: Sage.

Aronson, J. (1970). *The press and the Cold War.* Indianapolis, IN: Bobbs-Merrill.

Ash, T. G. (2005, May 12). Europe's never-ending memory wars. Retrieved May 12, 2005, from http://www.latimes

Barrett, E. W. (1953). *Truth is our weapon.* New York: Funk & Wagnalls.

Berelson, D. (1956). *Reader in public opinion and communication.* New York: Free Press.

Bohn, T. (1977). *An historical and descriptive analysis of the why we fight films.* New York: Arno.

Brody, G. H., & Stoneman, Z. (1983, June). The influence of television viewing on family interaction: A contextualist framework. *Journal of Family Issues, 4*(2), 329–348.

Chaiken, S., & Stangor, C. (1987). Attitudes and attitude change. *Annual Review of Psychology, 38,* 575–630.

Christenson, R. M., & McWilliams, R. (Eds.). (1967). *Voice of the people: Readings in public opinion and propaganda.* New York: McGraw-Hill.

Cushman, D. P., & McPhee, R. D. (1980). *Message-attitude-behavior relationship: Theory, methodology, and application.* New York: Academic Press.

Erenberg, L. A., & Hirsch, S. E. (Eds.). (1996). *The war in American culture.* Chicago: University of Chicago Press.

Ewen, S., & Ewen, E. (1982). *Channels of desire: Mass images and the shaping of American consciousness.* New York: McGraw-Hill.

Foster, M. S. (1989). *Henry J. Kaiser: Builder in the modern American West.* Austin: University of Texas Press.

Greenberg, B. S. (Ed.). (1980). *Life on television.* Norwood, NY: Ablex.

Heiner, A. P. (1989). *Henry J. Kaiser: American empire builder.* New York: Lang.

Jowett, G. S. (1987). Propaganda and communication: The re-emergence of a research tradition. *Journal of Communication, 37*(1), 97–114.

Joyce, W. (1963). *The propaganda gap.* New York: Harper & Row.

Katz, E., & Lazarsfeld, P. (1955). *Personal influence: The part played by people in mass communication.* Glencoe, IL: Free Press.

Katz, E., & Szecsko, T. (Eds.). (1981). *Mass media and social change.* Beverly Hills, CA: Sage.

Lang, J. S. (1979, August 27). The great American bureaucratic propaganda machine. *U.S. News and World Report,* pp. 43–47.

Lashmar, P., & Oliver, J. (1998). *Britain's secret propaganda war: 1948–1977.* Oxford, UK: Sutton.

Lasswell, H. (1935). *Propaganda and promotional activities.* Minneapolis: University of Minnesota Press.

Lerner, D., & Nelson, L. M. (Eds.). (1977). *Communication research: A half century appraisal.* Honolulu: University Press of Hawaii.

Littlejohn, S. W. (1989). *Theories of human communication.* Belmont, CA: Wadsworth.

Lowenthal, L. (1949). *Prophets of deceit: A study of the techniques of the American agitator.* New York: Harper.

Lutz, W. (1989, July 12). No one died in Tiananmen Square. *New York Times,* pp. A1, A9.

McGuire, W. J. (1969). The nature of attitudes and attitude change. In G. Lindzey & E. Aronson (Eds.), *The handbook of social psychology* (Vol. 3, pp. 136–314). Reading, MA: Addison-Wesley.

McQuail, D. (1975). *Communication.* New York: Longman.

McQuail, D. (1984). With the benefit of hindsight: Reflections on uses and gratifications research. *Critical Studies in Mass Communication, 1*(2), 177–193.

Meyerhoff, A. E. (1965). *The strategy of persuasion: The use of advertising skills in fighting the cold war.* New York: Coward McCann.

Oh, what a censored war! (1991, May). *Newsletter on Intellectual Freedom, 40*(69), 93–97.

Payne, D. (Ed.). (1965). *The obstinate audience.* Ann Arbor, MI: Foundation for Research on Human Behavior.

Petty, R. E., & Cacioppo, J. T. (1986). *Communication and persuasion: Central and peripheral routes to attitude change.* New York: Springer-Verlag.

PMU Farm Act, Regulation No. 217/70, Ontario (1968–1969).

Pool, I. D., Frey, F. W., Schramm, W., Maccoby, N., & Parker, E. B. (Eds.). (1973). *Handbook of communication.* Chicago: Rand McNally.

Premarin (PMU) controversy. (1997, March 27). Retrieved March 27, 1997, from http://home.earthlink.net/~ighahorseaid/pmu_link.html

Rogers, E. M., & Kincaid, D. L. (1981). *Communication networks: Toward a new paradigm for research.* New York: Free Press.

Rubin, B. (1973). *Propaganda and public opinion: Strategies of persuasion.* Columbus, OH: Xerox Education.

Sereno, K., & Martensen, C. D. (1974). *Foundations of communication theory.* New York: Harper & Row.

Shavitt, S., & Brock, T. C. (1994). *Persuasion: Psychological insights and perspectives.* Boston: Allyn & Bacon.

Short, K. R. M. (1990). *International broadcasting and the best interests of mankind: A historical perspective.* Unpublished manuscript.

Smith, C. R. (1998). *Rhetoric and human consciousness: A history.* Prospect Heights, IL: Waveland.

Stiff, J. B. (1994). *Persuasive communication.* New York: Guilford.

Stone, P. H. (1979, April 14). Muldergate on Madison Avenue. *The National,* pp. 390–393.

Taylor, P. M. (1999). *British propaganda in the 20th century: Selling democracy.* Edinburgh, UK: Edinburgh University Press.

Tutle, W. M. (1993). *Daddy's gone to war: The Second World War in the lives of America's children.* New York: Oxford University Press.

U.S. Information Agency. (1991). *USIA fact sheet.* Washington, DC: Author.

U.S. trying to limit damage of Koran story. (2005, May 17). *Los Angeles Times,* p. A3.

Whiteside, T. (1971, March 27). Selling death. *New Republic,* pp. 15–17.

Wyeth Prempro users can sue as a group. (2005, March 8). *Los Angeles Times,* p. C3.

'04 drug prices outpace inflation. (2005, April 13). *Orange County Register,* pp. 1, 4.

Author Index

Subject Index

About the Authors

Garth S. Jowett is Professor of Communication at the University of Houston. He obtained his Ph.D. in communications history from the University of Pennsylvania. He has served as Director for Social Research for the Canadian government's Department of Communication and has been a consultant to various international communication agencies. He was appointed a Gannett Center Fellow in 1987–1988 and has published widely in the area of popular culture and the history of communication. His book *Film: The Democratic Art* (1976) was an important benchmark in film history. His volume in Sage's Commtext series, *Movies as Mass Communication* (with James M. Linton), is a unique and widely appreciated study. His most recent publication, *Children and the Movies: Media Influences and the Payne Fund Studies* (with Ian C. Jarvie & Kathryn H. Fuller), is a detailed account of an important rediscovery of a hitherto lost episode in mass communication history in the United States. He is also on the boards of several communication and film journals. He is currently working on a social history of television in the United States.

Victoria O'Donnell is Professor Emeritus and former Director of the University Honors Program and Professor of Communication at Montana State University–Bozeman. Previously, she was the Chair of the Department of Speech Communication at Oregon State University and Chair of the Department of Communication and Public Address at the University of North Texas. In 1988, she taught for the American Institute of Foreign Studies at the University of London. She received her Ph.D. from the Pennsylvania State University. She has published articles and chapters in a wide range of journals and books on topics concerning persuasion, the social effects of media, women in film and television, British politics, Nazi propaganda, collective memory, cultural studies theory, and science fiction films of the 1950s. She is also the author (with June Kable) of *Persuasion: An Interactive-Dependency Approach, Propaganda and Persuasion* (with Garth

421

Jowett), and *Speech Communication*. She is currently writing a book on television criticism. She made a film, *Women, War, and Work: Shaping Space for Productivity in the Shipyards During World War II*, for PBS through KUSM Public Television at Montana State University. She has also written television scripts for environmental films and has done voice-overs for several PBS films. She served on editorial boards of several journals. The recipient of numerous research grants, honors, and teaching awards, including being awarded the Honor Professorship at North Texas State University and the Montana State University Alumni Association and Bozeman Chamber of Commerce Award of Excellence, she has been a Danforth Foundation Associate and a Summer Scholar of the National Endowment for the Humanities. She has taught in Germany and has been a visiting lecturer at universities in Denmark, Norway, Sweden, and Wales. She has also served as a private consultant to the U.S. government, a state senator, the tobacco litigation plaintiffs, and many American corporations.